MERRILL'S
INTERNATIONAL EDUCATION SERIES

Under the Editorship of

KIMBALL WILES

Dean of the College of Education

University of Florida

The Nature of
EDUCATIONAL
METHOD

JACK R. FRYMIER
The Ohio State University

The Nature of
EDUCATIONAL
METHOD

CHARLES E. MERRILL BOOKS, INC. COLUMBUS, OHIO

Library of Congress Catalog Card Number: 65—26117

PRINTED IN THE UNITED STATES OF AMERICA

3 4 5 6 7 8 9 10 11 12 13 14 15-76 75 74 73 72 71 70 69 68 67

To my mother
who encouraged me to disagree

Preface

This book describes a theory of educational method. Written for advanced undergraduates, graduate students, and professional educators, it attempts to do two things: first, it sets out to translate research results into educational principles and statements of practice. Second, it outlines a rough theory for pursuing research in educational method. In both instances it is designed to help teachers devise methods of working in classrooms by which they can achieve democratic ends in democratic ways.

This book assumes that democracy is both important and possible in our kind of schools. It also assumes that democracy has both rigor and power, and that an understanding of these ideas can enable teachers to extend their efforts in working with youth. Toward that end, research studies in education, psychology, social psychology, and sociology are fused into concepts and looked at from the point of view of educational method.

Chapter one maintains that schools are committed to particular objectives; they have a moral purpose. In Chapter two one specific end of education is described: democratic behavior, and all that the term implies. The third chapter outlines how the many facets of a culture impinge upon a growing youngster and mold his behavior. Learning from a perceptual point of view is examined in Chapter four and the nature of academic motivations in Chapter five. The sixth chapter outlines ways in which a teacher can structure his classroom by varying the factors inherent in the learning situation.

Beginning with Chapter seven, practical ways of incorporating educational principles into classroom practice are explored. Teachers are encouraged to devise different kinds of structure, according to their students' motivations and personalities. In the eighth chapter the contract way of grading is discussed in depth. Chapter nine encourages teachers to experiment within their own classrooms, and Chapter ten discusses the advantages of defining one's professional role precisely. This final chapter urges teachers to draw a circle around those activities which will enable them to achieve their purposes and exclude ways of working which may or may not be important, but which are not teaching. They are asked to focus their energies and their efforts for maximum effectiveness.

Throughout the book teachers are seen as the heart of educational method: their beliefs, their values, and their ways of behaving are the most powerful variables in any classroom. Teachers are encouraged to use the power of their own personalities as a teaching tool. Teachers are the most important instructional device. Improving instruction involves creating opportunities for teachers to become more intelligent, more creative, more inspiring people.

Several persons have read various parts of the manuscript, and their reactions and criticisms have been extremely helpful. I would like to take this opportunity to express my appreciation to some of them: Professors Allen Chapline, Arthur Combs, Roy Dwyer, Earl Kelley, Clara Olson, and David Sarner read portions of the manuscript and made many constructive suggestions. Professors Robert Bills, O. L. Davis, Jr., Alexander Frazier, Jack Hough, Paul Klohr, James Macdonald, Ross Mooney, Harry Passow, and Zelda Samoff tested many of these concepts in extended discussion over a period of years. Professors Kelly Duncan and Kimball Wiles both read the entire manuscript and offered criticisms of organization and content which were invaluable. Finally, thousands of teachers and students have reacted to these ideas in classrooms and workshops, and I want to express my heartfelt appreciation to them, too. Without their stimulation and response, this book could never have been written at all.

Not all of these persons agreed with or approved the ideas which are involved, of course, and responsibility for the content as presented here rests solely with the author.

JACK R. FRYMIER

Columbus, Ohio
July, 1965

Contents

xiii

Chapter One

Why We Have Schools

Schools exist to help children learn. In a society dedicated to the principles of freedom and built upon the ethical constructs of Christian-Judaic teachings, learning is essential. In a world of increasing numbers and awesome power, faced with problems sometimes completely beyond belief, teaching children how to learn and inspiring them in learning are absolute necessities.

THE FUNCTIONS OF EDUCATION

Educational purposes have evolved to the point that three functions seem especially important today: discovering information, sharing information, and affecting behavioral change (3).

A basic function of education is to encourage the search for truth and the discovery of new ideas. In our society this effort is generally concentrated in universities and in governmental and industrial research centers, where the challenge of the unknown and the desire to know assures us of scholars, however few, who accept this function as their own. Scientists, artists, and writers, especially, are continuously striving to understand and describe the universe of which we are a part. They are engaged in one aspect of education: discovering knowledge.

Once information has been procured, it must be shared. A second function of education involves the dissemination of knowledge. This function is normally accomplished by such diverse media as newspapers, magazines, books, and radio and television broadcasts. All of those who devote their energies to "promulgating the truth" are occupied in this second function. When the truth is known, it must be shared.

After the accumulation and distribution of facts, the final function of education is to help people behave according to the facts. Ideas and facts are worthwhile only if they affect behavior. To know is only half enough; one must do as well as he knows. Intelligent behavior is behavior which is in keeping with the facts. Persons whose lives reflect an awareness of and congruence with reality are intelligent and psychologically healthy. Those who are out of touch with reality are generally described in less positive terms.

This final function of education is extremely significant. For this reason alone, in fact, we have public schools: to foster intelligent behavior. Schools exist so that young people may experience and be affected by the best that we now know.

Some Examples of Educational Functions in Operation

During recent decades the question of the effect of heavy cigarette smoking upon health has been thoroughly explored. Research in hospitals and laboratories all over the world has resulted in an amassing of facts (9). Almost without exception, the evidence indicates clearly and forcefully that persons who are heavy cigarette smokers are more apt to die of lung cancer than those who do not smoke. The facts have been discovered; the first function of education has been accomplished.

Secondly, many groups and individuals have worked in many ways to bring these facts to the attention of the public. Radio and television programs, magazine articles, books, and public discussion everywhere have made most adult Americans aware of the effects of heavy cigarette smoking on health. The facts are known and few persons seriously question the validity of the findings.

But many persons still smoke. The plain truth is that their behavior has not been affected by the facts. Knowing one thing, they do another. They ignore the facts. Those who know that they ought not smoke but do are not engaged in intelligent behavior. For them, the third basic function of education has not been effective.

Consider another, more academic, example. The First Amendment to the Constitution of the United States is fact. It does exist. It guarantees certain freedoms to the citizens of our nation. Looked at as an educational problem, the three basic purposes are apparent once more.

As knowledge, the First Amendment to the Constitution has been discovered. Made clear to us by historians and others, the ideas involved in this segment of knowledge are also widely understood. Not all men, however, speak freely, write freely, worship freely, assemble freely, or petition freely. To the extent that Americans are not free to do these things, our schools have failed. Schools exist to help children learn. Helping children learn involves helping them behave according to the facts.

Education as Communication

If every generation is standing on the shoulders of the previous generation, as Sinnot suggests (8), then, except for communication, each generation would be no further advanced than were the men of an earlier age. Huxley describes it another way (5). Man "has developed a new method of evolution: the transmission of organized experience by way of tradition. . . ." It is the ability to communicate which distinguishes man from other animals.

To educate we must communicate. Education, concerned primarily with ideas, involves both the notion and the process of communication. One of the outstanding attributes of an educated person is his facility in the skills of communication: reading, writing, speaking, and listening. Sometimes listed as English, rhetoric, composition, public speaking, or literature, the core of any educational program invariably embraces the communicative skills.

Further, once these skills have been acquired, the primary activity in the educational enterprise becomes one of communication, too. Ideas are shared. The cultural heritage is transmitted. Books are read. Lectures are given. Pictures and music and poetry are enjoyed. Laboratory experiences are only efforts to make the material being commuicated more meaningful. Tests are simply indications of the extent to which communication has occurred.

Norbert Wiener's book (10), *The Human Use of Human Beings*, describes the problems and the theory of communication. In another book to explain this theory, Warren Weaver (7) allots three levels to the problems involved:

Level A. How accurately can the symbols of communication be transmitted? (The technical problem.)

Level B. How precisely do the transmitted symbols convey the desired meaning? (The semantic problem.)

Level C. How effectively does the received meaning affect the conduct in the desired way? (The effectiveness problem.)

The first level of communication involves the transmission and acquisition of information. The teacher demonstrates a problem and its solution and the child attempts to grasp the ideas. A child reads a book seeking to acquire information. Or a teacher says: "The First Amendment to the Constitution guarantees every citizen in the United States freedom of speech, press, religion, assembly, and petition." And the child says back: "Yes, I know. The First Amendment to the Constitution guarantees freedom of speech, press, religion, assembly, and petition." Learning has occurred, obviously, but just as obviously it is at a relatively low level.

For a student to hear and repeat what was said is not enough. An awareness of the contents of the First Amendment would represent such a level of accomplishment; but, even memorizing verbatim this important part of the Bill of Rights, being able to recite it or to write it out is not sufficient. Education has occurred, but it is not the kind of education which greatly influences personal action. It is not the kind of education which makes men better or alters the course of human events. Indeed, its most outstanding characteristic is its lack of influence on anybody, including the one who was supposed to have been affected most—the learner himself.

Archibald MacLeish (6) describes a letter which Lewis Mumford wrote to *The New York Times* about this problem. Mumford was complaining about the apathy of the American people regarding the possibility of another, perhaps final, holocaust of war. He was decrying the fact that Americans seem to be the best informed people on the globe, but they do not feel or act upon their information. They seem to be willing to see the whole world, themselves included, drawn into a devastating conflict with the end of human existence on earth as a possible consequence, and all without a note of protest. Americans are informed, Mumford complained, but the information has little impact upon their actions. They have not really been affected by the facts at all.

Understanding is a second level of the educational effort. To return to our previous example, for a child to know that the First Amendment guarantees freedom of speech, press, religion, assembly, and petition represents a first step in learning. Understanding the full significance of these ideas would be progress to a higher level.

In reference to the first item of the Bill of Rights, for example, children need to understand *why* we have freedom of speech guaranteed to the people in our country; why we believe that a full and vigorous examination of any idea leads to a clearer perception of the truth, if it is correct, or an opportunity to reject the notion should it be wrong. They need to understand, as Commager suggests (4), that liberty and freedom thrive on disagreement; that difference of opinion is the very essence of democracy. Without freedom of speech, without criticism, without dissent, democracy dies. Students probably should also know that the forces against open discussion today are much more pervasive and far more subtle than they were when our nation was founded. Chafee's interpretation may provide additional meaning (1):

> The First Amendment provides two kinds of interests in free speech. There is an individual interest, the need of many men to express their opinions on matters vital to them if life is to be worth living, and a social interest in the attainment of truth, so that the country may not only adopt the wisest course of action but carry it out in the wisest way. This social interest is especially important in war time. Even after war has been declared there is bound to be a confused mixture of good and bad arguments in its support, and a wide difference of opinion as to its objects. Truth can be sifted out from falsehood only if the government is vigorously and constantly cross-examined, so that the fundamental issues of the struggle may be clearly defined, and the war may not be directed to improper ends, or conducted with an undue sacrifice of life and liberty, or prolonged after its purposes are accomplished.

Young people also need to realize that it is only this freedom, fully exercised, which in the long run assures democratic peoples of survival in the face of totalitarian opposition. Unable to profit from criticism, authoritarian states do not know when they have erred. They are not able to correct a wrong course. Perhaps the fable of the emperor with no clothes on is the classic illustration of this idea. He even fooled himself. At any rate, understanding, or the semantic phase of communication, is a second level of education, however it is achieved.

Few persons would maintain that a mere knowledge of the content of the First Amendment is adequate for life in our complex society. Nor is an appreciation of the ideas for their own sake justifiable. Knowledge is simply not enough. Children need to comprehend and savor the full significance of these ideas; they need *to know* in the fullest sense of the term. Influencing behavior is the ultimate level of education. This is, as Weaver describes it in terms of communication theory, "the effectiveness problem." Being able to repeat the First Amendment is probably unimportant, as in fact is understanding it, *unless the knowledge affects what people do*. Unless citizens speak freely, worship freely, write freely, assemble freely, and petition freely, even complete understanding of this basic notion seems insignificant. Knowing that one has the right to speak out against oppression or evil is simply academic unless people *do* these things. Helping children improve their ability to transmit ideas is completely without significance unless they reflect this knowledge in their lives each day. Our schools must develop people who are free— not just people who know, understand, appreciate, and think about freedom, but people who behave in the ways of free men.

Schools Exert Control

To fulfill these purposes, men build schools. Schools are established by and maintained for society. Through them society attempts to provide an instrument whereby young people may acquire ideas of which the social order is aware, at the same time building into those same youths a genuine capacity for change. For these reasons, schools are concerned with providing experiences which will enable young people to translate vast amounts of information into actual behavior.

Considered in this context, schools effect a type of social control. Schools in America are expected to exert a kind of control which is based upon the principle of increasing the amount of information available to learners rather than restricting it; of opening up areas of inquiry rather than closing them off; of encouraging an examination of all pertinent data regarding any issue. Schools in a democratic society exert a control which forces people to be cognizant of "all sides of the issue." They do not permit one to ignore the facts. They are a positive, pulling kind of force. Rather than restricting an individual's opportunity to view broader horizons, education in its truest sense encourages—in fact, insists upon—the exploration of all possible facts. And education attempts to make facts so significant that the individual is aware of, understands, and behaves according to those facts.

Schools seek to contrive situations and foster experiences in which particular behavioral developments are encouraged. They try to teach children to be honest and kind, for example. They work toward helping children learn to spell correctly, compute accurately, and read with speed and comprehension. Schools and teachers attempt to help children delve into the depths of important ideas and to see their significance for themselves. Schools endeavor to develop in young people ways of behaving which are democratic. They are not willing, if they can help it, to let children develop authoritarian attitudes and undemocratic behavior. They are not willing to permit youth to acquire ways of behaving which are unacceptable socially or unrewarding personally if they can influence those same young people's growth and behavior in other directions.

SUMMARY

The major responsibility of schools is to take facts which have been made readily available, and help young people weave this information through the very fabric of their being so that it is reflected in everything they do. They have to help youth wrap ideas around their psychological backbones, so to speak, so that when they leave the classroom these youngsters will be affected by the facts.

Education is a moral process (2). The purposes of education imply direction. They assume that behavioral change is both an appropriate and a legitimate goal. Schools seek to effect such changes through communication; through persuasion rather than coercion; through influence rather than physical force. In a democracy, schools are committed to specific ends, but the ends are always predicated upon the dignity of man and the power of ideas. And the means must never violate the ends pursued. The next chapter will examine specific goals for schools. Once educators are clear about the goals of education, the major professional problem is one of method.

REFERENCES

1. Chafee, Zechariah Jr., "Freedom of Speech in the Constitution," *Primer of Intellectual Freedom*, Howard Mumford Jones, Ed. (Cambridge: Harvard University Press, 1949), 63.
2. Childs, John L., as quoted by Raymond C. Callahan in *An Introduction to Education in American Society* (New York: Alfred A. Knopf, 1957) 95-102.
3. Combs, Arthur W., "Personality Theory and Its Implications for Curriculum Development," *Learning More About Learning*, Alexander Frazier, Ed. (Washington, D. C.: Association for Supervision and Curriculum Development, 1959), 9.
4. Commager, Henry S., *Freedom, Loyalty, Dissent* (New Haven: Yale University Press, 1954).
5. Huxley, Julian, as quoted by Raymond C. Callahan in *An Introduction to Education in American Society* (New York: Alfred A. Knopf, 1957), 29.
6. MacLeish, Archibald, "The Poet and the Press," *The Atlantic Monthly*, CCIII (March, 1959), 44.
7. Shannon, Claude E. and Weaver, Warren, *The Mathematical Theory of Communication* (Urbana: University of Illinois Press, 1949), 96.
8. Sinnot, Edmund, "The Questing Heritage," *The Nature of Being Human*, Marie Rasey, Ed. (Detroit: Wayne University Press, 1959).
9. *The Consumers Union Report on Smoking and the Public Interest* (Mount Vernon: Consumers Union, 1963).
10. Wiener, Norbert, *The Human Use of Human Beings: Cybernetics and Society* (Garden City: Doubleday Anchor Books, 1954).

Chapter Two

Working Toward Democratic Behavior

If schools exist to help children learn, and if we are concerned about the kind of people children become, what should be our goal? In our society, *children must learn to behave in democratic ways.* Research in the social sciences may be of assistance here.

Concerned as science is with describing and predicting human behavior, one might not think to look there for goals. Philosophers have generally been the ones to tell us where we ought to go. With the advent of systematic and intensive investigation of man himself, however, a direct concomitant of such inquiry has been the observation that some kinds of behavior are beneficial to the individual and to the group as well, whereas others are detrimental. Research in the social sciences continuously emphasizes the desirability or undesirability of certain behaviors, the consequences of particular actions. Not to look at these data would be to ignore a source of significant information.

HISTORICAL BACKGROUND

For about two decades social scientists have probed man's inner being, including his cognitive, emotional, and personality structure, employing a frame of reference which has come to be called "authoritarian personality theory." Out of these investigations has recently evolved a mass of data which pertain to "authoritarian" people.

Several hundred years ago Machiavelli (162) first described in careful terms the authoritarian nature. This description, written as advice to a political leader, has become a classic statement of the totalitarian way. The book itself was primarily a statement of the most effective despotic

8

methods of that day. Christian Gauss, in his introduction to the Mentor edition (162), mentions that Mussolini selected *The Prince* as the thesis for his doctorate, and that Hitler kept the book for bedside reading.

Whether or not Hitler was influenced to any degree by *The Prince* we do not know, but of two things we are quite sure: Hitler did write a book himself (112), and he was a cruel and vicious authoritarian. Erich Fromm, a sensitive and literate observer who lived in Germany during the period of Hitler's rise, became alarmed at *Mein Kampf* and then at the actions of the German people themselves as they turned from freedom to an unbelievably harsh and inhuman dictatorship. The process both interested and bothered Fromm, who rushed his own *Escape from Freedom* (83) into print.

A timely book, written during the early part of World War II, this caused many astute social scientists, aroused by the brutal conduct of the Germans and the Japanese, to push deeper into their own studies of the nature of man. Maslow, a clinical psychologist who had been influenced by Fromm's analysis of the social scene, used his own experience as a clinician, and outlined the authoritarian character structure in detail. This statement (170), published at the height of the war in 1943, did much to focus attention on the problem of authoritarianism. Immediately inspired, a group in California undertook a study of authoritarian personality structure, and published, in 1950, a monumental work (1) on the subject. *The Authoritarian Personality*, entailing a study of many subjects by a variety of methods, did much to impel hundreds of other scientists into action.

Excited about the vistas into human nature opened before them, alarmed at the devastation of the war, and frightened by the ever-present possibility of another, more awesome, instant of destruction, social scientists all over the world attacked the problem of authoritarianism from many angles. Some did clinical investigations of a few individuals; others undertook broad, cross-cultural studies of thousands of persons. Investigation into every aspect of personality and behavior was inaugurated. Out of all these studies have come clarification and elaboration of authoritarianism, including extension and justification of the concept.

Rokeach's *The Open and Closed Mind* (203), for instance, is an effort to extend the concept of authoritarian behavior and make it at once more inclusive and more precise. Literally hundreds of other researches (39) have been reported, and though there is some concern about the assumptions and the logic of particular phases of authoritarian theory (40), there is fairly widespread acceptance of the idea itself. The theory, as outlined by Fromm, Maslow, Adorno, and others, has gradually come to generate fruitful ideas and assist researchers in the exploration of man himself.

Against this background of authoritarian theory and from this wealth of research, the following concepts of democratic behavior have evolved. It is also upon this information that the following assumption is predicated: *Schools must develop boys and girls who behave in democratic ways.* What, then, is the democratic way?

BEHAVIORAL TRAITS

The first, most striking, observation in reference to democratic behavior is its unity or its totality. Superficially this might seem a function of the theory itself (i.e., the idea of a personality syndrome was subsumed by the California group), but analysis of the data (1, 40, 86, 150, 203) indicates that a total personality pattern apparently does exist, although the evidence is by no means conclusive (86, 143, 168, 236).

Before we look at the total pattern, though, perhaps an examination of some specific behavioral traits would be appropriate. Many way of behaving might be described. The purpose here has been to select the most significant for the teaching profession. Neither time nor space would permit review of all factors, but an outline of the general pattern should gradually emerge.

It may be true, as Whorf (253) maintains, that behavior is a function of language. This idea has attracted wide attention in recent years. Our own language is unquestionably two-dimensional. Most of the words in our vocabulary present one aspect of a phenomenon which is generally conceived of as having two. The opposite, of course, is represented by the antonym. Synonyms represent the same or a related shade of meaning. Thus, for every right there is a wrong, for black a white, for hard a soft, for tall a short, for give a receive.

This may or may not be a correct description, but our language is so built that it forces our thought processes in one of two directions along some conceptual continuum. Since we have the kind of language that we do, and since continua are convenient tools with which to think (135, 136, 194), the material which follows will be described in those terms. For purposes of illustration, at least, the ideas will be expressed in terms of democratic or authoritarian attributes. It is assumed that these are polar aspects of human behavior, and though it may ultimately be that a more precise presentation of these same ideas would employ a holistic approach, they will not here be so viewed.

The discussion which follows, therefore, is predicated upon this bi-dimensionality of our language system, and the descriptions of behaviors are essentially those of the extremes of various behavioral continua. This does not mean that the characteristics undergoing study are different entities; they are simply opposite sides of the same factor. Break a stick in two, and it still has two ends.

More Perceptive

A democratic person is perceptive (1, 38). He is more open (86, 172, 211), has more perceptions, and is more accurate in the perceptual process than the authoritarian person (168). The quality and quantity of his perceptions are different from those of the undemocratic person (121). He sees reality more for what it actually is than for what he wishes it were. He is in harmony with the universe of which he is a part. A democratic individual is more able to bring his environment into his central nervous system and give it meaning (46, 119, 163, 186); a meaning which is closely allied with what is actually there. Rokeach says (203):

> This leads us to suggest a basic characteristic that defines the extent to which a person's system is open or closed; namely, the extent to which the person can receive, evaluate, and act on relevant information received from the outside on its own intrinsic merits, unencumbered by irrelevant factors in the situation arising from within the person or from the outside.

He recognizes that previous experiences tend to distort his perceptions (11, 55, 129, 130, 263), so he continuously subjects his interpretations to scrutiny.

The authoritarian, on the other hand, perceives as if he had a built-in mechanism for distortion (110, 142, 251). His perceptions are less accurate, and he has fewer of them (85). He seems to be less capable of seeing the world as it really is, but tends to see it as he wishes it were, or as he is afraid it might be (37, 72, 79, 120, 248). As Van Loon says (245), "happily lived mankind in the peaceful Valley of Ignorance."

Democratic people are not so handicapped. Being more perceptive, they act in a way which brings them closer to that which is true (2, 36). The truth seems to fascinate them; they are attracted toward it. They are concerned that in their search for truth they have the maximum opportunity to perceive with a minimum of restrictions (21). They therefore tend to value the opportunity to know different people and share their expressions of reality (100). They make almost no restrictions on another's efforts to discuss or describe (76) any aspect of his own experience. Freedom of speech and press are their bywords, and many are attracted to the academic life with its prevailing freedom—the "pursuit of truth." It might even be said that one of the democratic person's chief driving forces is this desire to know and comprehend; to understand, to see and hear what is—to know the truth.

Although the world is full of uncertainties and unknowns, for the democratic person they represent challenges and opportunities, never threats. The democratic person is not only able to tolerate the ambiguities of life, the unknown tomorrows, the uncertainties of modern existence, he even seems to enjoy them. Many times it is this uncertainty which is a prime motivating force in his own life (171). The true scientist represents the extremely democratic person. Able to live with the unknown, attracted toward it, in his scientific endeavors he is persistently but patiently mapping out the shady areas beyond the known.

An authoritarian, on the other hand, is the kind of person who is upset by uncertainty (81, 255). He wants to know where he stands. He wants to do something, even if it is wrong. He cannot tolerate what appears to him to be indecision, even though to the democratic person who insists on such procedures this is "suspending judgment." The authoritarian "runs a taut ship," as it were, and many of his actions which, on the surface, seem to reflect an efficient air of accomplishment, actually indicate a rigid set of relationships with things and people (150).

The democratic person appears to be more patient. He realizes that it is not always possible to ascertain immediately any bit of information, and he prefers to move steadily, if slowly, toward intelligent action (133) rather than strike out boldly but perhaps ignorantly toward some unforeseen fate.

This is not to imply that the democratic person is incapable of decisive action. He realizes that there is a time for waiting and a time for action (202), and though he may wait for an extended period, when he acts he may do so with great vigor and speed.

Witness the doctor who patiently listens to the sick person describe his symptoms. He looks, punches, feels, takes blood samples, and performs laboratory tests, all the while striving to be maximally perceptive. The patient, in his concern about his health, may repeatedly ask the doctor, "What's wrong?" The physician, however, bides his time, looking for additional evidence or symptomatic behavior.

If he decides to operate, he may move with great alacrity, even amazing the patient who all this time felt he was being ignored, or that the doctor did not know very much, after all. The doctor, however, was tolerating the ambiguities of the situation and endeavoring to resolve them into certainties. When that time came, he acted.

Ledley and Lusted emphasize the point (154) that ". . . the most brilliant diagnosticians . . . are the ones who remember and consider the most possibilities." In our society, effective medical doctors and scientists, especially, epitomize this democratic trait in their daily lives.

Another facet of this characteristic is the democratic person's disinclination to think in categorical terms (82), good or bad, right or wrong. Whereas the authoritarian tends to categorize things as black or white (15), the democratic person usually sees the world as "shades of gray."

Neither an extremist nor a moderate, the democratic individual sees things for what they really are (75), and though this is often "somewhere in between," he is not a moderate in the sense that he is looking for compromise or seeking to avoid the attention or persecution which might result from an extreme position. Should he see any facet of reality as a clear-cut extremity, he would not hesitate to describe it as such.

The fact that most aspects of reality are not extreme, however, means that he usually assumes a position or describes a phenomenon (32) which could be characterized as "middle ground." He recognizes that most of our undertakings are more successful if we have some part in their planning and execution. He strives to incorporate the best of all men's ideas into a social endeavor. That this may make him seem to be a compromiser is no more accurate than to say that he has no principles of his own. The careful observer, however, will note in the democratic person's behavior his constant struggle to get at reality, and since this reality is usually something less than jet black or lily white, his own efforts at action and decision are generally characterized by accuracy rather than boisterousness and by moderation rather than the extreme.

Basically secure, the democratic person does not suffer from the tensions which beset the authoritarian individual. Evidence of this is his realistic concern with time (203). Unlike the authoritarian, who is preoccupied with the past or future, the democratic person has a healthy awareness of all phases of time—past, present, and future. He recognizes the need to be cognizant of things which have happened before in order to benefit from other men's experiences, but at the same time he is not obsessed with the past nor does he look to long dead authorities for direction. Such people are concerned about the here and now, but they also are aware of the future, and set about making reasonable preparations for the days to come.

Fearful of the future or concerned for nothing else, the authoritarian has a different outlook. He is forever occupied with making preparations for tomorrow. He is, indeed, so busy preparing that he seldom finds an opportunity to enjoy today. Always working for tomorrow or living in the glorious past (206), the authoritarian wants desperately to resolve his conflicts with himself and his beliefs with respect to time. His attention, centered elsewhere, makes him less aware of the significance of daily events. He tends to be less able to assume responsibility for difficulties which arise, even though they may be of his own making. There is a tendency to seek scapegoats: parents, school board members, or just plain "they."

Positive Self Concept

A democratic person has a positive self-image (95, 149, 188). He feels that he is important and worthwhile, that he possesses dignity and worth. He is neither overly self-centered nor overly self-concerned. His attention generally lies outside his own concept of self. He recognizes the fact that he is unique and different from other persons (229), but he also recognizes that these differences are significant. He does not have to prove continuously that he is unique. He knows it. The democratic person seems to be aware, intuitively or intellectually, that differences among people are to be valued, therefore his own capabilities and differences must be so considered. He does not, however, feel compelled to act "bohemian" in order to convince himself of his importance. He comprehends that he is important simply because he is a human being.

Furthermore, the democratic person is more ready to accept himself (171, 186). He is able to assess his personal potentialities and weaknesses accurately (113). Neither deceived nor discouraged by his limitations, he accepts them as a part of his experience (122).

This is not to say that democratic people always approve of everything they do. They often make mistakes and regret them. They recognize that they have erred, and sincerely set about to eliminate such behavior (171).

The democratic person is responsible; he feels *able to respond;* able to cope with life and all that it implies (18, 153, 197, 204, 239). He seems to enjoy responsibility and on many occasions seeks it out. He sees the universe as a challenging and exciting opportunity to test himself (99, 102, 241). He is able to do this because of his faith in himself and his belief in his own abilities.

The authoritarian individual, however, has a different sort of self concept (56). Superficially it, too, may seem to be positive. Such a person may seem to be satisfied with himself and his efforts (6), even to the extreme. Conceit or bragging is not uncommon for these people.

In the final analysis, however, authoritarians are less sure of themselves (23, 70); they feel less able to cope with their environment without assistance (93, 223), and usually feel much less positive toward themselves than democratic individuals (1).

The basic reason for this is that they tend to see themselves as threatened by some portion of their circumstances (147, 207). Being threatened (145, 151), they feel less able to cope with the realities. The threat may be real or imagined (213, 261), but the authoritarian is adversely affected by it (55, 194). The result is a loss of status for himself in his own eyes. He is unable to respect himself unless he distorts his interpretation of things so that he can admit them into his awareness (237). Apprehensive because of inadequacy, he seeks opportunities to assign responsibility to others. If trouble occurs, the fault is never his. His attention is upon himself; he is so concerned with what he does and how he does it that he cannot take responsibility for his own actions. To be wrong would obliterate his self-picture (152). So inadequate does he feel, that he is continuously striving to present a positive picture of himself to others. Unable to accept the fact that he is unique and different, he feels compelled to justify his variances as "right" or "acceptable."

It is the democratic individual who recognizes and cherishes his uniqueness and that of others, and he also feels positively toward himself in a healthy, realistic manner (28). He is, as Combs and Snygg would say (47), an "adequate personality."

Positive Concept of Others

A democratic person also has positive relationships with other people. These might be described as "accepting" (96). He is giving of himself (220, 234). He extends the right hand of fellowship to all people (63, 84). He is a philanthropist in the original sense of the word—he loves mankind.

The problem of acceptance, of course, is not a simple one. Most studies to date have examined the impact of acceptance upon other people rather than the dynamics of being an accepting kind of person (12, 25, 26, 31, 42, 54, 60, 73, 78, 94, 139, 159, 181, 208, 249). That is, "who is accept*ed?*" "why are they accept*ed?*" "what are accept*ed* people like?" rather than "who is accept*ing?*" why are they accept*ing?*" "what are accept*ing* people like?" (96, 180)

This raises a fundamental question for teachers, for example, because if teachers are concerned about helping boys and girls become accept*ed,* they go about their teaching one way; but if they are concerned about helping youngsters become accept*ing,* they behave differently.

Most teachers are aware of the negative results of rejection. They know that if boys and girls are not accepted, they generate so much activity striving for acceptance (111, 137) that they have little psychological energy left over for learning (69). These statements, made by a young, delinquent girl, describe her personal feelings of rejection by her mother (212):

> My mother got all upset, and she called me a big horse, and said I didn't need a doll like that. I was too big to play with a doll like that. I cried, and I never forgot it. My parents just didn't understand how a little girl feels about such things. . . . My mother always called me a bad girl. She said one year near Christmas that if I wasn't a good girl, Santa Claus would put coal in my stocking instead of a gift. Then, on Christmas morning, when I woke up, there was coal all around me in my bed. I almost died when I saw that. I've never forgiven my mother for doing that.

Following his study of the differences in self-concepts of whites and Negroes in South Africa, Bloom reaches a conclusion equally pathetic (23):

> We cannot avoid stepping out of the sterile role of social scientist to deplore the lack of hope, the wastage of potential in a country with inadequate educational and social services, and few opportunities for the non-whites who comprise 75 per cent of the total population, and whose slender weight of opportunity is amply overweighed by the heavy and crushing burden of discouragement.

Unless people feel wanted, accepted, and secure in their relationships with other persons, they expend time and effort seeking such attention (87, 158, 215).

Teachers know this. Teachers recognize that a child who feels unwanted and alone is much less able to learn his science lesson than the one who has had his social yearnings satisfied (105, 264). However, in their efforts to increase students' social acceptance, many teachers have approached the problem from the reject*ed* child's point of view. If a particular youngster is rejected, they try to discover the cause and then try to help him to change. One soon realizes that inducing acceptance by changing the rejected person brings about a conforming type of behavior (140, 157, 200). If John rejects Billy, and if Billy feels that he must change in order to gain John's acceptance, the result is a loss of Billy's individuality. However, if John can accept Billy *for what he is*, this will create an air of acceptance and at the same time preserve Billy's uniqueness and individuality. By encouraging people to be more accept-

ing, teachers can eliminate the undesirable results which accompany rejection, and at the same time retain the individual differences which make life so worthwhile.

It is just on this factor that Drevdahl (65) quotes Bertrand Russell, when that sage gentleman implored mankind to be "a wise herd." Drevdahl continues:

> All deviates are not creative. As Russell points out, a number of these people are those that fall *below* average in one respect or another; but until we *know* that the deviate is non-productive and non-creative it behooves us to be tolerant of deviation of a non-violent sort, and to recognize that it may be years or decades before someone's "crazy" ideas can be demonstrated to be genuinely "crazy" or simply so far ahead of the rest of us that we take forever to catch up. I suppose that now tolerance may be the best we can hope for; but in order to avoid national suicide it *must* also be the *least* that we do.

The democratic person is accepting (9, 235, 245).

This does not mean that the democratic person must like or approve of all that other people do (74, 195). On the contrary, many persons' actions and attitudes often seem to him disgusting, but, because they are people, he accepts them. All people have worth and dignity to him (89). The democratic person seems able, as Maslow (171) says, "to give a certain quantum of respect to *any* human being, just because he is a human individual."

This notion approaches the Christian ethic (224) of "love thy neighbor." It is certainly not characterized by the negative behaviors so common among authoritarians: intolerance, rejection, stereotypy (77, 88, 192, 193), and discrimination. A democratic person seems unable to behave negatively towards other people (169). Even though they be despicable, he strives to accept them. He may not want to associate with certain persons (126, 184), but there is never, in his demeanor, anything which would communicate this to them. He attempts to give them every indication of consideration and acceptance. This is not a false kind of behavior; he genuinely wants to accept them and to be of help if he can. Concerning this point, Maslow says (172):

> Self-actualizing people, by definiton gratified in their basic needs, including the love need, should cease loving and wanting love, if the only determinant of love were the basic love need. But the finding is that they are *more* loving people than the average, rather than *less* loving, especially from the point of view of being able to give love as well as to receive it.

In all his relationships with others, the democratic individual tends to be supportive, encouraging, assisting, and positive in his associations (34, 47, 61, 80, 222). This manifests itself in cooperative rather than competitive behavior (97), and a general demeanor which seems to say: "I am a person who really tries to understand." In every way this acceptance goes beyond tolerance. He does not "put up with" other people, but makes every effort to see things from their point of view.

This effort causes democratic people to be more empathic (186). They are able to identify themselves with other people; able to see why and how they feel the way they do; able to appreciate their circumstances and feelings (105, 236). This ability to empathize comes about primarily as a result of the democratic person's exceptional ability to perceive (7, 10). Since he is better able to see reality for what it is, he is less often influenced by his biases and is more accurate in estimating the positions and feelings of others (13, 221).

This capacity to identify himself with other people—to put himself in the other fellow's shoes—wins for the democratic person many friends (246). Because he is accepting and perceptive, he is always willing to lend an ear and a helping hand. This means that such people are very social (189, 190). Not social or popular in the usual sense of the term (71), since they often associate with only one person, or a few at a time. Nonetheless, these people are in great demand and spend much time in the company of others. Since they are so accepting, they sometimes experience difficulty in finding opportunities to work on things which they themselves feel are important. Because they feel that people are so very important, and because they are so able to sense how others feel, their own desires and their concerns for others sometimes get confused.

These people may have difficulty in saying "no" when asked to be of assistance in any worthy cause. Feeling that people are worthwhile, they are apt to think that all people's efforts are likewise important. The result is that they expend time and effort working toward other people's goals.

Not all democratic people are so distracted for long, however, since their perceptual abilities permit them eventually to see their own objectives as worthy of pursuit. Because they are extremely skillful socially, they are usually able to terminate such relationships on a positive note, leaving the other person supported and accepted (167). This ability enables the democratic individual to help himself repeatedly by helping other people help themselves (125). Such efforts are very satisfying to all concerned.

This is the kind of behavior which Carl Becker felt was called for by *The Declaration of Independence.* As quoted by Howard Mumford

Jones (123), Becker described the ideas embodied in that great document as follows:

> It was a humane and engaging faith. At its best it preached toler-
> ation in place of persecution, goodwill in place of hate, peace in
> place of war. It taught that beneath all local and temporary diver-
> sity, beneath the superficial traits and talents that distinguished men
> and nations, all men are equal in the possession of a common hu-
> manity; and to the end that concord might prevail on the earth
> instead of strife, it invited men to promote in themselves the hu-
> manity which bound them to their fellows, and to shape their
> conduct and their institutions in harmony with it.

The authoritarian behaves in other ways. Rather than accepting people, he rejects them (3). This rejection may take the form of prejudice and ethnocentrism (1, 8, 22, 50, 131, 166, 196, 218, 219, 227, 232, 247, 259) or outright discrimination. He tends to say and do things which drive people apart. At first, these behaviors may exist at the verbal, gossip, or rumor level. In more serious instances (4), they manifest themselves in restrictions (115, 165), "Jim Crow laws," segregation, physical attack (59, 216), and even physical obliteration (51, 191) as with the Jews in Germany or the lynching of Negroes in the South.

Rokeach (203), for example, describes the pathetic humor of a cartoon in which a man at a bar is saying: "I hate everybody, regardless of race, creed, or color." When this researcher says that he is finding evidence for misanthropy—hatred of mankind—rather than simple discrimination, one realizes the significance of the notion. These actions occur because authoritarians are afraid (59, 72, 79, 129, 198). And the fact that such actions are *learned* (4) is both discouraging and hopeful.

Independent

It would be unthinkable, having come this far in an examination of the democratic person's behaviors, to imagine him as being anything but independent; and naturally he is. But he is independent in a mature and sophisticated way.

Whereas the authoritarian tends to be both dominating and submissive (1), sadistic and masochistic (84), the democratic person tends to relate to people in an entirely different way (92). The illustrations below may indicate some of the differences in the way these two kinds of people see other human beings. Although the authoritarian tends to see others as part of a social hierarchy, above and below him (106, 175, 176, 225),

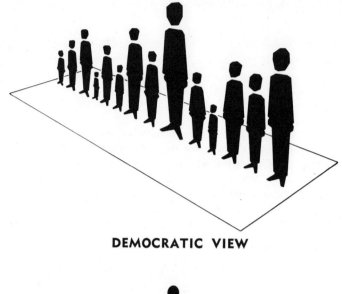

DEMOCRATIC VIEW

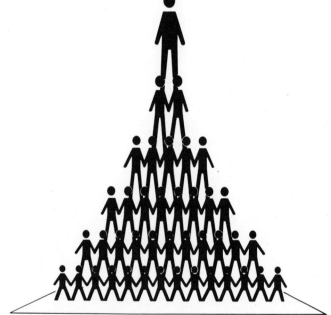

AUTHORITARIAN VIEW

Democratic and Authoritarian Persons' Perceptions
of Social Reality

the democratic person tends to see other people as different but on an equal plane (210).

Fromm describes the sadistic person in this respect (84):

> The sadistic person wants to escape from his aloneness and his sense of imprisonment by making another person part and parcel of himself. He inflates and enhances himself by incorporating another person, who worships him.
>
> The sadistic person is as dependent on the submissive person as the latter is on the former; neither can live without the other. The difference is only that the sadistic person commands, exploits, hurts, humiliates, and that the masochistic person is commanded, exploited, hurt, humiliated. There is a considerable difference in a realistic sense; in a deeper emotional sense, the difference is not so great as that which they both have in common: fusion without integrity.

The democratic person recognizes that there are differences among individuals, to be sure, but that these differences do not imply that some are better than, stronger than, or more important than, anyone else (171). The democratic person recognizes that while people are different, they are all worthwhile. Men do bad things, but all men possess worth and dignity. The college professor recognizes that the dean is his administrative superior but also his intellectual peer; that his students are academically less advanced but intellectually engaged in the same enterprise—the pursuit of truth.

The authoritarian has trouble with such an idea since he feels that everybody has his own place and ought to stay there. Or, if there is to be any moving around within the social milieu, changes will be the result of status and force. To the authoritarian, it's "dog eat dog," and "survival of the fittest." The authoritarian recognizes that there are differences among people but that all people are basically the same —bad (124). One dare not trust a stranger or a novice or a subordinate, since all of them are out to get all they can. Also, since children are bad, it becomes the responsibility of the school to make them good. And since they will not be good of their own accord (because by definition they are bad), the school must employ any means, including force, to make them that way. The authoritarian seems to feel that "there are two kinds of people in the world; the good and the bad. And the good decide which is which."

These notions come primarily from the authoritarian's distorted perception of social reality (30, 173). He assumes that we live in a world which is largely competitive and aggressive, not recognizing that competition always rests and operates on a broad, cooperative base. He fails to recognize that even the largest, most competitive organizations are unable to compete when their working force fails to maintain production, as happens during a strike. He feels that most men are dependent on a few rather than that all men are interdependent. He fails to recognize that ours is the most highly cooperative, interdependent, society which ever existed; that "getting along with other people" is more than a byword—it is an absolute necessity.

Deploring the decision to make and use the atom bomb, Lewis Mumford (182) says: "More than any other event that has taken place in modern times this sudden radical changeover from war to collective extermination reversed the whole course of human history."

He continues:

> Plainly, the acceptance of mass extermination as a normal outcome of war undermined all the moral inhibitions that have kept man's murderous fantasies from active expression. War, however brutal and devastating, had a formal beginning and could come to an end by some formal process of compromise or surrender. But no one has the faintest notion how nuclear extermination, once begun, could be brought to an end. . . . Most Americans . . . have no consciousness of either the magnitude of their collective sin or the fact that, by their silence, they have individually condoned it. It is precisely as if the Secretary of Agriculture had licensed the sale of human flesh as a wartime emergency measure and people had taken to cannibalism when the war was over as a clever dodge for lowering the cost of living—a mere extension of everyday butchery.

Obviously Mumford feels that as a nation we are moving away from those democratic principles, espoused in *The Delcaration of Independence* and elsewhere, directly toward an authoritarian way of life.

For the authoritarian, while professing individualism, is really very unindividualistic in the final analysis (45, 114, 228, 254, 255, 256). Seldom able to operate without support, he usually does not want to do anything different. Sometimes he represents what Benedict (16) calls "extreme development of the cultural type." Instead of exposing these persons, society

> . . . supports them in their furthest aberrations. They have a license which they may almost endlessly exploit. For this reason these persons almost never fall within the scope of any contemporary psychiatry. They are unlikely to be described even in the most careful manuals of the generation that fosters them. Yet from the point of view of another generation or culture they are ordinarily the most bizarre of the psychopathic types of the period.

The authoritarian's direction and support invariably comes either from some leader (20, 24) or from the group itself (200), or from the recognized "in-group" (66, 177); never from his own convictions about right and wrong (113). He usually accepts what is done without question, because some superior has implied that it should be so (179). This authoritarian is the same person who, as a school principal, will browbeat his teachers during faculty meetings, and then bow submissively to the superintendent.

The democratic person functions in a different manner. He recognizes his dependence on all people, but also realizes that it is this same interdependence which makes for satisfying human existence. He knows that differences and uniqueness among people makes for a fuller, more productive way of life. How boring things would be if all members of the opposite sex were identical. All of the joy and satisfaction which comes from courtship and marriage would disappear. And if all males were identical, what would we do for football games and other contests, which depend for their existence upon differences in ability and skill? The democratic person does not believe, to paraphrase George Orwell (187), that "all people are equal, but some are more equal than others."

But in addition to recognition of these variations in human attributes, the democratic person prizes these differences highly (65, 185, 199). He "cherishes uniqueness," as Kelley and Rasey (130) say. He recognizes his own individuality, but at a level which does not require a surface nonconformity. As mentioned before, he is not "bohemian" or "beatnik." He has faith in his own value so that he is able to do the things required for human existence like most other people. But he also knows that, should the need arise, he would be willing, as Maslow says (171), to "shed the cloak of conventionality" for concerted action, or break the law one time in a hundred, as Gandhi (214) professed:

> The right of civil disobedience, i.e., breaking of laws, accrues only to one who has willingly and scrupulously obeyed laws. Lawbreaking cannot be made a habit. . . . The law-breaker breaks the law surreptitiously and tries to avoid the penalty; not so the civil resister. He ever obeys the laws of the State to which he belongs, not out of fear of the sanctions, but because he considers them to be good for the welfare of society. But there come occasions, generally rare, when he considers certain laws to be so unjust as to render obedience to them a dishonour. He then openly and civilly breaks them and quietly suffers the penalty for their breach. And in order to register his protest against the action of the law-givers, it is open to him to withdraw his co-operation from the State by disobeying such other laws whose breach does not involve moral turpitude.

The democratic person realizes that his real strength as an individual comes from his contacts with other people. He knows that people are the main substance, the lifeblood, of his experience, and if he does things to other people which would be damaging or degrading in any way, what he really does is to deprive himself of a good perceptual source. He is aware that the only way in which he can improve his own lot in life is by helping other people. They are the stuff out of which he builds himself. When he hurts other people, he destroys the source of his own positive perceptions, but when he tries to make other people better, when he accepts and supports them, then he perceives a better psychological material. Out of these perceptions he builds a better self. He is, indeed, "his brother's keeper," and he knows it (130).

This concept of individualism for a democratic person is closely allied with Gandhi's idea of Satyagraha (214). Satyagraha means "soul force" or "love force," and as such was epitomized by Gandhi's own existence (214):

> This force is to violence, and therefore to all tyranny, all injustice, what light is to darkness. In politics, its use is based upon the immutable maxim that government of the people is possible only so long as they consent either consciously or unconsciously to be governed.

It represents a dynamic relationship between two parties which is characterized by neither domination nor submission; neither aggression nor appeasement (47). What this means in everyday politics has been well described by Kripalani (146) for India:

> Indian foreign policy before independence was confined to the enunciation of basic principles which would guide the country's diplomacy after independence. These principles, influenced as a matter of course by the principles that directed our whole struggle, were based on non-violence and truth. These are moral principles, but translated into political terms they mean disarmament and open diplomacy, principles enunciated by President Woodrow Wilson during World War I. India stood for the freedom of all nations and peoples and against all colonial or racial domination of one people over another . . .

Barrington outlines a similar position for Burma (14):

> . . . independence means complete independence, independence even from those countries which happen to adopt a line similar to the Union of Burma's in international affairs . . . [Burma's] policy

of judging each individual issue as it arises strictly on its merits causes her to vote sometimes with one side and sometimes with the other, or to abstain where the issue is not a clear-cut one.

Both in practice and theory what is involved is a statement something like this: "I am a man and you are a man. I will not hurt you, but I will not let you hurt me. I will make no effort to damage or destroy or degrade you, but neither will I permit you to do these things to me. We are both men, equally, and we are going to deal with each other on an equal plane. I will be honest and straightforward with you, and I expect you to be the same with me."

This profound idea embodies the very spirit of democracy. It recognizes the rights and responsibilities and equal worth of all individuals (62, 250). It is an active position which does not depend upon force to settle claims, but relies upon good will and rational thought to solve all problems. It is a concept which appeals to the democratic person because of the way he views the social scene (134). It is an idea which strikes the authoritarian as ridiculous or naïve, depending upon his estimate of the individual espousing it. Such a description of independence aptly applies to democratic people. This idea sounds similar to "peaceful co-existence," as outlined by Khrushchev (148):

> In its simplest expression it signified the repudiation of war as a means to solving controversial issues . . . The principle of peaceful coexistence signifies a renunciation of interference in the internal affairs of other countries with the object of altering their system of government or mode of life for any other motives. The doctrine of peaceful coexistence also presupposes that political and economic relations between countries are to be based upon complete equality of the parties concerned, and on mutual benefit.

Kennan, however, feels that Khrushchev's statement departs somewhat from the facts. He states acidly (128):

> There could be few propositions more amazing than the assertion that the Soviet state "from its very inception . . . proclaimed peaceful coexistence as the basic principle of its foreign policy," and that the initial Communist leaders in Russia were strong partisans of the view that peaceful coexistence could and should prevail among states with different social systems. . . . One turns reluctantly to the record of those early years of Soviet power . . . It is surprising that there should be so little respect for the true history of the Russian revolutionary movement on the part of those who profess today to be its custodians and protagonists that they are

willing to pervert it in this way for the sake of their own tactical convenience.

He continues:

> The fact is (and it is one we have had impressed upon us in painful ways over these past four decades) that there are more ways than outright military aggression or formal political intervention by which the fate of smaller peoples may be brought under subjection to the will of larger ones, and more devices than those of the classic nineteenth century colonialism by which people can be kept in that state.. There does exist, after all, such a thing as the science of insurrection—the science of the seizure of power by conspiratorial minorites, and of the conquest of the vital centers of power, of the control of the streets, of the manipulation of civil conflict.

A democratic person's leadership is defined by his attitudes toward the group and toward his role. He thinks of himself as somebody endeavoring to help others get a job done. He feels that one of his responsibilities is to act so that people are able to release their creative powers in solving problems (53). The democratic individual knows that leadership is both an individual and a group phenomenon, thus he strives to be aware of the sentiments and norms of the group with which he is associated (155, 156). In all of his efforts he consciously works at building morale, opening channels of communication, encouraging and assisting in the exploration of ideas, and struggling to minimize any potential threat (27, 68, 258).

He sees his own role of status leader primarily as one of "following ahead." This is how a democratic person tries to operate. It is in this realm of mutual trust, exploration, and group participation (123) that the individual whom we call democratic feels most at home. The idea is beautifully described by Judge Rosenman (29) in his portrayal of Roosevelt's turn from isolationism to internationalism. He quotes the president, who, having in his own mind failed at this very thing, said: "It's a terrible thing to look over your shoulder when you are trying to lead—and to find no one there."

The authoritarian's estimate of leadership is based on the "strong man" philosophy, and though actual physical force is frowned upon, more subtle ways of keeping people in their proper place are used. Recognition from the chair, appointments to key committees, or assignment to prize locations or important posts are all procedures whereby authoritarians achieve control. Less obvious but more devastating, are devices based on bringing group pressure to bear upon deviant members (116) or granting condescending recognition of individual accomplishments which also carries with it a note of denunciation. Other approaches involve general degradation of the parties involved (98, 101). Because he thinks his position is based on power in a "drive or be driven" situation, such a person resorts to practices which are predicated upon the essential inequality of man: fear (198), distrust (90, 91), shame, psychological force, or manipulation (108, 109). Carrying with him the assumption that men are inherently evil and basically degenerate, such authoritarians generally fail to recognize the leadership potential within a group. The result is that they "play the cards close to their chests," never divulging all they know or feel about any problem, and always seeking those who will support them to bring about change along predetermined lines. Because he is the authority, he feels that his actions should reflect his position, thus he tends to exalt his status. Insistence through overt means or covert indication assures him of the recognition and submission which he feels are due authorities. Proper use of titles or degrees, for example, will be quickly rewarded. Reflecting and supporting the leader's suggestions and position is not only appreciated but expected (49). Those who advance contrary notions are being disloyal and therefore suspect. Experimentation is discouraged, and inspiration and direction normally come from the past. Tradition becomes an authority in itself.

Communicative

Skill in communication is both a natural and an acquired characteristic of the democratic person (116). Because he is more open and perceptive, he apparently is aware of ideas with a minimum of effort (172). He knows that communication is the basic social activity, and he strives to improve himself in the processes of communication by working toward increasing the flow of information (238).

Combining his unusual perceptual abilities and his concerns for other people, the democratic person seriously tries to say things so that others can hear what he has to say. He is not as concerned that other people agree with him as he is with being understood. He seems to know that people have defensive psychological mechanisms (37, 120) which they employ to fend off ideas which could be threatening to their own concepts of themselves (217). The democratic individual endeavors to couch his concepts in terms that will "get through."

This is not to say that such a person would compromise his principles to be understood. He does not "straddle the fence" just to avoid debate.

On the contrary, he often professes his own beliefs with great tenacity. He strikes out vigorously for ideas which he believes are right.

These people are exceptionally good listeners. They seem to have a capacity to "reach out" and pull ideas into their own consciousness; to comprehend another's point of view. This is akin to the ability to empathize, since skillful listening is characteristic of empathic people. But this is also a way of behaving. The democratic person not only is concerned with other people as people, but seeks the full value of their ideas (43). He knows that people are what they have learned, and he knows that those who learn the most are most able to partake completely of their environment (164). For this reason, then, he makes a sincere effort, psychologically, to hear what other people have to say.

This effort manifests itself in several ways. First, in the receiving process the democratic person is less distracted than others. He is able to focus his perceptual energies upon the source of communication (118) and to concentrate upon what is being said. When distractions do occur, he strives to minimize them. He ignores or eliminates interruptions so that he can devote full attention to the ideas themselves.

The authoritarian individual, on the other hand, not only tolerates disturbances while listening, he may even create them. Talking in whispers to other people or leafing through a program at a lecture, watching the clock or looking for an opportunity to get away are examples.

The democratic person is willing to go the extra mile in his effort to understand a speaker. He is noticeably tolerant of imperfections or variations of speech production which may be disturbing to other people. He does not leave a lecture if the speaker rolls his "r's." He spends less effort criticizing a speaker's delivery than trying to understand what he has to say. When listening to a foreign accent, for example, he recognizes a challenge to his own comprehension, rather than an opportunity to "turn him off," as the authoritarian is apt to do.

The democratic person also uses the thought-speed advantage which a listener has over a speaker to maximum advantage. He knows that listeners can think much faster than talkers can speak, and he uses this differential to ask himself questions about the meaning of words or the logic of an argument. The authoritarian, however, frequently employs this time difference by daydreaming, preparing an answer to the idea being presented, or by simply looking about him, all the while blaming the speaker for not presenting the ideas more interestingly. The undemocratic person does not really listen (107); he is just quiet while others talk.

Democratic people recognize that by refusing to listen they are depriving themselves of ideas. They know that only bigots condemn an idea without having fully comprehended it. They realize, again intuitively, that people are built out of their perceptions, so they struggle to have as many and as rich perceptions as possible. Rather than limiting their opportunities to come in contact with varied notions, as do authoritarians, they continuously work toward having more (240).

This does not mean that democratic people are uncritical of ideas. It does mean that they are always striving to hear ideas out, to understand them, and then decide upon their fitness (132). A democratic person considers every idea before agreeing with it, and it is this consideration, which can only come after reception, which is important. The authoritarian often does not even receive the idea for consideration. His psychological barriers keep it away from his inner self.

The authoritarian, also, seems to have a built-in capacity for judging ideas primarily according to their source (174, 203). He feels that good people have good ideas and bad people have bad ideas, and that all he needs is to get close enough to good people to hear what they have to say. The authoritarian is concerned to keep bad people, and thus worthless ideas, far, far away. He even segregates himself from any who he feels are unworthy associates. The authoritarian seems unable to accept a good man having a bad idea or a bad man having a good idea. He has, however narrow it may seem, a tendency to examine and judge ideas by their source. (48).

To the democratic person this is appalling. He recognizes the fallibility of men, and realizes that ideas must stand or fall on their own merit. This behavior on the part of the democratic person sometimes shows as a distrust of any idea, whoever projects it. Ideas are hypotheses to be tested, not finalities; guideposts for action, not pillars of truth. It is not the purpose of communication to buttress one's present ignorance, but to eradicate more of the unknown from our world. The democratic person, however, also realizes that information available to any person on any issue usually comes to him through other people. He realizes that (242):

> Our dependence on facts turns out to be somewhat pathetic, since we do not know any facts at all except as they are involved in the experience of man. . . . The area of immediate experience open to any individual is extremely slight—a mere slit in the world's expanse. Thus to say that we shall believe only what we know directly at first hand is to reduce our belief in a fantastic manner. All history would be thereby eliminated and we should be confined to the *spe-*

cious present. A life so ordered would be intellectually poverty-stricken, if, indeed, it were possible at all.

Knowing this he still endeavors to get the facts, even though his efforts are limited. One way he attempts to overcome dependence on any one authority is to seek many authorities' observations on an issue. One person may be recognized as more authoritative than another, but the democratic person attempts to experience many men's reports of reality, especially those which apparently are opposed, thus reducing any personal bias which may have resulted.

The democratic person is first concerned about that which is true. But truth is reality, and the closer one can come to that which is, the closer he can come to achieving the "good life." Blanchard (21) describes this truth as follows:

> The truth which scientists seek is not something which lies dormant, waiting to be discovered. The atomic theory, relativity, and psychoanalysis are not concrete objects which are scratched from the intellectual soil like uranium. They are products of human creativity, and, as such, they are dependent upon the intellectual ability as well as the objectivity of the discoverer.

To live in harmony rather than in opposition to reality is an objective of the democratic individual. The way to do this involves improving communication and increasing information.

Another facet of his capacity to communicate is the democratic person's ability to resist suggestion (183, 265). He tends less to be thus misled and always strikes toward the heart of any matter (117). This is a function of his unusual perceptual abilities. Being less susceptible to status figures, he reflects a lower level of suggestibility (160, 161, 205).

Horowitz and Perlmutter (116) also recognize this same danger to conformity, and they maintain that ". . . although discussion obviously does not in itself make for a democratic procedure or a democratic decision, it is apparently the only path to that goal." They continue:

> This social pressure towards conformity with some group commitment, as a group, is sometimes confused with the establishment of a democratic decision. Making individuals feel guilty if they don't do what they decided as a group, and merely establishing those conditions, cannot strictly be called a democratic procedure.

A direct application of this idea, as described by Harriet Mills (178), is employed by a totalitarian state:

They know that only if people are truly persuaded of the justice and correctness of the Communist position will they release their spontaneous creative energy and cooperate, not from necessity but from conviction. To accelerate this persuasion the Chinese Communists have developed group study, or *hsueh-hsi*, in which everyone must participate—peasant, ex-landlord, city dweller, artisan, worker, peddler, merchant, housewife, producer, industrialist, even the political prisoner. Group study is a unique means for achieving critical rejection of old ideas in favor of new ones and a power weapon for ideological remolding.

The authoritarian is responsive to status figures (67) and symbols of prestige and power, and is thus more conforming (19). Although he is generally unaware of this himself, his actions usually reflect a current vogue. A victim of modern advertising, he finds himself entrapped by suggestion and innuendo, and readily responds to the dictates of others.

Because he sees himself and his reputation threatened, the authoritarian has his psychological apparatus tuned to pounce on suggestions from many sources (200). Any energy which he might have for surveying the situation and assessing the potentialities for action is actually converted to a sensitivity which will enable him to do the right thing at the right time according to the right sources. He is suggestible.

The Democratic Pattern

This chapter has described several democratic ways of behaving. In actuality they are all closely related (1, 170, 203). Many of these characteristics are directly dependent upon others. Taken together they represent a total pattern.

We could envision such a pattern in several ways, but only one will be discussed here. It might be called the "bundle" *continuum.* Such a concept would entail considering all specific behavioral characteristics as individual continua, and the total would then consist of all of them bound together in some psychological way. The chart which follows might clarify this idea.

This diagram sets forth a series of apparently discrete, but actually related, phenomena, each one signifying a different way of acting in a particular situation. Together, these might be considered as a bundle or cable of different factors which represent a totality of behavior, democratic or authoritarian, depending upon the tendency of an individual to be at one end of the dimensions.

Since evidence we have concerning the interrelations of these factors show that positive correlations exist (5, 35, 39, 86, 103, 138, 150, 168,

DEMOCRATIC		AUTHORITARIAN
More		Less
Accurate	**PERCEPTIVE**	Distorted
Realistic Time		Overconcern with Time
Positive		*Negative*
Challenged	**SELF**	*Threatened*
Adequate		*Inadequate*
Accepting		*Rejecting*
Tolerant	**OTHERS**	*Prejudiced*
Loving		*Hateful*
Independent		*Dependent*
Equalitarian	**INDEPENDENCE**	*Dominant-Submissive*
Autonomous		*Suggestible*
Listens		Does not listen
"Gets Thru"	**COMMUNICATIVE**	Arouses Barriers
Understands		Does Not Comprehend

Democratic-Authoritarian Continuum

209, 236), we would expect up and down relationships. There would be a pattern readily discernible which would represent an individual's tendency toward democratic behavior or authoritarianism.

Most people would tend in one direction or the other along all of the continua. Because of the nature of the phenomena under examination, most people would be found either in the extreme democratic or authoritarian directions, or occupy some middle ground. Those persons who are perceptive are also likely to be accepting, tolerant, communicative individuals. Those persons who are ethnocentric or prejudiced are most likely to be anxious, unperceptive, and defensive in communicative acts.

We are not concerned here with a theoretical structure for studying individual behavior, but rather are attempting to describe by analogy something which is psychologically so. This diagram should be taken as an effort at explanation rather than as an outline of behavioral theory. A much more adequate outline has already been made, as mentioned before (1, 83, 170, 203).

There is another significant factor about this pattern involving its relationship to the total life process. A study of those behaviors described as democratic immediately makes apparent the particular quality of action involved. Those things which facilitate human growth, such as perception, are also positively related to the idea of acceptance. Those things which tend to make people feel accepted, tend to be positive and good. The effect on existence is beneficial. Likewise, making it possible to partake maximally of available information is also enhancing to the individual involved. This seems to be true for all of the democratic characteristics.

Those characteristics which were outlined as authoritarian are based upon actions which result in human deprivation and degradation. To limit the number and quality of perceptions which an individual has, even if this stems from his own perceptual barriers, is to assure him of something less than the maximum in development and learning. When a person cuts himself off from associations and experiences with others, he will suffer as a result of this loss, as well as those who are rejected. By the suffering and hardship he produces in rejecting other people, he makes his own psychological self out of poorer perceptual material. Incidents of rejecting behavior like gossiping are not intended to bring people together and make them better; they are designed to drive little wedges which push them apart. Based as it is upon faulty or distorted communication, gossiping is incompatible with democratic behavior. The gossiping person's actions are destructive of other people—disintegrative rather than integrative. And the anxieties and feelings of inadequacy which accompany one's inability to resolve the unknowns of life without adequate information inevitably bring forth human misery and individual suffering. The story of Captain Queeg (262) in *The Caine Mutiny* is a well-known example.

Taken together, these ideas culminate in a fundamental notion directly related to the life process. It is this: those behaviors which are democratic are life-giving and life-supporting; those which are authoritarian are moving in the direction of death itself.

Expressed as a single continuum, it might look something like this:

Life	Death
Democratic ←——————————————→	**Authoritarian**
Homeostasis	**Entropy**

Democratic-Authoritarian Continuum

Wiener (257) mentions the relation between communication and the second law of thermodynamics, which states that all matter is continuously moving from a state of maximum organization toward a state of minimum organization, or entropy. The universe is continuously running downhill. Homeostasis, like communication, represents a tendency in the opposite direction. Democratic behavior would also seem to possess life-giving, life-supporting, homeostatic, or integrative attributes. The result of democratic behavior is to make all men better, to increase the quality and quantity of communication, and to maximize the organization. Such an idea has great significance for those who teach.

If one of the theses of this book is correct, that children learn from others, then for teachers to behave in authoritarian ways is both literally and figuratively to destroy the lives of those with whom they work. Noble intentions would be no excuse if this is true. To do things which result in personality disintegration has no place in American schools. Teachers must behave in democratic ways.

SUMMARY

Why do we have schools? To help children learn. What should be the goals of schools? Democratic behavior. What is democratic behavior? Openness to experience, a positive concept of self and others, the ability to communicate effectively, and a genuine sense of independence.

People who behave in democratic ways are psychologically healthy and have compassion for their fellow man. They believe in the worth of ideas and are open to learning and change and growth. Teachers who would be effective must both manifiest and teach these ways to all. Chapter Three describes what children learn from others, including their teachers.

REFERENCES

1. Adorno, T. W. et al., *The Authoritarian Personality* (New York: Harper and Brothers, 1950).
2. Albert, Robert S., "The Role of the Critic in Mass Communications: A Theoretical Analysis," *Journal of Social Psychology*, XLVIII, (November, 1958), 265-274.
3. Albert, Robert S. et al., "The Psychopathic Personality: A Content Analysis of the Concept," *Journal of General Psychology*, LX (January, 1959), 17-28.
4. Allport, Gordon W., *The Nature of Prejudice* (Cambridge, Massachusetts: Wesley-Addison, 1954).
5. Altus, W. D. and Tafejian, T. T., "MMPI Correlates of the California E-F Scale," *Journal of Social Psychology*, XXXVIII (August, 1953), 145-149.
6. Armstrong, John D., "The Search for the Alcoholic Personality," *The Annals of the American Academy of Political and Social Science*, CCCXV (January, 1958), 40-47.
7. Arnoff, F. N., "Ethnocentrism and Stimulus Generalization," *Journal of Abnormal and Social Psychology*, LIII (1956), 138-139.
8. Ash, Philip, "The Development of a Scale to Measure Anti-Negro Prejudice," *Journal of Social Psychology*, XXXIX (May, 1954), 187-199.
9. Ausubel, David P., "Reciprocity and Assumed Reciprocity of Acceptance Among Adolescents. A Sociometric Study," *Sociometry*, XVI (November, 1953), 339-348.

10. Ausubel, David P. and Schiff, Herbert M., "Some Intrapersonal and Interpersonal Determinants of Individual Differences in Socioempathic Ability Among Adolescents," *Journal of Social Psychology*, XLI (February, 1955), 39-56.
11. Ball, Thomas S. and Bernardoni, Louis C., "The Application of an Auditory Apperception Test to Clinical Diagnosis," *Journal of Clinical Psychology*, IX (1954), 54-58.
12. Barbe, Walter B., "Peer Relationships of Children of Different Intelligence Levels," *School and Society*, LXXX (August 21, 1954), 60-62.
13. Barrett-Lennard, G. T., "Dimensions of Perceived Therapist Response Related to Therapeutic Change," Unpublished dissertation (University of Chicago, 1959).
14. Barrington, James, "The Concept of Neutralism," *The Atlantic Monthly*, CCI (February, 1958), 126-128.
15. Belmont, Ira and Birch, Herbert G., "Personality and Situational Factors in the Production of Rigidity," *Journal of General Psychology*, LXII (January, 1960), 3-17.
16. Benedict, Ruth, *Patterns of Culture* (New York: Houghton-Mifflin Co., 1934), 254-255.
17. Bennett, Edward M., "A Socio-Cultural Interpretation of Maladjustive Behavior," *Journal of Social Psychology*, XXXVII (February, 1953), 19-26.
18. Bennett, Edward M. and Cohen, Larry R., "Men and Women: Personality Patterns and Contrasts," *Journal of General Psychology*, LIX (February, 1959), 101-155.
19. Bernberg, Raymond E., "Prestige Suggestion in Art as Communication," *Journal of Social Psychology*, XXXVIII (August, 1953), 23-30.
20. Bieri, James and Lobeck, Robin, "Acceptance of Authority and Parental Identification," *Journal of Personality*, XXVII (March, 1959), 74-86.
21. Blanchard, William H., "Intellectual Inhibition and the Search for Scientific Truth," *Journal of Social Psychology*, XLVII (February, 1958), 55-70.
22. Bloch, Herman D., "Recognition of Negro Discrimination: A Solution," *Journal of Social Psychology*, XLVIII (November, 1958), 291-295.
23. Bloom, Leonard, "Self Concepts and Social Status in South Africa: A Preliminary Cross-Cultural Analysis," *Journal of Social Psychology*, LI (February, 1960), 103-112.
24. Blum, Richard H., "The Choice of American Heroes and Its Relationship to Personality Structure in an Elite," *Journal of Social Psychology*, XLVIII (November, 1958), 235-246.
25. Bonney, M. E., Hoblit, R. E., and Dreyer, A. H., "A Study of Some Factors Related to Sociometric Status in a Men's Dormitory," *Sociometry*, XVI (November, 1953), 287-301.
26. Bonney, M. E., "Choosing Between the Sexes on a Sociometric Measurement," *Journal of Social Psychology*, XXXIX (February, 1954), 99-114.
27. Borgatta, Edgar F., "Analysis of Social Interaction and Sociometric Perception," *Sociometery*, XVII (February, 1954), 7-32.
28. Brandt, Richard M., "The Accuracy of Self-Estimate: A Measure of Self-Concept Reality," *Genetic Psychology Monographs*, LVIII (August, 1958), 55-100.
29. Brockway, Wallace, Ed., *High Moment* (New York: Simon and Schuster, 1955), 261.
30. Brown, Donald R. and Bystryn, Denise, "College Environment, Personality, and Social Ideology of Three Ethnic Groups," *Journal of Social Psychology*, XLIV (November, 1956), 279-288.
31. Buswell, Margaret M., "The Relationship Between Social Structure of the Classroom and the Academic Success of the Pupils," *Journal of Experimental Education*, XXII (September, 1953), 37-52.

32. Carleton, William G., "The Triumph of the Moderates," *Harper's Magazine*, CCX (April, 1955), 31-37.
33. Carter, Patricia, "An Exploratory Study of Relationships Existing Among Public School Principals' Background, Self-Concept, Role Concept, Values, and Pattern of Work," Unpublished dissertation (University of Florida, 1954).
34. Cartwright, Rosalind Dymond et al., "Patterns of Perceived Interpersonal Relations," *Sociometry*, XIX (September, 1956), 166-177.
35. Cattell, Raymond B. and Scheier, Ivan H., "Extension of Meaning of Objective Test Personality Factors: Especially into Anxiety, Neuroticism, Questionnaire, and Physical Factors," *Journal of General Psychology*, LXI (October, 1959), 287-315.
36. Chafee, Zechariah Jr., "The Encroachments on Freedom," *The Atlantic Monthly*, CXCVII (May, 1956), 39-44.
37. Chodorkoff, Bernard and Chodorkoff, Joan, "Perceptual Defense: An Integration with Other Research Findings," *Journal of General Psychology*, LVIII (January, 1958), 75-80.
38. Christie, R. and Garcia, J., "Subcultural Variation in Authoritarian Personality," *Journal of Abnormal and Social Psychology*, XLVI (October, 1951), 457-469.
39. Christie, Richard and Cook, Peggy, "A Guide to Published Literature Relating to the Authoritarian Personality Through 1956," *Journal of Psychology*, XLV (April, 1958), 171-199.
40. Christie, Richard and Jahoda, Marie, Eds., *Studies in the Scope and Method of "The Authoritarian Personality"* (Glencoe: The Free Press, 1954).
41. Christie, R., Havel, J., and Seidenberg, Berdard, "Is the F Scale Irreversible?" *Journal of Abnormal and Social Psychology*, LVI (1958), 143-159.
42. Clampitt, Richard R. and Charles, Don C., "Sociometric Status and Supervisory Evaluation of Institutionalized Mentally Deficient Children," *Journal of Social Psychology*, XLIV (November, 1956), 223-231.
43. Cohen, Arthur R., "Situational Structure, Self-Esteem, and Threat-Oriented Reactions to Power," *Studies in Social Power*, Dorwin Cartwright, Ed. (Ann Arbor: University of Michigan, Institute of Social Research, 1959), 35-52.
44. Cohn, T. S., "Is the F Scale Indirect?" *Journal of Abnormal and Social Psychology*, XLVII (July, 1952), 732.
45. Cohn, Thomas S., "The Relation of the F-Scale to a Response Set to Answer Positively," *Journal of Social Psychology*, XLIV (August, 1956), 129-133.
46. Cohn, Thomas S., "The Relation of the F-Scale to Intelligence," *Journal of Social Psychology*, XLVI (1957), 207-217.
47. Combs, Arthur W. and Snygg, Donald, *Individual Behavior* (New York: Harper and Brothers, 1959) (revised edition).
48. Cooper, Joseph B., "Perceptual Organization as a Function of Politically Oriented Communications," *Journal of Social Psychology*, XLI (May, 1955), 319-324.
49. Cooper, Joseph B., "Mobility Anticipation, Class Assignment, and Authoritarianism as Feld Determinants of Attitudes," *Journal of Social Psychology*, XLIII (February, 1956), 139-156.
50. Cooper, Joseph B. and Singer, David N., "The Role of Emotion in Prejudice," *Journal of Social Psychology*, XLIV (November, 1956), 241-247.
51. Corsini, Raymond, "Bernreuter Patterns of a Group of Prison Inmates," *Journal of Clinical Psychology*, II (1946), 283-285.
52. Coulson, Robert E., "Let's Not Get Out the Vote," *Harper's Magazine*, CCXI (November, 1955), 52-53.
53. Cunningham, Ruth, "Factors Affecting Group Behavior," *Baltimore Bulletin of Education*, XXIX (March-June, 1952), 9-15.
54. Dahlke, H. Otto, "Determinants of Sociometric Relations Among Children in the Elementary School," *Sociometry*, XVI (November, 1953), 327-338.

55. Davids, A., "Some Personality and Intellectual Correlates of Intolerance of Ambiguity," *Journal of Abnormal and Social Psychology*, LI (1955), 415-420.
56. Davids, Anthony and Murray, H. A., "Preliminary Appraisal of an Auditory Projective Technique for Studying Personality and Cognition," *American Journal of Orthopsychiatry*, XXV (July, 1955), 543-554.
57. Davidson, Helen H. and Kruglov, Lorraine P., "Some Background Correlates of Personality and Social Attitudes," *Journal of Social Psychology*, XXXVIII (November, 1953), 233-240.
58. Davis, Junius A., "Correlates of Sociometric Status Among Peers," *Journal of Educational Research*, L (April, 1957), 561-569.
59. Davitz, Joel R., "Fear, Anxiety, and the Perception of Others," *Journal of General Psychology*, LXI (July, 1959), 169-173.
60. DeVault, M. Vere, "Classroom Sociometric Mutual Pairs and Residential Proximity," *Journal of Educational Research*, L (April, 1957), 605-610.
61. Dickens, Sara Lee and Hobart, Charles, "Parental Dominance and Offspring Ethnocentrism," *Journal of Social Psychology*, XLIX (May, 1959), 297-303.
62. Douvan, Elizabeth, "The Sense of Effectiveness and Response to Public Issues," *Journal of Social Psychology*, XLVII (February, 1958), 111-126.
63. Dowling, Betty, "Some Personality Factors Involved in Tolerance and Intolerance," *Journal of Social Psychology*, XLI (May, 1955), 325-327.
64. Drevdahl, John E. and Cattell, Raymond B., "Personality and Creativity in Artists and Writers," *Journal of Clinical Psychology*, XIV (April, 1958), 107-111.
65. Drevdahl, John E., "The Wise Herd," *The Educational Forum*, XXIII (January, 1959), 135. Reprinted by permission of Kappa Delta Pi.
66. Drucker, Melvin B., "Authority and Ingroup Standards and Conformity Behavior," Unpublished dissertation (George Peabody College for Teachers, 1956).
67. Dudycha, George J., "Race Attitude and Esthetic Preference," *Journal of Social Psychology*, XXXVII (February, 1953), 61-68.
68. Ekman, Gösta, "The Four Effects of Cooperation," *Journal of Social Psychology*, XLI (February, 1955), 149-162.
69. Emerson, Richard M., "Deviation and Rejection: An Experiment in Replication," *American Sociological Review*, XIX (December, 1954), 688-693.
70. Fagan, Joen and Guthrie, George M., "Perception of Self and of Normality in Schizophrenics," *Journal of Clinical Psychology*, XV (April, 1959), 203-207.
71. Faulkner, William, "On Privacy: The American Dream," *Harper's Magazine*, CCXI (July, 1955), 33-38.
72. Faulkner, William, "On Fear: The South in Labor," *Harper's Magazine*, CCXII (June, 1956), 29-34.
73. Feinberg, Mortimer R. et al., "An Analysis of Expressions Used by Adolescents at Varying Economic Levels to Describe Accepted and Rejected Peers," *Journal of Genetic Psychology*, XCIII (September, 1958), 133-148.
74. Festinger, Leon, Schachter, Stanley, and Back, Kurt, *Social Pressures in Informal Groups* (New York: Harper and Brothers, 1950), 101-113.
75. Fields, Sidney J., "Discrimination of Facial Expression and Its Relation to Personal Adjustment," *Journal of Social Psychology*, XXXVIII (August, 1953), 63-71.
76. Fischer, John, "New Hope for Television?" *Harper's Magazine*, CCXX (January, 1960), 12-21.
77. Fishman, Joshua A., "An Examination of the Process and Function of Social Stereotyping," *Journal of Social Psychology*, XLIII (February, 1956), 27-64.
78. Forlano, George and Wrightstone, J. Wayne, "Measuring the Quality of Social Acceptability Within a Class," *Educational and Psychological Measurement*, XV (Summer, 1955), 127-136.

79. Frank, Jerome D., "The Great Antagonism," *The Atlantic Monthly*, CCII (November, 1958), 58-62.
80. Frenkel-Brunswik, Else, "A Study of Prejudice in Children," *Human Relations*, I, No. 3 (1948), 295-306.
81. Frenkel-Brunswik, Else, "Intolerance of Ambiguity as an Emotional and Perceptual Variable," *Journal of Personality*, XVIII (September, 1949), 108-143.
82. Frenkel-Brunswik, Else, "Tolerance Toward Ambiguity as a Personality Variable," *American Psychologist*, III (1948), 268.
83. Fromm, Erich, *Escape from Freedom* (New York: Farrar and Rinehart, 1941).
84. Fromm, Erich, *The Art of Loving* (New York: Harper and Row, 1956).
85. Frymier, Jack R., "Relationship of Aural Perceptions to Cultural Situations," *Perceptual and Motor Skills*, VIII (June, 1958), 67-70.
86. Frymier, Jack R., "Aural Perceptions of Authoritarians in Different Cultural Situations," *Journal of Experimental Education*, XXVIII (December, 1959), 163-169.
87. Frymier, Jack R., "The Relationship of Authoritarianism to Rejection," *Journal of Educational Research*, LIII (September, 1959), 33-34.
88. Frymier, Jack R., "The Relationship Between Church Attendance and Authoritarianism," *Religious Education*, LIV (July-August, 1959), 369-371.
89. Frymier, Jack R., "Analysis of Adolescents' Responses to the F-Scale," *Journal of Experimental Education*, XXIX (September, 1960), 73-80.
90. Frymier, Jack R., "Teachers' Estimates of Adolescents' Responses to F-Scale Items," *Journal of Educational Research*, LV (May, 1962), 353-357.
91. Frymier, Jack R., "Prospective Teachers' Estimates of Adolescents' Responses to the F-Scale," *Journal of Experimental Education*, XXIX (December, 1960), 183-188.
92. Gaier, Eugene L. and Bass, Bernard M., "Regional Differences in Interrelations Among Authoritarianism, Acquiesence, and Ethnocentrism," *Journal of Social Psychology*, XLIX (February, 1959), 47-51.
93. Gaier, Eugene L. and Wambach, Helen S., "Self-Evaluation of Personality Assets and Liabilities of Southern White and Negro Students," *Journal of Social Psychology*, LI (February, 1960), 135-143.
94. Gallagher, James J., "Peer Acceptance of Highly Gifted Children in Elementary School," *Education Digest*, XXIV (October, 1958), 24-26.
95. Gebel, Arnold S., "Self Perception and Leaderless Group Discussion Status," *Journal of Social Psychology*, XL (November, 1954), 309-318.
96. Gottheil, Edward, "Sociometric Technique and Experimental Method in Social Psychology," *Journal of Social Psychology*, XXXV (February, 1952), 9-21.
97. Gottheil, Edward, "Change in Social Perception Upon Competing or Cooperating," *Sociometry*, XVIII (May, 1955), 132-137.
98. Gough, Harrison G. et al., "Children's Ethnic Attitudes: Relationship to Certain Personality Factors," *Child Development*, XXI (June, 1950), 83-91.
99. Gough, Harrison G., "Predicting Social Participation," *Journal of Social Psychology*, XXXV (May, 1952), 227-233.
100. Gould, John, "Lazy Journalism," *The Atlantic Monthly*, CXCIX (June, 1957), 51-54.
101. Gray, J. Stanley and Thompson, Anthony H., "The Ethnic Prejudices of White and Negro College Students," *Journal of Abnormal and Social Psychology*, XLVIII (April, 1953), 311-313.
102. Greenberg, H. et al., "Authoritarianism as a Variable in Motivation to Attend College," *Journal of Social Psychology*, XLIX (February, 1959), 81-85.
103. Greenberg, H. and Fare, Don, "An Investigation of Several Variables as

Determinants of Authoritarianism," *Journal of Social Psychology*, XLIX (February, 1959), 105-111.

104. Gronlund, Norman E., "The Accuracy of Teachers' Judgments Concerning the Sociometric Status of Sixth-Grade Pupils," *Sociometry*, XIII (November, 1950), 329-357.

105. Grossack, Martin W., "Group Belongingness Among Negroes," *Journal of Social Psychology*, XLIII (February, 1956), 167-180.

106. Gump, Paul V., "Anti-Democratic Trends and Student Reaction to President Truman's Dismissal of General MacArthur," *Journal of Social Psychology*, XXXVIII (August, 1953), 131-135.

107. Gynther, Ruth A., "The Effects of Anxiety and of Situational Stress on Communicative Efficiency," *Journal of Abnormal and Social Psychology*, LIV (March, 1957), 274-276.

108. Harris, D. B. et al., "Children's Ethnic Attitudes: II. Relationship to Parental Beliefs Concerning Child Training," *Child Development*, XXI (September, 1950), 169-181.

109. Hart, I., "Maternal Child-Rearing Practices and Authoritarian Ideology," *Journal of Abnormal and Social Psychology*, LV (1958), 232-237.

110. Hartman, A. A., "Personality Factors in Perceptual Distortion," *Journal of General Psychology*, LXI (October, 1959), 181-188.

111. Havighurst, Robert J. et al., *Growing Up in River City* (New York: John Wiley and Sons, 1962).

112. Hitler, Adolph, *Mein Kampf* (New York: Reynal and Hitchcock, 1940).

113. Hochbaum, Godfrey M., "The Relation Between Group Members' Self-Confidence and Their Reactions to Group Pressures to Uniformity," *American Sociological Review*, XIX (December, 1954), 678-687.

114. Holder, Wayne B., "Value Conformity in Normal and Non-Normal Groups," *Journal of Social Psychology*, XLVIII (August, 1958), 147-154.

115. Holloway, John E., "Apartheid," *The Annals of the American Academy of Political and Social Science*, CCCVI (July, 1956), 26-37.

116. Horowitz, Milton W. and Perlmutter, Howard V., "The Discussion Group and Democratic Behavior," *Journal of Social Psychology*, XLI (May, 1955), 231-246.

117. Israeli, Nathan, "Social Interaction in Creation and Criticism in the Fine Arts," *Journal of Social Psychology*, XXXV (February, 1952), 73-89.

118. Jackson, Douglas N., "Cognitive Energy Level, Acquiescence, and Authoritarianism," *Journal of Social Psychology*, XLIX (February, 1959), 65-69.

119. Jacobson, Frank N. and Rettig, Salomon, "Authoritarianism and Intelligence," *Journal of Social Psychology*, L (November, 1959), 213-219.

120. Jenkin, Noel, "Affective Processes in Perception," *Psychological Bulletin*, LIV (March, 1957), 100-127.

121. Jenkins, David H. and Lippitt, Ronald, *Interpersonal Perceptions of Teachers, Students, and Parents* (Washington: Adult Education Service, NEA, 1951).

122. Jersild, Arthur T., *When Teachers Face Themselves* (New York: Teachers College, Columbia University).

123. Jones, Howard Mumford, *The Pursuit of Happiness* (Cambridge: Harvard University Press, 1953).

124. Jones, Marshall B., "Religious Values and Authoritarian Tendency," *Journal of Social Psychology*, XLVIII (August, 1958), 83-89.

125. Jones, Stewart and Gaier, Eugene L., "A Study of the Anti-Democratic Potential of Teachers," *Journal of Educational Research*, XLVII (September, 1953), 1-18.

126. Kaplan, Walter and Littman, Richard A., "Expectations and Social Attitudes," *Journal of Social Psychology*, XLII (August, 1955), 83-112.

127. Keehn, J. D., "An Examination of the Two-Factor Theory of Social Attitudes

in a Near Eastern Culture," *Journal of Social Psychology*, XLII (August, 1955), 13-20.
128. Kennan, George F., "Peaceful Coexistence: A Western View," *Foreign Affairs*, XXXVIII (January, 1960), 171-190.
129. Kelley, Earl C., *Education for What Is Real* (New York: Harper and Brothers, 1947).
130. Kelley, Earl C. and Rasey, Marie I., *Education and the Nature of Man* (New York: Harper and Brothers, 1952).
131. Kelly, James G. et al., "The Measurement of Attitudes Toward the Negro in the South," *Journal of Social Psychology*, XLVIII (November, 1958), 305-317.
132. Kelman, Herbert C. and Hovland, Carl I., " 'Reinstatement' of the Communicator in Delayed Measurement of Opinion Change," *Journal of Abnormal and Social Psychology*, XLVIII (July, 1953), 327-335.
133. Kemp, C. Gratton, "Effect of Dogmatism on Critical Thinking," Unpublished paper, read at the American Association for the Advancement of Science meeting, December 29, 1959. Chicago.
134. Kennedy, John F., "The Man Who Saved a President," *Harper's Magazine*, CCXI (December, 1955), 40-44.
135. Kerlinger, Fred N., "Progessivism and Traditionalism: Basic Factors of Educational Attitudes," *Journal of Social Psychology*, XLVIII (August, 1958), 111-135.
136. Kerr, Willard A., "Untangling the Liberalism-Conservatism Continuum," *Journal of Social Psychology*, XXXV (February, 1952), 111-125.
137. Kidd, John W., "Personality Traits as Barriers to Acceptability in a College Men's Residence Hall," *Journal of Social Psychology*, XXXVIII (August, 1953), 127-130.
138. Kingston, Albert J. and Newsome, George L., "The Relationship of Two Measures of Authoritarianism to the Minnesota Teacher Attitude Inventory," *Journal of Psychology*, XLIX (April, 1960), 333-338.
139. Kinney, Elva E., "A Study of Peer Group Social Accceptability at the Fifth Grade Level in a Public School," *Journal of Educational Research*, XLVII (September, 1953), 57-64.
140. Kipnis, David, "The Effects of Leadership Style and Leadership Power upon the Inducement of an Attitude Change," *Journal of Abnormal and Social Psychology*, LVII (September, 1958), 173-180.
141. Klausner, Samuel Z., "Social Class and Self-Concept," *Journal of Social Psychology*, XXXVIII (November, 1953), 201-205.
142. Kogan, Nathan, "Authoritarianism and Repression," *Journal of Abnormal and Social Psychology*, LIII (1957), 34-37.
143. Koontz, Miram E., "A Comparison of False Nonauthoritarians in Two Ethnic Groups," Unpublished dissertation (George Peabody College for Teachers, 1955).
144. Kouwenhoven, John A., "What's American About America?" *Harper's Magazine*, CCXIII (July, 1956), 25-33.
145. Knutson, Andie L., "The Concept of Personal Security," *Journal of Social Psychology*, XL (November, 1954), 219-236.
146. Kripalani, Acharya J. B., "For Principled Neutrality: A New Appraisal of Indian Foreign Policy," *Foreign Affairs*, XXXVIII (October, 1959), 46-60.
147. Kruglov, Lorraine P. and Davidson, Helen H., "The Willingness to Be Interviewed: A Selective Factor in Sampling," *Journal of Social Psychology*, XXXVIII (August, 1953), 39-47.
148. Khrushchev, Nikita A., "On Peaceful Coexistence," *Foreign Affairs*, XXXVIII (October, 1959), 1-18.
149. Kuenzli, Alfred E., Ed., *The Phenomenological Problem* (New York: Harper

and Brothers, 1959) (Chapter 2, "The Self, Its Derivative Terms, and Research," by Arthur W. Combs and Daniel W. Soper).

150. Lambert, Philip, "Interaction Between Authoritarian and Nonauthoritarian Principals and Teachers," *Genetic Psychology Monographs,* LVIII (November, 1958), 163-205.

151. Landfield, Alvin W., "Self-Predictive Orientation and the Movement Interpretation of Threat," *Journal of Abnormal and Social Psychology,* LI (November, 1955), 434-438.

152. Landfield, Alvin W., "A Movement Interpretation of Threat," *Journal of Abnormal and Social Psychology,* XLIX (October, 1954), 529-532.

153. Lecky, Prescott, *Self-Consistency* (New York: Island Press, 1945).

154. Ledley, Robert S. and Lusted, Lee B., "Reasoning Foundations of Medical Diagnosis," *Science,* CXXX (July 3, 1959), 9-21.

155. Lewin, Kurt, "Experiments on Autocratic and Democratic Atmospheres," *Social Frontier,* IV (July, 1938), 316-319, as quoted in Fullagar, William A. et al., *Readings for Educational Psychology* (New York: Thomas Y. Crowell Co.), 410-417.

156. Lewin, Kurt, et al., "Patterns of Aggressive Behavior in Experimentally Created 'Social Climates,' " *Journal of Social Psychology,* X (May, 1939), 271-299.

157. Lindzey, Gardner and Urdan, James A., "Personality and Social Choice," *Sociometry,* XVII (February, 1954), 47-63.

158. Lohman, Joseph D., "A Sociologist-Sheriff Speaks Out About Juvenile Delinquency," *Phi Delta Kappan,* XXXIX (February, 1958), 206-214.

159. Loomis, Charles P. and Proctor, Charles, "The Relationship Between Choice Status and Economic Status in Social Systems," *Sociometry,* XIII (November, 1950), 307-313.

160. Luchins, Abraham S. and Luchins, Edith H., "Previous Experience with Ambiguous and Non-Ambiguous Perceptual Stimuli Under Various Social Influences," *Journal of Social Psychology,* XLII (November, 1955), 249-270.

161. Luchins, Abraham S. and Luchins, Edith H., "On Conformity with True and False Communications," *Journal of Social Psychology,* XLII (November, 1955), 283-303.

162. Machiavelli, Niccolo, *The Prince* (New York: New American Library, 1952).

163. Mahrer, Alvin R., "Potential Intelligence: A Learning Theory Approach to Description and Clinical Implication," *Journal of General Psychology,* LIX (July, 1958), 59-71.

164. Maier, Norman R. F., "Screening Solutions to Upgrade Quality: A New Approach to Problem Solving Under Conditions of Uncertainty," *Journal of Psychology,* XLIX (April, 1960), 217-231.

165. Mann, John H., "The Relationship Between Cognitive, Affective, and Behavioral Aspects of Racial Prejudice," *Journal of Social Psychology,* XLIX (May, 1959), 223-228.

166. Mann, John H., "The Effect of Inter-Racial Contact on Sociometric Choice and Perceptions," *Journal of Social Psychology,* L (August, 1959), 143-150.

167. Marks, John B., "Authoritarianism, Intelligence, and Work Effectiveness Among Psychiatric Aides," *Journal of Social Psychology,* LIX (May, 1959), 237-242.

168. Masling, Joseph M., "How Neurotic is the Authoritarian?" *Journal of Abnormal and Social Psychology,* XLIX (April, 1954), 316-318.

169. Masling, Joseph et al., "Status, Authoritarianism, and Sociometric Choice," *Journal of Social Psychology,* XLI (May, 1955), 297-310.

170. Maslow, A. H., "The Authoritarian Character Structure," *Journal of Social Psychology,* XVIII (November, 1943), 401-411.

171. Maslow, A. H., *Motivation and Personality* (New York: Harper and Brothers, 1954).

172. Maslow, A. H., "Cognition of Being in the Peak Experiences," *Journal of Genetic Psychology*, XCIV (March, 1959), 43-66.
173. Melikian, Levon Hagop, "Some Correlates of Authoritarianism in Two Cultural Groups," Unpublished dissertation (New York: Columbia University, 1956).
174. Mellinger, Glen D., "Interpersonal Trust as a Factor in Communication," *Journal of Abnormal and Social Psychology*, LII (May, 1956), 304-309.
175. Miller, Delbert, "Decision-Making Cliques in Community Power Structures: A Comparative Study of an American and an English City," *American Journal of Sociology*, LXIV (November, 1958), 299-310.
176. Miller, Robert E. and Murphy, John V., "Social Interactions of Rhesus Monkeys: I. Food-Getting Dominance as a Dependent Variable," *Journal of Social Psychology*, XLIV (November, 1956), 249-255.
177. Millon, Theodore, "Authoritarianism and Acceptance of an Ingroup Set," *Journal of Social Psychology*, XLVIII (November, 1958), 199-204.
178. Mills, Harriet C., "Thought Reform: Ideological Remolding in China," *The Atlantic Monthly*, CCIV (December, 1959), 70-77.
179. Milton, O., "Presidential Choice and Performance on a Scale of Authoritarianism," *American Psychologist*, VII (1952), 597-598.
180. Moreno, J. L., "A Note on Sociometry and Group Dynamics," *Sociometry*, XV (August-November, 1952), 364-366.
181. Muldon, John F., "The Concentration of Liked and Disliked Members in Groups and the Relationship of the Concentrations to Group Cohesiveness," *Sociometry*, XVIII (February, 1955), 73-81.
182. Mumford, Lewis, "The Morals of Extermination," *The Atlantic Monthly*, CCIV (October, 1959), 38-44.
183. McKeachie, Wilbert J., "Individual Conformity to Attitudes of Classroom Groups," *Journal of Abnormal and Social Psychology*, XLIX (April, 1954), 282-289.
184. Nadler, Eugene B. and Morrow, William R., "Authoritarian Attitudes Toward Women and Their Correlates," *Journal of Social Psychology*, XLIX (February, 1959), 113-123.
185. Noble, Lois A. and Noble, Ransome E., "A Study of Attitudes of College Students Toward Civil Rights," *Journal of Social Psychology*, XL (November, 1954), 289-297.
186. Norman, Ralph D., "The Interrelationships Among Acceptance-Rejection, Self-Other Identity, Insight into Self, and Realistic Perception of Others," *Journal of Social Psychology*, XXXVII (May, 1953), 205-235.
187. Orwell, George, *Animal Farm* (New York: New American Library, 1956).
188. Pearl, David, "Ethnocentrism and the Self Concept," *Journal of Social Psychology*, XL (August, 1954), 137-147.
189. Plant, Walter T., "Changes in Ethnocentrism Associated with a Two-Year College Experience," *Journal of Genetic Psychology*, XCII (June, 1958), 189-197.
190. Plant, Walter T., "Sex, Intelligence, and Sorority or Fraternity Membership and Changes in Ethnocentrism over a Two Year Period," *Journal of Genetic Psychology*, XCIII (September, 1958), 53-56.
191. Prothro, E. Terry and Miles, Otha King, "Social Distance in the Deep South as Measured by a Revised Bogardus Scale," *Journal of Social Psychology*, XXXVII (May, 1953), 171-174.
192. Prothro, E. Terry, "Cross-Cultural Patterns of National Stereotypes," *Journal of Social Psychology*, XL (August, 1954), 53-59.
193. Prothro, E. Terry and Melikian, Levon H., "Studies in Stereotypes: V. Familiarity and the Kernel of Truth Hypothesis," *Journal of Social Psychology*, XLI (February, 1955), 3-10.
194. Rubin-Rabson, Grace, "Several Correlates of a Conservatism-Liberalism

Attitude Scale," *Journal of Social Psychology*, XXXIX (February, 1954), 47-55.

195. Rubin-Rabson, Grace, "Liberalism Toward Negroes as a Deviant Reaction in a Conservative Group," *Journal of Social Psychology*, XLI (February, 1955), 139-148.

196. Radke-Yarrow, Marian and Lande, Bernard, "Personality Correlates of Differential Reactions to Minority Group-Belonging," *Journal of Social Psychology*, XXXVIII (November, 1953), 253-272.

197. Reckless, Walter C. et al., "The Self Component in Potential Delinquency and Potential Non-Delinquency," *American Sociological Review*, XXII (October, 1957), 566-570.

198. Regan, John F., "The School Connected Fears of Children Under Authoritarian and Democratic Teachers," Unpublished dissertation (New York: Columbia University, 1958).

199. Remmers, H. H. and Radler, D. H., "Teenage Attitudes," *Scientific American*, CXCVIII (June, 1958), 25-29.

200. Riesman, David et al., *The Lonely Crowd* (New York: Doubleday Books, 1953).

201. Rodgers, Richard and Hammerstein, Oscar 2nd, "You've Got To Be Carefully Taught," from *South Pacific* (New York: Williamson Music Co., 1949).

202. Rokeach, Milton and Eglash, Albert, "A Scale for Measuring Intellectual Conviction," *Journal of Social Psychology*, XLIV (August, 1956), 135-141.

203. Rokeach, Milton, *The Open and Closed Mind* (New York: Basic Books, 1960).

204. Rosen, E., "Differences Between Volunteers and Non-Volunteers for Psychological Studies," *Journal of Applied Psychology*, XXXV (June, 1951), 185-193.

205. Runkel, Philip J., "Cognitive Similarity in Facilitating Communication," *Sociometry*, XIX (September, 1956), 178-191.

206. Sanai, M., "The Relation Between Social Attitudes and Characteristics of Personality," *Journal of Social Psychology*, XXXVI (August, 1952), 3-13.

207. Sarbin, T. R. and Rosenberg, B. G., "Contributions to Role-Taking Theory: IV. A Method for Obtaining a Qualitative Estimate of the Self," *Journal of Social Psychology*, XLII (August, 1955), 71-81.

208. Scandrette, Onas C., "Classroom Choice Status Related to Components of the California Test of Personality," *Journal of Educational Research*, XLVII (September, 1953), 291-296.

209. Schaefer, Earl S., "A Circumplex Model for Maternal Behavior," in press (*Journal of Abnormal and Social Psychology*).

210. Schlesinger, Arthur M., "America's Influence: Our Ten Contributions to Civilization," *The Atlantic Monthly*, CCIII (March, 1959), 65-69.

211. Scodel, A. and Mussen, P., "Social Perceptions of Authoritarians and Non-Authoritarians," *Journal of Abnormal and Social Psychology*, XLVIII (April, 1953), 181-184.

212. Sharp, E. Preston, "A Report on Delinquency from the Youth Study Center," reprinted from *The Philadelphia Inquirer*, CCLVII (December 12, 1957), 1.

213. Sherif, Muzafer and Harvey, O. J., "A Study in Ego Functioning: Elimination of Stable Anchorages in Individual and Group Situations," *Sociometry*, XV (August-November, 1952), 272-305.

214. Shukla, Chandrashanker, *Gandhi's View of Life* (Bombay: Bharatiya Vidya Bhavan, 1954).

215. Siegel, Arthur I. and Greer, F. Loyal, "A Variation of the Bogardus Technique as a Measure of Perceived Prejudice," *Journal of Social Psychology*, XLIII (May, 1956), 275-281.

216. Siegel, Saul M., "The Relationship of Hostility to Authoritarianism," *Journal of Abnormal and Social Psychology*, LII (1956), 368-372.

217. Singer, Jerome L. and Goldman, George D., "Experimentally Contrasted

Social Atmospheres in Group Psychotherapy with Chronic Schizophrenics," *Journal of Social Psychology*, XL (August, 1954), 23-37.

218. Sommer, Robert and Killian, Lewis M., "Areas of Value Difference: I. A Method for Investigation," *Journal of Social Psychology*, XXXIX (May, 1954), 227-235.

219. Sommer, Robert and Killian, Lewis M., "Areas of Value Difference: II. Negro-White Relations," *Journal of Social Psychology*, XXXIX (May, 1954), 237-244.

220. Sorokin, Pitrim A., "The Powers of Creative Unselfish Love," in *New Knowledge in Human Values*, A. H. Maslow, Ed. (New York: Harper and Brothers, 1959) 3-12.

221. Speroff, B. J., "Empathy and Role-Reversal as Factors in Industrial Harmony," *Journal of Social Psychology*, XXXVII (February, 1953), 117-120.

222. Speroff, B. J., "Problems and Approaches in Integrating Minority Group Work Forces," *Journal of Social Psychology*, XXXVII (May, 1953), 271-273.

223. Spilka, Bernard and Struening, E. L., "A Questionnaire Study of Personality and Ethnocentrism," *Journal of Social Psychology*, XLIV (August, 1956), 65-71.

224. St. Luke, The New Testament, Chapter 6, verses 27-31.

225. Stagner, Ross, "Attitude Toward Authority: An Exploratory Study," *Journal of Social Psychology*, XL (November, 1954), 197-210.

226. Stephenson, Chester M., "The Relation Between the Attitudes Toward Negroes of White College Students and the College or School in Which They Are Registered," *Journal of Social Psychology*, XXXVI (November, 1952), 197-204.

227. Stotsky, Bernard A. and Lachman, Sheldon J., "Differences in Political and Social Attitudes of Pro-Eisenhower and Pro-Stevenson Students," *Journal of Social Psychology*, XLIV (August, 1956), 143-144.

228. Stouffer, Samuel A., *Communism, Conformity, and Civil Liberties* (New York: Doubleday and Co., 1955).

229. Strauss, Anselm, *The Social Psychology of George Herbert Mead* (Chicago: University of Chicago Press, 1956).

230. Strout, Richard Lee, "The Next Election is Already Rigged," *Harper's Magazine*, CCXIX (November, 1959), 35-40.

231. Taft, Ronald, "Is the Tolerant Personality Type the Opposite of the Intolerants?" *Journal of Social Psychology*, XLVII (May, 1958), 397-405.

232. Taft, Ronald, "Ethnic Stereotypes, Attitudes, and Familiarity: Australia," *Journal of Social Psychology*, XLIX (May, 1959), 177-186.

233. Tear, Daniel Grant and Guthrie, George M., "The Relationship of Cooperation to the Sharpening-Leveling Continuum," *Journal of Social Psychology*, XLII (November, 1955), 203-208.

234. Thittila, Bhikkhu U., "The Meaning of Buddhism," *The Atlantic Monthly*, CCI (February, 1958), 142-145.

235. Thorpe, J. G., "An Investigation into Some Correlates of Sociometric Status Within School Classes," *Sociometry*, XVIII (February, 1955), 49-61.

236. Titus, H. Edwin and Hollander, E. P., "The California F-Scale in Psychological Research: 1950-1955," *Psychological Bulletin*, LIV (January, 1957), 47-64.

237. Torrance, Paul, "Rationalizations About Test Performance as a Function of Self-Concepts," *Journal of Social Psychology*, XXXIX (May, 1954), 211-217.

238. Torrance, E. Paul, "The Behavior of Small Groups Under the Stress Conditions of 'Survival,'" *American Sociological Review*, XIX (December, 1954), 751-755.

239. Torrance, E. Paul, "The Relationship of Attitudes and Changes in Attitudes Toward Survival Adequacy to the Achievement of Survival Knowledge," *Journal of Social Psychology*, XL (November, 1954), 259-265.

240. Torrance, E. Paul, "Perception of Group Functioning as a Predictor of Group Performance," *Journal of Social Psychology*, XLII (November, 1955), 271-282.

241. Torrance, E. Paul, "Interpersonal Aggression and Submission in Ability to Endure Pain and Discomfort," *Journal of Social Psychology*, XLVIII (November, 1958), 205-210.

242. Trueblood, D. E., *The Logic of Belief* (New York: Harper and Brothers, 1942).

243. Trumbull, Richard, "A Study of Relationships Between Factors of Personality and Intelligence," *Journal of Social Psychology*, XXXVIII (November, 1953), 161-173.

244. Van Aken, Elbert W., "An Analysis of the Methods of Operation of Principals to Determine Working Patterns," Unpublished dissertation (University of Florida, 1954).

245. Van Loon, Hendrick, *Tolerance* (New York: Liveright, 1927).

246. Vernon, Glenn M. and Stewart, Robert L., "Empathy as a Process in the Dating Situation," *American Sociological Review*, XXII (February, 1957), 48-52.

247. Vinacke, W. Edgar, "Explorations in the Dynamic Processes of Stereotyping," *Journal of Social Psychology*, XLIII (February, 1956), 105-132.

248. Walters, Richard H. et al., "A Test of the Perceptual Defense Hypothesis," *Journal of Personality*, XXVII (March, 1959), 47-55.

249. Wardlow, Mary E. and Greene, James E., "An Exploratory Sociometric Study of Peer Status Among Adolescent Girls," *Sociometry*, XV (August-November, 1952), 311-318.

250. Weeks, Edward, "How Big Is One?" *The Atlantic Monthly*, CCII (August, 1958), 25-30.

251. Weiner, Harold and Ross, Sherman, "Manifest Anxiety and Perceptual Judgment," *Journal of Social Psychology*, XLIV (August, 1956), 83-87.

252. Wexner, Lois B., "Relationship of Intelligence and the Nine Scales of the Minnesota Multiphasic Personality Inventory," *Journal of Social Psychology*, XL (August, 1954), 173-176.

253. Whorf, Benjamin Lee, *Language, Thought, and Reality* (New York: John Wiley and Sons, Inc., 1956).

254. Wiener, Morton et. al., "Some Determinants of Conformity Behavior," *Journal of Social Psychology*, XLV (May, 1957), 289-297.

255. Wiener, Morton, "Certainty of Judgment as a Variable in Conformity Behavior," *Journal of Social Psychology*, XLVIII (November, 1958), 257-263.

256. Wiener, Morton, "Some Correlates of Conformity Responses" *Journal of Social Psychology*, XLIX (May, 1959), 215-221.

257. Wiener, Norbert, *The Human Use of Human Beings: Cybernetics and Society* (Garden City: Doubleday Anchor Books, 1954).

258. Willard, Ruth A., "A Study of the Relationship Between the Value-Behaviors of Selected Teachers and the Learning Experiences Provided in their Classrooms," *Journal of Educational Research*, XLIX (September, 1955), 45-51.

259. Winder, Alvin E., "White Attitudes Toward Negro-White Interaction in a Number of Community Situations," *Journal of Social Psychology*, XLIV (August, 1956), 15-32.

260. Winfield, Don L., "The Relationship Between IQ Scores and Minnesota Multiphasic Personality Inventory Scores," *Journal of Social Psychology*, XXXVIII (November, 1953), 299-300.

261. Winthrop, Henry, "Self-Images of Personal Adjustment vs. the Estimate of Friends," *Journal of Social Psychology*, L (August, 1959), 87-99.

262. Wouk, Herman, *The Caine Mutiny*. (New York: Doubleday and Co. 1954).

263. Wittreich, Warren J., "Visual Perception and Personality," *Scientific American*, CC (April, 1959), 56-60.

264. Yablonsky, Lewis, "A Sociometric Investigation Into the Development of an Experimental Model for Small Group Analysis," *Sociometry*, XV (August-November, 1952), 175-205.
265. Young, Norman and Gaier, Eugene L., "A Preliminary Investigation into the Prediction of Suggestibility from Selected Personality Variables," *Journal of Social Psychology*, XXXVII (February, 1953), 53-60.

Chapter Three

Children Learn from Others

If the basic purpose of education is to help children behave in democratic ways, then it is imperative that we employ democratic means to
achieve this end. In schools we have one avenue available. To help
children learn to behave democratically, we must manipulate not the
children but the curriculum, not the students but the situation.

WHAT IS CURRICULUM?

Curriculum includes, among other things, the ideas which comprise
the substance of an experience, the way these ideas are organized, the
length of time allotted to consideration of them, and the ways in which
they are presented and received. We might also include community
sentiment and expectations along with national need as well as professional requirements, industrial demands, and college pressures.

Curriculum represents a pattern of all these factors interrelated in
such ways that there develops some sort of focus embodying all of the
component elements. The curriculum is all these things.

Ideas are the subject matter of curriculum. They are the data which
society deems important, and feels must be communicated to its young.
Sometimes when we manipulate the curriculum we modify the ideas
involved. If children do not seem to have an appreciation of their
cultural heritage, to cite an example, we require them to take a course
in American history. If they are not learning the precise ideas considered
essential in American history, we change textbooks or revise the syllabus.
If it is believed that children should be acquainted with the significant
minds of the past, they study the classics. To teach children to think
scientifically we have them study both the ideas and the methods of

47

the sciences. One obvious way in which we can manipulate the curriculum and thus affect children's behavior is by revising or manipulating the ideas. By adding to, deleting from, or otherwise altering subject matter, we reflect our concern for controlling the learners' actions.

Another way in which we change the curriculum is by reorganizing it. We might deal with the sequence of ideas, for example; which things come first, which next. Some persons may feel that by requiring geometry first and algebra later we can teach children more mathematics than by the opposite sequence. Since geometry is more concrete and algebra more abstract, by postponing the abstract experience until they have had more opportunity to develop concepts and understandings in mathematics, more children may be successful with algebra later. More children may thus proceed further in mathematics than if they had had an unsuccessful experience because of their inability to handle abstractions at too early an age.

Another illustration might involve the placement of a science course in a four-year high school schedule. If the particular course is biology, and if the compulsory age limit of sixteen is also considered, some persons might feel that, since many students will quit school at that age, it could be especially important for them to have experience with biology earlier. A required course for all ninth graders might be the result.

Likewise, teaching geography in the fifth grade rather than in the third might well be based on the assumption that nine-year-olds are less able to grasp the spatial concepts necessary to such a study than eleven-year-old children. These examples all represent attempts to manipulate the curriculum by organizing it.

Still another way in which we might attempt to influence behavior by changing the curriculum would be to modify the time factor. If we assume, as Aristotle (8) implied, that the quality of education is a direct function of the length of the educational experience, we may employ this concept. Requiring students to attend school through age sixteen is an example. Increasing the length of period of 42 to 55 minutes would be another. Combining two 45-minute periods into one 90-minute period three times each week would be a third example.

Changing classroom methods is yet a different approach. By going from lecture to recitation, or from discussion to laboratory work, or from group process to individual study in the classroom, we can vary the impact of a teacher's efforts on students' behaviors. The great bulk of professional literature is aimed at this very point. By describing procedures and techniques which were successful or effective in one situation, teachers try to convince their fellow workers that such approaches might succeed in their own classrooms.

We often vary several factors simultaneously to bring about more drastic change. Certain innovations in curriculum development incorporate such changes in several areas at the same time. The core curriculum (39), for example, is based upon the assumption that a longer period of time, a problem-solving approach, a broader inclusion of ideas, and a particular kind of teacher-pupil relationship are all-important. Team teaching and the nongraded school involve variations of a different kind.

The Main Idea

One thesis of this book is that children learn from others. In fact, they tend to become the kind of people their teachers are. Our concern, then, must be with several of the factors just discussed. Still accepting the premise that the best way in which we can influence children is by manipulating the curriculum, to look at that curriculum from a different angle might prove worthwhile. If the fundamental idea is that children tend to become the kind of people their teachers are, the problem becomes one of getting teachers to behave in appropriate ways.

Everything a teacher is and does is educational method. That is, from a child's vantage point, what a teacher says and does are inseparable. As Emerson supposedly said, "What you are speaks so loudly I cannot hear what you say." Or, looked at from the opposite point of view, the ideas embodied in the phrase "Don't do as I do, do as I say!" tend to be impossible by definition. Perhaps a diagram will clarify the idea.

Learning from the Student's Vantage Point

When a student is in a classroom, he really perceives two things: the ideas which the teacher is attempting to communicate, represented by the book, and the kind of person that the teacher is himself, including what he does. Methods and content are both materials of growth and learning. The way a teacher behaves and the ideas with which he works are both important because they are both perceptible. The student builds his own psychological being from both of these sources. To say that an idea, however basic, can be conceived apart from its manner of presentation is as absurd as to maintain that the way in which ideas are handled is the only factor which is really important in the learning process. Both must be included in any consideration of curricular effectiveness.

Most frequently, however, the overhauling of a curriculum consists of a lengthy consideration of the ideas which comprise the subject matter, with perhaps a quick glance at the time and sequence, and the change is made. New course descriptions and new textbooks are often chosen without regard to the nature of the people who will teach those courses. Note how many college courses, instituted by particular men under certain circumstances, remain on the schedule for years unquestioned. The inference is unmistakable that particular ideas are worthy material for study, regardless of how or by whom they are taught. Such a notion presupposes that the strength and logic of the ideas will be sufficient to overcome any other influence. Or, if other considerations do appear, they generally show up in the almost apologetic form of insistence that the ideas will always be presented in "the best way we know how," or that teachers always use "good" teaching methods.

For example, it is seldom realized that the learning experience in which a student engages when he undertakes a study of liberal ideas from an authoritarian person is bound to be confusing or downright damaging. It is not possible to teach democracy autocratically. And yet we do. At least we initiate activities which we call teaching but in which authoritarian people profess libertarian concepts. No wonder young people are not clear (82) about democracy. To learn two conflicting things simultaneously is certain to upset the equilibrium.

But to assume that presentation of liberal ideas will assure the development of liberal students is to assume that the impact of an instructor upon a growing mind is negligible. The notion has merit, but it is not without fault (59). We must direct our attention to other aspects of the curriculum.

Proof that instructors are more memorable than their courses is found in the fact that their names and personalities are often more firmly fixed in students' minds than the subject matter of their teaching. College students working at the graduate level, especially, choose their programs in terms of people rather than of courses or ideas. "I want to get a course with Professor _____," they say. And the emphasis is upon the *a*; any course will do, as long as they have an opportunity to *know the man*.

A teacher's personality and his ideas are perceived and absorbed, and become the basis for future behavior. What a teacher says and what he is are both content which can be learned.

These things imply that another way to change the curriculum would be to change the teacher. By providing children with a particular kind of teacher-personality, it should be possible to influence the kind of people they will become.

The impact of this idea is considerable. If children experience more than the ideas expressed by a teacher, then what a teacher is actually like becomes fundamental to the educational process. Educational method is everything a teacher is and does. The traditional difference which many persons supposed to exist is in name only. The notion of subject matter and method as distinct and separate arises only in the teacher's mind. Children learn what a teacher is just as they learn what he says.

This idea is logical. It seems reasonable to assume that children tend to become the kinds of people they experience. However, what kind of evidence is there to support such a contention? Do children learn from others, and if so, how? The next few pages are devoted to a review of research regarding what children learn from the persons around them.

Impact of the Culture

"They are as like their forebears as peas to peas," says Margaret Mead (69) in showing the profound influence a culture has upon its young. One of the indisputable conclusions anthropologists have reached in studies of man's existence is that the idea of induced conformity through experience is important for educators. Ruth Benedict (16) describes the same phenomenon in different terms:

> The life history of the individual is first and foremost an accommodation to the patterns and standards handed down in his community. From the moment of his birth the customs into which he is born shape his experience and behavior. By the time he can talk, he is a little creature of his culture, and by the time he is grown and able to take part in its activities, its habits are his habits, its beliefs his beliefs, its impossibilities his impossibilities . . .

Riesman's study (84) also describes the ways in which various societies induce conformity. Some do it by appealing to tradition, and shaming their young into appropriate modes of behavior. Others set up certain goals within the individual's own psychological mechanism, then resort to suggestions of guilt should he not succeed. Still others develop social awareness among their youth which enables them to respond sensitively to their environment, and in these societies anxiety becomes the lever employed by the elders. But all societies seek to promote similarity between generations.

Some studies also indicate that as the culture changes, so does the resultant behavior (49, 50, 61). Among the more interesting examples is a study by Richman and Schmeidler (83) of variations in the Hora, a Jewish folk dance, during the period of the Israelis' fighting with the Arabs after World War II. During the fighting, they noted, for instance, how dancers began to stamp instead of hopping, as was traditional. The participants would sometimes suddenly stop their usual circular motion in a particularly rapid tempo. Later, when the fighting had ended, the dance changed once again. This time the circle was the same, but the stamping and interruption of the rhythm dropped out, replaced by three little running steps. The authors summarized (83) by saying that "the change in the most popular form of this popular dance seems appropriate to the change in the needs of the nation and the cultural atmosphere."

Gladwin (44, 85), recounting his observations and study of the Truk Islanders' cognitive aspects of personality, contrasts the variations in thought processes of the islanders with those of the American servicemen stationed there. Especially intriguing is his description of the Truk navigator learning to pilot his sailing canoe across many miles of open ocean (44):

> Essentially the navigator relies on dead reckoning. He sets his course by the rising and setting of stars, having memorized for this purpose the knowledge gleaned from generations of observations. A heading toward a given island, when leaving another given island, is set at a particular season a trifle to the left, or perhaps the right, of a certain star at its rising or setting. Through the night a succession of such stars will rise or fall, and each will be noted and the course checked. Between stars, or when the stars are invisible because of daylight or storm, the course is held constant by noting the direction of wind and waves. A good navigator can tell by observing wave patterns when and by how much the wind is shifting its direction or speed. In a dark and starless night, the navigator can even tell these things from the sound of the waves as they lap upon the side of the canoe's hull and the feel of the boat as it travels through the water. . . .

What kind of information is he utilizing, how is he selecting it, and how does he have to manipulate and integrate it in order to produce a useful end product—*i.e.*, differential pressure on the steering paddle? His information consists of a large number of discrete observations, a combination of motion, sounds, feel of the wind, wave patterns, star relationships, and the like. Each is a concrete, largely unequivocal factual observation. Either the boat is heading toward the correct star or it is not. The wind is from a certain direction and of a certain velocity; although it takes practice to observe this accurately, the fact is unambiguous. The significance of each observation is established by a comparison with remembered observations from past experience, a result of training. . . .

The feat of the navigator, although remarkable and highly useful, is thus not one of logic and reasoning but rather one of using a succession of concrete criteria to assign appropriate weight to a set of data based upon predetermined categories of observation. The weighted data in turn fit into what we might refer to as a standard equation, which will permit of only one solution from one set of data.

Gladwin goes on to describe how these Truk navigators actually function like an electronic computer; they are being intelligent but are not thinking. This, he concludes, is primarily a result of the navigator's acculturation. The cultural experiences which the navigator has had have encouraged the development of particular cognitive processes and simultaneously discouraged the development of others.

In more restricted studies, Christie and Garcia (27) and Frymier (42, 43) examined the impact of certain cultural situations upon the development of young people, including the way in which they perceive. These studies and others (7, 52, 67) tend to support Kelley and Rasey's contention (60) that "man and his environment are one."

When the specific variations in socio-economic levels within a given culture are examined, we see that they do account for differences in actions of young people. Auld (9), for instance, reviewed 47 studies and found definite deviations among respondents' personality scores according to the different social levels from which they came. In her study of mothers and young children, Bayley (14) reported similar differences, noting especially that mothers of higher socio-economic status were more warm, understanding, and accepting of their children than mothers of lower status, who were more controlling, irritable, and punitive.

Others (4, 48) also reported that mothers from lower and middle class strata were more restrictive and used more punishment than mothers from higher social levels. Not all researchers were agreed upon this point, however, as Dahlke (30) found no difference in the extent to which parents from different socio-economic levels treated their children. Burchinal (26) did find, though, that children coming from higher class homes had fewer maladjustments, and Elder (37), who interviewed 32 Iowa fathers, noted that those from lower levels had more traditional concepts of child-rearing as compared to others whose views were described as developmental. Related to this latter study, Duvall (36) interviewed 433 mothers and likewise noted more traditional conceptions of child-rearing among lower-class and Negro mothers.

These findings are especially interesting when compared with McKee's (74) study indicating that children from lower socio-economic groups displayed more competitive, aggressive behavior than children from higher classes. It is not surprising that Sims (89) concluded from his observations of high school and college students that "there seems little doubt that . . . social class identification is an important positive correlate of . . . social adjustment."

Siegman (88) reported an investigation of the Rorschach performance of a group of Yeshivah students as compared to that of other college students. Boys who studied at a Yeshivah adhered to an extremely Orthodox religious way of life, and these particular students had been exposed to such orthodoxy from their earliest youth. The results indicated constrictiveness, defensiveness, rigidity, and lack of spontaneity. Siegman points out that the more rigidly predetermined behavior in the Yeshivah culture possibly accounts for the differences in personality which were found.

Obviously, particular portions of the culture mold the individual in different ways, but mold him nonetheless. The impact of the culture is both powerful and strange.

The Impact of the Family

"The apple never falls very far from the tree." Within a culture the family as a unit also makes its impression upon the growing organism. Such a point would hardly seem to need justification or documentation, though there are many relevant studies (10, 12, 13, 15, 57, 58, 77, 79, 96, 97).

Duncan (35), for example, studied the personality patterns of stutterers. She noted that these persons seemed to feel a lack of love and understanding from their parents. In a synthesis of the results of a number of studies which have been developing under his direction at Yale, Sarason (86) describes the home situation of childrn who are "test anxious." He says, for example, that the mothers of the highly anxious children are more concerned with what is right and wrong and with what other people will think of them and their children than are the mothers of those children who are less anxious about school tests. Further, mothers of anxious children tend to discourage the expression of aggression, and foster a dependent relationship between themselves and their children. Test anxiety, or the general apprehension which accompanies an examination in school, would seem to be partly related to the kind of home from which a child comes.

Dickens and others (32) studied 40 students and their mothers in a West Coast college and noted that a majority of the mothers of ethnocentric young people agreed with the statement that strict discipline is necessary to develop fine, strong character in children. Further, there was evidence that the mothers of those who were more ethnocentric were also more "ignoring" of their children than mothers of children who were less ethnocentric. That is, they tended to believe that a "good" child was one who required less time and attention from the parent.

Allport's (5) classic statement on prejudice, based upon an accumulation and interpretation of research, emphasizes the extent to which the family influences the prejudicial patterns a child acquires.

> There is no society on earth where the children are not thought to belong to the ethnic and religious group of their parents. By virtue of kinship, the child is expected to take on the prejudices of his parents, also to become the victim of whatever prejudice is directed against his parents.

> It is because of this fact that prejudice *looks* as though it were inherited, linked somehow to biological descent. Since children are identical with their parents in respect to memberships, we must expect ethnic attitudes to be handed down from parent to child. So universal and automatic is it that somehow heredity seems to be involved.

> Actually, the course of transmission is one of teaching and learning, not heredity. As we have seen, parents sometimes deliberately inculcate ethnocentrism, but more often they are unaware of doing so.

Bornston (21) studied 152 college students and their mothers and observed that the more domineering the mother was, the more aggressive the child. Likewise, Harris (48) reported that mothers of prejudiced children expected unquestioning obedience, offered rewards to get their children to obey, and actually preferred quiet and cautious children.

Clark (28) did a questionnaire study of college graduates and persons whose names appeared in "Who's Who." He concluded that the more successful of those in "Who's Who," came more frequently from ministers' families than did the college graduates. He inferred that it may have been because ministers' wives were superior as mothers. Other studies (18, 20, 44, 62, 99) support the inference that parental behavior arouses similar responses in children.

Several researchers have explored the influence of particular kinds of disciplinary action upon child development. Ahlstrom (3), reviewing educational research done in Sweden and other Scandinavian countries, pointed out that mothers who were less child-centered had boys who were more aggressive, disturbing, and careless. Meyer (70) also reported that children who encounter more friction in the home are apt to be more aggressive in nursery school. Emmerich (38) studied 31 Chicago children's patterns of identification with their parents. For the boys, mothers were seen as more permissive than fathers, but that both parents became more controlling as the child grew older. Drews (34) found the parents of good students to be less permissive and more restrictive.

A series of inquiries into the relationships between disturbed or maladjusted children and their parents is even more enlightening. Abbe (1) described the behavior of three-fourths of the mothers of disturbed children as restrictive, or lax and overindulgent, whereas all of the mothers of non-disturbed children were moderately permissive in their dealings with their children. McKeown (75) described the parents of schizophrenics, neurotics, and normal children as generally similar to their children. Further, he reported that parents of normal children more frequently were encouraging and supportive of their children than were the parents of the psychologically disturbed. In a similar study, Phillips (78) examined the data from several clinical cases and reported considerable overlap of symptoms between parent and a child with some type of personality disturbance.

These studies and others (2, 17, 19, 22, 26, 58, 66, 73, 76, 93, 95), with few exceptions indicate the extent to which family forces influence individual development.

The Impact of Teachers and Others

Interesting as they are, these studies are incomplete. Taken by themselves they present a formidable argument that children tend to become what they perceive. But there is still one breach in our logic. Even though children acquire the basic behavior of their culture, and even though parental personality and action patterns show up in young people, what assurance do we have that these are not really genetically determined? How do we know that these behaviors are really learned and not inherited?

Razran (81) reviewed some of Pavlov's writing on the Lamarckian notion of transmitting information genetically. In this paper he described how Pavlov reported in 1923, here in the United States, a study in which first generation white mice required 300 lessons to teach them to run to a feeding place upon hearing a bell ring. The second generation required only 100 repetitions, the third only 30, and the fourth only 10. The fifth generation learned the lesson after five repetitions, and Pavlov reported that he himself expected to produce a generation of mice which would run to the feeding place on hearing the bell with no previous lesson.

This is an intriguing idea and, if correct, would call for a complete reorientation of the human race. Razran goes on to point out, however, that although Pavlov apparently never formally renounced Lamarck's doctrine, the inference is clear that he did not expect positive results. He did not continue these studies, in fact. American observers, at least, are generally agreed that the Lamarckian theory is completely without basis.

Authorities, for instance, are fairly unanimous in agreeing that these ways of thinking and feeling and acting are really learned behaviors, not transmitted from parent to offspring by biological means. Sinnott (91) states their position beautifully:

> Biologists are generally agreed that the qualities a living thing acquires through responses to factors in its environment are unable to insinuate themselves into its basic heritable nature and thus cannot be transmitted from an individual to his offspring. Binding the feet of any number of generations of Chinese girls left no effect behind, once this unfortunate custom was abandoned. Bantam corn can be grown in rich Iowa soil to the greatest height of which it is capable, but no one can succeed by this means in making out of it a permanently taller race of corn. The claims of Messrs. Michurin and Lysenko that in Russia, at least, such things are possible have quite collapsed, despite the importance of such a theory for Soviet ideology.

> This failure of acquired characters to be inherited may seem unfortunate at first sight, for it prevents the permanent acquisition by our race of those valuable qualities gained in man's long ascent from barbarism. The changes that so distinguish him today from his progenitors at the dawn of civilization are not the result of biological evolution, as were the processes that made him man, but of cultural

development, and in regard to them every individual starts from scratch. Only one generation separates us from barbarism. We stand on the shoulders of our predecessors and our balance is precarious. This fact of life also has its bright side, however, for it means that although every generation has to start afresh and without benefit biologically from the experience of its ancestors, it also is free from the errors and tyrannies and prejudices which were theirs. It can gain Utopia at a single bound if it has the determination to do so. Its fate is in its own hands.

But to conclude that information is not transmitted by means of the genes is not to conclude that it is unmistakably learned. What evidence is there that children reared in different environments by foster parents or other teachers assume their behavioral ways? If we can furnish data relative to this last point, our thesis that children tend to become what their teachers are takes on real meaning.

First, what happens to children who are separated from their parents and placed in institutions? Do they develop in ways which are so atypical that we could make valid generalizations about the influence of the environment? Dennis (31) described a study of three institutions in Teheran, the capital of Iran. He observed that babies in two of the institutions were exceedingly retarded in their motor development, while children in the third showed but little lag behind the non-institutionalized. His analysis indicated that attendants in the first two failed to place the children in the sitting and prone positions, whereas those in the third had such assistance. He concluded: "The retardation of subjects in Institutions I and II is believed to be due to the restrictions of specific kinds of learning opportunities." Not guiding children in these experiences, therefore, seems to result in motor retardation.

Goldfarb (45) compared Rorschach patterns of fifteen children whose first three years of life had been in an infant institution compared with fifteen children whose experience had been in foster-family homes. The institutionalized children showed a greater trend to deviation from the "normal" Rorschach pattern than did the others. Further, this deviation manifested itself in an unusual adherence to concrete attitudes and in inadequate conceptualizations. Such differences would seem to be a direct result of restricted opportunities to perceive.

In a study of the language development of institutionalized and hospitalized children, Haggerty (46) noted that such children's speech patterns proved surprisingly similar to those of schizophrenics. He ended his report by noting that extended confinement apparently can damage personality integration, and may lead to inhibition of proper communicability.

Sarason and Gladwin (85), after reviewing several studies in which Southern Negroes who moved to Northern cities, and rural children who moved to urban areas, were studied for changes in IQ, concluded:

> The study of rural-urban differences, and particularly of children and adults who leave the country and arrive in cities with an apparent intellectual deficit, has great research promise for the exploration of subcultural mental retardation. We now know that many of these people are, in terms of the usual test criteria, retarded on their arrival, even though seldom very severely, and that *they appear rather consistently to improve intellectually to a level of parity with their new neighbors.* [Italics added.]

These data lend some respectability to the idea that the quality of the perceived environment is reflected in human behavior. It almost appears that, as the food they eat and the air they breathe becomes physical form, so do the sights they see and the sounds they hear become psychological form.

The Skeels and Dye (92) studies are also significant in this connection. In these inquiries, two matched groups of institutionalized children experienced differing amounts of social stimulation. In one group each child was given to six "mothers" who cared for it. These "mothers" were actually older children and women, retarded, who were living in the same institution. These "mothers" cared for each child, fondled it, and gave it a generous amount of social stimulation. The other group was cared for in the usual manner, with each attendant being responsible for approximately twenty children. Follow-up studies of these children indicated that those who had affectionate care increased their intelligence quotients markedly more than those who were cared for by a single attendant responsible for several children. Without doubt, such studies demonstrate the feasibility of "creating intelligence," as Combs (41) describes it. It would appear that to perceive some social substance, however poor its quality (the "mothers" were actually retardates themselves) is better than to have less of a better kind. Research in France (55) demonstrates a similar phenomenon.

Anderson's (7) study of more than 9,000 children in several different countries is also important in relation to this problem. Students from authoritarian and dominating cultures "hold images of the teacher that are significantly different from those held by children in less dominating, that is, more integrative or democratic cultures." The fact that children from the democratic countries had teachers who were more apt to believe them than children from more dominating cultures seems significant in itself. Regan's (82) investigation of fifth and sixth graders also indicated that students under authoritarian teachers had more school-related fears than those under non-authoritarian teachers.

Other efforts to assess the importance of a teacher's personality upon learners have met with varied success. Barr (11), in his review of the literature for teaching competencies, points out a great number of studies which have shown high correlations between teachers' personalities and teaching success. In a more recent publication, McCall (72) refers to an unpublished study by Krause in which the highest correlations obtained were between teacher personality and pupil personality. Washburne's (100) description of Heil's work also indicates the importance of teacher personality upon student achievement, as do other studies (33, 56).

Considering the influence of teachers' behavior as contrasted with teachers' personality, one is immediately confronted with Jacob's (59) reference to the impact of particular instructors upon college students' values. With important exceptions, college teachers are largely ineffective in helping students reformulate their value structure.

Some instructors, though, actually do exert a profound influence on some students, "even to the point of causing particular individuals to re-orient their philosophy of life and adopt new and usually more socially responsible vocational goals." Jacob goes on to say (59):

> What it is that ignites such influence can hardly be defined, so personal, varied, and unconscious are the factors at work. It is perhaps significant, however, that faculty identified as having this power with students are likely to be persons whose own value-commitments are firm and openly expressed, and who are out-going and warm in their personal relations with students. Furthermore, faculty influence appears more pronounced at institutions where association between faculty and students is normal and frequent, and students find teachers receptive to unhurried and relaxed conversations out of class.

Thistlethwaite's (98) own research into the productivity at different institutions sounds quite similar:

> The faculties of schools high in natural science productivity are described as follows: (1) their contacts with students are characterized by informality and warmth; open displays of emotion are not likely to embarrass them; in talking with students they frequently refer to colleagues by their first names; they are not as likely to be described as practical and efficient in dealing with students; students do not feel obliged to address them as professor or doctor. (2) they emphasize high academic standards: according to student reports their standards are exacting; they see through the pretenses and

bluffs of students; they push students to the limits of their capacities; and they give examinations which are genuine measures of the student's achievement and understanding. (3) they have high standards for evaluating faculty productivity and selecting new faculty members: the faculty values pure scholarship and basic research, and the course offerings and faculty in the natural sciences are outstanding. (4) the faculty does not play the role of Big Brother: students need not sit in assigned seats and attendance is not taken; student organizations are not closely supervised to guard against mistakes; faculty members are tolerant and understanding in dealing with violations of rules.

The classic study by Lewin, Lippitt, and White (64) gives additional evidence of the degree to which a teacher's behavior is reflected in his students. In this research, different groups of boys worked in different kinds of group atmosphere: democratic, autocratic, or laissez-faire. Lewin's (63) description of the situations follow:

> The autocrat always tried to be friendly and did not purposely suppress free expression. He merely told the children what to do, with whom to work, and how to do it. As a whole, this was an atmosphere not too much different from that created by a friendly teacher who believes in strict discipline. In the democratic group all problems of policy were put up to the children to decide. The leader acted as fully as possible as a regular member of the group. In laissez faire, no encouragement was given to cooperative decision. The leader stood entirely apart from the group, but ready to give technical information when approached.

Out of these studies came indications that children who experienced autocratic leadership were more dominating and less objective in behavior, while those in the democratic group showed more cooperative behavior. Those persons who participated in decision-making expressed matter-of-fact attitudes, as opposed to the personal feeling in the autocratic group. In conclusion, Lewin (63) notes:

> These experiments point anew to the great possibilities vested in education, and to the responsibility given to moulders of young lives which are so sensitive to the present socal climate and are so dependent upon it.

The inference is obvious that teachers' behavior profoundly influences their students' lives.

Lovell (65) assessed similar information in a normal rather than an artificially created group setting. He found that sub-group leaders imitated the modes of operating of their total group leaders, the teachers. In other studies, Fox (40) and Singer and Goldman (90) duplicated the essential features of the Lewin, Lippitt, and White studies. Singer and Goldman, working with two groups of schizophrenics, provided one with an "authoritarian" kind of therapy and the other with a "democratic" atmosphere. The groups met over a five-month period and generally produced results similar to the other studies. The authors note, for instance, that

> . . . as time passes, the "democratic" group shows a very definite increase in the relevance of their comments. The "authoritarian" group, on the other hand, after an originally high level of relevant comments, falls off rather strikingly . . . After the first eight sessions, despite continued efforts on the part of the therapists . . . the [authoritarian] group members . . . showed an increase in apathy, in autistic and irrelevant verbalization.

Other studies (23, 82) describe how teachers serve as models for students, how dominative behavior (6, 47) in teachers brings out dominative behavior in children, how students dislike (94) domineering teachers, and how autocratic classes (101) produce more frustration and aggressive behavior on the part of students. Some teachers even behave differently toward students from different socio-economic levels, according to one study (54). A national commission (102), endeavoring to describe the ideal high school teacher, suggested that teachers "be able to move from a dominant to a supplementary role and back, as necessary" with adolescents, who are moving from a period of dependence toward self-direction.

In summary, then, the research available indicates that children are the products of their perceptions. That is, partaking of the experiences provided in a given culture or family or school seems to foster the development or acquisition of certain ways of behaving. Children learn from others; they tend to become what their teachers are; they tend to acquire their teachers' behavioral and personality patterns as a result of perceiving them.

Some will maintain that the impact of the culture in general or the family in particular is so much more profound and lasting in its effect than the influence of a teacher or the school, that teachers have little hope of modifying students' personality or behavior to any great degree. The first portion of this statement is unquestionably correct. However, since it is impossible, or extremely difficult, to modify the culture of a student or his family, if teachers believe in the possibility and desirability of behavioral change (and they should, or they are unquestionably in the wrong profession), the only alternative open to them is to bring about such change by manipulating the curriculum. Helping students have a better home life may be a noble ambition, but attempting to realize it will probably bring cries of "meddling" and "keep your hands off" from the home.

The only realistic approach, therefore, is to attempt to provide the most desirable experiences in school that are professionally possible.

If schools exist to help children learn to behave in democratic ways, then teachers must be democratic, too. Presenting children with appropriate behaviors to perceive is more than a cliche: children learn from others. In fact, children tend to become the kind of people their teachers are.

REFERENCES

1. Abbe, Alice E., "Maternal Attitudes Toward Child Behavior and Their Relationship to the Diagnostic Category of the Child," *Journal of Genetic Psychology*, XCII (June, 1958), 167-173.
2. Adorno, T. W. et al., *The Authoritarian Personality* (New York: Harper and Row 1950).
3. Ahlström, Karl-George, "Scandinavian Countries: Denmark, Norway, and Sweden," *Review of Educational Research*, XXVII (February, 1957), 119-138.
4. Aldous, John and Kell, Leone, "Childrearing Values of Mothers in Relation to Their Children's Perceptions of Their Mothers' Control: An Exploratory Study," *Marriage and Family Living*, (February, 1956), 72-74.
5. Allport, Gordon W., *The Nature of Prejudice* (Cambridge, Massachusetts: Wesley-Addison, 1954).
6. Anderson, H. H. and Brewer, H. M., "Dominative and Socially Integrative Behavior of Kindergarten Teachers," *Studies of Teacher's Classroom Personalities, I*. Standford University Press, 1955.
7. Anderson, H. H. et al., "Image of the Teacher by Adolescent Children in Four Countries: Germany, England, Mexico, United States," *Journal of Social Psychology*, L (August, 1959), 47-55.
8. Aristotle, *Ethics*, as cited in *An Introduction to American Education* by Raymond E. Callahan (New York: Alfred A. Knopf, 1957), 336.
9. Auld, Frank Jr., "Influence of Social Class on Personality Test Responses," *Psychological Bulletin*, XLIX (July, 1952), 318-332.
10. Baldwin, A. L., "The Effects of Home Environment on Nursery School Behavior," *Child Development*, XX (June, 1949), 49-61.
11. Barr, A. S., "Teaching Competencies," *Encyclopedia of Educational Research* (New York: Macmillan, 1952), 1446-1454.
12. Bartlett, Claude J. and Horrocks, John E., "A Study of the Needs Status of Adolescents from Broken Homes," *Journal of Genetic Psychology*, XCIII (September, 1958), 153-159.
13. Bateman, Mildred M. and Jensen, Joseph S., "The Effect of Religious Background on Modes of Handling Anger," *Journal of Social Psychology*, XLVII (February, 1958), 133-141.

14. Bayley, Nancy and Shaefer, Earl S., "Relationships Between Socioeconomic Variables and the Behavior of Mothers Toward Young Children," *Journal of Genetic Psychology*, XCVI (March, 1950), 61-77.
15. Behrans, Marjorie L., "Child Rearing and Character Structure of Mother," *Child Development*, XXV (September, 1954), 225-238.
16. Benedict, Ruth, *Patterns of Culture* (New York: New American Library, 1934), 2.
17. Bieri, James and Lobeck, Robin, "Acceptance of Authority and Parental Identification," *Journal of Personality*, XXVII (March, 1959), 74-86.
18. Block, Jack, "Personality Characteristics Associated with Fathers' Attitudes Toward Child-Rearing," *Child Development*, XXVI (March, 1955), 41-48.
19. Blood, Robert O., "A Situational Approach to the Study of Permissiveness in Child-Rearing," *American Sociological Review*, (February, 1953), 84-87.
20. Body, Margaret, "Patterns of Aggression in the Nursery School," *Child Development*, XXVI (March, 1955), 3-11.
21. Bornston, Freida and Coleman, James, "Relationship Between Certain Parents' Attitudes Toward Child-Rearing and the Direction of Aggression of Their Young Adult Offspring," *Journal of Clinical Psychology*, XII (January, 1956), 41-44.
22. Brim, Orville G. Jr., "The Acceptance of New Behavior in Child-Rearing," *Human Relations*, VII (November, 1954), 473-491.
23. Bronfenbrenner, Urie, "The Study of Identification Through Inter-Perception," *Personal Perception and Interpersonal Behavior* (Stanford: Stanford University Press, 1958), 110-130.
24. Burchinal, Lee G., "Parents' Attitudes and Adjustment of Children," *Journal of Genetic Psychology*, XCII (March, 1958), 69-79.
25. Burchinal, Lee G., "Mothers' and Fathers' Differences in Parental Acceptance of Children for Controlled Comparisons Based on Parental and Family Characteristics," *Journal of Genetic Psychology*, XCII (March, 1958), 103-110.
26. Burchinal, Lee; Gardner, Bruce; and Hawkes, Glenn R., "Children's Personality Adjustment and the Socio-Economic Status of Their Families," *Journal of Genetic Psychology*, XCII (June, 1958), 149-159.
27. Christie, R. and Garcia, J., "Subcultural Variation in Authoritarian Personality," *Journal of Abnormal and Social Psychology*, XLVI (1951), 457-469.
28. Clark, W. H., "A Study of Some of the Factors Leading to Achievement and Creativity, with Special Reference to Religious Skepticism and Belief," *Journal of Social Psychology*, XLI (February, 1955), 57-69.
29. Cogan, Morris L., "The Behavior of Teachers and the Productive Behavior of Their Pupils: I," *Journal of Experimental Education*, XXVII (December, 1958), 89-124.
30. Dahlke, H. Otto, "Determinants of Sociometric Relations Among Children in the Elementary School," *Sociometry*, XVI (November, 1953), 327-338.
31. Dennis, Wayne, "Causes of Retardation Among Institutional Children: Iran," *Journal of Genetic Psychology*, XCVI (March, 1960), 47-59.
32. Dickens, Sara Lee et al., "Parents Dominance and Offspring Ethnocentrism," *Journal of Social Psychology*, XL (May, 1959), 297-302.
33. Dodge, Arthur F., "What Are the Personality Traits of the Successful Teacher?" *Journal of Applied Psychology*, XXVII (1943), 325-337.
34. Drews, Elizabeth M. and Teahan, John E., "Parental Attitudes and Academic Achievement," *Journal of Clinical Psychology*, XIII (October, 1957), 328-332.
35. Duncan, Melba H., "Home Adjustment of Stutterers Versus Non-Stutterers," *Journal of Speech Disorders*, XIV (September, 1949), 255-259.
36. Duvall, Evelyn M., "Conceptions of Parenthood," *American Journal of Sociology*, (November, 1946), 193-203.

37. Elder, Rachel Ann, "Traditional and Developmental Conceptions of Fatherhood," *Marriage and Family Living*, (Summer, 1949), 98-101.

38. Emmerich, Walter, "Parental Identification in Young Children," *Genetic Psychology Monographs*, LX (November, 1959), 257-308.

39. Faunce, Roland and Bossing, Nelson, *Developing the Core Curriculum* (Prentice-Hall, 1951).

40. Fox, William M., "Group Reaction to Two Types of Conference Leadership," *Human Relations*, X (August, 1957), 279-289.

41. Frazier, Alexander, Ed., *Learning More About Learning* (Washington: Association for Supervision and Curriculum Development, 1959), 5-20.

42. Frymier, Jack R., "Relationship of Aural Perceptions to Cultural Situations," *Perceptual and Motor Skills*, VIII (June, 1958), 67-70.

43. Frymier, Jack R., "Aural Perceptions of Authoritarians in Different Cultural Situations," *Journal of Experimental Education*, XXVIII (December, 1959), 163-169.

44. Gladwin, Thomas, "The Need: Better Ways of Teaching Children to Think," *Freeing Capacity to Learn*, Alexander Frazier, Ed. (Washington, D.C.: Association for Supervision and Curriculum Development, 1960), 25-28. Copyright © 1960 by the Association for Supervision and Curriculum Development.

45. Goldfarb, William, "The Effects of Early Institutional Care on Adolescent Personality," *Child Development*, XIV (May, 1943), 213-220.

46. Haggerty, Arthur D., "The Effects of Long-Term Hospitalization or Institutionalization Upon the Language Development of Children," *Journal of Genetic Psychology*, XCIV (June, 1959), 205-209.

47. Hanna, Paul R. and Lang, Arch D. "Integration," *Encyclopedia of Educational Research* (New York: Macmillan, 1952), 588-600.

48. Harris, D. B. et al., "Children's Ethnic Attitudes: Relationship to Parental Beliefs Concerning Child Training," *Child Development*, XXI (September, 1950), 169-181.

49. Havighurst, R. J.; Robinson, Myra Z.; and Dorr, Mildred, "The Development of the Ideal Self in Childhood and Adolescence," *Journal of Educational Research*, XL (December, 1946), 241-257.

50. Havighurst, R. J. and MacDonald, D. V., "Development of the Ideal Self in New Zealand and American Children," *Journal of Educational Research*, XLIX (December, 1955), 263-273.

51. Havighurst, R. J. and Davis, Allison, "A Comparison of the Chicago and Harvard Studies of Social Class Differences in Child-Rearing," *American Sociological Review*, (August, 1955), 438-442.

52. Hess, Robert and Handel, Gerald, "Patterns of Aggression in Parents and Their Children," *Journal of Genetic Psychology*, LXXXIX (December, 1956), 199-212.

53. Highberger, Ruth, "The Relationship Between Maternal Behavior and the Child's Early Adjustment to Nursery School," *Child Development*, XXVI (March, 1955), 49-61.

54. Hoehn, Arthur J., "A Study of Social Status Differentiation in the Classroom Behavior of Nineteen Third Grade Teachers," *Journal of Social Psychology*, XXXIX (May, 1954), 269-292.

55. Hotyat, Fernand A., "French-Speaking Countries: Belgium, France, Switzerland " *Review of Educational Research*, XXVII (February, 1957), 39-56.

56. Hunt, J. T., "School Personnel and Mental Health," *Review of Educational Research*, XXVI (December, 1956), 502-521.

57. Hunt, Jacob T., "The Adolescent: His Characteristics and Development," *Review of Educational Research*, XXX (February, 1960), 13-22.

58. Itkin, William, "Relationship Between Attitudes Toward Parents and Parent's

Attitudes Toward Children," *Journal Genetic Psychology*, LXXXVI (May, 1953), 399-452.

59. Jacob, Philip E., *Changing Values in College* (New York: Harper and Brothers, 1957), 8.

60. Kelley, Earl C. and Rasey, Marie I., *Education and the Nature of Man* (New York: Harper and Brothers, 1952), 50.

61. Laswell, Harold D., "The Method of Interlapping Observation in the Study of Personality in the Culture," *Journal of Abnormal and Social Psychology*, XXXII (March, 1937), 240-243.

62. Levin, Harry and Sears, Robert, "Identification with Parents as a Determinant of Doll Play Aggression," *Child Development*, XXVII (June, 1956), 135-153.

63. Lewin, Kurt, "Experiments on Autocratic and Democratic Atmospheres," *Social Frontier*, IV (July, 1938), 316-319. (as quoted in Fullagar, William A., et al., *Readings for Educational Psychology* (New York: Thomas Y. Crowell Co.), 410-417.

64. Lewin, K.; Lippitt, Ronald; and White, R. K., "Patterns of Aggressive Behavior in Experimentally Created 'Social Climates,'" *Journal of Social Psychology*, X (May, 1939), 271-299.

65. Lovell, John T., "A Study of the Relationship Between the Style of Teacher Participation in the Total Classroom Group and the Internal Structure of Sub-Groups in the Classroom," Unpublished dissertation (University of Florida, 1954).

66. Lowery, L., "The Family as a Builder of Personality," *American Journal of Orthopsychiatry*, VI (1936), 117-124.

67. Maller, J. B., "Superstition and Education," *Encyclopedia of Educational Research* (New York: Macmillan), 1367-1371.

68. Mayer, Martin P., *The Schools* (New York: Harper and Row, 1961).

69. Mead, Margaret, *Growing Up in New Guinea* (New York: Mentor, 1930), 126.

70. Meyer, Charlene T., "The Assertive Behavior of Children as Related to Parent Behavior," *Journal of Home Economics*, XXXIX (February, 1947), 77-80.

71. Milton, G. A., "A Factor Analytic Study of Child-rearing Behavior," *Child Development*, XXIX (September, 1958), 381-392.

72. McCall, William A. and Krause, Gertrude R., "Measurement of Teacher Merit for Salary Purposes," *Journal of Educational Research*, LIII (October, 1959), 73-75.

73. McGuire, Carson, "Factors Influencing Individual Mental Health," *Review of Educational Research*, XXVI (December, 1956), 451-478.

74. McKee, John P. and Leader, Florence B., "The Relationship of Socioeconomic Status and Aggression to Competitive Behavior of Preschool Children," *Child Development*, XXVI (June, 1955), 135-142.

75. McKeown, James E., "The Behavior of Parents of Schizophrenic, Neurotic, and Normal Children," *American Journal of Sociology*, LVI (September, 1950), 175-179.

76. Nakamura, Charles Y., "The Relationship Between Children's Expressions of Hostility and Methods of Discipline Exercised by Dominant Over-Protective Parents," *Child Development*, XXX (March, 1959), 109-117.

77. Payne, Donald and Mussen, Paul, "Parent-Child Relations and Father Identification Among Adolescent Boys," *Journal of Abnormal and Social Psychology*, LII (May, 1956), 358-362.

78. Phillips, Ewing L., "Parent-Child Similarities in Personality Disturbances," *Journal of Clinical Psychology*, VII (April, 1951), 188-190.

79. Radford, W. C., "Australia," *Review of Educational Research*, XXVII (February, 1957), 7-19.

80. Raven, Bertram H., "Social Influence on Opinions and the Communication

of Related Content," *Journal of Abnormal and Social Psychology*, LVIII (January, 1959), 119-128.

81. Razran, Gregory, "Pavlov and Lamarck," *Science*, CXXVIII (October 3, 1958), 758-760.

82. Regan, John F., "The School Connected Fears of Children Under Authoritarian and Democratic Teachers," Unpublished dissertation (Columbia University, 1958).

83. Richman, Marjorie and Schmeidler, Gertrude R., "Changes in a Folk Dance Accompanying Cultural Change," *Journal of Social Psychology*, XLII (November, 1955), 333-336.

84. Riesman, David, *The Lonely Crowd* (New York: Doubleday, 1953).

85. Sarason, Seymour B. and Gladwin, Thomas, "Psychological and Cultural Problems in Mental Subnormality: A Review of Research." *Genetic Psychology Monographs*, LVII (February, 1958), 3-290.

86. Sarason, Seymour B., "Test Anxiety," *National Education Association Journal*, (November, 1959), 26-27.

87. Sharp, George, *Curruculum Development as Re-education of the Teacher* (New York: Columbia University).

88. Siegman, Aron W., "A 'Culture and Personality' Study Based on a Comparison of Rorschach Performance,' *Journal of Social Psychology*, XLIV (November, 1956), 173-178.

89. Sims, Verner M., "Relations Between the Social-Class Identification and Personality Adjustment of a Group of High School and College Students," *Journal of Social Psychology*, XL (November, 1954), 323-327.

90. Singer, Jerome L. and Goldman, George D., "Experimentally Contrasted Social Atmospheres in Group Psychotherapy with Chronic Schizophrenics," *Journal of Social Psychology*, XL (August, 1954), 23-37.

91. Sinnott, Edmund W., "The Questing Heritage," *The Nature of Being Human*, Marie I. Rasey, Ed. (Detroit: Wayne State University Press, 1959). Reprinted by permission of Wayne State University Press.

92. Skeels, H. M. and Dye, H. B., "A Study of the Effects of Differential Stimulation on Mentally Retarded Children," *Proceedings of American Association on Mental Deficiency*, XLIV (1939), 114-136.

93. Staples, Ruth and Smith, J. W., "Attitudes of Grandmothers and Mothers Toward Child Rearing Practices," *Child Development*, XXV (June, 1954), 91-97.

94. Stiles, Lindley J. et al., "Methods of Teaching," *Encyclopedia of Educational Research* (New York: Macmillan), 745-752.

95. Stoke, Stuart, "An Inquiry Into the Concept of Identification," *Journal of Genetic Psychology*, LXXVI (March, 1950), 163-189.

96. Stout, Irving W. and Langdon, Grace, "A Study of the Home Life of Well Adjusted Children," *Journal Educational Sociology*, XXIII (April, 1950), 442-460.

97. Stout, Irving W. and Langdon, Grace, "A Report on Follow-Up Interviews with Parents of Well-Adjusted Children," *Journal Educational Sociology*, XXVI (May, 1953), 434-446.

98. Thistlethwaite, Donald L., "College Environments and the Development of Talent," *Science*, CXXX (July, 1959), 72-74.

99. Von Mering, Faye Higier, "Professional and Non-Professional Women as Mothers," *Journal of Social Psychology*, XLII (August, 1955), 21-34.

100. Washburne, Carleton et al., "What Characteristics of Teachers Affect Children's Growth?" *School Review*, LXVIII (Winter, 1960), 420-428.

101. Wattenberg, William W. and Redl, Fritz, "Mental Hygiene," *Encyclopedia of Educational Research* (New York: Macmillan 1952), 733-745.

102. Wiles, Kimball and Patterson, Franklin, *The High School We Need* (Washington: Association for Supervision and Curriculum Development, 1959), 18.

Chapter Four

How Students Learn

INTRODUCTION

If education has a purpose, and if its goal is democratic behavior, how do people learn to behave democratically? What is learning? What forces facilitate the process? What aspects impede its occurrence?

Some persons say that children "learn by doing." Others maintain that "if nothing has been learned, then nothing has been taught." Still others profess that "there are few who learn from the experiences of others, but few who do not learn from their own."

Learning is such a commonplace process that most of us tend not to give it much attention. Little children *learn* to walk and *learn* to talk and learn many other things. The very fact that most youngsters acquire desired ways of behaving leads some to believe that the learning process itself is very simple. Nothing could be further from the truth.

The purpose of this chapter will be to examine the concept of learning from a perceptual point of view (56, 144, 159). The major phases of learning will be examined in some detail. Next, certain factors which impede learning will be explored for insights which might prove useful to teachers. Finally, the nature of intelligence will be examined briefly, with a discussion of some of the inherent implications.

AN OVERVIEW OF THE LEARNING PROCESS

Learning involves behavioral changes. These changes may be either overt or covert. Changes in the behavior of an organism, however, may result from maturation or fatigue as well as from learning.

For example, we say that "children learn to read." Confronted with printed symbols, children "learn" to interpret and respond to such

68

phenomena. But learning to read can only follow certain developments in a child's maturational progress (131). Unless and until the fine muscles of the eye develop along with the neuro-muscular apparatus which controls their movements, no child can learn to read. In this sense, the intellectual aspects of learning must follow the physical aspects, and in thinking about learning as a school activity, it becomes necessary to separate them as completely as possible.

Consider another, less academic, example. A major problem of most young mothers is to teach their youngsters to control bowel movements. Very small babies do not control the defecation act consciously, and they must learn as early as possible.

Many mothers, accordingly, begin to "teach" their child this control at a very early age. What some of them do not know is that bowel movements in adults are controlled by voluntary contraction and relaxation of the sphincter muscles in the anus, and volitional control is not possible until certain neuro-muscular maturations have occurred. Very young children could not develop such habits even if they wanted to until their own body cells matured to the point that voluntary rather than involuntary contractions were possible. These developments with the child's neural and muscular tissues take place about eighteen or so months after birth, hence most youngsters about this age can begin to "learn" toilet training. Attempting to teach the child those skills before his body is physically ready may satisfy the mother's need for activity in that direction, but it will never result in any learned behaviors on the part of the child. Learning and maturation are different, although related, aspects of individual growth (170).

Many things which people do result in changes in behavior primarily caused by fatigue rather than by learning. For instance, as a simple experiment, do as many push-ups as you can. Now consider how these push-ups would have looked if you had recorded them on movie film. Would the first have "looked like" the last? Probably not, but the changes came about because of fatigue rather than learning. Even though your first push-up "looked different" than the last one, such a behavioral change could hardly be labeled learning.

Analysis of the Learning Process

To account for learning in terms of changes in the organism's behavior, then, is not enough. If such changes are attributable to maturation or fatigue, they are not "learned" in the schoolmen's sense. For their purposes, learning might best be defined as those changes in behavior which result primarily from experience.

Behavioral change attributable to experience narrows our problem, but what is experience? For the purposes of this book, experience is defined as those perceptions which each individual has of the stimuli which impinge upon his nerve endings. To clarify this idea let us look at the way in which the learning process occurs. The learning act consists of the segments or phases of a totality: *behavioral change* follows *perception*, which comes after the *reception* of *stimuli*. Looked at graphically, we have this kind of schema:

STIMULI are RECEIVED then PERCEIVED for LEARNING

This outline oversimplifies the complexities involved, but several things are evident.

First, there is a process or flow to the act of learning. It has direction. For learning to occur, certain events must precede others. Perceptions depend upon the existence of stimuli, and, as will be shown later, the availability and richness of stimuli profoundly affect behavioral changes.

Second, although learning is a total process, there are phases of it which are sufficiently discrete to be explored more minutely. What we will attempt to do in the following pages will be to "hold the learning process still" and look at its component parts. Because learning is dynamic, such an analysis has definite advantages, but the reader is cautioned to realize that the description of learning which follows is a static description of a non-static phenomenon undertaken for the purposes of illustration.

Third, learning is a very personal thing, similar to such personal processes as digestion or respiration. Kelley (157) and Mooney (287, p. 336) have both made this observation before. Because of the similarity, it may aid understanding if learning is sometimes described in terms of these other basic human processes.

Stimuli

Learning starts with stimuli (296). Learning cannot occur, in fact, unless there is some event or fact or symbol or other form of stimulation present. Generally such stimuli arise outside the organism, but not always (6). In an academic sense, stimuli are the ideas, facts, generalizations, books, suggestions, pictures, lectures, maps, graphs, and so forth which constitute the "subject matter" to be learned.

Stimuli are also those smiles or frowns which teachers have for certain students. "Pats on the back," kicks and blows or derogatory remarks from other children are also stimuli at school. In a still broader sense, the books in the library, each issue of the newspaper, the very people in his hometown are all stimuli for the youth in school. Movies, television programs, concerts and exhibitions, even the appearance of houses and buildings and streets and alleys are all stimuli for the learner.

All of the sights and sounds and smells and pressures within "receiving" distance of any learner are stimuli. In some lower organisms the time in life at which a stimulus is available also seems to produce a marked effect and a special learning called "imprinting" (137). There is some evidence that this imprinting may also occur in human learning, but the discussion here relates to the learning which most frequently occurs in schools.

In this connection, several things about stimuli seem especially worth noting. The *quantity* of stimuli available will affect learning. All other things being equal, situations which contain more stimuli will provide better learning than those which have less (38, 141, 232). Those situations in which the *quality* of stimuli available are better will also produce better learning (232, 271, 272).

The number of stimuli could include such factors as the number of books in a home or classroom, the number of people associated with the learner, the number of places visited, speakers heard, points of view expressed, newspapers and magazines available, and museum displays at hand. The point is that those situations offering a greater number of stimuli hold greater learning potential because there is more to be learned. Though quantity of stimuli is an extremely crude index of potential for learning, it is nevertheless a factor to be considered. It represents one variable in the learning situation which can be partially controlled and manipulated. Deutsch describes the disadvantages which a slum youngster has in these respects (232, p. 170):

> Visually, the urban slum and its overcrowded apartments offer the child a minimum range of stimuli. There are usually few if any pictures on the wall, and the objects in the household, be they toys, furniture, or utensils, tend to be sparse, repetitious, and lacking in form and color variations. The sparsity of objects and lack of diversity of home artifacts which are available and meaningful to the child, in addition to the unavilability of individualized training, gives the child few opportunities to manipulate and organize the visual properties of his environment and thus perceptually to organize and discriminate the nuances of that environment. These would include figure-ground relationships and the spatial organi-

zation of the visual field. The sparsity of manipulable objects probably also hampers the development of these functions in the tactile
area. For example, while these children have broomsticks and
usually a ball, possibly a doll or a discarded kitchen pot to play
with, they don't have the different shapes and colors and sizes to
manipulate which the middle class child has in the form of blocks
which are brought just for him, or even in the variety of sizes and
shapes of cooking utensils which might be available to him as
playthings.

Aside from the mere numerical availability of stimuli, the qualitative
aspects are even more important (64, 65, 80 232). Any discussion of
quality of events, things or people might refer to their moral or their
educational characteristics. Stimuli considered "good" educationally
would probably also be considered "good" morally, but the two notions
must not be confused.

"Good" books may sometimes mean that they are socially acceptable
and morally sound. More often than not, however, "good" books are
those which tradition or certain authorities have recognized as treating
significant events or ideas with insight. In this sense, "good" books may
or may not be acceptable (Darwin's *Evolution of Species* was considered
"bad" for many years), but the ideas they outline and the style in which
these ideas are expressed are generally considered as exceptionally
significant.

It is in the educational sense of "good" that some stimuli are here
described as being of high quality. Because stimuli do vary in quality as
well as quantity, this is another manipulable aspect of learning. All other
things being equal, students who partake of "better" stimuli will acquire
appropriate ways of behaving more often than those who experience
"poor" stimuli.

For the moment it may be enough to suggest that learning starts with
stimulation, and stimuli may vary in both quantity and quality. Any
adequate understanding of the process must take these factors into
account. Just as the physical body develops out of the food and air and
water which it consumes, so does the learner grow and change on the
basis of the number and kind of stimuli which he psychologically consumes. And this brings us to the second segment of our analysis.

Receiving Stimuli

Legend has it that shipwrecked sailors loudly bemoan the fact that
there is "water, water everywhere, nor any drop to drink." The sailors'

dilemma is like the problems which sometimes confront teachers: there are many good stimuli around, but they do not find their way into the experience of their students. Books on library shelves mean nothing compared to books in the hands of youngsters who want to learn.

Availability of stimuli is not enough. The stimuli must be received within the central nervous system of the student. The only way in which stimuli which are "outside" of the student can get "inside" is via his senses. The senses are the gateway to the mind.

Sense receptors are highly refined and differentiated nerve endings which enable the organism to partake of his environment. The eyes enable the individual to receive light waves reflected from a page of print and then such stimuli are sent on to the brain where they are processed for use. Just as the mouth and nose serve as entryways into the organism for the physical necessities of life, so do the eyes and ears and other sense receptors take in available stimuli for use in learning.

Three things seem important at this point about receptors. First, they are highly differentiated. Second, they function differently in terms of distance or space. Third, the point of input (receptor) is related only to the point of output (behavior evident) inside the central nervous system of the learner. By way of explanation, let us look at each of these notions in some detail.

Stimuli are physical phenomena. As actualities they occur in the form of sound waves (the spoken word), light waves (a painting), physical pressures (the weight of the body pressing downward in a chair), odors ($FeS + H_2SO_4 \rightarrow H_2S + FeSO_4$), or kinesthetic sensations (touching your nose with your finger while your eyes are closed). As realities, however, they come to the organism in a variety of ways. One of the outstanding characteristics of the human organism is that it has finely developed and highly discriminating receptor apparatus. It is not the purpose of this book to discuss how the eye or ear is constructed and functions. Suffice it to say that man has sensory apparatus which enables him to partake of his environment in many different ways. The first observation one might make about man's several sensory receptors is that they are sensitive to particular types of stimuli. They are differentiated.

Secondly, each of the various sense modalities responds differently in terms of spatial factors. Nerve endings uniquely sensitive to pain stimuli respond to only those aspects of their environment which are immediate and pressing. The point of a pin held even a fraction of an inch from the pain receptor does not cause the nerve to fire. No impulse is transmitted if the stimulus is not received, and some of those nerve endings within the human organism which receive stimuli do so only when the object emitting the stimulation is placed in direct contact with the neural tissue itself.

The eyes and ears, on the other hand, almost "reach out" and pull stimuli their way to facilitate learning. Of course, light waves and sound waves must impinge upon the nerve endings before there is any sensation of sight or hearing, but the eyes especially seem to pursue stimuli and bring them in for the organism to receive.

Finally, one of the most obvious characteristics of the sensory apparatus is that the connection between afferent and efferent neurons occurs only in the central nervous system. Though this may appear important only as a physiological fact, consider those academic ways of behaving called reading and writing, or speaking and listening. These four types of communication skills are the main body of any language arts program, and all occur along different neural pathways within the student's organism.

Reading and writing, for example, are corollary activities, but reading stimuli flow into the student by way of his eyes, while those activities which result in writing are manifest through the arms and fingers. Physically, reading and writing are completely unrelated phenomena. Psychologically, of course, the relationship is closer, but teachers dare not assume that progress in one is related to progress in the other. They are different in almost every way imaginable.

Think, too, about speaking and listening as learned behaviors. Listening involves sound waves impinging against the eardrums to activate the neural fiber by initiating an impulse which is carried the length of the nerve to the brain, where it is accorded some significance. For all practical purposes, listening involves one set of nerve fibers which are completely segregated from those involved in speaking, except where they unite within the brain, where the central neurons lie. To speak, the brain sends signals along various efferent neurons which cause dozens of muscles in the cheeks, lips, tongue, and diaphragm to contract and relax in such a way that air is expelled from the lungs through the larynx and the mouth in the form of particular sounds. Although this difference between neural activity and learning will be discussed in more detail later in this chapter, it is important here to point out that sensory receptors are the means by which stimuli are received by the organism, while learning (changes in behavior) is expressed along completely different pathways.

The basic purpose of this section has been to outline certain dimensions of the cognition segment of the learning process. Just as the organism takes food into itself through the mouth, so too does the organism take stimuli into itself by way of its many sensory receptors. These sense modalities might be likened to pathways to the brain, where learning occurs.[1] And this brings us to the third segment of the learning process.

Perceiving

Receiving stimuli is one thing. Perceiving them is another. For a stimulus to be received, the sensory apparatus of the organism must be functioning reasonably well and there must be no obstructions to or serious distortions of the stimulus itself. However, perception involves much more than the mere receipt of stimuli. Perceiving means that the organism *gives meaning to* a stimulus which it receives. That is, only *after* a stimulus has impinged upon the nerve ending in a sense modality can a percept occur.

Perceptions are a union of past and present. Attributing meaning to a stimulus involves drawing upon reservoirs of previous experience when new experiences present themselves (158).

Consider the psychological aspects of learning to read. Suppose that a youngster is confronted with the spoken word "dog." As far as the ear is concerned, this symbol is simply a variation in sound waves which have a particular pattern. Faithfully and accurately, the ear picks up the sound waves and sends the stimuli on their way to the youngster's brain. Once these stimuli are received, however, there is nothing more the ear can do.

While receiving the symbol "dog" the brain must also be receiving other stimuli which enable it to recognize a relationship between the sound "dog" and a real dog or at least a picture of one. Over a period of time the youngster begins to relate the pattern of sound waves which we call the spoken word "dog" to four-footed pets that run and jump and bark and play. Somewhere, somehow, deep within the recesses of the brain, a concept of "dog" develops which is gradually associated with the spoken word "dog." Eventually this union will occur so that hearing the word "dog" will enable the youngster to conjure up a mental image of dogs as a class or a dog in particular.

Now consider what happens when a child begins to learn to read. He is confronted with the printed word "dog" on a piece of paper. Certainly, as far as the eye is concerned, these symbols are just black shapes on white paper, with no meaning at all. If the presentation of the written

---

[1] W. Penfield reported in an article in *Science* (236) that stimulating temporal areas of the brain during the course of neurosurgical operations elicits recollections of experiences on the part of the patient which indicate that stimuli which have been received and stored within the brain may be accessible through physical stimulation when they are unavailable with normal efforts at recall.

word "dog" is accompanied by a picture of a dog or a teacher's saying the word "dog" aloud, then perceptions begin to occur. Drawing upon his previous experience with the sound of the word "dog" and an actual observation of dogs, when a student sees the written word "dog" accompanied by these other stimuli, then he begins to *give* meaning to the printed stimulus "dog."

Note that *meaning comes from the learner.* The printed symbol "dog" means nothing by itself. Only when it is added to the student's reservoir of previous experience do perceptions occur. Perceptions involve the giving of significance to stimuli by the learner, and such perceptions always follow, never precede, the reception of a stimulus.

Knowing is the result of perceiving, and knowledge comes after the fact and not before (158, 203, 206). Knowledge always rests behind the eyes of the perceiver, inside the human brain. Knowledge is not what is printed on pages or stated in lectures. Knowledge lies behind the production of those symbols in that the writer or speaker has had his own set of perceptions, but in no sense can one consider printed material or lectures or pictures as knowledge. Stimuli, yes. Knowledge, no.

The individual accumulates perceptions which are grouped in clusters within his mind (212). These groups of percepts occur around patterns of meanings, and as the individual adds to his experiential store and reorganizes his perceptions into larger clusters, he gains insights.

Insights represent perceptual groupings which have become both differentiated and integrated to the learner. Achieving an insight means recognizing both a "whole" idea and its many "pieces" in their precise relationships to one another (171).

Accumulating fact after fact after fact does not bring insightful learning. Only when a person is able to organize and reorganize discrete bits of information into larger and larger patterns of meaning can insights occur. Learning is insightful only when the individual obtains a valid generalization while still retaining the awareness of the specific details and the way in which they are functionally and psychologically related to each other and to the whole.

For example, in learning to drive a car one must learn the specific location and function of such things as the accelerator, brake pedal, steering wheel, clutch, and gear shift. Knowing the names of these parts and where they are is not enough. One must understand the process of depressing the clutch pedal, engaging the gears, releasing the clutch pedal, pressing downward on the accelerator, and steering the car in one continuous way. Mastering the nomenclature and operation of each of the specifics by themselves will never be enough. There must be insight and understanding of how these and other parts of the automobile must be utilized in pattern for one to become a skillful driver. Insights occur when the learner has built up a reservoir of specific perceptions to be related in his mind as they are in reality, so that recognition and understanding of the details as part of a larger whole give added meaning.

The process of perceiving might be likened to the digestion of food, as implied before. Within the digestive tract the human organism processes the food that comes its way so it has both utility and potential. Just as the organism combines food particles with enzymes and other juices, and propels them on their digestive way, so too does the human brain process the stimuli which are received and then perceived in some marvelous but as yet unknown way. Somehow the stimuli are given meaning and stored in the central nervous system for future use, but many factors affect the perceptual process.

Just as the body has a way of selecting from the food and water and air available the essentials which tend to perpetuate and enhance the physical self, so too does the central nervous system have a way of selecting from the multitude of stimuli available those which will be most likely to maintain and enhance the psychological self.

Whatever the life process is, it seems to show itself in what biologists and some psychologists call purpose. Life has direction and intent, and in those completely subconscious acts of digestion and elimination the human organism has a way of functioning which enables it to be selective in what it admits to or expels from itself for its own continued existence. Increased quantities of carbon dioxide in the blood, for example, cause the brain to stimulate the phrenic nerve which causes the diaphragm to contract. This in turn draws more fresh air into the lungs as the rib cage is expanded, then during exhalation the excess carbon dioxide is given off. Allowed to increase in quantity, carbon dioxide would first cause discomfort, then pain, and ultimately death. But the organism has its own physiological mechanisms for coping with just such an eventuality, and the process of life is actually a series of actions and counteractions initiated by various parts of the organism so that the aspects of the environment which are beneficial are drawn into the physical being, while those which are harmful are generally rejected by one means or another (157). There is even some evidence that the actual structure of the neural tissue itself predisposes the organism to respond to different types of stimuli because of the electro-chemical activity which is predominate within any given person's central nervous system (299, pp. 214 ff.).

It is this selective nature of the life process which is so important for teachers to understand, because learning follows the same general pattern (9, 56, 119). Certain restrictive forces sometimes deprive the physical organism of the things it needs for the continuance of life and health. If a person has pneumonia, the congestion in his lungs may act so that the oxygen essential for survival is cut off at that point in the body where it can be assimilated into the blood stream and used. In the same way, a negative self concept may serve to keep the psychological organism from receiving stimuli which might help the individual develop a different, more positive concept of himself which would facilitate learning. Bills says about this point (19):

> Our perceptions are influenced by several factors including our needs, values, threat, physiological state, opportunity, and beliefs about self and other people. Of these factors, the most important in forming our perceptions and, consequently, our behavior, are our self-concepts and the beliefs we have about other people.

There is little doubt that the way a person sees himself affects his total perceptual processes (8, 67, 124, 216, 289). And self concept is essentially a learned behavior (41, 96, 113, 164).

Hastorf and Cantrill's study of college students' perceptions of rule infractions in a football game (130) also demonstrates clearly how a person's values influence his perceptions. Other studies show the same (123, 146, 241). Extensive research on the effect of threat in conjunction with stimuli indicate beyond doubt that threat narrows one's perceptual field (4, 18, 43, 48, 54, 83, 91, 125, 129, 161, 180, 186, 194, 200, 205, 219, 258, 277, 300, 304, 310, 311, 314, 318).

Since threat, values, self concept, and need are all factors amenable to some variation and control, such information provides clues for teaching method. For the time being we will shift to the fourth segment of our learning process—behavioral change—but we will return to this problem.

Changes in Behavior Come from Acting on Perceptions

Learning is apparent in what people do. The only way teachers or students can ever know whether or not learning has occurred is by observing behavior. Think for a moment about the following illustration.

William Whatley teaches physical education to junior high school boys. One of his objectives is that all of them should learn to perform a headstand satisfactorily. The first day of class Mr. Whatley spreads out the tumbling mats, lines up his class alongside, and requests each student to do a headstand.

Now suppose that Mr. Whatley finds nine boys who are unable to maintain the inverted position on their heads and hands without falling. If, through verbal description, demonstration, and physical assistance, he is able to help each of these nine boys *do* a headstand, he can assume that learning has occurred. The change in behavior is obvious in this example. When a youngsters is trying to learn to stand on his head, and his teacher *shows* him how, *tells* him how, and helps him into a headstand by holding his legs while he is in the inverted position, the teacher's actions are all stimuli. As they are channeled into the student's central nervous system, he interprets each and gives it meaning. When he actually attempts to stand on his head himself, however, then he starts *acting* on his perceptions. Only by testing perceptions out in action can he really know whether his interpretations are correct.

In the process of testing his perceptions through action, what the student does is feed back more stimuli into the learning process. As he tries to raise his hips above his head in order to extend his legs, the boy learning to do a headstand is creating new stimuli (kinesthetic: "it feels as if my body weight is directly over my head;" visual: "I can see that my head and hands form an equilateral triangle," etc.) which feed back into his central nervous system, modifying experience still further.

Although overt behaviors are where learning itself becomes evident, they are also, from the learners' point of view, actually new stimuli to be perceived (158). In this sense the total learning process is really cyclical, continuously feeding back into itself and expanding the experiential store.

If an English teacher wants students to know the meanings of certain words, he may provide experiences followed by observation of their behavior. Can the students *tell him* what "procrastinate" means, telling being a behavioral act? Or can they *write out* the definitions of "elucidate" or "prowess"? The writing out of the definition would be an observable behavior.

The important point is that the only way teachers ever know whether learning has occurred is by observations of behavior. Comparing performance after the presentation of stimuli with performance before enables teachers to make inferences about the effectiveness of their instruction. Or comparing performance after stimuli to the professed objectives permits a teacher to know whether students are learning what they "ought to," when the "ought to" is described in behavioral terms. Observations of behavior are the *only* source of information relative to learning.

Even when educational objectives are described in covert terms— attitudes, appreciations, beliefs—teachers must look to behaviors for clues about learning. Many literature teachers profess the belief that students should learn to *like* poetry or *appreciate* Chaucer's writings. Though these may be both appropriate and legitimate objectives, what teachers really look for is a clue which demonstrates that students who *like* poetry will actually read it in their spare time. If so, it is assumed that such students have learned; their behavior has changed. Acting on perceptions results in behavioral change (274).

RESTATEMENT OF THE LEARNING PROCESS

Learning involves behavioral change. Behavior is a function of perceptions. Perceptions follow the reception of stimuli. Stimuli are the subject matter of experience.

Stimuli constitute the major portion of what schools teach. The sensory receptors constitute the pathway to the students' minds. Perceiving involves giving meaning to stimuli from previous experience, and this is where learning really occurs. Acting on perceptions and testing out personal meanings through behavior is where learning shows.

Learning is a process. It has both direction and force of flow. It is affected by many factors within the individual and outside. Some of these factors are known or knowable, and some are subject to manipulation and control. In the section which follows some of the detriments to learning are examined for suggestions to facilitate the learning process.

FACTORS WHICH IMPEDE LEARNING

Using the foregoing analysis, it should be possible now to look at each of the segments of the learning process. Certain things may impede learning at each segment of the process. Stimuli may be reduced in number or quality. Physical defects may impair the reception process. Many psychological forces operate to destroy or deny perceptions. Many people "know one thing but do another"; they have not really learned at all. This section explores the forces which work against learning.

Learning Impeded at the Source of Stimuli

Because learning starts with the nature and extent of stimuli available, anything which diminishes either their number or quality impedes the process. The term "cultural deprivation" assumes this point. Children whose early years are spent in homes or communities barren of stimuli begin their schooling with a distinct disadvantage (135, 232, 257).

Readiness tests in reading, for example, assess a youngster's threshold point in that subject. What such tests really measure is the extent and nature of his previous experience as these relate to learning to read. Those students who have had more experiences with symbolic stimuli and their manipulation, including contrived, intricate relationships, are "more ready" than those who have not. Children who grow up in homes where there are pictures, magazines and books, games, toys, and other stimuli develop a background of experience which they can take with them to school to help them learn to read. Young people whose environments lack these stimuli cannot gain such experience, hence are "less ready."

Because experiences affect perception, there are many other stimuli which influence the learning process in addition to the obvious symbolic type. As was pointed out in Chapter Three, a growing youngster's major perceptual material is people. Those persons whom a child perceives become part of his experience—their personalities, values, prejudices, aspirations, language patterns, morals, and mannerisms. Their ways of coping with frustration, responding to stress, dealing with strangers, discussing issues and attending church are all stimuli to the young child. In most cases, youngsters pattern their own behavior after that of the adults in the home and immediate community almost without change. Whether or not they adopt these identical responses does not negate the fact that they do perceive them. Their culture contains the only source of stimuli out of which they can build experience and shape their own perceptions. Later in life most young people will acquire skills, such as reading, which will enable them to extend their field of experience vicariously, but initially they are prisoners of their environment and profoundly affected by it. The more extensive and intensive a child's own early experiences are, the more background he brings to school and the more "ready" he is to learn those things which the school is prepared to teach.

Inasmuch as the richness and availability of stimuli are the seed bed of experience, an individual who grows up in a situation characterized by personal aspirations which are hedonistic and immediate, a lack of concern for ideas, and deprecation of the abstract, his experience is "loaded" against success in school. Through no fault of his own, he is bound to have problems. This does not mean that teachers cannot help such children have productive experiences. It does mean that children who have such a background must be provided with other stimuli in many forms so they can modify their experience and allow subsequent stimuli to have real meaning.

Deutsch describes how children from lower-class homes are denied opportunities to experience the spoken word, which illustrates this point (232, p. 171):

> The lower-class home is not a verbally oriented environment . . . While the environment is a noisy one, the noise is not, for the most part, meaningful in relation to the child, and for him most of it is background. In the crowded apartments with all the daily living stresses, there is a minimum of non-instructional conversation directed toward the child. In actuality, the situation is ideal for the child to learn inattention. Futhermore, he does not get practice in auditory discrimination or feedback from adults correcting his enunciation, pronunciation, and grammar. In studies at the Institute for Developmental Studies at New York Medical College, as yet unreported in the literature, we have found significant differences in auditory discrimination between lower-class and middle-class children in the first grade. These differences seem to diminish markedly as the children get older, though the effects of their early existence on other functioning remain to be investigated. Here again, we are dealing with a skill very important to reading. Our data indicate too that poor readers within social-class groups have significantly more difficulty in auditory discrimination than do good readers. Further, this difference between good and poor readers is greater for the lower-class group.

Though it will not be discussed here in much detail, it is important to recognize other factors related to stimuli which affect the learning process. The sequence in which stimuli are made available has profound influence on the degree and quality of learning.

Historical events have their own logical sequence in that they occurred under certain circumstances at certain times and in certain places. In learning history, however, the logical sequence of events as they occurred and the psychological sequences of stimuli as they should be made available to the learner are not necessarily identical. The logic of events and the logic of the mind are not the same. The ordering of stimuli for learning is a very important consideration in teaching, and the research in programmed learning demonstrates this point forcefully.

Repetition of stimuli is another factor which affects learning. Repeated exposure to a stimulus facilitates learning, if each experience is meaningful. "Practice makes perfect," at least practice which the learner feels is worthwhile and in which he gets feedback about his accomplishments.

Stimulus deprivation impedes learning. Desired behavior patterns are built out of different stimulus patterns. Anything which teachers do which limits stimuli restricts learning. To discourage discussion of controversial issues deprives students of opportunities to perceive, and thus to learn. Using just one textbook impedes learning in that the stimuli are beyond the capacity of some youngsters. Students whose reading level is below the level of the text are unable to give meaning to the unfamiliar symbols. Stimuli presented in a sequence which has no relation to a student's psychological needs cannot be perceived, and cannot affect learning.

Learning Impeded at the Senses

Since the blind cannot see, they cannot learn from visual stimuli. Many things may affect the sensory receptors, and these affect learning. If the cornea of the eye is misshapen or the optic nerve degenerated, learning is impeded. If the nerves to a man's leg are severed, he is unable to "know" where his foot is, kinesthetically. He must watch it with his eyes. The individual who is born deaf has extreme difficulty learning to read since he cannot first experience the sounds of words before attempting to comprehend the printed page. Anything which affects sensory receptors so that they are less effective in forwarding stimuli to the central nervous system impedes the learning process.

Perhaps an illustration will reinforce this point. In recent years ethical hypnotists have sometimes employed hypnosis to inhibit the reception of pain stimuli. Teeth have been pulled, surgery performed, babies delivered, cancer pain endured, all under hypnotic suggestion. Under certain conditions hypnosis results in depressed sensory awareness. Whatever hypnosis is or does, one thing seems certain: the capacity of the organism to receive certain stimuli may be inhibited. When a person "comes out of" hypnosis, his sensory receptors begin to function and he is able to receive stimuli as before. If educators could ever fully understand the forces which operate to "open up" the organism to stimuli when one leaves the hypnotic state, they might be in a position to expedite learning universally. Since learning demands an openness to stimuli and a sensitivity to the environment, understanding the dynamics of "coming out of" hypnosis might help teachers overcome certain problems.

Those children whom we call "handicapped" are generally youngsters afflicted by blindness, deafness, cerebral palsy, etc., whose perceptual apparatus has been impaired. Clearly, anything which restricts the flow of stimuli along the neural fibers restricts learning.

Learning Impeded at the Point of Perception

Although reducing the number or quality of stimuli and impairing the function of sensory receptors negatively affects learning, probably an even more important place in which it is impeded is at the point of perception—within the central nervous system itself. Even if stimuli are received they are often not perceived. Stimuli are sometimes so misperceived that a completely false idea is created. What causes such perceptual errors to arise? Why are some stimuli denied interpretations altogether? What forces operate to impede learning at the point of perception?

First of all, there may be certain types of brain damage, such as lesions or hemorrhage or hypoxia, which have affected the way in which the brain processes the stimuli received. Many children incur minor brain damage at birth, generally in the form of limited oxygen supply to the brain, which results in mild cases of aphasia and similar maladies sometimes not even apparent to the physician. In such cases reading difficulties, for example, almost inevitably arise. The central pathways in the brain cannot function adequately, and the experiences necessary to learn to read (i.e., see a reality, hear a sound, see a symbol, say a word) are garbled because of the damage within the brain where perceptions occur.

The proportion of these cases, however, is fairly small. Such factors as threat, aspirations and values held, an individual's image of himself, and his personal needs, all affect perception in a much more extensive way (56).

Threat limits perceptions (48, 129, 295, 304). When confronted with a threatening stimulus, the organism responds two ways. First, the threatening object is seized upon, perceptually, and held in sharp focus. Secondly, other stimuli which are simultaneously impinging upon the organism are denied perception. This increased awareness of the threat and decreased awareness of other factors results in "tunnel vision," a psychological phenomenon in which the senses seem to narrow their energies and aim them at the threatening stimulus. Although the available stimuli may have remained unchanged, for all practical purposes they have decreased in number because they are not now accessible to the organism to be perceived.

Threat in an educational context produces the same result that stimulus-deprivation creates. A child who is afraid of his teacher is less able to assimilate subject matter because his perceptual apparatus is atuned to the threatening object (the teacher) rather than the information to be acquired. If teachers threaten students, this demands the students' attention, but in a way that simultaneously restricts their perceptual field and limits learning.

The way an individual sees himself also affects his perceptions and his learning. Those whose experiences have enabled them to see themselves in essentially positive terms are less defensive and more open to experience than those whose concept of themselves is negative (56, 197). Those who hold less positive self concepts, who are insecure, afraid, feel incompetent or inadequate, are threatened, and their perceptions are therefore limited.

In a classroom a student whose concept of himself is generally negative, who may feel unwanted, stupid, disliked, unimportant, or slow, may be so preoccupied with his low valuations of himself that he feels it is useless to try to learn. Why put forth the effort when you know it will not result in gain? By not trying, he denies himself the practice and experience he needs to learn. When he does not learn, his teacher evaluates him as "doing poorly," and he says to himself, "See, I knew I could not do it, and I didn't" (56). Needless to say, *telling* him he ought to try will hardly help. Unless the student himself feels such an insight, outside judgment will make no difference.

Self concept works in circular fashion, forcing back into the self observations which substantiate the original convictions (20, 133, 174). The process works both positively and negatively. The student who feels he is competent, intelligent, desirable, and worthy approaches each new opportunity to learn with these positive images of himself. Because he feels he can, he tries; and because he tries, he usually gets the practice and experience which bring him into contact with the essential stimuli. Because he does experience the stimuli, and because his teacher also sees him make the effort, he is rewarded with positive valuations, "good work, keep it up," which confirm his first concept of himself (56). Some children, however, seldom have the kind of experiences which build up self concept in the positive sense. Deutsch says, for example (232, p. 172):

> Another area in which the lower-class child lacks pre-school orientation is the well-inculcated expectation of reward for performance, especially for successful task completion . . . In these impoverished, broken homes there is very little of the type of interaction seen so commonly in middle-class homes, in which the parent sets a task for the child, observes its performance, and in some way rewards its completion.

The way an individual sees himself affects the way he perceives other stimuli. If he feels threatened or inadequate in any way, his perceptions are limited with resulting deficiencies in learning. If he feels no threat, but is able to cope with his environment without being overwhelmed by it, his perceptions are expanded and learning increases.

Another factor which influences the perceptual process is the individual's value structure and his aspiration level. Pursuing certain goals and believing in certain things are themselves learned behaviors. Products of one's early years, essentially, goals and values give direction and sensitivity to the perceptual process. Such factors operate to increase the individual's awareness of certain stimuli and lessen that of others.

To the scientist who values truth, ideas are hypotheses to be tested rather than dogma to be embraced or denied. The person who believes that Negroes are inherently inferior will point to their lower IQ scores as proof. Those who believe that all persons are inherently equal will point to the environmental surroundings of most Negro families to show that the difference in IQ is not attributable to basic differences. The objectives for which men strive and the beliefs which they hold dear give both direction and intensity to their perceptual processes (70, 192).

Need structure affects perception, too. Man's needs are many and varied, but they all influence the interpretations he gives to stimuli. All needs affect perception (195).

Because the human organism is organized and organizing, Combs and Snygg (56) maintain that man's basic need is to preserve and enhance the self. Built as he is of systems (circulatory, respiratory, digestive), each of which accomplishes a specific function, the human is an integral entity. As long as this integration is preserved and perpetuated, some of man's basic needs are being satisfied.

However, man is also part of a larger whole—he belongs to a family, a community, a nation—and this larger whole also consists of organized entities.

Within this framework of reality man exists. He has both a physical and a psychological self, and his basic need is to preserve and improve them. Driven by this need, his perceptual energies are brought to bear upon stimuli seen as threatening or enhancing to the self. All stimuli are interpreted within this context. Those which are threatening are denied admission or distorted to complement the self of the perceiver. Those which are non-threatening and hold promise of satisfying the organism's needs are given meaning which builds the total self. Man's needs affect perception while they motivate his actions.

Any stimulus which threatens an individual's self concept or is seen as being contrary to his basic values, impedes learning. If the need to preserve and build the self is endangered, learning is also affected. Just as the body endeavors to rid itself through vomiting or expulsion of any foreign substance harmful to the physical self, so the psychological self strives to receive and process only those stimuli helpful and beneficial to its continued existence.

"Underachievement" is predicated upon these factors (88, 114, 156, 265, 266, 290). The aspects of an individual's being which cause him to do less well than expected are inextricably related to the perceptual inhibitors described above. A child's ability is probably a less significant determiner of his achievement than his own concept of his ability (13, 29, 58, 101). Furthermore, any element of the educational context which is seen as threatening limits the learning potential, regardless of the teacher's intentions. What a teacher means is always less important than what the student thinks the teacher means (62).

Factors Which Impede Learning at the Point of Action

Stuttering is a learned behavior. Long thought to be the result of changing handedness or genetic factors (39), recent research demonstrates that children are taught to stutter (26, 27, 30, 82, 152, 153). The whole process goes something like this.

In learning to speak and in perfecting the speaking process in early years, children sometimes hesitate or repeat certain words or parts of words. Such hesitations and repetitions are perfectly normal and all children have them. Any study of "normal" speech indicates numerous imperfections in the pronunciation and flow of words. Some parents or teachers, however, are especially conscious of these deviations. They perk up their ears to see if they heard what they thought they heard.

Children are sensitive, too. They note the increased attention of the adult to their speech patterns (16, 108, 164), and they wonder if something is wrong. Gradually at first, and then more strongly, they detect cues from the adults about their speech effort. Bits of conversation such as "Is Johnny stuttering there?" or "Don't stutter—say your words clearly and distinctly and do not stutter!" make the child aware that something about his speech needs correcting.

Hoping to please his parents or the teacher, the child who has been made aware of his normal speech hesitations vows: "I will not stutter." He decides to try very hard not to make mistakes which bring disapproval from the adults. Anxious now (107, 247), he works at perfect speech, and the tension produced from trying so hard not to err causes still more hesitations and repetitions.

And so it goes. The more he becomes aware of his imperfections, the harder he works to correct them. The harder he works, the more tense and anxious he gets. The more tense he gets, the more mistakes he makes, and the more mistakes he makes, the more his parents and teachers tell him not to stutter. The more they tell him not to, the more he does. Ultimately he will even detect aversion in their facial expressions, little cues which increase his anxieties and make normal speech more difficult, if not impossible.

This oversimplified description of how a child learns to stutter shows that stuttering really starts in the ear of the listener. But when the listener feeds information back to the speaker about his behavior, a chain reaction is initiated which is difficult to stop. It is the action and perception of the action by the behaver which creates conditions essential to *teach* children how to stutter, even though this perception comes indirectly from the elders.

This illustration is an example of an undesirable kind of learning, but it also shows how learning may be impeded at the point of action. Since learners must test their perceptions by acting on them, no significant learnings are possible without this final step. Perceptions are like hypotheses which must be tested. Those whose meaning survives when they are acted upon become more firmly learned. Those which do not hold up must be tested again and re-perceived before significant learning can occur.

In many classrooms children are expected to "consume" stimuli, but not allowed to act on their perceptions. Ideas are not fully explored, discussions are limited, the apparent necessity to "cover ground" allows the teacher to force the pace of stimulus presentation without allowing opportunity for perceptions and actions upon perceptions. Such efforts are wasted motion. The teacher may feel satisfied that he "got through the book," but unless students are provided with opportunities to interact with stimuli, give them meaning and test that meaning, behavioral change will never come about except by accident. Some students may test certain percepts on their own, and thus alter their patterns of behavior, but to trust such a happenstance arrangement when more systematic learning would be possible under the teacher's guidance hardly seems defensible. Teachers must create situations in which students act on their perceptions or there will be no real learning.

SUMMARY OF THE IMPEDING FACTORS

Learning may be slowed or halted at any point in the process. Intentionally or unintentionally limiting either the quantity or quality of stimuli impedes learning. If the physical organism is unable to receive stimuli by way of its sensory receptors, learning will be restricted at the point of reception. To the extent that threat is apparent or inadequate concepts of self develop among students, learning will be impeded at the point of perception also. Finally, if the student is denied the opportunity to explore or act upon his perceptions, or if he is induced to react in some undesirable way, then learning will also be affected at that point.

In most instances, learning difficulties are complicated at several points throughout the process, thus confounding the efforts of those who project simple solutions. Unbelievably involved, learning difficulties are seldom overcome by simple panaceas, and though this makes the teachers' role more difficult, the opportunities also make it more challenging and rewarding. Teachers can relish the fact that they are dealing with the most difficult of problems—influencing the mind of man.

WHAT IS INTELLIGENCE?

Any effort to describe learning should probably include discussion of intelligence. Schoolmen employ the concept of ability or intelligence in their considerations of teaching and learning so extensively, it would hardly seem reasonable not to explore the topic, if only briefly.

Intelligence as a human quality can be measured crudely, and an understanding of its properties would certainly be of immense value to any teacher (119). Since this is not a volume on learning theory, however, only a limited discussion seems appropriate here.

Like motivation and teaching method, intelligence affects learning. Equating intelligence and IQ scores, however, has unquestionably been one of the most insidious and devastating practices ever engaged in by teachers. Clark discusses this point cogently in a paper addressed to the problems of racially disadvantaged children. He writes (232, p. 149):

> Among many of the teachers who are required to teach children from culturally deprived backgrounds there exists a pervasive negative attitude toward these children. These teachers say repeatedly, and appear to believe, that it is not possible to teach these children. They offer, in support of their conclusion, the belief that these children cannot learn because of "poor heredity," "poor home background," "cultural deprivation," and "low IQ."
>
> Probably as disturbing as these examples of rejection of these children on the part of those who are required to teach them, are the many examples of well-intentioned teachers who point to the low intelligence and achievement-test scores of these children as the basis for their belief that these children cannot be educated . . .

They maintain that these children should not be expected to function up to the academic level of other children because the test scores clearly indicate that they cannot.

In this same vein, there is the story of a teacher who was shocked to find at the end of the school year that the numbers in his record book were not IQ's but locker numbers. That many teachers equate intelligence and IQ score can hardly be denied. In the author's experience, only those teachers who have taken intelligence tests themselves and then scored their own responses and interpreted the data, item by item and sub-score by sub-score, really come to respect both the advantages and disadvantages of the tests.

Consideration of intelligence is not out of place in a book on teaching. Overwhelmed by ever-growing numbers of children, faced with diversities almost beyond comprehension, teachers clutch at one straw after another to improve their teaching. Seldom willing to shy away from difficulties, teachers have steadily been inundated with pressures and demands. One important factor in any academic situation is the concept of ability—generally labeled intelligence or intellectual capacity or scholastic aptitude—and teachers should seek more information about their students in this connection.

Ability and capacity and potential are all similar terms. When intelligence is considered in these kinds of verbal terms, however, the notion is implicit that, like a bucket, the capacity can be measured fairly accurately in some way. Unlike gauging the capacity of the bucket, however, we have not yet found a way to "get inside" the human brain and measure precisely what is there. Indeed, the *only* way we have of measuring intelligence is by observing behavior. By looking at the human output, we attempt to infer backwards and determine what intellectual qualities are present inside the organism.

All things considered, measuring behaviors seems to be a reasonable way of assessing intelligence. However, since we do study behavior and not capacity directly, it would also seem reasonable to restrict our discussion to that. The moment we do, our whole basis for thinking about intelligence must change.

Since scores on intelligence tests are really considerations of the *responses* the individual made to certain problems, we ought to direct our attention to what affects behaviors. When we do we are immediately faced with the fact that it is the learning process we are considering, and what we are really measuring are *learned behaviors* (257). What we have called intelligence is really behavior, and since most behaviors can be learned or created, then so can intelligence be created (57). Or, as Kelley quotes Howard Lane (160), "dullness is therefore more an achievement than a gift," a negative achievement at that. "An individual's IQ varies, depending upon the kind of life he is able to live. Rich human environments raise individual scores, while starved environments lower them." The extensive research related to intelligence among various cultural groups attests to this fact (38, 53, 228, 231, 237, 257, 270, 271, 272, 317).

To press such a point would be to argue that environment is the sole answer to an understanding of human intelligence. The human qualities which an individual brings to his experience, however, do affect his learning (112). Someday it will probably be shown that variations in the quality of neural tissue itself are related to intelligence (299). That is, just as a copper wire conducts electricity more efficiently than a steel wire, there are probably variations in the cellular structure of the central nervous system, and undoubtedly differences in composition of other factors affect the way in which the impulses are communicated throughout the organism.

For instance, it may well be that the thickness or extent of the myelin sheath, which encompasses certain segments of the nervous system, affects the way in which an individual learner processes stimuli. Or, the precise temperature or chemical conditions existing at any given synapse may create conditions which affect learning. Since neural activity is electro-chemical in nature, the effect of different drugs or foods or shortages of certain elements may well result in increased or decreased function. Variations in calcium content in the blood, for example, result in marked changes in muscular activity. Perhaps such changes also affect learning more than we now suppose. Recent research regarding the so-called "PKU" disease, for instance, demonstrates that human use of proteins under unusual conditions creates mental retardation, which can be prevented if discovered in time.

There are certain realities within the human organism which affect learning and which are probably directly related to intelligence. But it is also true that we do not now have even crude ways of assessing these factors, and all of the devices which we do employ to measure intelligence actually measure behaviors. And behaviors are, for the most part, learned.

Maturation accounts for many changes in human behavior, but it is also true that these changes are relatively complete from person to person and are fairly uniform throughout all of the species, whereas behavioral changes resulting from learning are much more varied. If we study learned behaviors with the intention of inferring what the state of any person's intelligence is, we are proceeding on shaky ground.

In summary, intelligence is a reality—it does exist. Our present procedures for assessing it are all directed at its manifestations rather than the quality itself. The behaviors manifest, however, are also affected by many other factors: stimuli, sensory apparatus, self concept, motivation, values, goals, and needs, among others. To assume that intelligence tests measure anything other than such a complex of factors is to make a serious mistake. Those who would make a profession of helping people learn dare not allow themselves to be deluded by such a naïve generalization.

REFERENCES

1. Allen, Roben, "Nine Quarterly Rorschach Records of a Young Girl," *Child Development*, XXVI (March, 1955), 63-69.
2. Altus, William D., "Personality Correlates of Verbal-Quantitative Discrepancy Scores on the Scholastic Aptitude Test," *Journal of Psychology*, LXVIII (October, 1959), 219-225.
3. Anderson, Jeanette and Whealdon, Mary, "A Study of Blood Group Distribution Among Stutterers," *Journal of Speech Disorders*, VI (1941), 23-25.
4. Angelino, Henry and Shedd, Charles L., "Reactions to Frustration Among Normal and Superior Children," *Exceptional Children*, XXI (March, 1955), 215-230.
5. Anspaugh, G. E., "Qualities Related to High Scholarship in Secondary School," *School Review*, LXI (September, 1953), 337-340.
6. Aronoff, Joel, "Freud's Conception of the Origin of Curiosity," *Journal of Psychology*, LIV (July, 1962), 39-45.
7. Auria, Carl, "Differences in Specific Intellectual Functioning Among Children of the Same General Intellectual Ability but of Different Chronological Ages," Ph.D. Dissertation (University of Buffalo, 1961).
8. Ausubel, David P., "Prestige Motivation of Gifted Children," *Genetic Psychology Monographs*, XLIII (January-June, 1951), 52-117.
9. Ausubel, David P. et al., "The Influence of Intention on the Retention of School Materials," *Journal of Educational Psychology*, XLVIII (February, 1957), 87-92.
10. Ausubel, David P., "Learning by Discovery: Psychological and Educational Limitations," Paper read at the American Educational Research Association Convention, Atlantic City, 1962.
11. Banghart, Frank W., "Group Structure, Anxiety, and Problem-Solving Efficiency," *Journal of Experimental Education*, XXVIII (December, 1959), 171.
12. Barbe, Walter B., "A Study of the Family Background of the Gifted," *Journal of Educational Psychology*, XLVII (May, 1956), 302-309.
13. Barrett, Harry O., "An Intensive Study of 32 Gifted Children," *Personnel and Guidance Journal*, XXXVI (November, 1957), 192-194.
14. Beckham, Albert S., "A Study of the Intelligence of Colored Adolescents of Different Social Economic Status in Typical Metropolitan Areas," *Journal of Social Psychology*, IV (1933), 70-91.
15. Berkson, Gershon and Cantor, Gordon N., "A Study of Mediation in Mentally Retarded and Normal School Children," *Journal of Educational Psychology*, LI (April, 1960), 82-86.
16. Berlin, Charles, "Parents' Diagnoses of Stuttering," *Journal of Speech and Hearing Research*, III (1960), 372-379.

17. Berlo, David K. and Gulley, Halbert E., "Some Determinants of the Effects of Oral Communication in Producing Attitude Change in Learning," *Speech Monographs*, XXIV (1957), 10-20.
18. Bevan, William and Maier, Richard A., "Emotional Tension and the Generality of Its Effect upon Intellectual Performance," *Journal of Personality*, XXVI (September, 1958), 330-336.
19. Bills, Robert E., "About People and Teaching," *Bulletin of Bureau of School Service*, University of Kentucky, XXVIII, No. 2 (December, 1955).
20. Bills, Robert E., "Believing and Behaving: Perception and Learning," in *Learning More About Learning*, Alexander Frazier, Ed. (Washington, D.C.: Association for Supervision and Curriculum Development, 1959), 55-73.
21. Blatt, Burton, "The Physical, Personality, and Academic Status of Children Who Are Mentally Retarded Attending Special Classes as Compared with Children Who Are Mentally Retarded Attending Regular Classes," *American Journal of Mental Deficiency*, LXII (March, 1958), 810-818.
22. Bleckner, Janet E., "The Responses of Average and Gifted Students on the Group Rorschach Test," *California Journal of Educational Research*, X (November, 1959), 200-206.
23. Bleismer, Emery P., "Reading Abilities of Bright and Dull Children of Comparable Mental Ages," *Journal of Educational Psychology*, XLV (October, 1954), 321-331.
24. Blodgett, Elliott D., "A Comparative Study of Intellectually Gifted and Intellectually Average Children in a Problem-Solving Situation," Ph.D. Dissertation (Syracuse University, 1961).
25. Bloodstein, Oliver, "A Rating Scale of Conditions Under Which Stuttering Is Reduced or Absent," *Journal of Speech and Hearing Disorders*, XV (1950), 29-36.
26. Bloodstein, Oliver, "The Development of Stuttering: I. Changes in Nine Basic Features," *Journal of Speech and Hearing Disorders*, XXV (August, 1960), 219-238.
27. Bloodstein, Oliver, "The Development of Stuttering: II. Developmental Phases," *Journal of Speech and Hearing Disorders*, XXV (November, 1960), 366-377.
28. Bloom, Benjamin S. and Peters, Frank R., *The Use of Academic Prediction Scales*, (New York: The Free Press of Glencoe, 1961).
29. Bloom, Benjamin S., *Stability and Change in Human Characteristics* (New York: John Wiley and Sons, 1964).
30. Bluemel, C. S., "Concepts of Stammering: A Century in Review," *Journal of Speech and Hearing Disorders*, XXV (February, 1960), 24-32.
31. Bobroff, Allen, "Economic Adjustment of 121 Adults, Formerly Students in Classes for Mental Retardates," *American Journal of Mental Deficiency*, LX (January, 1956), 525-535.
32. Bonsall, Marcella R., "Introspections of Gifted Children," *California Journal of Educational Research*, XI (September, 1960), 159-165.
33. Bottorf, Barrie Olin, "An Experimental Study of the Speech Defectiveness of a Group of Slow Learners Based upon Two Scaling Methods," M.A. Thesis (The Ohio State University, 1959).
34. Bowman, Paul H. and Matthews, Charles V., "Motivations of Youth for Leaving School," Summary of Report of Completed Research in Cooperative Research Program, Project No. 200 (June, 1959).
35. Boyd, George F., "The Levels of Aspiration of White and Negro Children in a Non-Segregated Elementary School," *Journal of Social Psychology*, XXXVI (1952), 191-196.
36. Brazziel, William F. and Terrell, Mary, "An Experiment in the Development of Readiness in a Culturally Disadvantaged Group of First Grade Children," *Journal of Negro Education*, XXXI (1962), 4-7.

37. Brown, Fred, "Intelligence Test Patterns of Puerto Rican Psychiatric Patients," *Journal of Social Psychology*, LII (November, 1960), 225-230.
38. Brown, Fred, "An Experimental and Critical Study of the Intelligence of Negro and White Kindergarten Children," *Journal of Genetic Psychology*, LXV (1944), 161-175.
39. Bryengelson, Bryng, "A Comparative Study of Laterality of Stutterers and Non-Stutterers," *Journal of Speech Disorders*, II (March-December, 1937), 1-2.
40. Burr, Helen G. and Mullendore, James M., "Recent Investigations on Tranquilizers and Stuttering," *Journal of Speech and Hearing Disorders*, XXV (February, 1960), 33-37.
41. Buswell, Margaret M., "The Relationship Between Social Structure of the Classroom and the Academic Success of the Pupils," *Journal of Experimental Education*, XXII (September, 1953), 37-52.
42. Cantor, Gordon N. and Girardeau, Frederick L., "Rhythmic Discrimination Ability in Mongoloid and Normal Children," *An Investigation of Discrimination Learning Ability in Mongoloid and Normal Children of Comparable Mental Age* (George Peabody College for Teachers: Nashville, 1958), 2-12.
43. Carrier, N. A., "Relationship of Certain Personality Measures to Examination Performance Under Stress," *Journal of Educational Psychology*, XLVIII (December, 1957), 510-520.
44. Carrier, N. A., "A Note on the Effect of Filling Out an 'Anxiety Scale' on Examination Performance," *Journal of Educational Psychology*, L (December, 1959), 293-294.
45. Carrigan, Patricia M., "Implications of a Chemical Theory of Reading Disability," *The Education Digest*, XXVII (February, 1962), 47-49.
46. Cassidy, Viola and Phelps, Harold R., "Postschool Adjustment of Slow-Learning Children," Bureau of Special and Adult Education (The Ohio State University, March, 1955).
47. Charles, Don C., "Ability and Accomplishments of Persons Earlier Judged Mentally Deficient," *Genetic Psychology Monographs* (February, 1953), 3-71.
48. Chodorkoff, Bernard and Chodorkoff, Joan, "Perceptual Defense: An Integration with Other Research Findings," *Journal of General Psychology*, LVIII (January, 1958), 75-80.
49. Clapper, Cassie C., "A Study of Mentally Retarded Students in San Diego High School," *American Journal of Mental Deficiency*, LIX (1954), 44-45.
50. Cline, Marion, "Achievement of Bilinguals in Seventh Grade by Socioeconomic Levels," *Dissertation Abstracts*, XXII (1962), 3113-3114.
51. Cogan, Morris L., "The Behavior of Teachers and the Productive Behavior of Their Pupils: I. Perception Analysis," *Journal of Experimental Education*, XXVII (December, 1958), 89-105.
52. Cogan, Morris L., "The Behavior of Teachers and the Productive Behavior of Their Pupils: II. Trait Analysis," *Journal of Experimental Education*, XXVII (December, 1958), 107-124.
53. Coleman, William and Ward, Anne W., "A Comparison of Davis-Eells and Kuhlmann-Finch Scores of Children from High and Low Socio-Economic Status," *Journal of Educational Psychology*, XLVI (December, 1955), 465-469.
54. Combs, Arthur W. and Taylor, Charles, "The Effect of the Perception of Mild Degrees of Threat on Performance," *Journal of Abnormal and Social Psychology*, XLVII (1952), 420-424.
55. Combs, Arthur W., "A Comparative Study of Motivations as Revealed in Thematic Apperception Stories and Autobiography," *Journal of Clinical Psychology*, III (1947), 65-75.
56. Combs, Arthur W. and Snygg, Donald, *Invidivual Behavior* (New York: Harper and Bros., 1959).

57. Combs, Arthur W., "Personality Theory and Its Implications for Curriculum Development," in *Learning More About Learning*, Alexander Frazier, Ed. (Washington, D. C.: Association for Supervision and Curriculum Development, 1959), 5-20.
58. Combs, Arthur W., Ed., *Personality Theory and Counseling Practice* (Gainesville, Florida: Materials Diffusion Project, 1961).
59. Croxton, W. C., "Pupils' Ability to Generalize," *School Science and Mathematics*, XXXVI (June, 1936), 627-634.
60. Cunningham, Anne, "Relation of Sense of Humor to Intelligence," *Journal of Social Psychology*, LVII (June, 1962), 143-147.
61. Davidson, Helen H. and Balducci, Dom, "Class and Sex Differences in Verbal Facility of Very Bright Children," *Journal of Educational Psychology*, XLVII (December, 1956), 476-480.
62. Davidson, Helen H. and Lang, Gerhard, "Children's Perceptions of Their Teachers' Feelings Toward Them Related to Self-Perception, School Achievement and Behavior," *Journal of Experimental Education*, XXIX (December, 1960), 107-118.
63. Delp, Harold A. and Lorenz, Marcella, "Follow-up of 84 Public School Special Class Pupils with I. Q.'s below 50," *American Journal of Mental Deficiency*, LVIII (July, 1953), 175-182.
64. Dennis, Wayne, "Causes of Retardation Among Institutional Children: Iran," *Journal of Genetic Psychology*, XCVI (March, 1960), 47-59.
65. Dennis, Wayne, "The Human Figure Drawings of Bedouins," *Journal of Social Psychology*, LII (November, 1960), 209-219.
66. D'Huerle, Adma et al., "Personality, Intellectual, and Achievement Patterns in Gifted Children," *Psychological Monographs*, LXXIII, No. 13 (1959), 1-28.
67. Douvan, Elizabeth, "Social Status and Success Strivings," *Journal of Abnormal and Social Psychology*, LII (March, 1956), 219-223.
68. Downing, Elliot R., "Does Science Teach Scientific Thinking?" *Science Education*, XVII (April, 1933), 87-89.
69. Downing, Elliot R., "Some Results of a Test on Scientific Thinking," *Science Education*, XX (October, 1936), 121-128.
70. Drevdahl, John E. and Cattell, Raymond B., "Personality and Creativity in Artists and Writers," *Journal of Clinical Psychology*, XIV (April, 1958), 107-111.
71. Drevdahl, John E., "A Wise Herd . . . " *The Educational Forum*, XXIII (January, 1959), 133-140.
72. Dugan, Ruth, "An Investigation of the Personal, Social, Educational, and Economic Reasons for Success and Lack of Success in School as Expressed by 105 Tenth Grade Biology Students," *Journal of Educational Research*, LV (August, 1952), 544-553.
73. Durrell, Donald D., "The Influence of Reading Ability on Intelligence Measures," *Journal of Educational Psychology*, XXIV (September, 1933), 412-416.
74. Dye, Myrtle G., "Attitudes of Gifted Children Toward School," *Educational Administration and Supervision*, XLII (May, 1956), 301-308.
75. Edwards, T. Bentley, "Measurement of Some Aspects of Critical Thinking," *Journal of Experimental Education*, XVIII (March, 1950), 263-278.
76. Eisenson, Jon and Horowitz, Esther, "The Influence of Propositionality on Stuttering," *Journal of Speech Disorders* (1945), 193-197.
77. Emerick, Lonnie, "Extensional Definition and Attitude Toward Stuttering," *Journal of Speech and Hearing Disorders* (1960), 181-185.
78. Enos, Francis A., "Emotional Adjustment of Mentally Retarded Children," *American Journal of Mental Deficiency*, LXV (March, 1961), 606-609.
79. Eschenbach, A. E. and Dupree, L., "The Influence of Stress on MMPI Scores," *Journal of Clinical Psychology*, XV (January, 1959), 42-45.

80. Farber, Maurice L., "English and Americans: Values in the Socialization Process," in *Studies in Motivation* by David McClelland, Ed. (New York: Appleton-Century-Crofts, Inc., 1955), 323-330.

81. Ferrell, Guy V., "Comparative Study of Sex Differences in School Achievement of White and Negro Children," *Journal of Educational Research*, XLIII (October, 1949), 116-121.

82. Feidler, Fred E. and Wepman, Joseph M., "An Exploratory Investigation of the Self Concept of Stutterers," *Journal of Speech Disorders* (1942), 111-114.

83. Flanders, Ned A., "Personal-Social Anxiety as a Factor in Experimental Learning Situations," *Journal of Educational Research*, XLV (October, 1951), 100-110.

84. Flanders, Ned A., *Teachers Influence, Pupil Attitudes, and Achievement*, Final Report, Cooperative Research Project No. 397 (University of Minnesota, November, 1960).

85. Fitch, Mildred et al., "Frequent Testing as a Motivating Factor in Large Lecture Classes," *Journal of Educational Psychology*, XLII (January, 1951), 1-20.

86. Fort, Gerald M., "Subject: Comparison of Top Two Percent on Twelfth Grade Tests with Results on Ninth Grade Tests," *South Dakota Education Association Journal*, XXXII (February, 1957), 202-219.

87. Fox, David J. and Lorge, Irving, "The Relative Quality of Decisions Written by Individuals and by Groups as the Available Time for Problem Solving Is Increased," *Journal of Social Psychology*, LVII (June, 1962), 227-242.

88. Frankel, Edward, "A Comparative Study of Achieving and Underachieving High School Boys of High Intellectual Ability," *Journal of Educational Research*, LIII (January, 1960), 172-180.

89. Friedman, Kopple C., "Time Concepts of Junior and Senior High School Pupils and of Adults," *The School Review*, LII (April, 1944), 233-238.

90. Frymier, Jack R., "A Study of Students' Motivation to Do Good Work in School," *Journal of Educational Research*, LVII (January, 1964), 239-244.

91. Fulkerson, S. C., "Individual Differences in Reaction to Failure-Induced Stress," *American Psychologist*, X (1955), 336-337.

92. Furfey, Paul et al., "The Mental Organization of the Newborn," *Child Development*, I (1930), 48-51.

93. Gaier, E. L., "Students' Perceptions of Factors Affecting Test Performance," *Journal of Educational Research*, LV (August, 1962), 561-566.

94. Galanter, Eugene, Ed., *Automatic Teaching: The State of the Art* (New York: John Wiley and Sons, Inc., 1959).

95. Gallagher, James J. and Crowder, Thora, "Gifted Children in the Regular Classroom," *Exceptional Children*, XXIII (April, 1957), 306-319.

96. Gallagher, James J., "Peer Acceptance of Highly Gifted Children in Elementary School," *Elementary School Journal*, LVIII (June, 1958), 465-470.

97. Gallagher, James and Lucito, Leonard, "Intellectual Patterns of Gifted Compared with Average and Retarded," *Exceptional Children*, XXVII (1961), 479-482.

98. Geer, William C., "Education of Mentally Retarded Children Fourteen Years of Age and Beyond," *American Journal of Mental Deficiency*, LXI January, 1952), 560-569.

99. Gemignani, Barbara Parslow, "The Gifted Child in Art," *Research in Art Education* (NAEA 7th Yearbook, 1956), 8-17.

100. George, F. H., "Machines and the Brain," *Science*, CXXVII (May 30, 1958), 1269-1274.

101. Getzels, Jacob and Jackson, Phillip, *Creativity and Intelligence: Exploration with Gifted Students* (New York: John Wiley and Sons, 1962).

102. Ghiselin, Brewster, Ed., *The Creative Process* (New York: New American Library of World Literature, Inc., 1952).

103. Gibboney, Richard A., "Socioeconomic Status and Achievement in Social Studies," *Elementary School Journal*, LIX (March, 1959), 340-346.
104. Giolas, Thomas and William, Dean, "Children's Reactions to Non-fluencies in Adult Speech," *Journal of Speech and Hearing Disorders* (1958), 86-93.
105. Girardeau, Frederic L., "The Formation of Discrimination Learning Sets in Mongoloid and Normal Children," *An Investigation of Discrimination Learning Ability in Mongoloid and Normal Children of Comparable Mental Age* (George Peabody College for Teachers: Nashville, 1958), 13-30.
106. Gladis, Michael, "Grade Differences in Transfer as a Function of the Time Interval Between Learning Tasks," *Journal of Educational Psychology*, LI (August, 1960), 191-194.
107. Glasner, Philip, "Personality Characteristics and Emotional Problems in Stutterers Under the Age of Five," *Journal of Speech and Hearing Disorders*, XIV (June, 1949), 135-138.
108. Glasner, Philip, "Parental Diagnosis of Stuttering in Young Children," *Journal of Speech and Hearing Disorders*, XXII (June, 1957), 288-295.
109. Glaser, Edward M., *An Experiment in the Development of Critical Thinking* (New York: Bureau of Publications, Teachers College, Columbia University, 1941).
110. Gleason, Gerald T., "A Study of the Relationship Between Variability in Physical Growth and Academic Achievement Among Third and Fifth Grade Children," Ph.D. Dissertation (University of Wisconsin, 1956).
111. Goldberg, Murray A., "Can Reading Ability Be Improved More Effectively Through Wide Reading or Intensive Drill?" *High Points*, XXVIII (February, 1946), 21-27.
112. Goslin, David A., *The Search for Ability* (New York: Russell Sage Foundation, 1963).
113. Grace, Harry A. and Booth, Nancy L., "Is the 'Gifted' Child a Social Isolate?" *Peabody Journal of Education*, XXXV (January, 1958), 195-196.
114. Gray, Benjamin G., "Characteristics of High and Low Achieving High School Seniors of High Average Academic Aptitude," Ph.D. Dissertation (University of Southern California, 1960).
115. Gray, Susan W., "The Relation of Individual Variability to Emotionality," *The Journal of Educational Psychology*, XXXV (May, 1944), 274-283.
116. Gray, Susan W., "The Relation of Individual Variability to Intelligence," *The Journal of Educational Psychology*, XXXV (April, 1944), 201-210.
117. Greenberg, Paul and Gilliland, A. R., "The Relationship Between Basal Metabolism and Personality," *Journal of Social Psychology*, XXXV (February, 1952), 3-7.
118. Grener, Norma and Raths, Louis, "Thinking in Grade III," *Educational Research Bulletin*, XXIV (February, 1945), 38-42.
119. Guilford, Joy P., "The Structure of Intellect," *Psychological Bulletin*, LIII (1956), 267-293.
120. Gyr, John W., "An Investigation Into, and Speculations About, the Formal Nature of a Problem-Solving Process," *Behavioral Science*, V (January, 1960), 39-57.
121. Haddad, Raef K., "The Effect of Distribution of Trials on Problem Solving," *Dissertation Abstracts*, XX (February, 1960), 3398.
122. Hahn, Eugene, "A Study of the Relationship Between the Social Complexity of the Oral Reading Situation and the Severity of Stuttering," *Journal of Speech Disorders*, V (1940), 5-14.
123. Haigh, G. V. and Fiske, D. W., "Corroboration of Personal Values as Selective Factors in Perception," *Journal of Abnormal and Social Psychology*, XLVII (1952), 394-398.
124. Hall, William E. and Gaeddert, Willard, "Social Skills and Their Relationship

to Scholastic Achievement," *Journal of Genetic Psychology*, XCVI (June, 1960), 269-273.

125. Harleston, Bernard W., "Test Anxiety and Performance in Problem-Solving Situations," *Journal of Personality*, XXX (December, 1962), 557-573.

126. Harlow, H. F. et al., "Learning Motivated by a Manipulation Drive," *Journal of Experimental Psychology*, XL (1950), 228-234.

127. Harrison, E. C., "Achievement Motivation Characteristics of Negro College Freshmen," *Personnel and Guidance Journal*, XXXVIII (October, 1959), 146-149.

128. Harrison, M. Lucile, "The Nature and Development of Concepts of Time Among Young Children," *Elementary School Journal*, XXXIV (March, 1934), 507-514.

129. Hartman, A. A., "Personality Factors in Perceptual Distortion," *Journal of General Psychology*, LXI (October, 1959), 181-188.

130. Hastorf, A. H. and Cantrill, H., "They Saw a Game: A Case Study," *Journal of Abnormal and Social Psychology*, XLIX (1954), 129-134.

131. Havighurst, Robert J., *Developmental Tasks and Education* (New York: Longmans, Green and Co., 1952).

132. Havighurst, R. J. and MacDonald, D. V., "Development of the Ideal Self in New Zealand and American Children," *Journal of Educational Research*, XLIX (December, 1955), 263-273.

133. Havighurst, Robert J. et al., *Growing Up in River City* (New York: John Wiley and Sons, 1962).

134. Heber, Rick F., "The Relation of Intelligence and Physical Maturity to Social Status of Children," *Journal of Educational Psychology*, XLVII (March, 1956) 158-162.

135. Henson, Owen M., "A Descriptive Study of Factors Influencing the Status of Selected Students in Secondary Education Who Are Affected by an Area of Urban Renewal," *Dissertation Abstracts*, XXII (1962), 3288-3289.

136. Herskovits, Melville J., "On The Relation Between Negro-White Mixture and Standing in Intelligence Tests," *Journal of Genetic Psychology*, XXXIII (1926), 30-42.

137. Hess, Eckhard H., "Imprinting," *Science*, CXXX (July 17, 1959), 133-141.

138. Hicks, J. Allan, "The Acquisition of Motor Skill in Young Children," *Child Development*, III (1932), 90-105.

139. Hollingsworth, Leta S., *Children Above 180 I.Q.* (Yonkers-on-the-Hudson: World Book Co., 1942).

140. Hone, Elizabeth, "Identification of Children Gifted in Science," *California Journal of Educational Research*, X (March, 1959), 64-67.

141. Hotyat, Fernand A., "French-Speaking Countries: Belgium, France, Switzerland," *Review of Educational Research*, XXVII (February, 1957), 39-56.

142. Hoyt, Kenneth B., "A Study of the Effects of Teacher Knowledge of Pupil Characteristics on Pupil Achievement and Attitudes Toward Classwork," *Journal of Educational Psychology*, XLVI (May, 1955), 302-310.

143. Hyram, George H., "An Experiment in Developing Critical Thinking in Children," *Journal of Experimental Education*, XXVI (December, 1957), 125-132.

144. Ittelson, William H. and Cantrill, Hadley, *Perception: A Transactional Approach* (Garden City, New York: Doubleday, 1954).

145. Jacobs, James N., "A Study of Performance of Slow Learners in the Cincinnati Public Schools on Mental and Achievement Tests," *American Journal of Mental Deficiency*, LXII (1957-1958), 238-243.

146. Jenkin, Noel, "Affective Processes in Perception," *Psychological Bulletin*, LIV (March, 1957), 100-127.

147. Jenkins, Martin D., "A Socio-Psychological Study of Negro Children of Superior Intelligence," *Journal of Negro Education*, V (April, 1936), 175-190.

148. Jenkins, Martin D., "Case Studies of Sixteen Negro Children of Binet I. Q. of 160 or Above," *Journal of Negro Education*, XII (April, 1943), 159-166.
149. Jensen, Vern H., "Influence of Personality Traits on Academic Success," *Personnel and Guidance Journal*, XXXVI (March, 1958), 497-500.
150. Johnson, G. Orville, "A Study of the Social Position of Mentally Handicapped Children in the Regular Grades," *American Journal of Mental Deficiency*, LV (July, 1950), 60-89.
151. Johnson, Wendell and Ainsworth, Stanley, "Studies in the Psychology of Stuttering: Constancy of Loci of Expectancy of Stuttering," *Journal of Speech Disorders*, III (March-December, 1938), 101-104.
152. Johnson, Wendell, "A New Look at Stuttering," *Child Study*, XXXVI, No. 4 (Fall, 1959), 14-18.
153. Johnson, Wendell, "A Study of the Onset and Development of Stuttering," Chapter 3 in *Stuttering in Children and Adults* (Minneapolis: University of Minnesota Press, 1955), 37-73.
154. Johnson, Wendell, "Measurements of Oral Reading and Speaking Rate and Disfluency of Adult Male and Female Stutterers and Non-Stutterers," *Journal of Speech and Hearing Disorders, Monograph Supplement 7* (1961), 20 pp.
155. Karlin, Robert, "Physical Growth and Success in Undertaking Beginning Reading," *Journal of Educational Research*, LI (November, 1957), 191-201.
156. Karnes, Merle B. et al., *Factors Associated with Underachievement and Over-achievement of Intellectually Gifted Children* (Champaign, Illinois: Champaign Community Schools, July, 1961). Mimeographed.
157. Kelley, Earl C., "Communication and the Open Self," *ETC.: Review of General Semantics*, XI (Winter, 1954), 96-100.
158. Kelley, Earl C., *Education for What Is Real* (New York: Harper and Bros., 1947).
159. Kelley, Earl C. and Rasey, Marie I., *Education and the Nature of Man* (New York: Harper and Bros., 1952).
160. Kelley, Earl C., *In Defense of Youth* (Englewood Cliffs: Prentice-Hall, Inc., 1962), 109, 129.
161. Kemp, C. Gratton, "Effect of Dogmatism on Critical Thinking," *School Science and Mathematics*, LX (April, 1960), 314-319.
162. Kent, Louise R. and Williams, Dean E., "Use of Meprobamate as an Adjunct to Stuttering Therapy," *Journal of Speech and Hearing Disorders*, XXIV (February, 1959), 64-69.
163. Kern, William H. and Heinz, Pfaeffle, "A Comparison of Social Adjustment of Mentally Retarded Children in Various Educational Settings," *American Journal of Mental Deficiency*, LXVII (November, 1962), 407-413.
164. Kinstler, Donald B., "Covert and Overt Maternal Rejection in Stuttering," *Journal of Speech and Hearing Disorders*, XXVI (May 1961), 145-155.
165. Klausmeier, Herbert J., "Physical, Behavioral, and Other Characteristics of High- and Lower-Achieving Children in Favored Environments," *Journal of Educational Research*, LI (April, 1958), 573-581.
166. Klausmeier, Herbert J. and Loughlin, Leo J., "Behaviors During Problem Solving Among Children of Low, Average, and High Intelligence," *Journal of Educational Psychology*, LII (June, 1961), 148-152.
167. Klausmeier, Herbert J., "Psychological Research and Classroom Learning," in *New Dimensions in Learning*, Walter Waetjen, Ed. (Washington, D. C.: Association for Supervision and Curriculum Development, 1962), 66-82.
168. Klausmeier, Herbert J. and Chick, John, "Relationship Among Physical, Mental, Achievement, and Personality Measures in Children of Low, Average, and High Intelligence at 113 Months of Age," *American Journal of Mental Deficiency*, LXIII (1958-59), 1058-1068.
169. Kolstoe, Oliver P., "A Comparison of Mental Abilities of Bright and Dull

Children of Comparable Mental Ages," *Journal of Educational Psychology*, XLV (March, 1954), 161-168.

170. Krogman, Wilton M., "Physical Growth as a Factor in the Behavioral Development of the Child," in *New Dimensions in Learning*, Walter Waetjen, Ed. (Washington, D. C.: Association for Supervision and Curruculum Development, 1962), 8-23.

171. Kuhn, T. S., "Historical Structure of Scientific Discovery," *Science*, CXXXVI (June, 1962), 760-764.

172. Lacey, Joy M., *Social Studies Concepts of Children in the First Three Grades*, (New York: Bureau of Publications, Teachers College, Columbia University, 1932).

173. Lapp, Esther R., "A Study of the Social Adjustment of Slow Learning Children Who Were Assigned Part-Time to Regular Classes," *American Journal of Mental Deficiency*, LXII (September, 1957), 254-262.

174. Leckey, Prescott, *Self Consistency* (New York: Island Press, 1945).

175. Lesser, Gerald S. et al., "The Identification of Gifted Elementary School Children with Exceptional Scientific Talent," *Educational and Psychological Measurement*, XXII (1962), 349-364.

176. Lessinger, Leon M. and Martinson, Ruth A., "The Use of the California Psychological Inventory with Gifted Pupils," *Personnel and Guidance Journal*, XXXIX (March, 1961), 572-575.

177. Lewit, D. W., "Attitudes in Discrimination Learning," *Journal of Social Psychology*, LII (November, 1960), 315-327.

178. Liddle, Gordon, "Overlap Among Desirable and Undesirable Characteristics in Gifted Children," *Journal of Educational Psychology*, XLIX (August, 1958), 219-224.

179. Long, H. H., "Tests of Results of Third Grade Negro Children," *Journal of Negro Education*, IV (October, 1935), 523-552.

180. Longnecker, E. D., "Perceptual Recognition as a Function of Anxiety, Motivation, and the Testing Situation," *Journal of Abnormal and Social Psychology*, LXIV (1962), 215-221.

181. Lorge, Irving and Solomon, Herbert, "Group and Individual Performance in Problem Solving Related to Previous Exposure to Problem, Level of Aspiration, and Group Size," *Behavioral Science*, V (January, 1960), 28-38.

182. Machertzman, J., "The Relation of Individual Variability to General Ability as Measured by Mental Tests," *Journal of Educational Psychology*, XXVII (1936), 134-144.

183. Maddox, James, "Studies in the Psychology of Stuttering: The Visual Cues in the Precipitation of Moments of Stuttering," *Journal of Speech Disorders*, III (March-December, 1938), 90-94.

184. Mahler, Fred L., "A Study of Achievement Differences in Selected Junior High School Gifted Students Heterogeneously or Homogeneously Grouped," *Dissertation Abstracts*, XXII (1926), 2267.

185. Maier, Norman R. F., "Reasoning in Children," *Journal of Comparative Psychology*, XXI (June, 1936), 357-366.

186. Mandler, George and Sarason, Seymour B., "A Study of Anxiety and Learning," *Journal of Abnormal and Social Psychology*, XLVII (1952), 166-173.

187. Mannello, George, "Attitude as a Conditioner of the Acquisition of New Facts Among Eighth Grade Pupils," *Journal of Genetic Psychology*, LXXXV (September, 1954), 85-103.

188. Mann, Horace, "How Real Are Friendships of Gifted and Typical Children in a Program of Partial Segregation?" *Exceptional Children*, XXIII (February, 1957), 199-206.

189. Marsh, Patrick O., "An Empirical Study of the Effects of Two Types of Conflict-Arousing Arguments upon Retention and Attitude Change," *Dissertation Abstracts*, XXII (May, 1962), 4119.

190. Martin, Barclay, "The Measurement of Anxiety," *Journal of General Psychology*, LXI (October, 1959), 189-203.

191. Martinson, William D. and Stamatakos, Louis C., "An Attempt to Motivate Potentially Superior Students," *School and Society*, LXXXVII (April 11, 1959), 173-175.

192. Martire, John G., "Relationship Between the Self-Concept and Differences in the Strength and Generality of Achievement Motivation," *Journal of Personality*, XXIV (June, 1956), 364-375.

193. Martyn, Kenneth A., "The Social Acceptance of Gifted Students," *Dissertation Abstracts*, XVII (1957), 2501-2502.

194. Maslow, A. H. et al., "A Clinically Derived Test for Measuring Psychological Security-Insecurity," *Journal of General Psychology*, XXXIII (July, 1945), 21-41.

195. Maslow, A. H., *Motivation and Personality* (New York: Harper and Bros., 1954).

196. Maslow, A. H., "Deficiency Motivation and Growth Motivation," *Nebraska Symposium on Motivation*, Marshall R. Jones, Ed. (Lincoln: University of Nebraska Press, 1955), 1-30.

197. Maslow, A. H., "Cognition of Being in the Peak Experiences," *Journal of Genetic Psychology*, XCIV (March, 1959), 43-66.

198. Metraux, Ruth, "Speech Profiles of the Pre-School Child 18 to 54 Months," *Journal of Speech and Hearing Disorders*, XV (March, 1950), 37-53.

199. Miller, Jemima and Weston, Grace, "Slow Learners Improve in Critical Thinking," *Social Education*, XIII (November, 1949), 315-316.

200. Miller, Kent S. and Worchel, Phillip, "The Effects of Need-Achievement and Self-Ideal Discrepancy on Performance Under Stress," *Journal of Personality*, XXV (December, 1956), 176-190.

201. Miller, Neal E., "Fear as Motivation and Fear-Reduction as Reinforcement in the Learning of New Responses," *Journal of Experimental Psychology*, XXXVIII (1948), 89-101.

202. Miller, Robert V., "Social Status and Socioempathic Differences Among Mentally Superior, Mentally Typical, and Mentally Retarded Children," *Exceptional Children*, XXIII (December, 1956), 114-119.

203. Mooney, Ross L., "Perception and Creation," Paper delivered at the Summer Seminar in Creative Engineering, Massachusetts Institute of Technology, Summer, 1956. Mimeographed. (Columbus: Bureau of Educational Research, The Ohio State University).

204. Mooney, Ross L., "Evaluating Graduate Education," *The Harvard Educational Review*, XXV (Spring, 1955), 85-94.

205. Mooney, Ross L., "Cultural Blocks and Creative Possibilities," *Educational Leadership*, XIII (February, 1956), 273-278.

206. Mooney, Ross L., "The Perceptive Process in Reading," *The Reading Teacher*, XIII (October, 1959), 34-39.

207. Mooney, Ross L., "Creation and Teaching," in *Creativity and College Teaching*, XXXV Bulletin of the Bureau of School Service (Lexington: University of Kentucky, 1963), 45-62.

208. Morris, Charles et al., "Values of Psychiatric Patients," *Behavioral Science*, V (October, 1960), 297-312.

209. Morrison, Ernest B., "A Comparison of Mental Abilities of Average—Bright and Dull Children with Comparable Mental Ages," *Dissertation Abstracts*, XVII, Ph.D. Dissertation (University of Iowa).

210. Mowrer, O. H. and Viek, P., "An Experimental Analogue of Fear from a Sense of Helplessness," *Journal of Abnormal and Social Psychology*, XLIII (1948) 193-200.

211. Muehl, Siegmar, "The Effects of Visual Discrimination Pretraining on Learn-

ing to Read a Vocabulary List in Kindergarten Children," *Journal of Educational Psychology*, LI (August, 1960), 217-221.

212. Murphy, Gardner, *Human Potentialities*, (New York: Basic Books, Inc. 1958).
213. McBee, George and Duke, Ralph L., "Relation Between Intelligence, Scholastic Motivation, and Academic Achievement," *Psychological Reports*, VI (February, 1960), 3-8.
214. McClelland, David C. et al., *The Achievement Motive* (New York: Appleton-Century-Crofts, Inc. 1953).
215. McClelland, David C. et al., *Talent and Society* (Princeton, New Jersey: D. Van Nostrand Co., 1958).
216. McDavid, John Jr., "Some Relationships Between Social Reinforcement and Scholastic Achievement," *Journal of Consulting Psychology*, XXIII (April, 1959), 151-154.
217. McElwee, Edna W., "A Comparison of the Personality Traits of 300 Accelerated, Normal, and Retarded Children," *Journal of Educational Research*, XXVI (September, 1932), 31-34.
218. McGuire, Carson et al., "Dimensions of Talented Behavior," *Educational and Psychological Measurement*, XXI (Spring, 1961), 3-38.
219. McKeachie, W. J. et al., "Relieving Anxiety in Classroom Examinations," *Journal of Abnormal and Social Psychology*, L (1955), 93-98.
220. McKeachie, W. J., "Motivation, Teaching Methods, and College Learning," in *Nebraska Symposium on Motivation*, Marshall R. Jones, Ed. (Lincoln: The University of Nebraska Press, 1961), 111-142.
221. McKee, John P., "A Test of Primary Mental Abilities Applied to Superior Children," *Journal of Educational Psychology*, XLIII (January, 1952), 45-56.
222. McKee, John P. and Leader, Florence B., "The Relationship of Socio-economic Status and Aggression to the Competitive Behavior of Preschool Children," *Child Development*, XXVI (June, 1955), 135-142.
223. Neilson, Patricia, "Shirley's Babies," *Journal of Genetic Psychology*, LXXIII (October, 1948), 175-186.
224. Neville, Donald, "A Comparison of the WISC Patterns of Male Retarded and Non-Retarded Readers," *Journal of Educational Research*, LIV (January, 1961), 195-197.
225. Norman, Ralph D. et al., "Age, Sex, I.Q., and Achievement Patterns in Achieving and Nonachieving Gifted Children," *Exceptional Children*, XXIX (1962), 116-123.
226. Oakden, E. C. and Sturt, Mary, "The Development of the Knowledge of Time in Children," *British Journal of Psychology*, XII (April, 1922), 309-336.
227. Osborn, Wayland W., "An Experiment in Teaching Resistance to Propaganda," *Journal of Experimental Education*, VIII (September, 1939), 1-17.
228. Osborne, R. T., "Racial Differences in Mental Growth and School Achievement: A Longitudinal Study," *Psychological Reports*, VII (1960), 233-239.
229. Pachelman, Kathleen E., "A Comparative Study of Special Class and Regular Class Teacher Responses About Slow Learning Adolescent Children," M.A. Thesis (The Ohio State University, 1958).
230. Pallone, Nathaniel J., "Effects of Short and Long-Term Developmental Reading Courses upon S.A.T. Verbal Scores," *Personnel and Guidance Journal*, XXXIX (April, 1961), 654-657.
231. Papania, Ned et al., "Responses of Lower Social Class, High-Grade Mentally Handicapped Boys to a 'Culture Fair' Test of Intelligence—the Davis-Eells Games," *American Journal of Mental Deficiency*, LIX (January, 1955), 493-499.
232. Passow, A. H., Ed., *Education in Depressed Areas* (New York: Bureau of Publications, Teachers College, Columbia University, 1963).
233. Patterson, R. Melcher, "Analysis of Practice Effect on Readministration of the Grace Arthur Scale in Relation to Academic Achievement of Mentally

Deficient Children," *American Journal of Mental Deficiency*, LII (April, 1948) 337-342.

234. Peckham, Ralf A., "Problems in Job Adjustment of the Mentally Retarded," *American Journal of Mental Deficiency*, LVI (October, 1951), 448-453.

235. Pegnato, Carl V. and Birch, Jack W., "Locating Gifted Children in Junior High Schools; A Comparison of Methods," *Exceptional Children*, XXV (March, 1957), 300-304.

236. Penfield, W., "The Interpretive Cortex," *Science*, CXXIX (June 26, 1959), 1719-1725.

237. Peters, James S., "A Study of the Wechsler-Bellevue Verbal Scores of Negro and White Males," *The Journal of Negro Education*, XXIX (Winter, 1960), 7-16.

238. Pistor, Frederick, "How Time Concepts Are Acquired by Children," *Educational Method*, XX (November, 1940), 107-112.

239. Porter, Rutherford B. and Milazzo, Tony C., "A Comparison of Mentally Retarded Adults Who Attended a Special Class with Those Who Attended Regular School Classes," *Exceptional Children*, XXIV (May, 1958), 410-420.

240. Porterfield, O. V. and Schlichting, Harry F., "Peer Status and Reading Achievement," *Journal of Educational Research*, LIV (April, 1961), 291-297.

241. Postman, L. and Schneider, B. H., "Personal Values, Visual Recognition, and Recall," *Psychological Review*, LVIII (1951), 271-284.

242. Pottharst, Barbara S. C., "The Achievement Motivation and Level of Aspiration After Experimentally Induced Success and Failure," *Dissertation Abstracts*, XVII (1957), 171-172.

243. Quarrington, Bruce and Douglass, Ernest, "Audibility Avoidance in Non-vocalized Stutterers," *Journal of Speech and Hearing Disorders*, XXV (November, 1960), 358-365.

244. Radaker, Leon D., "The Visual Imagery of Retarded Children and the Relationship to Memory for Word Forms," *Exceptional Children*, XXVII (May, 1961), 524-530.

245. Ray, Wilbert S., "A Preliminary Report on a Study of Fetal Conditioning," *Child Development*, III (1932), 175-177.

246. Red, S. B. et al., "A Study of the Relationship Between Aspirational Levels and Academic Achievement," *Journal of Educational Research*, LV (December, 1961), 159-163.

247. Richardson, La Vange Hunt, "A Personality Study of Stutterers and Non-Stutterers," *Journal of Speech Disorders*, IX (1944), 152-160.

248. Ritzman, C. H., "A Cardiovascular and Metabolic Study of Stutterers and Non-stutterers," *Journal of Speech Disorders*, X (1945), 180-183.

249. Roberts, Helen Erskine, "Factors Affecting the Academic Underachievement of Bright High-School Students," *Journal of Educational Research*, LVI (December, 1962), 175-183.

250. Robinson, Mary L. and Meenes, Max, "The Relationship Between Test Intelligence of Third-Grade Negro Children and the Occupations of Their Parents," *Journal of Negro Education*, XVI (1947), 136-141.

251. Rokeach, Milton, *The Open and Closed Mind* (New York: Basic Books, Inc. 1960).

252. Rosebrook, Wilda, "Identifying the Slow Learning Child," *American Journal of Mental Deficiency*, L (October, 1945), 307-312.

253. Rosenzweig, Louis, "Report of a School Program for Trainable Mentally Retarded Children," *American Journal of Mental Deficiency*, LIX (October, 1954), 181-205.

254. Rust, Velma I. et al., "A Factor-Analytic Study of Critical Thinking," *The Journal of Educational Research*, LV (March, 1962), 253-259.

255. Sander, Erik K., "Counseling Parents of Stuttering Children," *Journal of Speech and Hearing Disorders*, XXIV (August, 1959), 262-271.

256. Sarason, S. B., Mandler, G., and Craighill, P. G., "The Effect of Differential Instructions on Anxiety and Learning," *Journal of Abnormal and Social Psychology*, XLVII (1952), 561-565.
257. Sarason, Seymour B. and Gladwin, Thomas, "Psychological and Cultural Problems in Mental Subnormality: A Review of Research," *Genetic Psychology Monographs*, LVII (February, 1958), 3-289.
258. Sarason, Seymour B. et al., *Anxiety in Elementary School Children: A Report of Research* (New York: John Wiley and Sons, Inc., 1960).
259. Schaaf, Oscar, "Student Discovery of Algebraic Principles as a Means of Developing Ability to Generalize," *Mathematics Teacher*, XLVIII (May, 1955), 324-327.
260. Schuell, Hildred, "Sex Differences in Relation to Stuttering," *Journal of Speech and Hearing Disorders*, XII (1947), 23-38.
261. Schultz, Raymond E., "A Comparison of Negro Pupils Ranking High with Those Ranking Low in Educational Achievement," *Journal of Educational Sociology*, XXXI (March, 1958), 265-270.
262. Scott, Flora and Myers, Garry C., "Children's Empty and Erroneous Concepts of the Commonplace," *Journal of Educational Research*, VIII (November, 1923), 327-334.
263. Seib, Charles B. and Otten, Alan L., "The Case of the Furious Children," *Harper's Magazine*, CCXVI (January, 1958), 56-61.
264. Shauel, Howard J. and Street, Roy F., "Prostigimin and the Chronic Stutterer," *Journal of Speech and Hearing Disorders* (March-December, 1949), 143-146.
265. Shaw, Merville C. and Black, M. D., "The Reaction to Frustration of Bright High School Underachievers," *California Journal of Educational Research*, XI (May, 1960), 120-124.
266. Shaw, Merville C. et al., "The Self Concept of Bright Underachieving High School Students as Revealed by an Adjective Check List," *Personnel and Guidance Journal*, XXXIX (November, 1960), 193-196.
267. Shaw, Merville C., "Need Achievement Scales as Predictors of Academic Success," *Journal of Educational Psychology*, LII (December, 1961), 282-285.
268. Shechtman, Audrey M., "The Relationship of Variability in Children's Verbal and Non-Language Test Performance to Current and Later Behavioral Functions," *Dissertation Abstracts*, XXII, Ph.D. Dissertation (University of Minnesota, 1961).
269. Sheldon, Paul M., "Isolation as a Characteristic of Highly Gifted Children," *The Journal of Educational Sociology*, XXXII (January, 1959), 215-221.
270. Skeels, Harold M. and Fillmore, Eva A., "The Mental Development of Children from Underprivileged Homes," *Journal of Genetic Psychology*, L (June, 1937), 427-439.
271. Skeels, H. M. and Dye, H. B., "A Study of the Effects of Differential Stimulation on Mentally Retarded Children," *Proceedings, American Association on Mental Deficiency*, XLIV (1939), 114-136.
272. Skeels, H. M., "A Study of the Effects of Differential Stimulation on Mentally Retarded Children: A Follow Up Study," *American Journal of Mental Deficiency*, XLVI (1941), 340-350.
273. Skinner, B. F., "Teaching Machines," *Science*, CXXVIII (October 24, 1958), 969-977.
274. Skinner, B. F., "Teaching Machines," *Scientific American*, CCV (November, 1961), 90-102.
275. Skinner, B. F., "Behaviorism at Fifty," *Science*, CXL (May 31, 1963), 951-958.
276. Smith, Joseph G., "Influence of Failure, Expressed Hostility, and Stimulus Characteristics on Verbal Learning and Recognition," *Journal of Personality*, XXII (June, 1954), 475-493.
277. Smock, Charles, "The Relationship Between Test Anxiety, Threat-Expectancy,

and Recognition Thresholds for Words," *Journal of Personality*, XXV (December, 1956), 191-201.

278. Smode, Alfred F., "The Motivating Effect of Knowledge of Performance Information on Learning and Performance in a One-Dimensional Compensatory Tracking Task," *Dissertation Abstracts*, XVII (1957), 2323-2324.

279. Sobel, Max A., "Concept Learning in Algebra," *Mathematics Teacher*, XLIX (October, 1956), 425-430.

280. Spaulding, Patricia, "Comparison of 500 Complete and Abbreviated Revised Stanford Scales Administered to Mental Defectives," *American Journal of Mental Deficiency*, L (July, 1954), 81-88.

281. Spriestersbach, Duane C., "An Objective Approach to the Investigation of Social Adjustment of Male Stutterers," *Journal of Speech and Hearing Disorders* (1951), 250-257.

282. Stachowiak, James G, "Hypnosis, the Principle of Congruity, and Attitude Change," *Dissertation Abstracts*, XXII (May, 1962), 4107.

283. Stevenson, Ian, "The Uncomfortable Facts About Extrasensory Perception," *Harper's Magazine*, CCXIX (July, 1959), 19-25.

284. Steward, Joseph L., "The Problem of Stuttering in Certain North American Indian Societies," *Journal of Speech and Hearing Disorders*, Monograph Supplement 6 (April, 1960), 1-87.

285. Stewart, Lawrence H., "Interest Patterns of a Group of High Ability, High Achieving Students," *Journal of Counseling Psychology*, VI (1959), 132-139.

286. Taba, Hilda, "Learning by Discovery: Psychological and Educational Rationale," Paper read at the American Educational Research Association Annual Convention, Atlantic City, February, 1962. Mimeographed.

287. Taylor, Calvin W. and Barron, Frank, Eds., *Scientific Creativity: Its Recognition and Development* (New York: John Wiley and Sons, Inc., 1963).

288. Theman, Viola and Witty, Paul, "Case Studies and Genetic Records of Two Gifted Negroes," *Journal of Psychology*, XV (April, 1943), 165-181.

289. Thistlethwaite, Donald L., "Effects of Social Recognition upon the Educational Motivation of Talented Youth," *The Journal of Educational Psychology*, L (June, 1959), 111-116.

290. Thorndike, Robert L., *The Concepts of Over- and Underachievement* (New York: Bureau of Publications, Teachers College, Columbia University, 1963).

291. Tomlinson, Helen, "Differences Between Pre-School Negro Children and Their Older Siblings on the Stanford-Binet Scales," *Journal of Negro Education*, XIII (October, 1944), 474-479.

292. Torrance, E. Paul, *Guiding Creative Talent*, (Englewood Cliffs, New Jersey: Prentice-Hall, Inc., 1962).

293. Tyler, Ralph W., "Permanence of Learning," *Journal of Higher Education*, IV (April, 1933), 203-205.

294. Van Riper, C., "A Study of the Stutterer's Ability to Interrupt Stuttering Spasms," *Journal of Speech Disorders*, (1940), 117-119.

295. Waetjen, Walter B., Ed., *Human Variability and Learning* (Washington, D. C.: Association for Supervision and Curriculum Development, 1961).

296. Waetjen, Walter B., "Curiosity and Exploration: Roles in Intellectual Development and Learning," Paper read at the Curriculum Research Institute, Washington, D. C., December, 1962. Mimeographed.

297. Waite, R. R. et al., "A Study of Anxiety and Learning in Children," *Journal of Abnormal and Social Psychology*, LVII (November, 1958), 267-270.

298. Walter, Verne A., "The Effect of Need for Academic Achievement on the Performance of College Students in Learning Certain Study Skills," *Dissertation Abstracts*, XVII (1957), 1384.

299. Walter, W. Grey, *The Living Brain* (New York: W. W. Norton, Co., 1953).

300. Walter, Richard H. et al., "A Test of the Perceptual Defense Hypothesis," *Journal of Personality*, XXVII (March, 1959), 47-55.

301. Watson, Gladys H., "Emotional Problems of Gifted Students," *Personnel and Guidance Journal*, XXXIX (October, 1960), 98-105.
302. Watson, Goodwin, "What Psychology Can We Feel Sure About?" *The Education Digest*, XXV (May, 1960), 18-20.
303. Weiner, Bluma B., "A Report on the Final Academic Achievement of Thirty-Seven Mentally Handicapped Boys Who Had Been Enrolled in a Prolonged Pre-Academic Program," *American Journal of Mental Deficiency*, LIX (October, 1954), 210-219.
304. Weiner, Harold and Ross, Sherman, "Manifest Anxiety and Perceptual Judgment," *Journal of Social Psychology*, XLIV (August, 1956), 83-87.
305. Weiss, Robert F., "Aspirations and Expectations: A Dimensional Analysis," *Journal of Social Psychology*, LIII (April, 1961), 249-254.
306. Wendahl, Ronald and Cole, Jane, "Identification of Stuttering During Relatively Fluent Speech," *Journal of Speech and Hearing Disorders*, IV (1961), 281-286.
307. Werner, Heinz, "Abnormal and Subnormal Rigidity," *The Journal of Abnormal and Social Psychology*, XLI (1946), 15-25.
308. Wert, J. E., "Twin Examination Assumptions," *Journal of Higher Education*, VIII (March, 1937), 136-140.
309. Wexner, Lois B., "Relationship of Intelligence and the Nine Scales of the Minnesota Multiphasic Personality Inventory," *Journal of Social Psychology*, XL (August, 1954), 173-176.
310. Wiener, Gerald, "The Effect of Distrust on Some Aspects of Intelligence Test Behavior," *Journal of Consulting Psychology*, XXI (April, 1957), 127-130.
311. Wiener, Gerald, "The Interaction Among Anxiety, Stress Instructions, and Difficulty," *Journal of Consulting Psychology*, XXIII (August, 1959), 324-328.
312. Wilson, Frank T., "Some Special Ability Test Scores of Gifted Children," *Journal of Genetic Psychology*, LXXXII (March, 1953), 59-68.
313. Winitz, Harris, "Repetitions in the Vocalizations and Speech of Children in the First Two Years of Life," *Journal of Speech and Hearing Disorders*, Supplement 7 (June, 1961), 55-61.
314. Wittreich, Warren J., "Visual Perception and Personality," *Scientific American*, CC (April, 1959), 56-60.
315. Witty, Paul A. and Jenkins, Martin D., "The Educational Achievement of a Group of Gifted Negro Children," *Journal of Educational Psychology*, XXV (November, 1934), 585-597.
316. Witty, Paul A. and Theman, Viola, "The Follow-up Study of the Educational Attainment of Gifted Negroes," *Journal of Educational Psychology*, XXXIV (January, 1943), 35-47.
317. Young, Florene and Bright, Howard A., "Results of Testing 81 Negro Rural Juveniles with the Wechsler Intelligence Scale for Children," *Journal of Social Psychology*, XXXIX (May, 1954), 219-226.
318. Zweibelson, I., "Test Anxiety and Intelligence Test Performance," *Journal of Consulting Psychology*, XX (December, 1956), 479-481.

Chapter Five

Motivation

Motives flow from the wellspring of life itself. They are energy in action; philosophy and physiology fused. Motives are a part of what biologists call purpose (241). They develop to satisfy needs, of which the human organism has many different kinds. Maslow (200) maintains that there are seven graded levels of them, higher needs emerging as more basic ones are satisfied: physiological, safety, love, esteem, self-actualizing, intellectual, and aesthetic. Those things we recognize as motivation in the classroom are but one part of any person's total motivational structure. They bear a distinct relation to an individual's abilities to satisfy his needs, but even so, they do not give a teacher much help in working with his students.

The purpose of this chapter will be to explore students' motivations toward school. Since this is a book about schooling, it seems appropriate to delve deeply into young people's motives as directly reflected in their eagerness to do good work in school.

McClelland (204) describes the need to achieve as learned behavior. Learned behaviors unquestionably stem from the basic drives which biologists postulate, but what a child brings with him to the classroom is essentially a collection of acquired characteristics. No child is born either liking or disliking mathematics. No child hates school naturally. No youngster approaches the world of ideas with apprehension without having had unpleasant experiences which preceded these fears. These are negative motivations, but the same is true of positive ones. No learner comes into the world with a taste for literature or mechanical drawing or geography. Children also learn these things. Motivation to do good work in school is a learned behavior.

THE BASES OF MOTIVATION

What aspects of motivation are included in a person's desire to do good work in school? Values, personality structure, and curiosity, among other things, affect motivations toward school experiences. Each of these will be explored in the pages which follow.

Values

Values involve beliefs and worth; according certain phenomena greater significance than others. The extent to which an individual cherishes some things as opposed to others reflects his value pattern. Values represent any individual's scale of differences; things at the top including facets of experience which are valued more dearly; things at the bottom being particulars which are considered of less worth.

Consider this simple test of values. Listed below are three words which represent concepts with which we are all familiar:

HEALTH   WEALTH   HAPPINESS

Assume for the moment that there is agreement about what each of these verbal symbols means. Now arrange these three words in the order in which you feel they are most important, putting at the top that which you cherish most and at the bottom that which you desire least. If you ranked them

HEALTH
HAPPINESS
WEALTH

this represents one kind of value pattern. If you ranked them

WEALTH
HEALTH
HAPPINESS

it means an entirely different structure.

This illustrates an elementary approach to the study of values. Actually people may establish one kind of hierarchy in their minds, but live another. Many persons say that health is more important than money, then forthwith engage in activities detrimental to their health in order to accumulate material possessions.

Human motivations are not as simple as this illustration. Many factors may have significance simultaneously. Some are close in time and space, and others distant. On certain factors the individual has a great deal of information while on others he is relatively ignorant. Each phenomenon has a relative position in any person's scale of values, however, exerting its influence as part of his total value structure.

Values influence human behavior. If people value social approval more than behavior in keeping with the facts, then they may do things which will insure social acceptance even if they ought to do otherwise. Many young persons start to smoke because the threat of social ostracism is more apparent than the possible dangers resulting from smoking, which appear remote. The dangers of heavy cigarette smoking, which almost any teenager knows, have been pushed completely out of consciousness to attain more immediate social approval. Values influence what people do.

Likewise, many intelligent people behave in prejudiced ways. Many persons whose behavior is usually characterized by a congruence with the facts are unable to behave reasonably as far as Negroes or Jews are concerned. Their value patterns do not permit an awareness of certain facts, but rather lead to pre-judgment. Even though abundant evidence indicates clearly that such things as rejection and discrimination increase social problems, their values prevent their perception of these facts.

In the same way, values influence what people do in school. Those who cherish the exploration of new ideas more than material things will manifest certain behaviors in the classroom, while their opposites will demonstrate an entirely different kind. This is not to say that either value pattern is necessarily "better" than the other. Both are probably important, but one generates one kind of human activity and the other, another.

Because they are different, the individual who values ideas will learn in a different way from a person with the other set of values (249). Each will respond to the opportunities to examine ideas in a unique manner (131). Each will respond to suggestions and directions from the teacher according to his own peculiar value pattern.

Personality

We have already devoted considerable space to various aspects of personality structure. You can predict with considerable accuracy what we will have to say here about the relationship of personality structure to motivation. The personality of any individual influences profoundly that person's approach to the world of ideas and his own conception of his ability to deal with them. The openness and adequacy of people, which are two generalized aspects of personality structure, directly affect people's motivation to do good work in school.

In a classic statement, Kelley (161) describes the "open self" as that aspect of existence represented in the ability to perceive clearly and accurately: the "willingness" of the organism to permit stimuli to be received and accorded significance. The very nature of the structure of the organism enables the individual to assimilate information (171).

The opposite of openness is "closed-mindedness" or "narrow-mindedness." These terms aptly describe an individual's reluctance to be receptive and to consider unfamiliar experiences (251).

The tendency to openness and its opposite is a deep-seated function of personality structure and seldom lies within the realm of will. The ability to behave in an "open" or "closed" manner is not something which the organism can turn off or on voluntarily. Rather, it is a reflection of the total personality structure, amenable to change which generally takes place over an extended period of time, and primarily according to a person's sense of adequacy.

Adequacy has been described in detail by Combs and Snygg (60). It is an individual's personal interpretation of his ability to cope with a situation. The extent to which he feels threatened, or unable to respond either to eliminate or modify threatening stimuli, is an indication of his feeling of inadequacy. The extent to which he feels capable of coping with himself and his surroundings without being threatened reflects a sense of adequacy. Adequacy includes both the way an individual perceives a situation and his interpretation of his own capacity to preserve and improve his unique self under the circumstances.

In learning, adequacy is manifest as the way in which an individual behaves in experiencing new ideas. When presented with new or unusual stimuli, some persons are attracted, others repelled. The very act of confronting people with something new may give teachers clues as to a student's motivational pattern. Those who withdraw from new experience and evade new stimuli, who typically and perceptually retreat to the more familiar, are reflecting inadequate behavior.

On the other hand, those persons who seem fascinated by the unknown, who apparently are drawn toward that which they have not experienced before, and who have the capacity to cope with new situations, are open, adequate personalities.

In the schoolroom this notion becomes much more involved. A teacher may attempt to present new ideas in an old way, but if the student has experienced frustration and dissatisfaction with this old way before, he may be unwilling to expend much perceptual energy pursuing the new ideas. If a teacher is really concerned that a learner learn, then he will be sensitive to a student's apparent reluctance to experience new ideas by examining his own methods, including himself, for clues which will enable him to "get through."

In summary, an individual's personality structure, harnessed to his value pattern, results in curiosity, be it great or little.

Curiosity

Any parent realizes that almost every child is curious. Little children seem to want to know, to be obsessed with the desire to explore themselves and their surroundings. They want to know what everything looks like, how it feels, what it tastes like, whether it will break, and on and on. But what is curiosity? Where does it come from? What may it lead to?

It is, first and foremost, a result rather than a cause. It follows naturally after satisfaction of physical, safety, and social needs of the individual. It is an observable expression of biological purpose. Curiosity is the individual's awareness of unusual problems coupled with a high energy output directed toward their solution. It is predicated upon a value pattern which includes cherishment of knowing. Curiosity is only possible in an organism which has a personality structure which enables it to be open and adequate.

Confronted with the unknown, the curious person recognizes that a problem exists. He probes and explores. He has an inner physical and physiological desire to discern its solution. Typically, the curious individual has been immersed in a particular medium for some considerable while (222). This immersion generally results in a high degree of awareness of the intricacies of the situation, physical, social, or otherwise. Existence in the world of force or tone or color or words may develop a sensitivity to them all so that incomplete aspects are recognizable to the curious person. He sees a problem.

Once perceived, these problems incubate within the central nervous system of the curious one. There is persevering mental activity aimed at resolving the component segments of the problem into a new and reasonable relationship (297). This activity, sometimes called divergent thinking, seeks new relationships. Ideas are re-assessed in terms of different assumptions. They are extended to their logical extremes, and beyond. There is an intense effort to recombine old notions into more significant patterns than conventional experience would provide. This effort is accompanied by a constant examination of the resulting combinations for indications of developments (73). Roller (61) describes the efforts of early observers to solve the riddles of electricity. For several centuries men observed the attractive or positive aspects of what we now recognize as magnetized iron. They also noted the repelling qualities, but they were not able to perceive completely the relationship of the positive and negative forces. There is both a pull and a push to magnetism, but it was hundreds of years before the relationship was recognized.

Recognizing relationships is insight. Insight follows the periods of immersion in the medium and the incubation of the experiences, and usually comes as a sudden awareness of the pattern of the total situation. The curious person hastens this process by persistently re-examining the particulars to recognize any logical relationships which might exist. He tries to find relationships which are consistent with both the inner logic of the material and the logic of his mental processes.

This pressing, trying, probing, teasing human effort is apparent in an individual's desire to know. Curiosity is a high level expression of human energy. It represents a physical and mental effort to comprehend all of the intricacies of any situation in their most significant relationships. Curiosity results in creativity, and curiosity is the lifeblood of motivation to do good work in school.

Motivation and Submission

Before we go further it might be appropriate to distinguish between motivation to do good work in school and submission to a teacher's will. There has been growing concern in recent years that some youngsters attempt to do good work by bending to authority. In studies of highly intelligent children compared with highly creative children, Getzels and Jackson (111) noted, almost with alarm, that fewer teachers wanted creative children in their classrooms than wanted intelligent ones. There were definite indications that teachers preferred obedient, docile, sub-missive children. Many students certainly learn early that most teachers give good grades to those who do exactly what the teacher says.

This does not mean that all students who do what the teacher directs are submissive, but that any consideration of student motivation should point out the fact that submissiveness may be involved.

Schools are complex social institutions, and the motives of all their participants are many and varied. Without question there are many youngsters whose experience both at home and at school has taught them that the way to be "successful" and to get good grades (which are often taken as direct evidence of learning) is to perform the proper tasks in the proper fashion at the proper time (99). This is not the type of motivation to which we are referring, however.

ASSESSING MOTIVATION

As it has been described thus far, motivation is something which a student *has*. It is not something which a teacher *does to* his students directly. This notion may disturb those who assume it is their responsibility to motivate students toward good work. The basic tenets of this book imply that a teacher should capitalize upon the forces within the individual for maximum learning, but to try to do things which motivate students is ineffective in most cases. Teachers need to arrange their activities and organize their classrooms so that these operations function in harmony with students' motivations rather than against them. This does not mean that teachers cannot arouse interest in a subject. It does mean, however, that it is generally more effective to design instruction so that the forces in the learner which are seeking expression are tied to the learning process directly rather than indirectly.

A second point about motivation, however, seems pertinent here. Submissiveness expressing itself as motivation to do good work illustrates the thesis that teachers are obliged to encourage children to develop higher levels of motivation. It is not desirable for a child to study because he is afraid of the teacher. But it does happen. Observing this, a teacher must endeavor to help that child move to a higher level of motivation. A good teacher recognizes that he must start with his students where they are, but also that it is imperative to help them move on. The teacher who can assist students to understand their fears and help them feel good about themselves and others may be able to help them move along the continuum toward a higher motivation.

A teacher faces two problems when he tries to use the concept of motivation in his teaching: how to organize his classroom and his techniques for effective instruction, and how to help students develop better motivational patterns. These problems are not mutually exclusive. It is important for the teacher to achieve both ends. Chapter Seven will attempt to provide specific suggestions about the first point. It will be left to the reader to attack the second, more profound, problem.

In the meantime, if we want to couple the teaching effort to the learner's motivation, how will we know who is highly motivated and who is not?

Psychologists have done very little research in the area of motivation toward school. Writing in the *Encyclopedia of Educational Research* in 1958 Marx noted (198):

Unfortunately we are handicapped by the relatively small amount of relevant material available in the educational literature; this dearth was made obvious by data reported by Ryans. He sampled topics treated in selected educational psychology textbooks published from 1925 to 1930 and in 1954, and in the *Journal of Educational Psychology* for the same periods. The percent of papers devoted to motivation in the journals was 0 and 1, for the two periods, the corresponding percent of pages devoted to the topic in the textboks was 2 and 10. An independent check of the 1955 to 1957 issues of the *Journal of Educational Research* and the *Journal of Experimental Education* gave essentially the same results (0 and 2 percent).

Other Motivation Studies

Reporting a series of research conferences on creativity, Taylor (296) stressed the need for new tests in motivation, drives, and values. There have been efforts to assess motivation for many years (20, 53, 54, 71, 100, 101, 102, 103, 179, 188, 193, 205, 233, 295, 311) but McClelland's studies of the achievement motive (204) is one of the recent major contributions. Rejecting certain ιᵗ eoretical models as incomplete or inefficient (e.g., survival model, stimulus intensity model), he ultimately selected affect as a basis for motives and then proceeded to conceptualize a theoretical framework which makes possible the measurement of motives through fantasy.

Developing a Motivation Index

In an effort to develop an instrument simple enough for any classroom teacher to administer yet valid enough to furnish precise data about a student's motivational level, the author undertook a series of studies of junior high school students. The details of this research are reported elsewhere (101, 102, 103), but a summary follows.

The responses of several hundred junior high school students, identified by experienced teachers as extremely high-motivated or extremely low-motivated out of a group of more than 9000, were analyzed to see which items discriminated most consistently and most effectively in repeated studies. From an original list of more than 300 such items, 50 were finally isolated which seemed to differentiate students according to their desire to do good work as reflected in teachers' estimates, other experts' judgments, and achievement on standardized examinations. Taken together, these items comprise the Junior Index of Motivation or the JIM Scale. It has been appended to this chapter (see Appendix A), along with specific instructions for administering and scoring. Representative items are listed below according to the way high-motivated students tended to respond, "D" indicating disagreement.

ITEMS REPRESENTING VALUES

6. Pupils who try should get good grades even if they make mistakes. (D)
7. Successful people are those who make the most money. (D)
9. Most young people do not want to go to school. (D)
60. Looking good is just as important as being good. (D)
62. Famous people usually have a lot of money. (D)
76. Quick thinking is always better than being polite. (D)
44. It is better to forget than to forgive. (D)

ITEMS REPRESENTING PERSONALITY

16. A person's feelings on a topic are not as important as the facts. (D)
21. Many youngsters often want to run away from home. (D)
29. The world we live in is a pretty lonesome place. (D)
35. Life seems to be one big struggle after another. (D)
48. The present is all too often full of unhappiness. (D)
53. There is a real limit to man's intelligence. (D)
70. Not many people in the world are really kind. (D)

ITEMS REPRESENTING CURIOSITY

5. School is more fun when teachers let students do things they want to. (D)
12. Knowing the answer is more important than knowing where to get the answer. (D)
18. It does not really help much to study about people from other lands. (D)
33. There is nothing new under the sun. (D)
46. Young people should be free to follow their own desires. (D)
57. People who are quick thinkers usually jump to conclusions. (D)
69. Asking questions usually gets you into trouble. (D)

This conception of motivation presupposes a very personal point of view. It assumes that highly motivated children are attracted toward the whole world of ideas according to their own personality and sense of values. The degree to which they are propelled toward learning in school is directly related to their openness to experience, their personal sense of adequacy, and the things they cherish. Motivation is not something which a teacher does to students, but something which students already have. Their motivational patterns may be changed, but this can occur only over an extended period of time. Interest and motivation are related in that interests are relatively short-term phenomena, subject to modification by appropriate stimulation and procedural variations. Motivation, on the other hand, changes slowly as personality and value structure are modified by experience and social interaction. From a teacher's point of view, motivation in students is a force to be understood and utilized.

A PICTURE OF LOW-MOTIVATED STUDENTS

This study of adolescents tends to substantiate the notion that high-motivated and low-motivated youngsters are basically different: they think differently, feel differently, behave differently.

To present this picture in sharper relief, a composite low-motivated student is described below. If we can understand why young people are not motivated to learn—why they hate school sometimes—we may be able to infer certain things about the nature of motivation itself. This hypothetical youngster is drawn from an analysis of the responses of several hundred low-motivated students to JIM Scale items.

In studying responses to the 50 JIM Scale items, five characteristics of the low-motivated students emerge: they are unhappy and afraid, they lack confidence in themselves, they resist change and new ideas, they are unduly concerned with the objective and the materialistic, and they dislike school intensely.

Low-Motivated Students Are Unhappy

Students who are not highly motivated to do good work respond positively to the following JIM Scale items: many young people feel grouchy, many youngsters often want to run away from home, no one seems to understand young people, the world we live in is a pretty lonesome place, most people just don't give a "darn" for others, the present is all too often full of unhappiness, people who are insulted generally deserve to be, life is mostly sorrow with just a little joy, not many people in the world are really kind, we are never really as happy as we think we are, hope is really no better than worry, and people who dream at night are apt to be crazy.

Taken together these ideas represent these students' negative social outlook. They are downhearted, pessimistic, and sad. Preoccupied with a series of discouraging developments, it is little wonder that they are not interested in formal education. Social needs are much more basic than the need to know (200). Rebuffed and defeated in their social relations, these students are evidently striving to combat or improve their relationships with other people; they have neither the energies nor the desires to pursue learning in school.

Low-Motivated Students Are Thing-Oriented

Youngsters who are not highly motivated to do good schoolwork respond positively to the following JIM Scale items: successful people are those who make the most money, a person's feelings on a topic are not as important as the facts, knowing the answer is more important than knowing where to get the answer, the best way to achieve security is for the government to guarantee jobs, it is better to forget than to forgive, looking good is just as important as being good, famous people usually have a lot of money, one can never desire too much of a good thing, quick thinking is always better than being polite, and familiarity breeds contempt so one should never be too friendly.

Adolescents who are not motivated toward school seem to be unduly obsessed with specifics and material things, having little concern for the subjective, human facets of life. These reactions are indicative of only one aspect of their motivational structure, but the pattern seems unmistakable.

Low-Motivated Students Lack Confidence

Among adolescents negatively motivated toward school there is a tendency to agree with the following JIM Scale items more frequently than do highly motivated students: life seems to be one big struggle after another, there is a real limit to man's intelligence, experience may be a good teacher but schools are better, people who are quick thinkers usually jump to conclusions, most people do not have good ideas until they grow up, most people cannot learn from the experience of others, the best people refuse to depend on other persons, our whole trouble is that we won't let God help us, all those who fail have worked in vain, and everything that people do is either right or wrong.

Taken together, these statements describe young people who are disillusioned about their own capacities, who lack confidence, and who reflect something of a fatalistic philosophy—"Things are predetermined, regardless of what I do."

Low-Motivated Students Resist Change

Very few of the low-motivated young people studied in this research possess a burning desire to know the truth or to adapt to change. The opposite actually seemed more characteristic. Students who were not highly motivated toward school agreed with these ideas: it does not really help much to study about people from other lands, social progress can only be achieved by returning to our glorious past, there is nothing new under the sun, some new ideas are interesting but most of them are not, it is very foolish to advocate government support of education, the dreamer is a danger to society, being a liar is better than being a gossip, asking questions usually gets you into trouble, and many ideas are not worth the paper they are printed on.

This obsession with the past and reluctance to change have been described by Rokeach (251) as characteristic of dogmatic, closed-minded persons. Certainly unwillingness to experience new ideas or admit the dynamic status of our society would seem appropriate behavior for persons who resist school. By definition, education implies a suscepti-bility to information and a congeniality toward change. This research seems to substantiate that notion by underlining the fact that young people who are not motivated toward school lack these aspects of personality structure.

Low-Motivated Students Dislike School

Finally, as might be expected, young people who are not highly motivated to do good work express an active distaste for several aspects of school life. For example, the pupils included in the JIM Scale study who were identified as low-motivated tended to agree with these items: most young people do not want to go to school, school is more fun when teachers let students do things they want to, most people would like school better if teachers did not give grades, some teachers seem to enjoy making students suffer, pupils who try should get good grades even if they make mistakes, most teachers like to drive students if they have the chance, teachers know more and do less than most other people, school is not all that it's cracked up to be, and young people should be free to follow their own desires.

Certainly the pervading theme throughout all of these reactions is that this particular group did not like school and held teachers in fairly low esteem. Whether these feelings are cause or effect—do students dislike teachers because they are low-motivated or are they low-motivated because they dislike teachers?—is a problem worth more than mere speculation.

Young people's varied motivations toward school are reflected in differing degrees of self-confidence, happiness, concern with material things, attitudes toward school, and personal and social adjustment. A person's desire to strive in school is rooted firmly in his value structure and his personality structure, both of which combine to generate his own curiosity level.

INFERRING THE NATURE OF MOTIVATION FROM OTHER RESEARCH

Up to this point we have reviewed some theoretical considerations and one study in detail. Perhaps it would be helpful now to look at several studies and attempt to infer from them the nature of motivation as compared to our findings thus far.

Students who leave school represent a valuable source of information about school motivation. Studying drop-out data should help us understand what generates the desire to try in school. There are many drop-out studies because there are many drop-outs.

Drop-Out Studies

The seriousness of the problem of early school-leavers is described by one official as follows (248):

> Our high school dropout rate has reached fantastic proportions: Two and one half million of the 10,800,000 students enrolled in grades 9 through 12 of the Nation's public and non-public schools this fall will drop out before graduation.
>
> This is a national problem of frightening implication representing a terrible waste of our youth, and it is found—not just in the big cities—but *in every State*. The dropout rate ranges from 20 to 40 percent in the 50 States.

These figures refer only to those drop-outs who actually enter high school. Other studies indicate only half of all who start fifth grade eventually graduate (51, 105). "Two out of three never reached senior high school" (329). In a society dedicated to universal education, these indices of negative motivations toward school reflect a fundamental rift between the teachers and the students.

Some drop-outs, when questioned about their reasons for leaving
school, say only that they dislike a certain teacher, but others are
able to define their grievances specifically. In a California study of
drop-outs, pupils complained that lessons were insufficiently explained and that they did not get enough individual help from the
teacher. Some of them were honest enough to say that they could
have gotten more help, but they were afraid to ask for it. What they
wanted most was more personal contact from the teacher. They
mentioned often that teachers were not consistent in disciplinary
practices, that they were lax and strict without reason, or that the
whole class was sometimes punished for the misdeeds of one or two
members. (226)

Johnson (156), analyzing teachers' comments about why secondary
students failed, noted that the six major reasons listed by teachers
blamed the student: does not do required work, is absent excessively,
has indifferent attitude, is uncooperative, lacks initiative, and fails to
make up back work. Not one of the eighteen cited reasons placed
responsibility on teachers or the school. This is especially pertinent in
view of the fact that "many factors besides intelligence and achievement
influence teachers' marks; among these are attitudes, neatness, degree
of interest, personality, speech, appearance of written work, and quality
of accomplishment" (225).

College students, asked to describe what motivated them in their
studies (336), responded that their major reasons for striving in school
were because of the practical value of the course in earning a living,
the instructor's knowledge, well-defined course objectives, instructor's
enthusiasm, and sympathetic understanding of the student. Asked to
point out things which brought forth opposite reactions, these same
students listed fear and the use of sarcasm by the instructor as inhibiting
factors.

Regardless of where the responsibility for student success rightfully
lies, teachers and students obviously blame each other for students'
unsuccessful experiences in school. Considering the implications of
having half the population quit school because they could not stand it,
teachers would do well to redirect their professional efforts toward those
factors over which they have most immediate control: themselves and
their methods.

One of the most obvious and often recurring factors in studies of
why students quit school is their lack of participation in extracurricular
programs and activities 40, 41, 42, 70, 78, 80, 164, 189, 203, 224,
226, 232, 238, 277, 278, 307, 310, 312, 318, 333). In comparing grad-

uates with drop-outs from a Chicago high school, Thomas noted (303) that *"not one person who dropped before completing the third year had engaged in even one activity,* and that 89 percent of those who finished had." Whether lack of participation reflects cause or effect is not too clear, though at least some students of drop-out studies maintain that "lack of money or rejection by their classmates" (226) are contributing factors. The fact that extracurricular programs are the one phase of a compulsory school program where personal involvement and individual choice are most possible would seem to imply that students who dislike school have *no* place within the educational enterprise where they feel a sense of belonging and a spirit of personal commitment.

Any review of drop-out studies uncovers two types of reasons for students leaving school: those over which the school has some control, and those over which the school has no control. It has been suggested before in this book that an understanding of the implications of causative factors which lie beyond the realm of teacher control may be enlightening. However, teachers who hope to be effective must devote most of their professional energies to factors within the educational system on which they have some influence. Whether a teacher should even attempt to improve a "poor" home situation has both practical and philosophical implications. Teaching students to learn how to learn (300), a noble goal, is probably best accomplished if teachers confine themselves to the role for which they are best prepared—instruction. Social welfare and psychotherapy are important, but they are other fields. The job of the teacher is to teach. Assuming this, and recognizing that students who leave school of their own volition generally reflect negative motivation toward school, what reasons do they give for leaving early?

Factors Beyond the School's Control

First, perhaps foremost, young people who drop out of school often come from poor home conditions (34, 40, 42, 66, 70, 76, 78, 120, 174, 180, 186, 203, 232, 238, 239, 275, 277, 278, 287, 304, 309, 312, 321, 333). This sometimes means lower socio-economic sections of the community, sometimes uneducated parents. Depending upon how the researcher defined his terms, "poor" home conditions include separated parents, unemployed father, exceptionally large family, or overcrowded living conditions. Most frequently what is implied in all the studies is that youngsters who quit school are from homes in which friction or lack of love is evident, parental concern with and belief in education is lacking, and the general atmosphere is one of short term goals and low level aspirations. Changing these conditions is very difficult. Recognizing that they exist, and working on those factors which are manipulable by the teacher, is realistic and rewarding.

Many students quit school to work (40, 42, 65, 74, 129, 144, 149, 155, 174, 180, 194, 203, 230, 238, 239, 266, 277, 278, 304, 307, 324, 333, 334). In some few cases the need for money is real. If the breadwinner dies, a boy may need to go to work to maintain the family. Others have to supplement a sagging family income. Even these reasons, however, have diminished in number in recent years.

But many students still drop out and go to work. Why? Again the reasons are not always clear. Most schools conduct an exit interview with departing students, and frequently these interviews hinge on the terminology in the administrative forms provided. If the official form lists such reasons as "transfer to another school outside the district," "voluntary withdrawal to enter employment," "voluntary withdrawal for reasons of marriage," or "voluntary withdrawal to enter armed services," the person recording the reason is apt to be more guided by the form than by the facts of the situation.

For example, the student may not have had any friends in school (40, 69, 74, 80, 115, 180, 186, 224, 278, 307, 310), or he may have been the butt of a sarcastic comment by a teacher. In either case, the real reason is probably lost from the official record.

When questioned after dropping out, many young people express extreme dissatisfaction with teachers or the school (50, 129). And the same youngsters who "would not work" and were "too lazy to do their lessons" are the ones who leave school to seek regular jobs, often badly paid jobs which are difficult and tiring. It hardly seems reasonable to assume that they are afraid of hard work. Many stated they "preferred work to school" when asked why they left. The kind of work they had in school evidently was neither rewarding nor satisfying.

These drop-outs may be unrealistic. Certainly we have some evidence that students who are not motivated to do good work in school are more materialistic and object-centered than highly motivated youngsters (101, 102, 103). Whether this is because they have never had as many material possessions as the more highly motivated pupils or whether it reflects a basic difference in orientations has not been established. Considering their poor home background, it is probably safe to assume that it is partly because these desires have never been satisfied. Persons who already have many possessions are probably less interested in objects than ideas because they already have the objects. Since this is only speculation, subsequent studies might explore the hypothesis in greater detail.

Many students leave school in order to marry (40, 65, 129, 168, 203, 239, 266, 277, 278, 287, 304, 307, 310, 324, 332, 333, 334). By far the most of these are girls. Boys frequently drop out of school to enter the armed services (129, 168, 266, 332), and though these figures vary according to the era involved, in recent years the number who leave for this reason has steadily diminished.

It may be that the school should not concern itself with these problems. Remmers' research (246) with thousands of teenagers dramatizes the fact that sex and vocational ambitions are their major problem areas. In most schools the first problem is ignored almost completely, and the second one "tolerated" for certain students. In very few cases are they deliberately and thoughtfully made a part of most students' educational experiences.

Ability is another factor which evidently affects students' motivations toward school. Many studies point up the fact that drop-outs have lower ability as measured by conventional paper and pencil intelligence tests than students who remain in school (78, 80, 174, 189, 226, 232, 277, 278, 287, 307, 310, 312, 321). Many other studies, however, indicate that early school leavers as a group possess average ability (70, 74, 76, 180, 212, 215, 238, 275, 281, 282, 303, 309), and some underline the fact that many drop-outs are exceptionally able (74, 281, 282, 287, 304, 310). The real problem is much more knotty.

Many youngsters who can handle educational programs do not, for one reason or another, do so. Assuming that some of their reasons lie within the jurisdiction of the school, let us turn our attention first to their less fortunate fellows. What about students who do not possess academic aptitude? Why do they leave?

Two reasons appear obvious: either they cannot succeed with the educational opportunities available, or they get no satisfaction from the experiences even if they can succeed. In either instance, these factors probably influence a young person's desire to try to do good work. Ability is not something over which a teacher has much immediate control, but how a teacher relates to youngsters with these abilities is another problem. This will be explored more fully in the next section.

Factors over Which the School Has Some Control

Teachers can exercise relatively little influence over young people's home environments or their needs for money. Students' academic abilities are also often assumed to be beyond a teacher's immediate influence. A teacher's relationships with students of poor ability or from poor home situations, however, is a problem of an entirely different order. Here we are confronted with factors which lie within a teacher's realm: his own behavior.

Consider the matter more specifically. Students who stay in school are generally successful academically, while those who leave often have poor records of scholastic achievement (15, 34, 40, 42, 50, 58, 64, 65, 70, 74, 76, 78, 80, 104, 119, 144, 147, 152, 164, 168, 174, 180, 189, 194, 203, 218, 224, 225, 226, 230, 238, 268, 278, 281, 287, 307, 310, 312, 318, 324, 329, 334). It may be that low motivation causes successive failures, but it seems equally plausible that failure in school causes low motivation.

When one views achievement in relation to ability, the problem takes on even more significance. Many students who quit school have low ability levels and poor achievement records. Students with below average IQ's who get poor marks frequently drop out. Compelling all children to go to school and then providing experiences which guarantee failure for many raises serious moral and philosophical questions. If teachers "fail" students with below-average ability who do not "measure up to standard," is this not something like grading God because he made a child who was unable to learn? This problem will be examined in more detail in Chapter Eight. It may be sufficient to say here that compulsory attendance laws place a definite moral responsibility on teachers to provide educational experiences in which all children can succeed. Forcing youngsters to attend school and then providing an educational diet beyond their ability level is poor teaching.

It is safe to say that one of the causes of low motivation is related to failures, and whether students succeed or fail is more within the jurisdiction of the teacher than the learner—the teacher makes out grades. The old adage to the contrary, students cannot depend on being able to "get just what you earn." There is evidence to indicate that the grades students receive depend more upon where they live (115) or whether their values correspond to their teachers' (121) than how much they learn, however disturbing this notion may be to those who hold the concept of absolute standards.

Another factor frequently cited as characterizing drop-outs is their poor attendance records (40, 50, 64, 70, 74, 76, 78, 80, 164, 170, 203, 212, 216, 224, 238, 278, 281, 312). Looked at objectively, whether students attend school regularly or not is at least partially a school responsibility. Home conditions and economic factors are certainly important. However, the adequacy of attendance workers, reporting procedures, and community relationships are also important.

Even more significant is the effort an individual teacher makes to maintain a classroom atmosphere charged with significant ideas, friendliness and acceptance. Inferring that students who repeatedly miss school do so because they do not enjoy the experience is not unreasonable, considering the record of failure cited earlier. Missing school is evidently an avoidance mechanism, perfectly understandable from the point of view of a child who has been repeatedly subjected to failure experiences. Who wants to enter an intellectual arena day after day where the opportunities for success are limited in many ways? Skipping school is simpler and much more fun. That the absence insures further failure is beside the point. From the learner's point of view, "playing hookey" is better than being told how poor you are, no matter how nice the tone. If teachers think that students should learn to fail because failure is a part of life, why not fail everybody? Why deprive even the highest achiever of a desirable experience if it is really educational?

Without question, many drop-outs dislike school, and some dislike it with a passion (39, 74, 76, 80, 129, 144, 194, 203, 226, 230, 266, 275, 278, 287, 307, 321, 329, 332, 333). This feeling often shows itself in direct resistance to school authorities. Sometimes buildings are mutilated or books destroyed. It is not uncommon for delinquents, rejected by society, to strike back at rejecting social institutions—the school (190, 243). Defacing school property and calling teachers names are obvious reflections of low motivation, and though some youngsters later repent and wish they had finished their education, many others would never go back, whatever the circumstances. Hating school is a learned behavior, and it is clearly learned at school.

Self Concept Affects Motivation

The way students view themselves influences their motivation toward school (38, 41, 97, 117, 143, 160, 167, 197, 208, 259, 270, 305). Overachievers have higher opinions of themselves than underachievers (172), and more frequently have parents who show interest, affection, and pride in their children.

How an individual sees himself and the kinds of values he develops are patterns set early in life (136, 268). In terms of achievement patterns, Bloom states the issue as follows (35):

> We may conclude from our results on general achievement, reading comprehension, and vocabulary development that by age 9 (grade 3) at least 50% of the general achievement pattern at age 18 (grade 12) has been developed, whereas at least 75% of the pat-

tern has been developed by about age 13 (grade 7). The evidence from the Ebert-Simmons (1943) study as well as studies of vocabulary development suggest that about one-third has been developed by the time the individual has entered school.

These patterns are subject to modification in later years, but change then is both slower and more difficult. There is evidence (35) that "school and home environments are most effective in determining the growth of the individual in periods of rapid growth and are least effective in the periods of less rapid growth." These clues suggest that such periods as adolescence present unique opportunities to educators concerned with influencing young people's development.

Studies in changes of the "ideal self" indicate progression from self concepts related to parents through glamorous and attractive young adults to a composite, imaginary self concept, embodying selected characteristics from various sources.

In an interesting cross-cultural study of American, Indian, and Chinese graduate students, Singh and others (273) reported extensive value differences related to early cultural background. Considering the extent to which values influence perception (55, 126, 131, 154, 279, 317), it is hardly surprising that different perceptions of the school arise. Other researches show similar results (26, 264). Sartain (261), for example, reported that values and interest were much more highly related than school marks and interest. A separate study (173), however, reported that attitudes toward school and academic achievement were positively related.

Parental Influence

Home environments help to mold motivations. Waetjen (315), reviewing several studies, observed the varying impact parents had in affecting their children's motivations:

> Fathers of sons with high achievement motivation give more autonomy on the descision-making process, but the reverse is true in the case of mothers. . . . Mothers of high achievement motivated boys express significantly more warmth to their sons than mothers of low achievement boys with low motivation. . . . Fathers of high achievement motivated boys tend to beckon from ahead (independence training) while mothers of these same boys push from behind (achievement training).

Pierce reached this conclusion (236):

It appears from this study and the earlier study that boys achieve best when parents (both fathers and mothers) are less authoritarian, more democratic and affectionate in attitudes toward children and family life. Girls appear to achieve well when mothers are more authoritarian and fathers somewhat cold and strict in attitudes toward children and family life.

These studies all indicate that the forces which cause young people to try to do good work are complex and varied (24, 113, 289). Coming from homes where definite value patterns are instilled often results in particular kinds of motivation toward school (206). Liddle describes this process as follows (186):

> Children growing up in homes and neighborhoods in which middle class values prevail are taught early in life that life is a long series of hurdles to be jumped . . . Many lower class adults, particularly mothers, at least partially share these values, but most of the parents of drop-outs do not. Rather, they teach their children that life is a long series of trying situations to be avoided if possible. It is important to get by, but achievement is neither valued in itself, nor is it seen as the road to a better life.

Working in the same study with Liddle, Bowman (40) reported that "dropouts viewed self, father, and the school as less valuable than did the controls. They also saw self and school as less industrious than did the controls."

Mothers relate to children in different ways (57, 314). Some see their role as doing things to or for the child (83); others are more concerned about the development of the person rather than any specific form of behavior (85). High achievers tend to come from homes in which the parents are approving, affectionate, and less restrictive (160, 172, 219). Children who come from homes of higher socio-economic status have fewer problems of maladjustment (47). When children grow up in a home where one parent is dead and where they tend to receive less recognition and affection from adults, they "compensate for this lack of recognition [by] striving for attention from the opposite sex" (25). Studies of well-adjusted children indicate generally "good" parental relationships prevail (292).

Clearly no single pattern of family living is conducive to generating achievement motivation in young people. Rosen (252) in a study of several hundred boys also concluded that demographic factors such as size of family, ordinal position of boy, mother's age, and occupation-education characteristics of the father "have relevance for the development of achievement motivation, but their effects are complicated, interconnected, and interdependent upon one another, and difficult to assess individually."

Variations Between Sexes

Without doubt, one of the most baffling problems related to motivation centers around the differences between boys and girls. In an effort to identify items which would discriminate between high and low motivated adolescents, this author (102, 103) consistently experienced difficulty because of the way in which young people responded according to sex. In similar manner, Davidson (68) noted in his study of anxious children that many items would differentiate between high and low anxious boys and many others between high and low anxious girls, but not a single item discriminated between the sexes. The forces which operate to cause girls to try to do good work are evidently different from those which cause boys to strive in school.

In a study of achievement motivation of able high school students, Pierce observed a similar discrepancy (236):

> The girls who sought no educational training beyond high school scored highest on achievement motivation, those who sought short term job preparation (e.g., business training, laboratory technician, beauty academy, etc.) scored next highest, and those who actually attended college the first year out of high school scored lowest of all and significantly lower than those seeking no post-high school training.

Bendig (28) experienced similar dissatisfactions with McClelland's need achievement measure.

In a study of 1300 subjects, Bennett and Cohen (29) compared self concepts, motivation, and values of men and women. They concluded:

> Women feel a greater social benevolence, social propriety, personal inadequacy of functioning, greater lack of self-protection, greater personal satisfaction, greater controlled rate. Men feel greater personal capacity, intelligence, imagination, etc. Masculine thinking is oriented more in terms of the self while feminine thinking is oriented more in terms of the environment; masculine thinking shows more desire for personal achievement and accomplishment while female thinking shows more concern for social love and friendship.

In another study Baer (22) reported that girls were consistently rated higher than boys by their teachers on such traits as "attitude toward school regulations" and "dependability," and though it was not reported in the original papers, this author also observed (101, 102, 103) that when teachers were asked to rate students on a motivational scale, about three fourths of those nominated as most highly motivated were generally girls whereas about three fourths of the low-motivated were boys. Other studies report these differences between the sexes, too (1, 2, 5, 23, 84, 88, 135, 139, 191). Whether these differences are real or simply observed is not apparent, but it is reasonable to assume that cultural expectations of males and females differ sufficiently to appear in motivation toward school (234), especially when one considers the fact that most youngsters' elementary years involve almost complete domination by female teachers. Perhaps more basic factors are operating also, however, since variations in basal metabolic rate (316), for instance, appears to be different between the sexes, as well as other factors.

Boys who mature late show drives toward aggression and social acceptance more strongly than boys who mature early (220). Klausmeier reported (165) that although high and low achieving elementary school children had significantly different mental ages, no significant differences were apparent in height, weight, strength, dentition, or carpal age.

The learning conditions which induce motivation toward school for boys must also be different than those for girls. Teachers who would be effective must tailor relationships which foster positive attitudes toward school on the part of each child.

Motivation Among Gifted Students

In a study of gifted youngsters Bishton (32) reported that boys tend to take over the value system of their fathers. Wedemeyer (322) noted that gifted under-achievers frequently had outside employment. Nason (223) compared high and low achieving gifted students and found that high achievers evidenced a distinct pattern of circumstances which included personal and parental expectations for college, specific vocational plans, and that they were personally and socially adjusted. These observations are similar to those reported by Terman (298, 299) almost two decades earlier.

Other studies indicate that special grouping and acceleration seem to spur very able students (158, 159, 176). In a study of high interest and high ability secondary students, however, Lazarus (183) noted that interest was obviously a more powerful determinant of achievement than ability. Other studies of gifted children indicate their preferences for more abstract learning (36). Honors classes (91), frequent testing (89), a "personal factor" resulting in increased communication between teacher and student (213), and opportunity to advance (262) all apparently affect students' achievement.

Thistlethwaite (301) observed that teacher traits causing college students to strive in particular disciplines varied from field to field. Since Stern and Masling (286) reported that teachers' own unconscious motivations for entering teaching range along a continuum from teacher-centered to student-centered, these results might be expected.

Vocational Objectives

Any careful look at young people's interests and expectations indicates that by adolescence boys and girls are already thinking primarily in vocational terms (6, 99, 157, 227, 246, 274, 285, 293, 336). Most young people view school as a means to a vocational end. Even those aspiring to college are chiefly interested in higher education as vocational preparation; few think of it otherwise. More and more young people plan to go to college (63). People choose certain vocations because the job role satisfies personality need patterns (272). Considering the fact that differing personality characteristics are attributed to different occupational groups (67), such a conclusion seems reasonable.

Aspiration Level

There is a relationship between a student's level of aspiration and his success in school (10, 21, 325). Faced with a problem, learners respond differently (94, 95). Those who seek to avoid failure do less well than those who refuse to perceive failure (263). Levels of aspiration also affect problem solving (192).

Many studies report that youngsters who are less well adjusted achieve at lower academic levels than students without personality problems (13, 16, 128, 142, 169, 235, 240). It is important to note, however, that responses to personality tests are evidently affected by social class factors (19), though how this influence reveals itself is hardly clear.

Low achieving students show greater improvement after failing to reach goals set by the teacher, whereas high achieving students show marked improvement after failing to reach goals they set for themselves (327).

The immediate problems involved in striving for grades are often complex. Some students work hard to learn, but many others strive to please their parents, to avoid punishment, to satisfy their teachers' expectations, or sometimes just because they "are told to" (56, 86, 98, 99, 288). Teachers' marks obviously influence students' attitudes toward school

(98, 199, 207, 330, 336), but not always the way teachers hope (175, 336).

Thought Processes

Being attracted toward ideas and learning may be affected by values and social acceptance, but it apparently is also a function of the structure of the intellect itself (125). Burgess noted that good "grade getters" were both more constricted and more cautious (48). Using Guilford's concepts, Getzels and Jackson (110, 111) reported that creative young-sters showed more divergent thinking than high IQ youngsters, and that they achieved as well despite a mean difference in IQ of more than 25 points. Torrance (305) made similar observations.

Related to this power of psychological productivity, Maslow elabo-rated in detail upon the greater perceptual abilities of self-actualizing persons (202):

> In [Cognition of Being] the experience or the object tends to be seen as a whole, as a complete unit, detached from relations, from possible usefulness, from experience, and from purpose. It is seen as if it were all there was in the universe, as if it were all of Being, synonymous with the universe. . . . Where there is B-Cognition, the percept is exclusively and fully attended to. This may be called "total attention". . . . This kind of perception is in sharp contrast to normal perception. Here the object is attended to simultaneously with attention to all else that is relevant. It is seen imbedded in its relationships with everything else in the world, and as part of the world.

Divergent thinking is related to openness. Only those who are most perceptive are able to consider many possible courses of action and create many new solutions. Aronoff's (14) interpretation of Freud's notions about curiosity and problem solving seem severely limited in this kind of framework.

Curiosity is rooted in a fundamental concern with truth (12, 33, 43, 118, 181), and susceptibility of ideas inevitably is associated with willing-ness to change (170, 250, 253, 254, 308). Information must penetrate the inner self, however, if it is to influence human behavior. Lawton and Goldman's study of cigarette smoking and attitudes among scientists toward lung cancer dramatizes this point (182):

> Involvement in lung cancer—smoking research per se, and the more intense opinions that it generates toward the controversy, did

little to modify, or even make one desire to modify, the smoking habit . . . There were a large number of subjects who believe in causation and yet did not quit smoking.

In a similar fashion, dogmatic college freshman tend to have more problems than those who are less dogmatic (162), revealing, perhaps, an inability on the part of closed-minded persons to avail themselves of information essential for problem solving. This is probably also due to more perceptual energy being available (153, 166). Persons who are more authoritarian also express less interest in attending college than persons who are less authoritarian (122).

Sense of Involvement

Being involved in a school's activities affects learner's attitudes (116). Students who are active participants in a college community have higher academic records and score higher on measures of critical thinking than non-participants (328), although participation itself is evidently neither satisfying nor effective for certain types of students (276). Those persons who feel they can exert some influence on big public issues are more alert to national issues and reveal more constructive and differentiated thought about them (79). An individual's personal sense of involvement and worth is reflected in his motivation.

Conversely, students who have unsuccessful experiences in school group up nurturing dislike for education. In a study of juvenile delinquents in Detroit, Wattenberg (320) noted that students who had repeated in school asserted that they got along poorly in school, had trouble with teachers, had trouble with classmates, and considered themselves poor spellers more frequently than those who had not failed. Reviewing other studies Wattenberg (319) also pointed out the problems which a "martinet who rules by fear" creates within the classroom. "Furious children" are beyond the realm of conventional classroom control (267), but most students who dislike school strongly simply leave when the opportunity presents itself (9, 18, 40, 108). Since students' perceptions of school are apparently influenced more by the grades they receive than by the extent of their learning as measured by standardized tests (195), this places a greater burden upon the teacher. Some gifted students feel, in fact, that only extracurricular opportunities offer challenges and satisfactions (81).

High need for achievement may manifest itself in student acceptance of responsibility (231). On the other hand, certain students who are motivated by fear frequently demonstrate avoidance behavior (210), which generally insures poor achievement, thus reinforcing the negative motivations.

Social Relationships

Social acceptance affects achievement (8, 27, 30, 72, 127, 160, 207, 302, 335), and achievement affects social acceptance (49, 137, 237). The way in which an individual views himself affects how he sees other people (59, 85, 177, 178, 283) and his general sense of security (45, 199, 242). Children under authoritarian teachers experience more fear than children under non-authoritarian teachers (245), and fears evoke children's needs for social affiliation (145, 260). Low achievers seek social affiliation (106, 107, 136); their need for acceptance is apparently greater than their need to achieve. They are motivated by a desire for social approval (75, 119, 247).

Under-achievers sometimes demonstrate "better adjustment or more extroverted response than over-achievers" (277). This author observed (98), however, that over-achievers had better "adjustment" scores on the California Test of Personality, and there was a marked tendency for greater dependence among under-achievers as compared to independence among over-achievers. Talented children are also less likely to be maladjusted (185, 289).

Frankel (93) found that under-achievers were more recalcitrant and less conforming than achievers, a conclusion also reached by others (7, 44, 184). Artists and writers known to be both productive and creative also differ from the average in several ways (37, 82). They are both introverted and bold, and often not "pleasant personalities." Drives for power, resentment, and aggression may accompany academic achievement aspirations among college students also (214, 269). Apparently anxiety also plays some part in motivation. Certain degrees of anxiety seem actually to facilitate learning (4, 140, 255); under other circumstances, development is obviously impeded (4, 54, 77, 87, 98, 209, 211, 257, 258); in still other studies no relationships were found (196, 244).

Other Factors

Flanagan's (90) early analysis of the data from almost half a million students tested in Project Talent indicates that for most tests of information 25 to 30 per cent of the 9th graders already exceed the average of the 12th grade students. If one adds the observation that many 9th grade students will probably drop out of school before the 12th grade (and the odds are that those who drop out are not those who will be high achievers), then the differences are reduced still more. In all probability, variations in achievement are far greater within any given grade level than they are between grade levels, even those that are some years apart, e.g., 9th and 12th.

Smith's studies (11) of college admissions practices at the University of Kansas indicate that many students succeed in college who had low entrance scores on the American Council of Education Psychological Examination and a Speed of Reading Examination. He states:

> Two hundred and eight out of one thousand and six graduating seniors in June 1955 were found to be in this lower group. They represented almost every academic discipline and every college or school in the University.

> In passing, it may be mentioned that the School of Fine Arts, of all the divisions, had the highest proportion of graduates (35 per cent) in this lower half while the School of Medicine (11 per cent) and the School of Engineering (16 per cent) had the lowest.

Smith concludes with these observations (11):

> If restrictions for admissions had eliminated all those who scored below the fiftieth percentile of both the A.C.E. and the Speed of Reading Examination, and provided, of course, that these students had not gone elsewhere to school, the loss to the state and to the nation would have been over 1100 individuals in only five graduating classes.

> With estimates included for the graduating classes of 1956 and 1957, the loss to the state and the nation would have been 202 teachers, 176 engineers, 22 journalists, 31 lawyers, 25 medical doctors, 43 pharmacists and 482 graduates of the College of Liberal Arts and Sciences and the School of Business who majored in areas where the supply of trained manpower is in equally short supply.

The desire to succeed in school is a powerful force when it exists. One is reminded of Toynbee's concept of environmental challenge (306), which through the ages has brought out the best in men.

According to Havighurst's notion of developmental tasks (133), there are "teachable moments" within the lives of all persons. These points in time represent that moment when an individual's psychological, physical, and social developments intersect. He is ready to learn. These are the moments which teachers must seek.

Motivation toward school is a complex, learned behavior. Teachers must understand and use to educational advantage this force which is built on values and reflected through cognition. Chapters Six and Seven offer suggestions to achieve these ends.

Appendix A

STUDENT QUESTIONNAIRE

DIRECTIONS

We are trying to find out how students think and feel about a number of important topics. In order to do this, we would like to ask you to answer some questions. This is not an intelligence test nor an information test. There are no "right" or "wrong" answers. The best and only correct answer is YOUR PERSONAL OPINION. Whatever your answer is, there will be many who agree and many who disagree. What we really want to know is HOW YOU FEEL about each statement.

Read each statement very carefully, and then indicate your agreement or disagreement by marking it, according to the following scale, in the appropriate space on the answer blank.

+1 slight support, agreement   −1 slight opposition, disagreement
+2 strong support, agreement   −2 strong opposition, disagreement

Please do not make any marks on the questionnaire booklet itself. You may have as much time as you need, so read each statement very carefully and answer it the best way you can. When you finish close your questionnaire booklet and turn your answer sheet over as a signal that you have finished.

1. Late afternoon is the best time of day.
2. Many children have often been punished without cause.
3. Students should be made to go to school until they are 18 years old.

136

4. Being right is more important than being kind.
*5. School is more fun when teachers let students do things they want to.
*6. Pupils who try should get good grades even if they make mistakes.
*7. Successful people are those who make the most money.
8. The best way to spend a free evening is with a good book.
*9. Most young people do not want to go to school.
*10. Some new ideas are interesting, but most of them are not.
11. Practical people are usually highly respected.
*12. Knowing the answer is more important than knowing where to get the answer.
*13. Many young people feel grouchy.
14. The best people refuse to depend on other persons.
15. Some teachers make school more interesting than others.
*16. A person's feelings on a topic are not as important as the facts.
17. There are more important things in the world than making money.
*18. It does not really help much to study about people from other lands.
19. Life is mostly sorrow with just a little joy.
20. Some students have to study more than others.
*21. Many youngsters often want to run away from home.
22. Being a good speaker is just as important as being a good speller.
*23. Some teachers seem to enjoy making students suffer.
24. Our whole trouble is that we won't let God help us.
25. Most people worry more before they take a test than during the test.
*26. No one seems to understand young people.
27. Learning to cooperate is more important than learning to compete.
*28. Most people would like school better if teachers did not give grades.
*29. The world we live in is a pretty lonesome place.
*30. Social progress can only be achieved by returning to our glorious past.
*31. It is very foolish to advocate government support of education.
32. Most people's hardest battles are with themselves.
*33. There is nothing new under the sun.
34. Helping other people is the key to happiness.
*35. Life seems to be one big struggle after another.
*36. Most people just don't give a "darn" for others.
*37. The best way to achieve security is for the government to guarantee jobs.
38. Some people do not appreciate the value of an education.

39. Most young people feel uncomfortable around someone of the opposite sex.
*40. Many new ideas are not worth the paper they are printed on.
41. Many teachers are not considerate of students' feelings.
42. Teachers are generally underpaid.
43. Being unhealthy is worse than being unhappy.
*44. It is better to forget than to forgive.
45. Pupils who copy during an examination should fail the test.
*46. Young people should be free to follow their own desires.
47. Listening to a good speaker is the best way to learn.
*48. The present is all too often full of unhappiness.
49. Most people just don't know what is good for them.
50. Understanding yourself helps one understand others.
*51. People who dream a lot at night are apt to be crazy.
*52. Familiarity breeds contempt, so one should never be too friendly.
*53. There is a real limit to man's intelligence.
*54. People who are insulted generally deserve to be.
*55. Experience may be a good teacher, but schools are better.
56. Wasting time is even worse than wasting money.
*57. People who are quick thinkers usually jump to conclusions.
*58. Most people do not have good ideas until they grow up.
59. When people are unhappy they should talk to someone about it.
*60. Looking good is just as important as being good.
61. The best part of education is that which people teach themselves.
*62. Famous people usually have a lot of money.
*63. Most people cannot learn from the experience of others.
*64. The dreamer is a danger to society.
*65. Most teachers like to drive students if they have the chance.
66. God helps those who help themselves.
*67. One can never desire too much of a good thing.
*68. Being a liar is better than being a gossip.
*69. Asking questions usually gets you into trouble.
*70. Not many people in the world are really kind.
71. The biggest part of being successful is determination.
*72. Teachers know more and do less than most other people.
*73. Hope is really no better than worry.
*74. School is not all that it's cracked up to be.
*75. Everything that people do is either right or wrong.
*76. Quick thinking is always better than being polite.
77. The gentle person often treats himself severely.
78. Everybody ought to do something worthwhile everyday.
*79. We are never really as happy as we think we are.
*80. All those who fail have worked in vain.

GENERAL INSTRUCTIONS TO TEACHERS

(Please read carefully)

The attached STUDENT QUESTIONNAIRE is the *Junior Index of Motivation* (Jim Scale) for assessing students' motivation toward school. It has been carefully developed from a study of hundreds of adolescents' responses to these particular items. Although there are 80 items, only 50 are scored. These are marked with an asterisk. Be sure *not* to reproduce this asterisk if you mimeograph the instrument yourself. The others are filler items, but should be included.

Although the questionnaire is not timed, it will probably take about 30 minutes for all students to complete the items. DO NOT explain the basic purpose of the test to students; that is, do not make any mention of the fact that this is designed to ascertain their motivation toward school. Explain rather, that *it is an instrument for studying students' attitudes and values.*

In administering the STUDENT QUESTIONNAIRE to your classes, give each student an answer blank and a set of questions. Then, ask each student to fill out the information called for on the answer blank *according to your instructions.*

Read the DIRECTIONS on the front of STUDENT QUESTION-NAIRE aloud, then permit students to complete the questionnaire at their own pace. Encourage each student to answer every question, but do not offer assistance of any kind.

TO SCORE THE PAPERS, PROCEED AS FOLLOWS:

First, prepare a key. Note that all 50 items are scored minus.

Next, add each student's scores for these 50 items algebraically. Then, *REVERSE* the sign (if it is +27, say, change it to −27. If it is −16, then change it to +16), and add this raw score value to +100 algebraically. THIS SCORE IS THE STUDENT'S *CONVERTED* MOTIVATION SCORE. Higher scores indicate higher motivational level. Low scores indicate low motivation level.

REFERENCES

1. Ahlström, Karl-Georg, "Scandanavian Countries: Denmark, Norway, and Sweden," *Review of Educational Research*, XXVII (February, 1957), 119-138.

2. Allen, Robert M. and Satz, Paul, "A Study of the Edwards Personal Preference Schedule: Regional Normative Approach," *Journal of Social Psychology*, LIII (April, 1961), 195-198.
3. Allport, Gordon W., *Becoming* (New Haven: Yale University Press, 1955).
4. Alpert, Richard and Haber, Ralph, "Anxiety in Academic Achievement Situations," *Journal of Abnormal and Social Psychology*, LXI (September, 1960), 207-215.
5. Amatora, Sister Mary, "Comparisons in Personality Self-Evaluation," *Journal of Social Psychology*, XLII (November, 1955), 315-321.
6. Amatora, Sister Mary, "Interests of Pre-Adolescent Boys and Girls," *Genetic Psychology Monographs*, LXI (February, 1960), 77-113.
7. Ames, Viola, "Factors Related to High-School Achievement," *Journal of Educational Psychology*, XXXIV (April, 1943), 229-236.
8. Ames, Viola C., "Socio-Psychological Vectors in the Behavior and Attitudes of Children," *Journal of Educational Psychology*, XXXVI (May, 1945), 271-288.
9. Anderson, Harold A., "Another Study of Drop-Outs," *The School Review*, LVIII (September, 1950), 318-319.
10. Anderson, Kenneth E., "The Relationship of Self-Rating Items on Intellectual Curiosity and Persistence to National Merit Scholarship Test Scores," Unpublished paper read at the American Association for the Advancement of Science meeting, December 29, 1959, Chicago, Illinois.
11. Anderson, Kenneth E., Ed., *The Coming Crisis in the Selection of Students for College Entrance* (Washington, D. C.: American Educational Research Association, 1960).
12. Anderson, William F. Jr., "Attitudes of University Students Toward Cheating," *Journal of Educational Research*, L (April, 1957), 581-588.
13. Arnholter, E. G., "School Persistence and Personality Factors," *The Personnel and Guidance Journal*, XXXV (October, 1956), 107-109.
14. Aronoff, Joel, "Freud's Conception of the Origin of Curiosity," *The Journal of Psychology*, LIV (July, 1962), 39-45.
15. Aronow, Miriam S., "Some Figures on Promotion," *High Points*, XXXV (December, 1953), 5-12.
16. Assum, Arthur L. and Levy, Sidney J., "A Comparative Study of the Academic Ability and Achievement of Two Groups of College Students," *Journal of Educational Psychology*, XXXVIII (1947), 307-310.
17. Atkinson, John W., Ed., *Motives in Fantasy, Action, and Society: A Method of Assessment and Study* (Princeton, New Jersey: Van Nostrand, 1958).
18. Aukerman, Dana W., "A Survey of Dropouts in Shelby County, Ohio, Between 1947-1952," Unpublished Master's Thesis (The Ohio State University, 1953).
19. Auld, Frank Jr., "Influence of Social Class on Personality Tests Responses," *Psychological Bulletin*, XLIX (July, 1952), 318-332.
20. Ausubel, David P., "Prestige Motivation of Gifted Children," *Genetic Psychology Monographs*, XLIV (February, 1951), 53-117.
21. Ausubel, David P.; Schpoont, Seymour H.; and Cukier, Lillian, "The Influence of Intention on the Retention of School Materials," *Journal of Educational Psychology*, XLVIII (February, 1957), 87-92.
22. Baer, Clyde J., "The School Progress and Adjustment of Underage and Overage Students," *Journal of Educational Psychology*, XLIX (February, 1958), 17-19.
23. Barlow, Bruce Marvin, "A Study of the Interests, Study Habits and Attitudes of Eleventh Grade Achieving and Under-Achieving Students," Unpublished Master's Thesis (The Ohio State University, 1960).
24. Barrett, Harry O., "An Intensive Study of Thirty-Two Gifted Children," *Personnel and Guidance Journal*, XXXVI (November, 1957), 192-194.
25. Bartlett, Claude J. and Horrocks, John E., "A Study of the Needs Status of

Adolescents from Broken Homes," *Journal of Genetic Psychology*, XCIII (September, 1958), 153-159.

26. Bateman, Mildred M. and Jensen, Joseph S., "The Effect of Religious Background on Modes of Handling Anger," *Journal of Social Psychology*, XLVII (February, 1958), 133-141.

27. Beach, Leslie R., "Variation of Whole-Part Methods of Learning," *Journal of Educational Psychology*, LI (August, 1960), 213-216.

28. Bendig, A. W., "Comparative Validity of Objective and Projective Measures of Need Achievement in Predicting Students' Achievement in Introductory Psychology," *Journal of General Psychology*, LX (April, 1959), 237-243.

29. Bennett, Edward M. and Cohen, Larry R., "Men and Women: Personality Patterns and Contrasts," *Journal of General Psychology*, LIX (February, 1959), 101-155.

30. Berkowitz, Leonard and Levy, Bernard I., "Pride in Group Performance and Group-Task Motivation," *Journal of Abnormal and Social Psychology*, LIII (November, 1956), 300-306.

31. Berkowitz, Leonard; Levy, Bernard I; and Harvey, Arthur R., "Effects of Performance Evaluations on Group Integration and Motivation," *Human Relations*, X (August, 1957), 195-208.

32. Bishton, Rodger, "A Study of Some Factors Related to Achievement of Intellectually Superior Eighth Grade Children," *Journal of Educational Research*, LI (November, 1957), 203-207.

33. Blanchard, William H., "Intellectual Inhibition and the Search for Scientific Truth," *Journal of Social Psychology*, XLVII (February, 1958), 55-70.

34. Bledsoe, Joseph C., "An Investigation of Six Correlates of Student Withdrawal from High School," *Journal of Educational Research*, LIII (September, 1959), 3-6.

35. Bloom, Benjamin, *Stability and Change in Human Characteristics* (New York: John Wiley and Sons, 1964).

36. Bonsall, Marcella R., "Introspections of Gifted Children," *California Journal of Educational Research*, XI (September, 1960), 159-166.

37. Borg, Walter R., "Personality Characteristics of a Group of College Art Students," *Journal of Educational Psychology*, XLIII (March, 1952), 149-156.

38. Borgatta, Edgar F., "Rankings and Self-Assessments: Some Behavioral Characteristics Replication Studies," *Journal of Social Psychology*, LII (November, 1960), 279-307.

39. Bowman, Paul H., "Effects of a Revised School Program on Potential Delinquents," *The Annals of the American Academy of Political and Social Science*, CCCXXII (March, 1959), 53-61.

40. Bowman, Paul H. and Matthews, Charles V., "Motivations of Youth for Leaving School," *Cooperative Research Program*, OE-24004, Project No. 200, United States Department of Health, Education, and Welfare, Office of Education.

41. Brim, Orville G., "College Grade and Self-Estimates of Intelligence," *Journal of Educational Psychology*, XLV (December, 1954), 477-484.

42. Broggan, Earl J., "What Are the Major Causes of Student Drop-Outs and What Should the School Do About the Present Condition?" *National Association of Secondary School Principals Bulletin*, XXXIX (April, 1955), 84-85.

43. Bronowski, Jacob, "The Values of Science," in *New Knowledge in Human Values*, A. H. Maslow, Ed. (New York: Harper and Bros., 1959).

44. Brown, William F.; Abels, Norman; and Iscoe, Ira, "Motivational Differences Between High and Low Scholarship College Students," *Journal of Educational Psychology*, XLV (April, 1954), 215-223.

45. Bruce, Paul, "Relationship of Self-Acceptance to Other Variables with Sixth Grade Children Oriented in Self-Understanding," *Journal of Educational Psychology*, XLIX (October, 1958), 229-237.

46. Bunch, Marion E., "The Concept of Motivation," *Journal of General Psychology*, LVIII (April, 1958), 189-206.
47. Burchinal, Lee; Gardner, Bruce; and Hawkes, Glenn R., "Children's Personality Adjustment and the Socio-Economic Status of Their Families," *Journal of Genetic Psychology*, XCII (June, 1958), 149-159.
48. Burgess, Elva, "Personality Factors of Over and Under-Achievers in Engineering," *Journal of Educational Psychology*, XLVII (February, 1956), 89-99.
49. Buswell, Margaret M., "The Relationship Between Social Structure of the Classroom and the Academic Success of the Pupils," *Journal of Experimental Education*, XXII (September, 1953), 37-52.
50. Caravello, S. J., "The Drop-Out Problems," *The High School Journal* (May, 1958), 335-340.
51. Carlson, Theodora, "More Years in School," *School Life*, XXXIX (April, 1957), 13.
52. Castaneda, Alfred; Palermo, David S.; and McCandless, Boyd R., "Complex Learning and Performance as a Function of Anxiety in Children and Task Difficulty," *Child Development*, XXVII (September, 1956), 327-332.
53. Cattell, Raymond B., *Personality and Motivation Structure and Measurement* (New York: World Book Co., 1957).
54. Cattell, Raymond B. and Baggaley, A. R., "The Objective Measurement of Attitude Motivation: Development and Evaluation of Principles and Devices," *Journal of Personality*, XXIV (June, 1956), 401-423.
55. Chodorkoff, Bernard and Chodorkoff, Joan, "Perceptual Defense: an Integration with Other Research Findings," *Journal of General Psychology*, LVIII (January, 1958), 75-80.
56. Clark, Russel A.; Teevan, Richard; and Ricciuti, Henry N., "Hope of Success and Fear of Failure as Aspects of Need for Achievement," *Journal of Abnormal and Social Psychology*, LIII (September, 1956), 182-186.
57. Clark, Walter Houston, "A Study of Some of the Factors Leading to Achievement and Creativity with Special Reference to Religious Skepticism and Belief," *Journal of Social Psychology*, XLI (February, 1955), 57-69.
58. Coffield, William H. and Blommers, Paul, "Effects of Non-Promotion on Educational Achievement in the Elementary School," *Journal of Educational Psychology*, XLVII (April, 1956), 235-250.
59. Coleman, James S., *The Adolescent Society* (New York, The Free Press of Glencoe, 1961).
60. Combs, Arthur W. and Snygg, Donald, *Individual Behavior: A Perceptual Approach* (New York: Harper and Bros., 1959).
61. Conant, James B., Ed., *Case Histories in Experimental Science*, Vol. 2. (Cambridge: Harvard University Press, 1957).
62. Condon, Margaret E., "Drop Out Study of Disabled Students," *Personnel and Guidance Journal*, XXXVII (April, 1959), 598-608.
63. Conference Board, "Road Maps of Industry," No. 1274, May 27, 1960.
64. Cook, Edward S. Jr., "An Analysis of Factors Related to Withdrawal from High School Prior to Graduation," *Journal of Educational Research*, L (November, 1956), 191-196.
65. Cumings, Edgar C., "Causes of Student Withdrawals at DePauw University," *School and Society*, LXX (September 3, 1949), 152-153.
66. Dale, Thomas W., "A Study of the Drop Out of the Columbus, Ohio, Public Schools: Data Derived from the Original Members of the Graduating Class of 1955," Unpublished Master's Thesis (The Ohio State University, 1955).
67. Davidson, Helen H; Riessman, Frank; and Meyers, Edna, "Personality Characteristics Attributed to the Worker," *Journal of Social Psychology*, LVII (June, 1962), 155-160.
68. Davidson, Kenneth et al., "Differences Between Mothers' and Fathers' Ratings

of Low Anxious and High Anxious Children," *Child Development*, XXIX (March, 1958), 155.

69. Davis, Donald A., "An Experimental Study of Potential Dropouts," *The Personnel and Guidance Journal*, XL (May, 1962), 799-802.
70. Delaney, John F., "That Vacant High School Seat," *American School Board Journal*, CXXI (November, 1950), 22-23.
71. DeCharms, Richard, "A Self-Scored Projective Measure of Achievement and Affiliation Motivation," *Journal of Consulting Psychology*, XXII (June, 1958), 172.
72. Deutsch, Morton, "Some Factors Affecting Membership Motivation and Achievement Motivation in a Group," *Human Relations*, XII (February, 1959), 81-95.
73. Dewey, John, *Experience and Education* (New York: Macmillan Co., 1938).
74. Dillon, Harold J., *Early School Leavers, A Major Educational Problem* (New York: National Child Labor Committee, 1949).
75. DiVesta, Francis J. and Cox, Landon, "Some Dispositional Correlates of Conformity Behavior," *Journal of Social Psychology*, LII (November, 1960), 259-268.
76. Dodds, Lafayette II, "A Profile of the Drop-Out Students at West Junior-Senior High School During the School Year 1959-60," Unpublished Master's Thesis (The Ohio State University, 1961).
77. Doris, John, "Test Anxiety and Blame-Assignment in Grade School Children," *Journal of Abnormal and Social Psychology*, LVIII (March, 1959), 181-190.
78. Doron, Warren, "Who Are Most Likely to Drop Out of High School?" *School Science and Mathematics*, LIV (March, 1954), 185.
79. Douvan, Elizabeth, "The Sense of Effectiveness and Response to Public Issues," *Journal of Social Psychology*, XLVII (February, 1958), 111-126.
80. Dresher, Richard H., "Factors in Voluntary Drop Outs," *Personnel and Guidance Journal*, XXXII (January, 1954), 287-289.
81. Dressel, Paul L. and Grabow, John M., "The Gifted Evaluate Their High School Experience," *Exceptional Children*, XXIV (May, 1958), 394-396.
82. Drevdahl, John E. and Cattell, Raymond B., "Personality and Creativity in Artists and Writers," *Journal of Clinical Psychology*, XIV (April, 1958), 107-111.
83. Drews, Elizabeth M. and Teahan, John E., "Parental Attitudes and Academic Achievement," *Journal of Clinical Psychology*, XIII (October, 1957), 328-331.
84. Durflinger, Glenn W., "The Prediction of College Success—A Summary of Recent Findings," *College and University Journal*, XIX (October, 1943), 68-78.
85. Duvall, Evelyn M., "Conceptions of Parenthood," *American Journal of Sociology*, (November, 1946), 193-203.
86. Ericksen, Stanford C., "An Experimental Study of Individual Differences in Scholastic Motives," *Journal of Educational Psychology*, XXXI (October, 1940), 507-516.
87. Farber, I. E. and Spence, Kenneth W., "Complex Learning and Conditioning as a Function of Anxiety," *Journal of Experimental Psychology*, XLV (1953), 120.
88. Fenton, Norman, "Problem Children and Delinquents," *Encyclopedia of Educational Research*, Walter S. Monroe, Ed. (New York: Macmillan Co., 1952), 868-874.
89. Fitch, Mildred I. et al., "Frequent Testing as a Motivating Factor in Large Lecture Classes," *Journal of Educational Psychology*, XLII (January, 1951), 1-19.
90. Flanagan, John C., "Project Talent: Preliminary Findings," Paper prepared for presentation at the annual meetings of the AERA and AASA, Atlantic City, New Jersey, February 20, 1962. Mimeographed.

91. Fliedner, L. J., "A Comparison of the Achievement of an Honor School Class and a Regular Class in Chemistry," *High Points*, XXVIII (November, 1946), 67-70.

92. Foshay, Arthur W. and Wann, Kenneth D., *Children's Social Values: An Action Research Study* (New York: Horace Mann-Lincoln Institute of School Experimentation, Columbia University, 1954), 323.

93. Frankel, Edward, "A Comparative Study of Achieving and Underachieving High School Boys of High Intellectual Ability," *Journal of Educational Research*, LIII (January, 1960), 172-180.

94. French, Elizabeth G., "The Interaction of Achievement Motivation and Ability in Problem-Solving Success," *Journal of Abnormal and Social Psychology*, LVII (November, 1958), 306-309.

95. French, Elizabeth G. and Thomas, Francis H., "The Relation of Achievement Motivation to Problem Solving Effectiveness," *Journal of Abnormal and Social Psychology*, LVI (January, 1958), 45-48.

96. Frenkel-Brunswik, E., "Motivation and Behavior," *Genetic Psychology Monographs*, XXVI (1942), 121-265.

97. Frymier, Jack R. et al., "A Case Study of Achievement," *Educational Leadership*, XVII (November, 1959), 119-122.

98. Frymier, Jack R., "A Study of Certain Factors Related to Motivation and Achievement Among Fifth Grade Students," Paper prepared for presentation at the annual meeting of the AERA in Atlantic City, New Jersey, February 21, 1962.

99. Frymier, Jack R., "A Study of Students' Motivations to Do Good Work in School," *Journal of Educational Research*, LVII (January, 1964), 239-244.

100. Frymier, Jack R., "Assessing Junior High School Students' Motivation," *The High School Journal*, XLV (April, 1962), 302-305.

101. Frymier, Jack R., "The Development and Validation of a Motivation Index: A Progress Report," Paper prepared for presentation at the annual meeting of the AERA in Chicago, Illinois, February, 1961. Mimeographed.

102. Frymier, Jack R., "The Development and Validation of a Motivation Index: A Further Report," Unpublished paper (The Ohio State University, Columbus, Ohio). Mimeographed.

103. Frymier, Jack R., "The Development and Validation of a Motivation Index: A Third Report," Unpublished paper (The Ohio State University, Columbus, Ohio). Mimeographed.

104. Gaumnitz, Walter H. and Tomkins, Ellsworth, *Holding Power and the Size of the High School* (Washington, D. C.: Federal Security Agency, U. S. Office of Education, 1950).

105. Gaumnitz, Walter H., "High School Retention by States" (Washington, D. C.: U. S. Office of Education, Circular No 398, June, 1954).

106. Gebhart, Gary G. and Hoyt, Donald P., "Personality Needs of Under- and Over-Achieving Freshmen," *Journal of Applied Psychology*, XLII (1958), 125-128.

107. Geberich, J. R., "Factors Related to the College Achievement of High Aptitude Students Who Fail of Expectations and Low Aptitude Students Who Exceed Expectations," *Journal of Educational Psychology*, XXXII (April, 1941), 253-265.

108. Gekoski, Norman and Schwartz, Soloman, "Student Mortality and Related Factors," *Journal of Educational Research*, LIV (January, 1961), 192-194.

109. Getzels, J. W., "Social Values and Individual Motives: The Dilemma of the Gifted," *The School Review*, LXV (Spring, 1957), 60-63.

110. Getzels, J. W. and Jackson, P. W., "The Highly Intelligent and the Highly Creative Adolescent: A Summary of Some Research Findings," Unpublished paper read at the University of Utah Conference on Creativity, June 11, 1959.

111. Getzels, J. W. and Jackson, P. W., *Creativity and Intelligence: Explorations with Gifted Students* (New York: John Wiley and Sons, Inc. 1962).
112. Goldberg, Miriam L., "Motivation of the Gifted," in *Education for the Gifted*, 1957 Yearbook, Part II (Chicago: National Society for the Study of Education), 87-107.
113. Goldberg, Miriam, "Studies in Underachievement Among Academically Talented," in *Freeing Capacity to Learn*, Alexander Frazier, Ed. (Washington: Association for Supervision and Curriculum Development, 1960).
114. Goode, William J. and Fowler, Irving, "Incentive Factors in a Low Morale Plant," *American Sociological Review*, XIV (October, 1949), 618-624.
115. Goodlad, John I., "Some Effects of Promotion and Non-Promotion upon the Social and Personal Adjustment of Children," *Journal of Experimental Education*, XXII (June, 1954), 301-328.
116. Gough, Harrison G., "Predicting Social Participation," *Journal of Social Psychology*, XXXV (May, 1952), 227-233.
117. Gough, Harrison G., "What Determines the Academic Achievement of High School Students," *Journal of Educational Research*, XLVI (January, 1953), 321-331.
118. Gould, John, "Lazy Journalism," *The Atlantic Monthly*, CXCIX (June, 1957), 51-54.
119. Gragg, William L., "Some Factors Which Distinguish Drop-Outs from High School Graduates," *Occupations*, XXVII (1959), 457-459.
120. Gragg, William, "Utilization of Census Data in Statistical Analysis of School Drop-Out Problems," *Journal of Experimental Education*, XVIII (December, 1949), 147-151.
121. Gragg, William L., "Findings in Ithaca's Continuous Survey of Drop-Outs," *Clearing House*, XXVI (March, 1952), 413-414.
122. Greenberg, H.; Marvin, C.; and Bivins, B., "Authoritarianism as a Variable in Motivation to Attend College," *Journal of Social Psychology*, XLIX (February, 1959), 81-85.
123. Greenberg, Paul and Gilliland, A. R., "The Relationship Between Basal Metabolism and Personality," *Journal of Social Psychology*, XXXV (February, 1952), 3-7.
124. Gruhn, William T. and Douglass, Harl R., *The Modern Junior High School* (New York: The Ronald Press Co., 1956).
125. Guilford, Joy P., "The Structure of Intellect," *Psychological Bulletin*, LIII (July, 1956), 267-293.
126. Haigh, G. V. and Fiske, D. W., "Corroboration of Personal Values as Selective Factors in Perception," *Journal of Abnormal and Social Psychology*, XLVII (1952), 394-398.
127. Hall, William E. and Gaeddert, Willard, "Social Skills and Their Relationship to Scholastic Achievement," *Journal of Genetic Psychology*, XCVI (June, 1960), 269-273.
128. Hancock, John W. and Carter, Gerald C., "Student Personality Traits and Curriculae of Enrollment," *Journal of Educational Research*, XLVIII (November, 1954), 225-227.
129. Hanthorn, J. N., "A Study of Major Causes for Quitting High School," *School and Community*, XXX (October, 1944), 272-273.
130. Harris, Dale B., "How Children Learn Interests, Motives, and Attitudes," in *Learning and Instruction*, 49th Yearbook, National Society for the Study of Education, Part I (Chicago: University of Chicago Press), 129-155.
131. Hastorf, A. H. and Cantrill, H., "They Saw a Game: A Case Study," *Journal of Abnormal and Social Psychology*, XLIX (1954), 129-134.
132. Havighurst, R. J.; Robinson, Myra Z. and Dorr, Mildred, "The Development of the Ideal Self in Childhood and Adolescence," *Journal of Educational Research*, XL (December, 1964), 241-257.

133. Havighurst, Robert J., *Developmental Tasks and Education* (New York: Longmans, Green and Co., 1952).
134. Havighurst, R. J. and MacDonald, D. V., "Development of the Ideal Self in New Zealand and American Children," *Journal of Educational Research*, XLIX (December, 1955), 263-273.
135. Havighurst, R. J. et al., *Growing Up in River City* (New York: John Wiley and Sons, 1962).
136. Hawkes, Glenn R., "Use of the Minnesota Multiphasic Personality Inventory in Screening College Students for Counseling Purposes," *Journal of Educational Psychology*, XLI (1950), 116-121.
137. Heber, Rick F. and Heber, Mary E., "The Effects of Group Failure and Success on Social Status," *Journal of Educational Psychology*, XLVIII (March, 1957), 129-134.
138. Heck, Arch O., "Pupil Personnel Work—II. School Attendance," *Encyclopedia of Educational Research*, Walter S. Monroe, Ed. (New York: Macmillan Co., 1952), 915-923.
139. Hicks, J. Allen and Hayes, Margaret, "Study of the Characteristics of 250 Junior High School Children," *Child Development*, IX (1938), 219-242.
140. Hieronymus, A. N., "A Study of Social Class Motivation: The Relationship Between Anxiety for Education and Certain Socio-Economic and Intellectual Variables," *Journal of Educational Psychology*, XLII (1951), 193-205.
141. Hills, John R., "Needs for Achievement, Aspirations, and College Criteria," *Journal of Educational Psychology*, XLIX (June, 1958), 156-161.
142. Hinkelman, Arthur Emmet, "Relation of Certain Personality Variables to High-School Achievement," *The School Review*, LX (1952), 532-534.
143. Hochbaum, Godfrey M., "The Relation Between Group Members' Self-Confidence and Their Reactions to Group Pressures to Uniformity," *American Sociological Review*, XIX (December, 1954), 678-687.
144. Holbeck, Elmer S., "Seven Ways to Help Prevent Drop-Outs," *Nation's Schools*, XLV (September, 1950), 16-33.
145. Holder, Wayne B., "Value Conformity in Normal and Non-Normal Groups," *Journal of Social Psychology*, XLVIII (August, 1958), 147-153.
146. Hollingworth, Leta S. and Cobb, Margaret V., "Children Clustering at 165 IQ and Children Clustering at 146 IQ Compared for Three Years in Achievement," 27th Yearbook, Part II, National Society for the Study of Education, 1928, 3-33.
147. Holmes, Darrell, "An Investigation of Student Attitudes Which May Be Related to Leaving College," *Journal of Educational Research*, LII (September,1958), 17-21.
148. Holtzman, Wayne H., "Adjustment and Leadership: A Study of the Rorschach Test," *Journal of Social Psychology*, XXXVI (November, 1952), 179-189.
149. Hopkins, Wilbur Allen, "A Survey of Student Reactions to the Columbus Evening High School Program, Reasons for Drop outs, and Interest in an Upward Extension of Public Secondary Education," Unpublished Master's Thesis (The Ohio State University, Columbus, 1958).
150. Hoyt, Jean S. and Blackmore, Dorthy S., "Fifty Seventh Graders: A Comparison of Their Reading Achievement and Expected Achievement in Grades One Through Seven," *Journal of Educational Research*, LIII (January, 1960), 163-171.
151. Hurley, John R., "Achievement Imagery and Motivational Instruction as Determinants of Verbal Learning," *Journal of Personality*, XXV (March, 1957), 274-282.
152. Iffert, Robert, *Retention and Withdrawal of College Students* (Washington, D. C.: U. S. Office of Education, 1958).
153. Jackson, Douglas N., "Cognitive Energy Level, Acquiescence, and Authoritarianism," *Journal of Social Psychology*, XLIX (February, 1959), 65-69.

154. Jenkin, Noël, "Affective Processes in Perception," *Psychological Bulletin*, LIV (March, 1957), 100-127.
155. Johnson, Elizabeth S. and Legg, Caroline E., "Why Young People Leave School," *National Association of Secondary School Principals Bulletin*, XXXII (November, 1948), 14-24.
156. Johnson, William H., "Reducing Failure in High School Subjects," *American School Board Journal*, CI (October, 1940), 23-28.
157. Jones, Mary Cover, "A Comparison of the Attitudes and Interests of Ninth-Grade Students over Two Decades," *Journal of Educational Psychology*, LI (August, 1960), 175-186.
158. Justman, Joseph, "Academic Achievement of Intellectually Gifted Accelerants and Non-Accelerants in Junior High School," *The School Review*, LXII (March, 1954), 142-150.
159. Justman, Joseph, "Academic Achievement of Intellectually Gifted Accelerants and Non-Accelerants in Senior High School," *The School Review*, LXII (November, 1954), 469-473.
160. Karnes, Merle B. et al., *Factors Associated with Underachievement and Overachievement of Intellectually Gifted Children* (Champaign, Illinois: Champaign Community Unit Schools, July, 1961). Mimeographed.
161. Kelley, Earl C., "Communication and the Open Self," *Etc.: Review of General Semantics*, XI (Winter, 1954), 96-100.
162. Kemp, C. Gratton, "Influence of Dogmatism on Counseling," *Personnel and Guidance Journal*, XXXIX (April, 1961), 662-665.
163. Kenkel, William F., "Dominance, Persistence, Self-Confidence, and Spousal Roles in Decision Making," *Journal of Social Psychology*, LIV (August, 1961), 349-358.
164. Kirkland, Lee A., "A Study of the Early School Leavers in Mechanicsburg, Ohio, Exempted Village, 1949-1953 and the City of Urbana and Champaign County, 1952-1953, Grades 7-12," Unpublished Master's Thesis (The Ohio State University, 1954).
165. Klausmeier, Herbert J., "Physical, Behavioral, and Other Characteristics of High- and Lower-Achieving Children in Favored Environments," *Journal of Educational Research*, LI (April, 1958), 573-581.
166. Knapp, Robert H. and Green, Helen B., "The Judgment of Music-Filled Intervals and Achievement," *Journal of Social Psychology*, LIV (August, 1961), 263-267.
167. Knutson, Andie L., "The Concept of Personal Security," *Journal of Social Psychology*, XL (November, 1954), 219-236.
168. Koelsche, Charles L., "A Study of the Student Drop-Out Problem at Indiana University," *Journal of Educational Research*, XLIX (January, 1956), 357-364.
169. Kooker, E., "An Investigation of Security, Insecurity, Achievement, and Boredom in Elementary School Children," Unpublished Doctoral Dissertation (Iowa State University, 1951).
170. Kruglov, Lorraine P. and Davidson, Helen H., "The Willingness to Be Interviewed: A Selective Factor in Sampling," *Journal of Social Psychology*, XXVIII (August, 1953), 39-47.
171. Kuenzli, Alfred E., *The Phenomenological Problem* (New York: Harper and Bros., 1959).
172. Kurtz, John J. and Swenson, Esther J., "Factors Related to Over-Achievement and Under-Achievement in School," *The School Review*, LIX (November, 1951), 472-480.
173. Kurtz, John J. and Swenson, Esther J., "Student, Parent, and Teacher Attitude Toward Student Achievement in School," *The School Review*, LIX (May, 1951), 273-279.
174. Lafferty, H. M., "The Reasons for Pupil Failure; A Progress Report," *School Board Journal*, CXVII (July, 1948), 18-20.

175. Lambert, Philip, "Interaction Between Authoritarian and Non-authoritarian Principals and Teachers," *Genetic Psychology Monographs*, LVIII (November, 1958), 163-205.
176. Lamson, Edna Emma, *A Study of Young Gifted Children in Senior High School*. Contributions to Education, No. 424 (New York: Bureau of Publications, Teachers College, Columbia University, 1930).
177. Landfield, Alvin W., "A Movement Interpretation of Threat," *Journal of Abnormal and Social Psychology*, XLIX (October, 1954), 529-532.
178. Landfield, Alvin W., "Self-Predictive Orientation and the Movement Interpretation of Threat," *Journal of Abnormal and Social Psychology*, LI (November, 1955), 434-438.
179. Lang, Gerhard, "An Experimental Scale to Measure Motives for Teaching," *Journal of Educational Research*, LI (March, 1958), 687-693.
180. Lanier, Armand J., "A Guidance-Faculty Study of Student Withdrawals," *Journal of Educational Research*, XLII (November, 1949), 205-212.
181. Lawson, Douglas E., "Truth, Values, and the Scientific Attitude," *The Educational Forum*, XXIV (November, 1959), 85-93.
182. Lawton, M. Powell and Goldman, Alfred E., "Cigarette Smoking and Attitude Toward the Etiology of Lung Cancer," *Journal of Social Psychology*, LIV (August, 1961), 235-248.
183. Lazarus, Arnold L., "Grouping Based on High Interest Vs. General Ability: A Senor High School Teacher's View-Point," *California Journal of Secondary Education*, XXX (January, 1955), 38-41.
184. Leipold, L. E., "Who Are Our Good Students?" *Journal of Educational Research*, XXXVIII (March, 1945), 529-533.
185. Liddle, Gordon, "Overlap Among Desirable and Undesirable Characteristics in Gifted Children," *Journal of Educational Psychology*, XLIX (August, 1958), 219-223.
186. Liddle, Gordon P., "Psychological Factors Involved in Dropping Out of School," *The High School Journal*, XLV (April, 1962), 276-280.
187. Liddle, Gordon, "The California Psychological Inventory and Certain Social and Personal Factors," *Journal of Educational Psychology*, XLIX (1958), 144.
188. Lindzey, Gardner, Ed., *Assessment of Human Motives* (New York: Rinehart and Co., 1958).
189. Livingston, A. Hugh, "High School Graduates and Drop Outs; A New Look at a Persistent Problem," *The School Review*, LXVI (June, 1958), 195-203.
190. Lohman, Joseph D., "A Sociologist-Sheriff Speaks Out About Juvenile Delinquency," *Phi Delta Kappan*, XXXIX (February, 1958), 206-214.
191. Long, Louis and Perry, James D., "Mortality Study of College Students," *School and Society*, LXXVII (February, 1953), 103-105.
192. Lorge, Irving and Solomon, Herbert, "Group and Individual Performance in Problem Solving Related to Previous Exposure to Problem, Level of Aspiration, and Group Size," *Behavioral Science*, V (January, 1960), 28-38.
193. Lynch, William W. Jr., *An Approach to the Study of Motivational Problems in Education* (Bloomington: School of Education, Indiana University, 1955).
194. Mack, A. Russell, "A Study of Drop Outs," *National Association of Secondary School Principals Bulletin*, XXXVIII (February, 1954), 49-51.
195. Malpass, Leslie, "Some Relationships Between Students' Perceptions of School and Their Achievement," *Journal of Educational Psychology*, XLIV (December, 1953), 475-482.
196. Martin, Barclay, "The Measurement of Anxiety," *Journal of General Psychology*, LXI (October, 1959), 189-203.
197. Martire, John G., "Relationships Between the Self Concept and Differences in Strength and Generality of Achievement Motivation," *Journal of Personality*, XXIV (June, 1956), 364-375.

198. Marx, Melvin A., "Motivation" in *The Encyclopedia of Educational Research,* Chester W. Harris, Ed. (New York: The Macmillan Co., 1960), 895.
199. Maslow, A. H.; Hirsh, Elisa; Stean, Marcella; and Honigmann, Irma, "A Clinically Derived Test for Measuring Psychological Security-Insecurity," *Journal of General Psychology,* XXXII (1945), 21-41.
200. Maslow, A. H., *Motivation and Personality* (New York: Harper and Bros., 1954).
201. Maslow, Abraham H., "Deficiency Motivation and Growth Motivation," *Nebraska Symposium on Motivation, 1955,* Marshall R. Jones, Ed. (Lincoln: University of Nebraska Press, 1955), 1-30.
202. Maslow, A. H., "Cognition of Being in the Peak Experiences," *Journal of Genetic Psychology,* XCIV (March, 1959), 43-66.
203. Masys, Paul John, "A Study of Student Dropouts from Linden McKinley Junior-Senior High School, Columbus, Ohio, 1954-1956," Unpublished Master's Thesis (The Ohio State University, 1956).
204. McClelland, David C. et al., *The Achievement Motive* (New York: Appleton Century Crofts, Inc., 1953).
205. McClelland, David C., Ed., *Studies in Motivation* (New York: Appleton Century Crofts, Inc., 1955).
206. McClelland, David C. et al., *Talent and Society; New Perspectives in the Identification of Talent* (Princeton, N. J.: D. Van Nostrand Co., 1958).
207. McDavid, John Jr., "Some Relationships Between Social Reinforcement and Scholastic Achievement," *Journal of Consulting Psychology,* XXIII (April, 1959), 151-154.
208. McGee, Roger, "A Comparison of 26 'Troublemakers' with 26 'Good School Citizens,'" Unpublished study (The Ohio State University, 1962).
209. McKeachie, Wilbert J. et al., "Relieving Anxiety in Classroom Examinations," *Journal of Abnormal and Social Psychology,* L (January, 1955), 93-98.
210. McKeachie, Wilbert J., "What Do the Research Findings from Behavioral Sciences Suggest by Way of the Improvement of Teaching and Learning?" Paper presented at the Fifteenth National Conference on Higher Education, Chicago, March 8, 1960. Mimeographed.
211. McKeachie, W. J., "Motivation, Teaching Methods and College Learning," in *Nebraska Symposium on Motivation,* Marshall R. Jones, Ed. (Lincoln: University of Nebraska Press, 1961), 111-142.
212. McKinney, Donovan Ewing, "A Study of the Early School Leavers from the Public School of Putnam County, Ohio, in Grades Seven Through Twelve for the School Year 1951-1952," Unpublished Master's Thesis (The Ohio State University, 1952).
213. McVitty, Lawrence F., "An Experimental Study on Various Methods in Art Motivations at the Fifth Grade Level," *Research in Art Education,* NAEA 7th Yearbook, 1956, 74-82.
214. Middleton, George, Jr., and Guthrie, George M., "Personality Syndromes and Academic Achievement," *Journal of Educational Psychology,* L (April, 1957), 66-70.
215. Miller, Joseph, "Causes of Failure and Success in Schools I," *Educational Method,* X (March, 1931), 327-333.
216. Miller, Joseph, "Causes of Failure and Success in School II," *Educational Method,* XII (March, 1933), 364-366.
217. Miller, Lebern N., "Using Law Case Materials to Teach Ethical Behavior," *Journal of Educational Research,* LI (September, 1957), 349-354.
218. Miller, Leonard M., "How Can a School Increase its Holding Power of Youth?" *National Association of Secondary Principals Bulletin,* XXXVI (March, 1952), 117-125.
219. Morrow, William R. and Wilson, Robert C., "Family Relations of Bright

High-Achieving and Under-Achieving High School Boys," *Child Development*, XXXII (September, 1961), 501-510.
220. Mussen, Paul Henry and Jones, Mary Cover, "The Behavior-Inferred Motivations of Late- and Early-Maturing Boys," *Child Development*, XXIX (March, 1958), 61-67.
221. Murphy, Gardner, *Personality: A Biosocial Approach to Origins and Structure* (New York: Harper and Bros., 1947).
222. Murphy, Gardner, *Human Potentialities* (New York: Basic Books, 1958).
223. Nason, Leslie J., *Academic Achievement of Gifted High School Students* (Los Angeles: University of Southern California Press, 1958).
224. *NEA Research Bulletin*, "High School Dropouts," February, 1960, 11-14.
225. NEA Research Division, "Pupil Failure and Nonpromotion," February, 1959. Mimeographed.
226. NEA Research Division, "School Drop-Outs," August, 1961. Mimeographed.
227. Novak, Daniel F., "A Comparison of Delinquent and Nondelinquent Vocational Interests," *Exceptional Children*, XXVIII (September, 1961), 63-66.
228. Owens, William A. and Johnson, Wilma C., "Some Measured Personality Traits of Collegiate Underachievers," *Journal of Educational Psychology*, XL (January, 1949), 41-46.
229. Park, Joe "How They Thought They Were Motivated," *Journal of Educational Research*, XXXIX (November, 1945), 193-200.
230. Patterson, Walter G., "Reasons for Dropping Out of Drury High School," *National Association of Secondary School Principals Bulletin*, XXXIX (April, 1955), 85-88.
231. Patton, Joseph A., "A Study of the Effects of Student Acceptance of Responsibility and Motivation on Course Behavior," Doctor's Thesis (Ann Arbor: University of Michigan, 1955). Reported by McKeachie, Wilbert J. in "Students, Groups, and Teaching Methods." *American Psychologist*, XIII (September, 1958), 580-584.
232. Pausch, Ruth W., "Determining the Probable Causes of Drop-Outs in a Rural School," Unpublished Master's Thesis (The Ohio State University, 1961).
233. Perkins, Hugh V., "Motivation," *CAPCI Bibliography*, Washington, D. C.: Association for Supervision and Curriculum Development, December, 1960. Mimeographed.
234. Pierce, James V. and Bowman, Paul H., "The Educational Motivation Patterns of Superior Students Who Do and Who Do Not Achieve in High School," Final Report of Research Project No. 208, U. S. Office of Education. Mimeographed.
235. Pierce, James V., "Personality and Achievement Among Able High School Boys," *Journal of Individual Psychology*, XVII (May, 1961), 102-107.
236. Pierce, James V., "Sex Differences in Achievement Motivation of Able High School Students," Unpublished paper. Cooperative Research Project No. 1097, U. S. Office of Education, December, 1961.
237. Porterfield, O. V. and Schlichting, Harry F., "Peer Status and Reading Achievement," *Journal of Educational Research*, LIV (April, 1961), 291-297.
238. Probst, Merlin C., "The Problem of Early School Leavers, with Special Reference to Factors Which Influenced Dropouts Who Left High Schools of Crawford County, Ohio During the School Year, September, 1950 to September, 1951," Unpublished Master's Thesis (The Ohio State University, 1952).
239. Puthoff, Francis Urban, "A Study of the Early School Leavers of Butler Township, Montgomery County, Ohio, in Grades Seven Through Twelve for the School Years 1943-1952," Unpublished Master's Thesis (The Ohio State University, 1953).
240. Rabinowitz, Ralph, "Attributes of Pupils Achieving Beyond Their Level of Expectancy," *Journal of Personality*, XXIV (March, 1956), 308-317.

241. Rasey, Marie I., Ed., *The Nature of Being Human* (Detroit: Wayne State University Press, 1959).
242. Reckless, Walter C., "Juvenile Delinquency," *Encyclopedia of Educational Research*, Walter S. Monroe, Ed. (New York: Macmillan Co., 1952), 643-646.
243. Reckless, Walter C.; Dinitz, Simon; and Kay, Barbara, "The Self Component in Potential Delinquency and Potential Non-Delinquency," *American Sociological Review*, XXII (October, 1957), 566-570.
244. Reese, Hayne W., "Manifest Anxiety and Achievement Test Performance," *Journal of Educational Psychology*, LII (June, 1962), 132-135.
245. Regan, John F., "The School Connected Fears of Children Under Authoritarian and Democratic Teachers," Unpublished Doctor's Thesis (New York: Columbia University, 1958), as cited in *Dissertation Abstracts*, XVIII (1958), 2079.
246. Remmers, H. H. and Radler, D. H., *The American Teenager* (Indianapolis: Bobbs-Merrill Co., 1957).
247. Remmers, H. H. and Radler, D. H., "Teenage Attitudes, with Biographical Sketches," *Scientific American*, CXCVIII (June, 1958), 25-29.
248. Ribicoff, Abraham, "Plain Words from Mr. Ribicoff on Dropouts," *School Life*, XLIV (November-December, 1961), 14-15.
249. Rockefeller Brothers Fund, Inc., *The Pursuit of Excellence: Education and the Future of America*, Chapter V, "Motivation and Values," as published in paperback, *Prospect for America: The Rockefeller Panel Reports* (New York: Doubleday and Co., 1961), 387-392.
250. Rokeach, Milton, "A Scale for Measuring Intellectual Conviction," *Journal of Social Psychology*, XLIV (August, 1956), 135-141.
251. Rokeach, Milton, *The Open and Closed Mind* (New York: Basic Books, 1960).
252. Rosen, Bernard C., "Family Structure and Achievement Motivation," *American Sociological Review*, XXVI (August, 1961), 574-585.
253. Rosen, E., "Difference Between Volunteers and Non-Volunteers for Psychological Studies," *Journal of Applied Psychology*, XXXV (1951), 185-193.
254. Sanai, M., "The Relation Between Social Attitudes and Characteristics of Personality," *Journal of Social Psychology*, XXXVI (August, 1952), 3-13.
255. Sarason, Seymour B. and Mandler, George, "Some Correlates of Test Anxiety," *Journal of Abnormal and Social Psychology*, XLVII (1952), 810-817.
256. Sarason, Seymour B. et al., "Rorschach Behavior and Performance of High and Low Anxious Children," *Child Development*, XXIX (June, 1958), 277-283.
257. Sarason, Seymour B., *Anxiety in Elementary School Children: A Report of Research* (New York: John Wiley and Sons, Inc., 1960).
258. Sarason, Seymour B., "Test Anxiety," *NEA Journal*, XLVIII (November, 1959), 26-27.
259. Sarbin, T. R. and Rosenberg, B. G., "Contributions to Role-Taking Theory: IV. A Method for Obtaining a Qualitative Estimate of the Self," *Journal of Social Psychology*, XLII (August, 1955), 71-81.
260. Sarnoff, Irving and Zimbardo, Phillip, "Anxiety, Fear and Social Affiliation," *Journal of Abnormal and Social Psychology*, LXII (1961), 356-363.
261. Sartain, A. Q., "Relation of Marks in College Courses to the Interestingness, Value, and Difficulty of the Courses," *Journal of Educational Psychology*, XXXVI (December, 1945), 561-566.
262. Schlesser, George E., "Gains in Scholastic Aptitude Under Highly Motivated Conditions," *Journal of Educational Psychology*, XLI (April, 1950), 237-242.
263. Schroder, Harold M. and Hunt, David E., *Failure Avoidance in Situational Interpretation and Problem Solving*, *Psychological Monographs*, LXXI,

(Washington, D. C.: American Psychological Association, 1957), Whole No. 432.

264. Schwitzgebel, Robert, "The Performance of Dutch and Zulu Adults on Selected Perceptual Tasks," *Journal of Social Psychology*, LVII (June, 1962), 73-77.

265. Scully, Mark, "Possibilities of a Summer Reading Improvement Program for Entering Sophomores," *High School Journal*, XXXIX (November, 1955), 118-123.

266. Segel, David and Schwarm, Oscar J., "Retention in High Schools in Large Cities," (Washington, D.C.: U. S. Dept. of Health, Education and Welfare, September, 1957), Bulletin No. 15.

267. Seib, Charles B. and Otten, Alan L., "The Case of the Furious Children," *Harper's Magazine*, CCXVI (January, 1958), 56-61.

268. Shaw, M. C. and McCuen, John T., "The Onset of Academic Underachievement in Bright Children," *Journal of Educational Psychology*, LI (June, 1960), 103-108.

269. Shaw, Merville C. and Black, Michael Doris, "The Reaction to Frustration of Bright High School Underachievers," *California Journal of Educational Research*, XI (May, 1960), 120-124.

270. Shaw, Merville C.; Edson, Kenneth; and Bell, Hugh M., "The Self Concept of Bright Underachieving High School Students," *Personnel and Guidance Journal*, XXXIX (November, 1960).

271. Siegel, Laurence and Macomber, Freeman G., "Comparative Effectiveness of Televised and Large Classes and of Small Sections," *Journal of Educational Psychology*, XLVIII (October, 1957), 371-382.

272. Siegelman, Marvin and Peck, Robert F., "Personality Patterns Related to Occupational Roles," *Genetic Psychology Monographs*, LXI (May, 1960), 291-349.

273. Singh, Paras Nath et al., "A Comparative Study of Selected Attitudes, Values, and Personality Characteristics of American, Chinese, and Indian Students," *Journal of Social Psychology*, LVII (June, 1962), 123-132.

274. Slocum, W. L., "Educational Planning by High School Seniors," *Journal of Educational Research*, LI (April, 1958), 583-590.

275. Smith, Harry P., "Syracuse Youth Who Did Not Graduate," (Syracuse, N. Y.: Board of Education, 1959).

276. Smith, Henry Clay and Dunbar, Donald, "The Personality and Achievements of the Classroom Participant," *Journal of Educational Psychology*, XLII (February, 1951), 65-83.

277. Snepp, Daniel W., "Why They Drop Out: 8 Clues to Greater Holding Power," *Clearing House*, XXVII (April, 1953), 492-494.

278. Snepp, Daniel W., "Can We Salvage the Dropouts?" *Clearing House*, XXXI (September, 1956), 49-54.

279. Sorokin, Pitrim A., "The Powers of Creative Unselfish Love," in *New Knowledge in Human Values*, A. H. Maslow, Ed. (New York: Harper and Bros., 1959), 3-12.

280. Spivak, Monroe L., "School Problems Reported by Seventh and Ninth-Grade Children Entering the Same Junior High School," *Journal of Educational Research*, L (April, 1957), 631-633.

281. Springer, David Elton, "School Drop Out Problem in a Rural Mennonite Community," Unpublished Master's Thesis (The Ohio State University, 1951).

282. Stalnaker, Elizabeth M., "A Four Year Study of the Freshman Class of 1935 at the West Virginia University," *Journal of Educational Research*, (October, 1942), 100-118.

283. Steele, Terry A. and McCloughan, Jack W., "The Responses of Delinquent Girls to the Junior Index of Motivation," Unpublished study (The Ohio State University, 1962).

284. Steffrle, Buford, "Psychological Factors Associated with Aspirations for Socio-Economic Mobility," *California Journal of Educational Research*, VI (1955), 55-60.
285. Stephenson, Richard M.,"Occupational Aspirations and Plans of 443 Ninth Graders," *Journal of Educational Research*, XLIX (September, 1955), 27-35.
286. Stern, George C. and Masling, Joseph M., *Unconscious Factors in Career Motivation for Teaching*, Final Report, June 30, 1958, U. S. Department of Health, Education, and Welfare, Office of Education Contract No. SAE 6459, Syracuse University Research Institute, Psychological Research Center. Mimeographed.
287. Stetler, Henry G., "Comparative Study of Negro and White Dropouts in Selected Connecticut High Schools," (State of Connecticut: Commission on Civil Rights, 1959).
288. Stivers, Eugene, "Motivation for College in High-School Boys," *The School Review*, LXVI (September, 1958), 341-350.
289. Stivers, Eugene, "Motivation for College in High-School Girls," *The School Review*, LXVII (Autumn, 1959), 320-334.
290. Stoner, William Gerald, "Factors Related to the Underachievement of High School Students," *Dissertation Abstracts*, XVII (1957), 96-97.
291. Stotland, Ezra, "An Expectancy Approach to Security as a General Aspect of Motivation," *Journal of General Psychology*, LXI (October, 1959), 253-268.
292. Stout, Irving W. and Langdon, Grace, "A Report on Follow-Up Interviews with Parents of Well-Adjusted Children," *Journal of Educational Sociology*, XXVI (May, 1953).
293. Strang, Ruth, "Adolescents' Views on One Aspect of Their Development," *Journal of Educational Psychology*, XLVI (November, 1955), 423-432.
294. Sutton-Smith, B. and Rosenberg, B. G., "A Scale to Identify Impulsive Behavior in Children," *Journal of Genetic Psychology*, XCV (December, 1959), 211-216.
295. Sweney, Arthur B. and Cattell, Raymond B., "Relationships Between Integrated and Unintegrated Motivation Structure Examined by Objective Tests," *Journal of Social Psychology*, LVII (June, 1962), 217-226.
296. Taylor, Calvin W., *Scientific Creativity: Its Recognition and Development* (New York: John Wiley and Sons, 1963).
297. Taylor, Calvin W., "Some Completed and Current Utah Research Activities on Creativity," Unpublished paper.
298. Terman, Lewis M. and Oden, Melita H., "The Significance of Deviates, III: Correlates of Adult Achievement in the California Gifted Group." 39th Yearbook, Part I, NSSE, 1940, 74-84.
299. Terman, Lewis M., "The Occupational Success of Intellectually Gifted Individuals," *Occupations*, XX (1942), 493-498.
300. Thelen, Herbert A., *Education and the Human Quest* (New York: Harper and Bros., 1960).
301. Thistlethwaite, Donald L., "College Press and Changes in Study Plans of Talented Students," *Journal of Educational Psychology*, LI (August, 1960), 222-234.
302. Thistlethwaite, Donald L., "Effects of Social Recognition upon the Educational Motivation of Talented Youth," *Journal of Educational Psychology*, L (June, 1959), 111-116.
303. Thomas, Robert J., "An Empirical Study of High School Drop-Outs in Regard to Ten Possibly Related Factors," *Journal of Educational Sociology*, XXVIII (September, 1954), 11-18.
304. Thomas, William Dale, "A Study of the Drop-Out of the Columbus, Ohio, Public Schools: Data Derived from the Original Members of the Graduating Class of 1955," Unpublished Master's Thesis (The Ohio State University, 1955).

305. Torrance, Paul, "Rationalizations About Test Performance as a Function of Self-Concepts," *Journal of Social Psychology*, XXXIX (May, 1954), 211-217.
306. Toynbee, Arnold J., *A Study of History* (New York: Oxford University Press, 1946), 88-139.
307. Trimmer, Wilbur D., "A Study of the Drop-Outs and Potential Drop-Outs of Marion Franklin High School, Columbus, Ohio," Unpublished Master's Thesis (The Ohio State University, 1959).
308. Trumbull, Richard, "A Study of Relationships Between Factors of Personality and Intelligence," *Journal of Social Psychology*, XXXVIII (November, 1953), 161-173.
309. U. S. Department of Labor, Washington, D. C., "School Dropouts and Their Employment Problems," (March, 1956).
310. Van Dyke, L. A. and Hoyt, K. B., "The Drop Out Problem in Iowa High Schools" (Iowa City: State University of Iowa, 1958).
311. Vinacke, W. Edgar, "The Drive-Modification Theory of Human Motivation," *Journal of Genetic Psychology*, XCVI (June, 1960), 245-268.
312. Visci, Leonard A., "A Study of the Early School Leavers in Grades Seven Through Twelve for the School Years 1950-1954 of the Frank B. Willis High School, Delaware, Ohio," Unpublished Master's Thesis (The Ohio State University, 1955).
313. Viteles, Morris S., *Motivation and Morale in Industry* (New York: W. W. Norton and Co., 1953).
314. Von Mering, Fay Higier, "Professional and Non-Professional Women as Mothers," *Journal of Social Psychology*, XLII (August, 1955), 21-34.
315. Waetjen, Walter B., "Motivation," *Educational Leadership*, XIX (October, 1961), 55-80. Copyright © 1961 by the Association for Supervision and Curriculum Development.
316. Waetjen, Walter B., "Is Learning Sexless?" *National Educational Association Journal*, LI (May, 1962).
317. Walters, Richard H.; Banks, Robin K.; and Ryder, Robert R., "A Test of the Perceptual Defense Hypothesis," *Journal of Personality*, XXVII (March, 1959), 47-55.
318. Warren, Doron L., "A Study of Drop-Outs in Austin," *Minnesota Journal of Education*, XXXVIII (May, 1958), 23-24.
319. Wattenberg, William W. and Redl, Fritz, "Mental Hygiene," *Encyclopedia of Educational Research*, Walter S. Monroe, Ed. (New York: Macmillan Co., 1952), 733-745.
320. Wattenberg, William W., "Relationship of School Experiences to Delinquency," Cooperative Research Program, OE-25022, Project No. 201. U. S. Department of Health, Education, and Welfare, Office of Education.
321. Watts, Yvonne C., "A Study of High School Failures," *National Association of Secondary School Principals Bulletin*, XLIII (October, 1959), 69-75.
322. Wedemeyer, Charles A., "Gifted Achievers and Non-Achievers," *Journal of Higher Education*, XXIV (January, 1953), 25-30.
323. Weinrich, Ernest F., "How Can a School Increase Its Holding Power of Youth?" *National Association of Secondary School Principals Bulletin*, XXXVI (March, 1952), 125-130.
324. Weintraub, Ruth G. and Sally, Ruth E., "Graduation Prospects of an Entering Freshman," *Journal of Educational Research*, XXXIX (October, 1945), 116-126.
325. Weiss, Robert Frank, "Aspirations and Expectations: A Dimensional Analysis," *Journal of Social Psychology*, LIII (April, 1961), 249-254.
326. Wheeler, D. K., "Development of the Ideal Self in Western Australian Youth," *Journal of Educational Research*, LIV (January, 1961), 163-167.
327. Williams, John E., "Mode of Failure, Interference Tendencies, and Achieve-

ment Imagery," *Journal of Abnormal and Social Psychology*, LI (November, 1955), 573-580.
328. Wilson, Everett K., "Determinants of Participation in Policy Formation in a College Community," *Human Relations*, VII (August, 1954), 287-312.
329. Wolfbein, Seymour L., "Transition from School to Work: A Study of the School Leaver," *Personnel and Guidance Journal*, XXXVIII (October, 1959), 98-105.
330. Wolins, Leroy; Mackinney, A. C.; and Stephans, Paul, "Factor Analyses of High School Achievement Measures," *Journal of Educational Research*, LIV (January, 1961), 173-177.
331. Woodruff, Asahel D., "Motivation Theory and Educational Practice," *Journal of Educational Psychology*, XL (January, 1949), 33-40.
332. Wooster, George F. and Stover, W. Wallace, "Lost—Students," *Educational Research Bulletin*, XXXVII (April, 1958), 85-90.
333. Yoder, Mary Jane, "A Study of the Drop Out in the City of Canton, Ohio, During the School Year 1958-1959," Unpublished Master's Thesis (The Ohio State University, 1960).
334. Young, Joe M., "Lost, Strayed, or Stolen," *The Clearing House*, XXIX (October, 1954), 89-92.
335. Zaleznik, A.; Christensen, C. R.; and Roethlisberger, F. J., *The Motivation, Productivity, and Satisfaction of Workers* (Cambridge: Harvard University Press, 1959).
336. Zimmerman, Joseph, "What Motivates Students?" *Journal of Higher Education*, XXVII (November, 1956), 449-453.

Chapter Six

Structure

During the course of a day a teacher may have to work with as many as a hundred different students, or even more. Finding the most effective relationship with each learner presents a real problem. There appear to be conflicting tasks: how to teach democratically but effectively. How can a teacher work with many students so that his teaching will be both democratic and effective?

Asked another way this question might read: How much "structure" should a teacher employ in his teaching? Or, how should a teacher structure his classroom for maximum learning?

WHAT IS STRUCTURE?

Structure is that aspect of educational method which includes the various activities and relationships which develop in a classroom. A schoolroom, first of all, means a group of students. How this grouping was determined is very important. Several other specific things are also significant: the patterns of communication, the nature of the decision-making process, the kind of thought process and problem-solving which occurs, the expectations which are present and the limitations which are imposed from without or developed within. Finally, the relationships which exist between the teacher and the students and among the students themselves are also important.

For purposes of this book, structure is thought of abstractly as a series of factors, each of which represents a continuum. To think of structure as a continuum is difficult but helpful. The basic dimension, however, is not the "progressive" and "traditional" one (81); it is more involved than that. Neither is it the "liberal" and "conservative" continuum (82), since it embodies a different set of qualities than is conventionally included in these terms.

156

The extent to which a teacher predetermines the various activities in learning determines the amount of structure which is involved. The word *structure* is used throughout this book primarily as a verb, and as such, expresses what a teacher, as status leader, *does to* the classroom; the extent and way in which he consciously and unconsciously controls various aspects of the process and thus influences the learning.

Some of these aspects of structure and the ways in which teachers manipulate them are described below. As these ideas are intended to serve as an operational definition of structure, they are described in light of some of the research from which they come. They should be especially pertinent to the young teacher, since college methods courses seldom provide prospective teachers with experiences consistent with the basic ideas included in the course (51, 75). College professors who teach methods courses do not always "practice what they preach," so understanding the principles of structure becomes even more important if they are not to be experienced in any other way.

Grouping

Schools organize children into groups for instructional purposes. Having too few Mark Hopkinses and preferring something else to logs, the American people have encouraged the development of schools in which several students are assembled with one teacher for varying lengths of time to help them learn. Traditionally the number of students has varied from a mere handful to several hundred, although thirty seems to be an average size today. There is, admittedly, little experimental basis for having groups of this number, but they will probably continue to be about this size for years to come. Two reasons account for this. First there is tradition itself, and second, most of the classrooms already built in America will each hold about thirty students. The permanency of existing classroom space has a way of overriding other arguments.

So we have groups. How shall these groups be constituted? What criteria shall be employed in bringing students together for educational purposes? Should the members of each group be as similar as possible or different in various respects? Should they all be of the same sex? same age? same size? same experience? same reading ability? same interests? same race? same motivations? same socio-economic level? same intellectual ability? same personality?

In the matter of sex, obviously, we can get clear-cut agreement about whether a particular youngster is male or female. The other factors, however, impose some kinds of limits. When is a six-year-old a six-year-old for educational purposes? Are we talking about the period of time between his sixth and seventh birthdays, or will we include, as many school systems do, all youngsters who will be six on or before a certain arbitrary date, say January 1st? Or shall we confine our discussion only to chronological age or broaden it to include mental age? reading age? social age?

From the standpoint of curriculum, grouping is significant in the educational process because it is a manipulable variable. Groups also enable youngsters to satisfy deep psychological needs if they learn in a democratic group (138). Perhaps these are the reasons public and professional attention has been so concentrated on this point, or perhaps why, as Davis says (28), "it is on the issue of democracy that much of the controversy about grouping centers." In a democratic state, schools must be democratic, and in a democratic school, grouping must be democratic. But democracy is many things, especially ways of behaving. Grouping is not an end in itself or a way of behaving. It is a means to an end.

Any way of grouping students together to learn which enables them to grow up behaving in democratic ways is democratic. Being democratic means being perceptive and open to experience, able to learn and to grow, and skillful in communication. If putting students together who are similar in certain traits will facilitate this, then this is democratic. If grouping children who are especially different will help them acquire these ways of behaving, then this is democratic. If grouping children together who are alike in some respects but different in others will expedite the process, then this should be our means. Logical arguments like "the slow are holding back the bright" or "children need to rub elbows with all kinds of people" should be substantiated by research. If these ideas are worthwhile, they will withstand experimental scrutiny. If they are common sense arguments which seem sound when described but which have no experimental base, they ought to go.

The history of science is the story of men discarding antiquated ideas which sounded reasonable but which were not really true: the flat earth, the geocentric universe, bleeding people to help them recover from illness. What does research say about ability grouping of pupils for instructional purposes? Goodlad, for instance, reviewing research for the 1960 *Encyclopedia of Educational Research*, had this to say (52):

> Research suggests the following generalizations concerning the extent to which ability grouping reduces variability in achievement: (a) Ability grouping only imperceptibly reduces student variability when a broad range of academic, intellectual, physical, and social

traits is considered. (b) When students of a given grade level are divided into A and B classes or A, B, and C classes according to general ability, variability in school achievement is reduced about 7 and 17 per cent respectively. (c) When this kind of grouping is accompanied by vertical regrouping so that bright and slow students advance on separate promotional tracks, attainment variability is reduced about 10 per cent more. . . . For example, children with IQ above 120 and below 90 were removed from a fifth grade class, but the range of reading ability still spread 2.7 to 11.2. . . . The evidence, of limited value as indicated above, slightly favors ability grouping in regard to academic achievement, with dull children seeming to profit more than bright children in this regard.

Other studies generally report similar findings (25, 54, 66, 91, 125). Even this kind of conclusion, however, ought to be qualified because of the different kinds of research upon which it is based. Passow (108) pointed out some of the reasons for difficulties in generalizing from research on ability grouping, including differences among the studies themselves regarding the aims of the research, number of students and groups involved, size of classes, duration, adequacy of selection bases, experimental "treatments" included and evaluation techniques. This problem faces any student in education who hopes to make valid generalizations from different research studies, but it should also serve to highlight what may be a false concern with grouping as it has been traditionally viewed, that is, with age and ability as paramount factors.

Another kind which has long interested educators is achievement grouping. Achievement has often been considered an important factor in grouping practices, although its precise relationship to age and ability has seldom been clarified. Promotion and acceleration are crude ways of grouping students for instructional purposes according to their achievement levels. Research generally supports the idea of acceleration (4, 7, 35, 40, 149), though retention or failure as a corollary means does not seem to prove as successful (153). After studying practices in 148 school systems, Cook states the point well (24):

> It was found that schools which have relatively high standards of promotion (retard the dull and accelerate the bright) tend to have a higher proportion of over-age slow-learning pupils, since such pupils remain in school from one to several years longer. The higher proportion of such pupils reduced significantly the mean mental age and achievement level of grade groups in these schools. . . . *the retention of a large number of low-ability pupils through nonpromotion tends actually to reduce grade standards and aggravate the range of ability problems.* [Italics added.]

Shane (126) reports several types of classroom grouping schemes which have been employed in American schools. Procedures vary from combination grade level experiments (1) and multigrade teaching (72) to individualized instruction (145, 150) and the non-graded school (53). Surveys show (78) that some schools make more provisions than others, but educators have generally recognized grouping as a means to an end, and perhaps one which has received undue attention.

The thesis of this book, of course, is that the heart of educational method lies in the teacher himself. One conclusion from any intensive study of grouping research is that the one variable which is infinitely more significant than the type of grouping employed is the teacher (126).

The problem, then, is not whether to group or not to group, but rather which groups to place with which teachers (92). This problem will be explored in much more detail in Chapter Seven. For the present, it should simply be recognized that teachers work with groups of students, and probably always will. Traditional efforts at improving instruction through various kinds of grouping have proved only moderately successful, but new ways of organizing classroom groups hold real promise.

Now for a closer look at some of the fundamentals of structure itself.

Communication

Within any group the communication pattern may take many forms. Generally, however, such a pattern would represent primarily a teacher-centered or group-centered phenomenon. The diagrams below depict two situations in which the flow of communication has been plotted, one representing a single-source, the other a multi-source communication network.

Throughout this book the single source type of communication will be referred to as *high* structured or *more* structure.[1] The extent to which the teacher master-minds the communication flow and directs the communication patterns which develop represents more structure.

In the teacher-centered communication pattern it is obvious that the teacher is the person primarily concerned with the flow of ideas. Information is funneled in toward, and out from, him. Classroom recitation or lecture exemplifies such a pattern in operation. In a recitation the teacher asks the questions, students respond, then the teacher passes judgment

---

[1] Some persons might prefer to call this a different kind of structure rather than more or less, since structure of some kind is present in any situation. This view would be perfectly acceptable, but in an effort to consider structure from a point of view which will ultimately be manipulable, the other definiton has been employed.

Figure 1

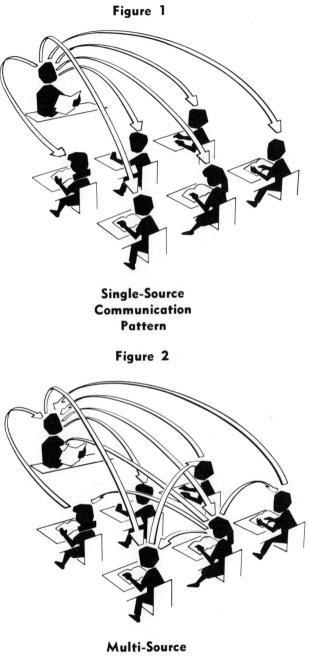

**Single-Source
Communication
Pattern**

Figure 2

**Multi-Source
Communication
Pattern**

upon the response. In all phases of the process the teacher is directly responsible for the way ideas are used, the kinds of ideas which are selected for consideration, and the manner of response to these ideas.

Discussion, however, provides a situation in which ideas come from many sources. The flow of communication is not always to and from the teacher. Ideas move around the room with a question here and an answer there. This is multi-source communication. There are learners who even use discussion effectively by not listening attentively (135):

> Some persons do not slavishly follow the flow of the discussion, but instead, they apparently listen (or perhaps even turn off their listening for awhile) and think at "right angles" on an unusual train of thought. Later they may come back into the discussion and send it down fresh routes.

Neither kind of communication pattern is considered good or bad, effective or ineffective, right or wrong. The purpose of this chapter will be to develop a framework within which either more or less structure might be most appropriate, depending upon the other factors present.

Single-source communication as high structure, and multi-source communication as low structure, however, are easy to describe in the abstract but difficult to isolate in actuality, because so many subtle factors are involved.

Telling, for example, is a very simple, honest, straightforward approach to teaching, the success of which depends upon a whole host of factors. Whether lecturing or telling is more effective than discussion (120, 131) also depends not so much on the obvious distinction between the two techniques as on the subtleties which may be a part of the total process.

Students and teachers who "see things the same way" at the beginning of an experience are much more apt to have successful communication than those who do not (121). The extent to which students trust an instructor will undoubtedly affect communication (101). Leaders are generally recognized as being more active in discussions, whether they are highly structured (16, 127) or leaderless (11, 47). Participation furthers the flow of communication (60, 93), though it probably is more important psychologically than actually (9, 146, 147). If persons involved feel they are an integral part or are adequately represented in what is going on, it is probably more important than overt participation. However, to control circumstances so that involvement in the communication network is more readily possible certainly affects morale and the sense of belonging (50, 109). Who sits where, and how the chairs are arranged has much to do with impeding or facilitating the flow of information. The size of a group also makes a difference (59).

People are seldom changed by information alone (77, 78), but by how information is presented (10, 80, 96, 105, 128). Studies of groups under extreme stress conditions of survival (141) indicate the importance of clear communication both before and during the event. However, having all persons participate is not necessarily democratic or effective in itself. Horowitz and Perlmutter discuss this problem in some detail (70):

> The rejected member is not a participant in the group in a real sense because his right to influence the group process is severely limited, while others, perhaps more conforming members, are allocated a greater degree of influence, not necessarily commensurate with their skill, knowledge, or ability. . . . frequent interchanges of opinion in the group are lost—not agreed with, not disagreed with, but simply not listened to. Here exists one of the most subtle, most prevalent, and most insidious of all intra-group processes.

The authors go on to describe the rights of members in a democratic group:

> There is the right to talk, the right to be heard, the right to be listened to, the right to benefit others, and the right to influence others. . . . We know that there exist great forces toward conformity in the group. . . . If a democratic decision requires representativeness of individual opinion, it follows that strongly-knit or cohesive groups give rise to anti-democratic forces which make disagreement with the majority undesirable and even "dangerous." Groups that feel they must reach decisions frequently use devices and techniques to insure conformity.

These are disturbing statements. No longer can we define lecturing as authoritarian and discussion as democratic. Indeed, under certain circumstances the exact opposite may very well be true. Discussion groups can be extremely autocratic. Harriet Mills' description of Communist technique in China, for example, delineates the authoritarian nature of such discussions beautifully (104):

> The Chinese Communists are attempting to remold the mind as well as the face of China. Their approach combines standard techniques of the authoritarian state with a system of their own invention. . . . However, the Chinese Communists are well aware that, effective as such regimentation may be in conditioning habits of

action and response, it does not necessarily achieve genuine reorientation.

Two main lines of experience have gone into group study, one Chinese, one Communist. During their twenty-odd years as guerrilla fighters, the Chinese Communists stumbled, through necessity, on one basic element of what is now group study. In teaching uneducated peasant recruits to use weapons, obey commands, live together, and protect the country people, the Communists gradually found that small discussions groups were the best way to make sure each man understood not only how but why. These small groups went patiently over all questions, objectives, or counter-suggestions until the best method had been found and agreed upon. . . . The second objective in group study—namely, the study of Marxist theory and the discipline of criticism and self-criticism— has long been standard practice in Communist cells around the world. Out of the gradual fusion of these two traditions—Chinese persuasion and Communist dogma—contemporary group study has evolved as the ubiquitous working mechanism of thought reform in China.

Complex interplay of psychological and personal factors gives the technique its special character and power. First, the study group is official. . . . Second, everyone must express an opinion; there is no freedom of silence. . . . Third, parroting theory or the official line is not enough. . . . The weapon the group uses is criticism. The ideas of each member are criticized by others against the correct standard. In this way everyone is forced actively to apply that standard to someone else's problem and is not permitted simply to receive it passively . . . . Self-criticism is as important as, if not more important than, criticism. One cannot merely reveal his thoughts. He must detail convincing reasons why he thinks they are wrong.

These sections have been quoted at length because communication is the heart of education. The nature and conditions of this communication are very important to the achievement of democratic educational objectives. Teachers have control of factors which will assure more effective communication or less. Encouraging trust among students and arranging the classroom for desirable communication flow are two factors.

Most important, however, are the teacher's own actions. The example he sets and the way he behaves is crucial. The kind and frequency of his comments, for instance, and the nature of the resulting relationships are fundamental. The way a teacher raises his voice or furrows his brow, how he pauses for emphasis or looks around the room, whether he requires students to raise their hands, respond informally, or stand to recite are little ways of behaving which have a profound effect upon the quantity and quality of communication within the room (99).

Flanders has found (39) that most teachers talk most of the time and, further, that most of their talk is directing and negating rather than facilitating and supporting. An understanding of the importance and function of communication as a part of structure is imperative for an understanding of educational method.

Direction

The direction which a classroom group takes represents another segment of structure. Direction may come primarily from the teacher or from the group itself, including both teacher and students.

If direction is determined primarily by the teacher, this is considered greater structure. The extent to which students participate either by themselves or in conjunction with the teacher to determine the direction in which the class should go would be indicative of less structure.

In schools, direction manifests itself mainly in the selection of ideas for study or the way in which they will be studied; what is usually called course content and classroom technique. In a history class, for example, it is not possible to include all salient information during any given course. Which ideas shall be studied and the way the class shall go are illustrations of the idea of direction. Which stories not to read in a literature class would be a negative aspect of the same thing.

One way to consider direction would be from the decision-making process. If most or all of the decisions regarding content and procedures are decided upon primarily by the instructor, such a classroom would be highly structured. If the students and the teacher explore the possibilities for action together and effect joint decision-making, such a classroom would be less highly structured. Neither procedure should be thought of as desirable apart from the other factors.

In deciding who should study what and how, persons concerned with structure consider direction. Direction is closely related to communication, in that the determination of content and procedures involves sharing information.

One of the schools in the Eight Year Study described one of its efforts to determine direction as follows (114):

> As part of our general program of evaluation, a questionnaire was devised to try to find out how much the students valued the Nursery experience, which parts of the work they enjoyed most, and why they thought spending so much time in the Nursery was important.

A careful study of the responses to this questionnaire showed that the girls in grade IX, as a group, liked the work in the Nursery better than the older girls, that they were more ready to learn various routines which are necessary in the life of a baby, and that they had a desire to learn the reasons for various aspects of child care. Other evaluation materials showed that our students were rather confused and inconsistent in their attitudes about family relationships. We also found that some of the material about New York City which we had been using was too mature for many of the freshman girls. At this time a small group of ninth graders had elected a course called "Nursery-Biology," and the enthusiasm with which they had approached the study of human biology, in relation to the babies in the Nursery, suggested that work in biology might be more valuable to freshmen than the kind of science they had been studying.

It was therefore decided to experiment for a year with a freshman program, built around the work in the Nursery as a center. Human biology was taught in relation to the Nursery, which was placed in charge of a teacher of biology who had had experience in babies' hospitals. Each freshman spent a week in each semester in the nursery, as a "worker," and was free to use the babies as an "observation laboratory" at any time. The work with the social studies teacher was still focused on trips about the city, but more emphasis was placed on the city as an environment in which individuals developed and lived many different kinds of lives.

The experimental year proved this program so successful that it has been continued.

This passage describes the activities of a staff, working with students, to determine course content for a particular school. It exemplifies low structure. Note, however, that the teachers initiated the action. Even low structure cannot be carried out except by way of the teacher. Teachers structure classrooms one way or another, either by design or by default.

Consider another illustration. It has been said that when Woodrow Wilson was a professor of American History at Princeton University he was so successful as a lecturer that students used to wait outside his classroom until after roll was called, then rush to get the vacant chairs. As a professor, Wilson was superb in lectures, but mediocre in discussion or with individual students. Lecture material is generally decided upon by the instructor, thus the ideas, the order in which they were covered, the illustrations and examples were left entirely to his discretion. This was high structure, but it was neither ineffective nor undemocratic. Those who heard the lectures considered Wilson a superb teacher of history, and felt his methods were extremely appropriate and unusually effective. These two examples may help to illuminate the basic differences in that aspect of structure we call direction. It is impossible at this point to say that either greater or lesser direction from the teacher is appropriate in any given situation unless we also consider other factors.

The classic study of the effect of a leader's actions upon a group's function was by Lewin, Lippitt, and White (89). This has been replicated in other situations (44, 64). These studies all indicate that achievements and interpersonal relations are most satisfactory when leaders assume a positive, helping role rather than a dominating or passive one. Perkins' study (110) of in-service teachers produced similar results.

Many contemporary researchers have explored the problem of teaching method by noting variations in achievement, acceptance and satisfaction in teacher-centered and student-centered classrooms (3, 5, 8, 12, 19, 34, 38, 41, 56, 98, 102, 117, 130, 143). Other efforts to assess the value of direct involvement through experimentation (17, 84, 86) and activity (62, 65, 77) or by noting the value of homework (96, 122), which is typically teacher-determined, all illustrate concern with this aspect of educational structure. Encouraging students to study in particular ways has also been examined (6), as has been a comparison of individual and group study practices (14).

The results of these studies are conflicting. Some indicate better results with student-centered, some with teacher-centered situations, and some report no differences at all. It would appear that students' expectations and previous experiences have as much to do with educational outcomes as the factors under study. Students sometimes do better in classrooms characterized by much structure and others better where it is held to a minimum.

There is also some evidence that all teachers cannot function equally well both ways (73). Certain teachers, at least, are more "comfortable" with one approach than the other. This "comfortableness" evidently influences their own activities in the classroom. Knowing exactly when and how much to vary structure becomes an essential skill for the democratic classroom teacher who wants to be effective.

Because there are many variables, the general tendency through the years has been to experiment with most of the manipulables other than the teacher. Making the time longer or shorter, or treating subject matter in highly departmentalized fashion or through some types of correlation are some of the experiments. Studying lecture versus discussion, or large and small group accomplishments are still other efforts to manipulate classroom variables in order to note educational results. Much of the research in core curriculum is of this type (20, 21, 36, 37, 46, 132, 140, 152).

Most of these studies are disappointing. In the main they indicate little difference in educational attainment, regardless of the method employed or the objectives measured. Some of the technical reports even carry an air of defeatism when they state that such and such a procedure "apparently did no worse than" some other approach. Many of the innovations themselves are sound, of course.

These slight differences are understandable, however, since the most important variable—the teacher—has seldom been studied either intensively or extensively in research. There are many reasons for this, not the least of which is the general tendency of some teachers to think that they may lose their positions if they appear ineffective in the study. The reluctance to look at the most important ingredient, the teacher, may very well have cost us years in educational progress. Working hard at changing the things that do not count has little to offer in the way of improving education itself.

Kinds of Problem-Solving

One can get the answer to any question in one of several ways. If he proceeds from given premises to valid conclusions, he is operating deductively. Should he go from specific information to valid generalizations, he is functioning inductively. In classrooms children may be taught to solve problems by appealing to an authority (premise), and thence deduce appropriate facts. On the other hand, they may be taught to accumulate their factual data systematically by making careful observations, and then develop from this information their own conclusions (generalizations).

When a teacher employs and encourages the processes of deductive logic, this is considered more structure. If he attempts to have students make their own observations, collect their own information, and draw their own conclusions, he would be using less structure.

There are times when it is appropriate for teachers to employ greater structure in the way they teach children to solve problems. At other times they need to use less structure. The problem-solving process is another facet of the concept of structure in an educational situation.

Many of the innovations in curriculum materials currently being advocated are based upon inductive and intuitive thinking and upon the psychological notion of discovery (18). Materials prepared in this fashion lead students through a series of experiences and help them "discover" basic generalizations themselves. For example, teaching children to memorize the multiplication tables calls for a deductive thought process on their part: $6 \times 3 = 18$ because it is in the tables that way. Memorizing number combinations by stating the problem, $6 \times 3 = \underline{\hspace{1cm}}$, and providing the answer, 18, represents high structure.

On the other hand, leading children through experiences in which they learn that six, three times, equals 18, i.e., 6 plus 6 plus 6 equals 18, or three, six times, i.e., 3 plus 3 plus 3 plus 3 plus 3 plus 3 equals 18, may help them understand multiplication as repeated addition. In this way they may "discover" that multiplying really involves adding numbers over and over again. The child who learns multiplication this way is experiencing less structure. He is being helped to understand multiplication as a concept and as a process. The mental activity being encouraged is inductive as opposed to deductive, hence less structure. Neither way is better than the other, except as other factors are considered.

Just as a classroom is structured, so is a discipline structured. Thinking about a particular body of information requires the student to proceed in particular ways. Foshay states it this way (76):

> If a discipline is a way of knowing its particular body of knowledge in its appropriate way, then a school subject can be thought of as a pattern of learning activities, worked out by an educationist (a teacher, if you please) which has as its purpose the introduction of students into the discipline.

He then goes on to describe the characteristics of a discipline:

> In order that there be a discipline, it is necessary among other things that people be in agreement on the field of phenomenon in question—the domain of the discipline. . . . Second, the members of a discipline agree upon a set of rules which are to apply to the scholar's attempt to create knowledge within his field of inquiry. . . . In many of the disciplines, the history of the discipline itself is of importance . . . The more one deeply understands the history of one's own field, the more nearly one can be in control of the effectiveness of one's own efforts.

From this discussion, Foshay urges educators to be concerned about "disciplines" as well as about "problems."

> What, you say, of the discipline of practical judgment, of the method of intelligence, of problem solving taken simply as orderly thinking? It is necessary, once more, to remember that each way of knowing has its own rules. The method of intelligence does not really help one to become an effective biologist, for it does not take

into account some real problems (such as multiplicity of unknown variables operating in a given biological experiment) that the biologist has to live with. Similarly, the method of intelligence does not give the literary critic the means to deal at the required level of sophistication with the phenomena he tries to comprehend and explain. The method of intelligence, or the method of problem solving, has to be a meta-method—a way of describing what thoughtful people have in common, not what they do in particular. It does not provide an adequate set of rules for the operation of scholars within particular fields.

There are many ways to view thought processes. Some studies provide helpful clues for teachers about how lecture secures attention readily, whereas discussion evokes complex problem-solving thought more effectively (13). Screening possible solutions carefully (94) expedites the process. Other investigations (45, 85) hold even greater promise. Understanding fully the kinds of thought processes being encouraged among learners is one part of structure. Knowing how cultural and other factors affect cognitive functioning is another. Determining precise procedures for fostering specific types of mental activity under given conditions is a third. The effective teacher is one who comprehends accurately the interplay of all of these forces, and structures the learning situation carefully and knowingly for maximum learning.

Expectations and Limitations

Everybody associated with education has certain expectations. Parents expect their children to learn to write and read and draw, for example. Children themselves expect and hope to become proficient at these as well as other ways of behaving. Teachers expect certain things from their students.

Parents also expect certain things not to take place within the school, so definite limitations are inherent in education. Students are expected not to be rowdy, or to leave the building, or to smoke or swear. Teachers, too, have definite limitations which they associate with the classroom: restrictions involved in accepting late assignments, how many students may talk at one time and procedures for leaving the room.

These factors, the positive and negative aspects of educational purpose, are examples of different aspects of structure. The extent to which expectations and limitations are imposed from without, either by or through the teacher, is indicative of high structure. If expectations and limitations are developed and imposed by the classroom group upon itself, this represents less structure.

What a teacher expects of a class and what students expect of themselves are handles on the conceptual framework of structure. These factors illustrate the concreteness of a relatively nebulous concept. The extent to which these factors are manipulated by the teacher or some outside source reflects the amount and kind of structure present in the classroom.

Clarifying expectations increases group members' effectiveness (23, 48, 129). Clarifying expectations, however, can occur at a general or a specific level. For example, suppose a teacher says to his class: "We will have major tests once each grading period, with shorter quizzes in between. Your grade will include an average of all of these examinations plus your classroom participation." These statements are an effort of the teacher to clarify what will be expected of his students, but it is a general approach.

Consider the above statement in comparison to this one: "Examinations will be given every Friday. Each weekly examination will consist of ten objective questions and one essay question covering the week's work. These papers will be scored but not graded. Your final examination, which will constitute fifty per cent of your grade, will be made up entirely of the questions included in the weekly tests. The other half of your grade will be determined subjectively by me. I will consider such factors as class attendance, participation, progress on your individual project, punctuality, dependability, and neatness. I will try to have short conferences with each of you at least twice during the grading period so we can discuss your activities in this class in some detail. Are there any questions?"

This statement, like the first, represents high structure on the part of the teacher. It is more detailed and more specific, however, even though it deals with such undefined concepts as "participation," "dependability," and "neatness." If this instructor can make these terms more precise, he will have achieved still greater clarity. Regardless of the type of structure, expectations and limitations must be clear.

If the things which students are expected to do and not to do are determined by the teacher or staff alone, this is high structure. If the rules and regulations as well as hopes and aspirations are designed in conjunction with students, however, this is low structure. Teachers and pupils planning together a system of student government or an honors system for examination periods would be illustrations of low structure.

Studies of teachers' own needs indicate that many of them have personal qualities which probably result in high structure in their classrooms: high deference, orderliness, and exacting demands (22, 74). These studies are apparently supported by teachers' desires to be allowed to administer corporal punishment. In one study (106), more than three-fourths of the elementary teachers, and almost 40 per cent of the secondary teachers involved, desired such opportunities. Even most superintendents (107) believe teachers should be permitted to use some type of corporal punishment in their classrooms. Since corporal punishment is directly related to high structure, these studies reflect a basic inclination by many professionals for highly structured classrooms with the teacher clearly and forcefully in control.

Some studies indicate that the group itself places severe limitations upon any member through constraints and restraints (61, 134). When asked in a nation-wide poll, almost 70 per cent of the teenagers queried favored a code of behavior for young people *if they could help write it* (49).

How limitations are imposed and where they come from are indicative of the kind and degree of structure in learning. Teachers who assume this prerogative for themselves employ high structure. Those who involve their students use low structure. Whether one is more effective than the other depends upon the other factors present.

Relationships Within the Classroom

Group activities involve inter-personal relationships. Several people living and learning together acquire ways of behaving, attitudes toward other members, values from the interactions, and a sense of being a part of the on-going process. These same persons also develop sentiments and norms as a result of their group experience, which affect their subsequent actions. How the class group sees the status leader (teacher), and how he sees himself are both influenced by the experience.

Requiring students to stand when an adult enters the classroom indicates high structure. So does insistence upon such titles as "Doctor," "Professor," or "Sir." Any action which tends to set teachers apart from students is higher structure. Allowing or encouraging informality within the classroom, laughing *with* students at an instructor's error, or sitting down in a chair on the students' level all indicate low structure. In the first case there is a distinct effort to establish and maintain a manageable distance between teacher and students. In the other there is a definite effort to bridge that distance and work with students on the same plane.

There have been many studies (32, 61, 64, 68, 69, 90, 148) of the classroom "atmosphere" or "climate," terms which encompass the relationships between teachers and pupils and the feelings these generate. Students' attitudes toward teachers are partly a result of the attitudes they hold toward their fathers (133), and teachers' attitudes toward their students are colored by the way in which they think these children are accepted within the group (100). Homans' (67) comprehensive theory identified four basic elements of group activity: interaction, sentiments, activity, and norms. Internal group factors are often more important in understanding individual behavior than external ones. Wolman (151), for example, studying relationships in a group involving college students, found that some who were very able but rejected by their peers could still exercise power over the group's activities because of their ability. Cohesiveness and acceptance within the group evidently contribute to group accomplishment (29, 45, 57, 137), and cooperation rather than competition, especially, fosters these characteristics within groups (30, 55, 111, 136). Core classes seem to develop better relationships than conventional classroom groups (42, 79).

Hanna and Lang, (58), in a review of research, concluded that "dominative behavior by teacher or child induced dominative behavior in other children; similarly, integrative behavior induced integrative behavior in others." Dominating students entering new groups, however, have to adjust to the new group and accept some of their customs before exerting influence (103).

Since the teacher is the principal agent in establishing climate (26, 43) and setting the pattern, he is the one person who most profoundly affects group members' morale (124). Some teachers favor themselves and their own actions (15, 112), rejecting children or their viewpoints. Others are more learner-supportive, and the teacher-pupil relations in these classrooms differ sharply. There is also some evidence that teachers are more authoritarian and more conservative than other members of the profession (144), (e.g., principals, guidance counselors, supervisors).

Teachers who are able to engender esprit in their groups by establishing desirable relationships and free communication (119) and who let students know of their personal interest in them (27), help their students learn more effectively. Teachers exert influence (116), and participatory leadership evidently affects group judgment to a greater degree than supervisory leadership (114).

There are evidently some disadvantages among groups whose cohesiveness and inter-personal acceptances become too strong (77, 83, 123). We have already quoted the Horowitz and Perlmutter reference on this point (70). One final study might be relevant. Torrance (142), studying bomber crews, noted that the most "effective crews differ from ineffective crews in that their members less frequently perceived harmony and more frequently perceived discord." He concludes:

The energy which goes toward the maintenance of friendly interaction and achieving hedonistic pleasure may reduce the total
amount of energy available for carrying out the crew's major purpose. It may also mean that the better combat crews are more
tolerant of disagreement, are less threatened by it, and thus utilize
less energy in trying to maintain these friendly, pleasurable relationships.

These studies suggest that there may be some type of a statistical
concept between "good" classroom climate and a group's effectiveness.
"Poor" relationships between pupils and teachers impede educational
accomplishments, "good" relationships facilitate them, but relationships
which are "too good" apparently produce at least moderately negative
effects upon a group's progress.

In summary, more structure implies a teacher-determination of ideas,
expectations, communication patterns, decisions and the ways in which
they are reached, and the nature of the problems employed. On the
other hand, if the content of the experience, the techniques employed,
and the evaluative procedures are decided upon and implemented to
some considerable degree by the students and the teacher working coop-
ratively, such a situation would be less structured. If the patterns of
communication tend to be multi-source rather than teacher-centered, if
the problems which make up the basic content of the course are genuine,
are solved by experimentation and examination, are developed and
refined and decided upon by the students and the teachers together,
and if the relationships fostered are basically equalitarian, these things
would also denote less structure.

Requiring students to use certain kinds of mathematical materials
represents high structure, but if these same materials and the teacher's
activities encouraged inductive thinking, this would be low structure.
Any learning situation, therefore, is a blend of many kinds of structure.
A mere averaging of these factors would not accurately reflect the nature
of the structure being employed, since certain aspects exert greater
influence than others. For the time being, we can only be aware of this
dilemma, and hope that future studies can pinpoint the relationships
more precisely.

Structure means the extent to which the various aspects of learning
are effected by the teacher—more structure implying more teacher-
determination, less structure implying a greater degree of joint teacher-
student determination. Neither more nor less structure is better or more
effective in and of itself, but only in context.

WHAT TYPES OF STRUCTURE ARE POSSIBLE?

In the preceding pages we have looked at the research related to structure and tried to identify its components. Having some understanding of what structure is, the next question is: "What kinds of structure can I use in my classroom?" In the following pages are described six different types of structure which might be employed. Four of these ways of structuring are both appropriate and legitimate. The other two are either immoral or so ineffective that they should not be utilized by a teacher under any circumstances. Once the other kinds of structure are understood, however, the problem is one of determining when and how to use each one. These latter problems will be explored in subsequent chapters.

First, a listing of the various kinds of structure possible:

Manipulative
Directive
Persuasive
Discussive
Supportive
Non-Directive

In one sense these various ways might be though of as deviations along a single continuum moving from high structure to low. In another sense they are entirely different ways of working with classroom groups. In any event, both the first and last ways to be described represent untenable positions—untenable either because they violate democratic theory or learning theory or both.

Manipulative

If there is any kind of classroom structure which is truly authoritarian, it is the manipulative. Here we see a group moving in a given direction with the teacher as part of that group. Manipulation has many and devious forms, but in essence it means that members of the group are moved in a predetermined direction by the leader, but think they are participating in the decision-making process themselves. The leader, who has endeavored to make himself appear part of the group, functions so that the members actually come to feel that their ideas and concerns are being heard and considered. They accept the leader as an equal; they feel that he is working *with* them toward a goal which they have all defined and for which they all feel genuine concern.

This kind of structure is the most insidious because it is predicated upon either one or both of two assumptions: people are ignorant, or honesty is not important. Consider an illustration.

A professor of a graduate course enters the classroom on the first day and proceeds to establish rapport with the members of the group. This class meets for a weekly three-hour session. He attempts to learn everybody's name and to call them by their first names. He encourages the students to call him "George" rather than "Dr. _____." After a series of introductions, the instructor asks the class what they feel would be worthwhile to study for the coming semester. "This is a problems course," he says. "What problems are of most concern to you? What ideas would you like us to discuss during the weeks ahead?"

Figure 3

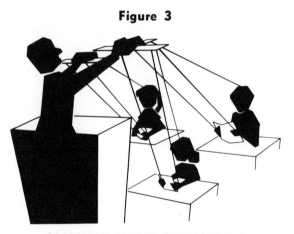

MANIPULATIVE STRUCTURE

As the session wears on, a list of problems begins to develop on the blackboard. Finally a set of criteria is discussed in preparation for selecting topics which will be most significant for the group as a whole. When it comes time to choose, a list of fourteen suggested problems of study is finally narrowed to five by the group. It is suggested that these five might constitute fruitful areas of inquiry for the weeks ahead, and the decision is made. All vote and all agree that this is right.

At this point the instructor pulls from his brief case pages of mimeographed material relative to the five topics. "I just happened to have these materials ready," he says.

Imagine these students' chagrin. They have been duped, and they know it, but only a slight slip on the part of the instructor made it apparent. Had he withheld the printed material until the next meeting, they all would have assumed that everything was straightforward. Nobody would have felt upset. As it is, many feel that the democratic process of discussion and voting, which they themselves had actually participated in, has failed. They are unable to differentiate between means and end.

How many times had just such an instance gone unnoticed? How many times had that same instructor hoodwinked most of his students into believing that they had participated in the decision-making when in actuality he had manipulated them for his own purposes?

The manipulative way of working with groups involves the use of ideas by a leader to achieve his own ends, regardless of the purposes or desires of the group. It involves a process in which the teacher actually moves the group in directions which he selects, while encouraging the students to believe they are really involved in the process. Such an instructor is "letting them think" that they are participating in the choice of topics for study, whereas he has already mapped out the course in detail. This "letting them think they have made the decision" eloquently characterizes the manipulator.

In practice manipulation may take many forms. In some instances it involves the refusal of a teacher to recognize persons whose opinions and ideas would be contrary to his own. As the status leader he may simply avert his eyes from them during the meeting, and not call on them for their discussion of the point in question. Such behavior may also take some form of paternalism. Group members may be given so much attention that they are unable to consider the significant problems at hand. They are not free.

Other manipulators in administrative roles may frown on proposals from various committees until their own notions are incorporated, and then laud them for adherence to the "democratic way." Such committees often wind up asking themselves: "What is it that he wants, anyway? Let's find out how he wants this thing done and do it his way. He is not going to approve it until it suits him, anyhow."

At other times, leaders may line up the votes on an issue before it has actually appeared for discussion in the group. Then, having persuaded people to commit themselves before they have fully comprehended the idea, they do not even participate in the "floor fight" when it develops. They let their lieutenants carry the leadership load.

Manipulation is a way of working with people which seems to be democratic but which is actually authoritarian. The superficialities of the democratic processes are invariably present, but the real spirit of democracy is never there. The harmful thing about such structure is that many persons may be misled, even for long periods of time, by a skillful manipulator, only to lose faith, both in themselves and the democratic way, when and if they discover the true nature of the procedure.

Some manipulators function undetected for years, and in all probability many such persons are not even completely aware themselves of exactly what they are doing. Some are so wrapped up in what they do and believe, they are unable to trust the genius of the group or any individual to make any contrary decisions.

However, when the time does come that some member presses his ideas to their logical extreme, the true nature of the manipulator may come to the surface. Gently prodded by the group to accept an idea alien to his own, he becomes evasive and ultimately resentful. Finally, as he slams his fist down on the table and violently swears while *insisting* on having his own way, then and only then do many recognize the true nature of the person with whom they have been working.

In a classroom, such a time may never come, but in school faculties and other groups it frequently does. The idea is described here to acquaint the reader with some of the aspects of manipulation; not to urge or even suggest that he employ them, but only to sharpen his awareness for such behaviors in himself or others.

The essential immorality of such a structure is that is assumes a way of dealing with people which is dishonest. It involves withholding or distortion of the facts. It presupposes that people are not sufficiently intelligent to make a good decision, hence need someone to make it for them. It makes a mockery of the democratic processes by perverting time-honored procedures for ulterior ends. There is no room for manipulation in a democratic school.

Directive

Seemingly similar yet really alien from manipulative structure is a way of working with groups which might be described as directive. In this situation the status leader openly asserts himself as the person initiating direction and communication patterns. He drives the group along paths wholly of his own selection, and in the process he uses ideas as levers to achieve his ends. The outstanding characteristics of this type of structure are one-way communication, a distinct superior-inferior kind of social relationship, and allowing information to serve both as a vehicle and commodity for facilitating "movement" of the group. Getting a group from one intellectual place to another is frequently described as "learning" by such a leader, and if he can effect such a change, he generally feels that students have learned and that he has been successful.

Figure 4

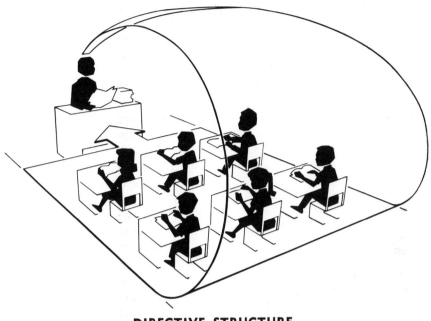

DIRECTIVE STRUCTURE

Some of the major differences between the directive and manipulative structure hinge upon the notion of openness. A directive leader is conspicuous by what is sometimes called his "autocratic" behavior. He openly commands and drives and is honest in the way he strives to achieve his purposes. An outstanding distinction between the manipulative and directive revolves around the ability of group members to recognize and relate to the different processes.

With the directive teacher, group members are able to assess the leader's position and relative significance clearly. They are able to adapt their own behavior without much difficulty. Many men, for instance, enter the armed forces and fulfill their obligations readily. They do not necessarily like or approve of the directive structure of these services, but it does not confuse them. They know exactly where they stand. They recognize their own relationships with the members of the military hierarchy and are able to fit in. In this same sense many persons are able to accept a political dictatorship, even though it may obviously be a means of working with people which is harsh or even brutal. It is when people do not know where they stand with their leaders and do not know if and when they are being used that they become confused and distrustful.

Directive behavior is legitimate in a democracy as long as members are free to leave if they wish, and as long as the leader exercises consideration for them. Lecture, for instance, is an appropriate instructional technique as long as the individual students really want to hear what the speaker has to say.

In this sense, directive structure represents an instance of high structure in the educational undertaking. Though it is sometimes described as "autocratic" or "authoritarian" by various writers, it is, in this connection, not only democratic but highly efficient under certain circumstances. It is important, however, that these circumstances exist. In the main, students must be very highly motivated, and really want to hear what this teacher has to say. Otherwise, such a procedure is almost certain to fail.

Persuasive

A third kind of structure frequently observed is one which might best be described as persuasive. Here, as suggested in the diagram, the teacher strives to become a part of the group. He works toward moving himself from a position of unearned authority towards one of earned authority. He strives to have his ideas accepted, not because he advances them or because he happens to be the leader, but rather because his ideas have worth. He seeks acceptance by the members of the group based upon their respect for him as a thinker and scholar and teacher. In this sense the persuasive person does not insist upon respect because he is the teacher, but, because he is, he seeks to earn the respect of his students by his ways of behaving. He becomes an authority but not an authoritarian.

The persuasive person is generally effective in convincing others of the worth of his ideas. Operating openly, and striving to earn the respect of the group, persuasive teachers are often quite successful in projecting their own ideas. Their ways of behaving are somewhat different from persons using directive structure. These persuasive people are effective in a pulling sort of way. Rather than driving a group along a path, they use a positive, pulling kind of force. They are able to convince members by persuasion that their suggestions are desirable. By the strength of their logic and the power of their personality, they are able to accomplish their ends.

The distinction between a persuasive and a manipulative teacher is often subtle. Both may appear congenial, pleasant, convincing and kind.

Figure 5

PERSUASIVE STRUCTURE

The real difference may only appear in that moment of crisis when the leader's authority must be exerted to its full limit. At such a time the manipulator drives forward relentlessly, demanding that things be done his way, while the persuader pauses, shrugs his shoulders, and lets the group move off in its own direction. With the manipulator, such a crisis invariably creates hard feelings between group members and the leader. The persuasive person, however, still remains an important part of the group, still able to present his ideas through the process of communication.

Discussive

When a teacher encourages a maximum of participation by all members of the group so that ideas are pooled, the structure takes on the characteristics of discussion. This results in activities which are like the "New England Town Meeting." Everybody who is present participates by projecting his own notions and by weighing the ideas of others. The result of such activity reflects the thinking of many persons in general and none in particular. When ideas are carefully explored and considered and modified, the resultant product represents the thinking of many individuals. When a teacher structures a classroom in such a fashion, the major activity is discussion.

To the novice, discussion and recitation may seem to be similar. Actually they are strikingly different. In a genuine discussion the leader's primary concern is one of thoughtful consideration of whatever ideas are introduced. A recitation repeats some particular point of view or statement of fact.

There are also at least two kinds of discussion: exploratory and decisive. In the first, the emphasis is upon understanding what is said, comprehending and considering the points of view of others. In the

Figure 6

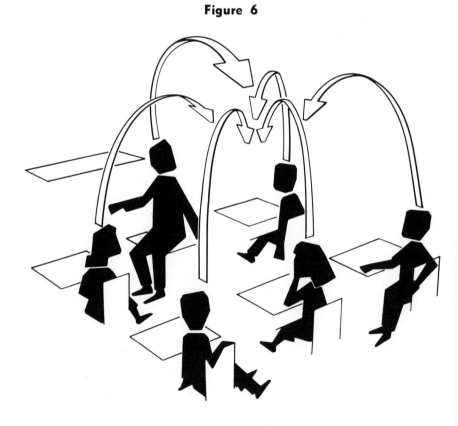

DISCUSSIVE STRUCTURE

decision type (like most legislatures, for example) discussion exists, but its purpose is to convince rather than to allow one to think through and understand. In both types there is extensive participation, but in the exploratory discussion the pace is slower. Group members strive intently to make themselves fully aware of the flow of ideas. In the decision type of discussion, on the other hand, conversation strikes out at a vigorous pace, and one is impressed with the feeling that more is being said than is being heard.

Either way, however, is discussive, and this structure is characteristic of many classrooms. Out of such experiences new directions frequently develop which neither the teacher nor class members had previously considered. From the power of group interaction, new thinking and new ideas open up new avenues of thought.

Whoever teaches in such a manner, naturally, is skillful in evoking participation and facilitating multi-source communication. He is sensitive to the slightest response, and always shows his students how to listen by being a good listener. Such a teacher inevitably moves from a position of unearned respect to one of earned respect.

Supportive

Sometimes a teacher helps and supports students to move out in directions in which they are vitally interested. Supportive structure is frequently found in seminar courses at the graduate level or in individualized study programs in secondary schools. Here students map out areas of individual concern, and then proceed to examine them by themselves. In every instance the instructor is available and helpful. The student goes his own way, but with extensive encouragement from the teacher. This support comes in the form of suggestions for reading, personal contact, individual conferences, praise and helpful ideas about techniques or procedures.

When a teacher employs supportive structure he enables students to move in their own directions at their own pace, but he is ever present with advice and counsel to make the experience more significant and personal.

Non-Directive

A final type of structure which has been studied extensively is the non-directive kind. Usually referred to as laissez-faire, this structure truly permits students to "do as they please." The non-directive and supportive have certain superficial similarities. Both permit students to pursue topics of their own choice. Both result in many people going in

Figure 7

SUPPORTIVE STRUCTURE

many directions at the same time. However, the teacher who uses supportive structure realizes the need learners have for mature assistance, whereas the non-directive teacher apparently feels that children can do no wrong, and anything they do will be all right for learning. Non-directive structure has no place in an educational institution, though it is very reasonable for mature and competent adults. Students, however, not only need but want assistance and support. They need "walls to push against," as some psychiatrists say. They need to know where they are and how far they can go. The vagueness of the non-directive classroom overwhelms all but the most mature and stable students, leaving them exhausted and uncertain.

SUMMARY

Structure is many things and shows up in many ways. Its basic elements include both the kind and amount of communication present, the

Figure 8

NON-DIRECTIVE STRUCTURE

type of mental activity sponsored, an understanding of what must be done and what cannot be done, and the extent and quality of human relationships which exist within the group.

Highly structured programs have lecture and recitation, encourage memorization and deductive logic, insure social distance between teachers and students, and have clearly defined purposes of learning determined before the students arrive. When teachers involve their students in determining directions and limitations by means of discussion and inductive thinking, they are using less structure.

Teachers have at their disposal a variety of teaching techniques and procedures. Whether they are directive, persuasive, discussive, or supportive, democratic teaching involves emphasis on both information and individual choice. The purpose of structure in a classroom is to facilitate the flow of ideas so that the most information is available. Ideas are important, and the more ideas the better. Any approach to the problem of classroom teaching which tends to increase the quantity and quality of ideas, and simultaneously enable students to gain experience and practice in exercising wise choice, is truly democratic.

Choice, of course, can come at several times and places in the educational scheme. Choosing for its own sake is not important. Teaching children to make wise choices is fundamental. The problem of structuring the learning experience so that choice can occur will be explored in Chapter Seven.

REFERENCES

1. Adams, Joseph J., "Achievement and Social Adjustment of Pupils in Combination Classes Enrolling Pupils of More Than One Grade Level," *Journal of Educational Research*, XLVII (October, 1953), 151-155.
2. Aiken, Wilford M., *The Story of the Eight Year Study* (New York: Harper and Bros., 1942).
3. Alexander, William M. and Ersoff, Samuel, "Schools for Adolescents: Instructional Procedures," *Review of Educational Research* (February, 1954), XXIV, 54-65.
4. Alltucker, Margaret M., "Is the Pedagogically Accelerated Student a Misfit in the Senior High School?" *School Review*, XXXII (1924), 193-202.
5. Anderson, Robert P. and Kell, Bill L., "Student Attitudes About Participation in Classroom Groups," *Journal of Educational Research*, XLVIII (December, 1954), 255-267.
6. Arnold, Henry F., "The Comparative Effectiveness of Certain Study Techniques in the Field of History," *Journal of Educational Psychology* (December, 1954), 449-457.
7. Baldauf, Robert J., "A Comparison of the Extent of Educational Growth of Mentally Advanced Pupils in the Cedar Rapids Experiment," *Journal of Educational Research*, LII (January, 1959), 181-183.
8. Banning, Evelyn, "Teacher Attitudes Toward Curriculum Change: The Effect of Personal Relationships on the Degree of Favorableness," *Journal of Experimental Education*, XXIII (December, 1954), 133-142.
9. Bass, Bernard M., "Feelings of Pleasantness and Work Group Efficiency," *Personal Psychology*, VII (Spring, 1954), 81-91.
10. Bennett, Edith B., "Discussion, Decision, Commitment and Consensus in 'Group Decision,' " *Human Relations*, VIII (August, 1955), 251-273.
11. Biggs, K. M. and Miller, J. B., "Attitude Change Through Undirected Group Discussion," *Journal of Educational Psychology*, XLIX (1958), 224-228.
12. Bills, Robert E., "An Investigation of Student Centered Teaching," *Journal of Educational Research*, XLVI (December, 1952), 313-319.
13. Bloom, B. S., "Thought-Processes in Lectures and Discussion," *Journal of General Education*, VII (April, 1953), 160-169.
14. Blue, John T., Jr., "The Effects of Group Study on Grade Achievement," *Journal of Educational Psychology*, XLIX (June, 1958), 118-123.
15. Bogen, Isidore, "Pupil-Teacher Rapport and the Teacher's Awareness of Status Structures Within the Group," *Journal of Educational Sociology*, XXVIII (November, 1954), 104-114.
16. Borgatta, Edgar F., "Analysis of Social Interaction and Sociometric Perception," *Sociometry*, XVII (February, 1954), 7-32.
17. Brown, Sanford, C., "Do College Students Benefit from High School Laboratory Courses?" *American Journal of Physics*, (May, 1958).
18. Bruner, Jerome S., *The Process of Education* (Cambridge: Harvard University Press, 1960).
19. *The Bulletin of the National Association of Secondary School Principals*, XLVI (February, 1962).

20. Burnett, Lewie W., "Core Programs in Washington State Junior High Schools," *The School Review*, (February, 1951), 97-100.
21. Capehart, Bertis E., "An Objective Evaluation of a Core Program," *The School Review*, LX (February, 1952), 84-89.
22. Chansky, Norman M., "The Attitudes Students Assign to Their Teachers," *Journal of Educational Psychology*, XLIX (July, 1958), 13-16.
23. Cohen, Arthur R., "Situational Structure, Self-Esteem, and Threat-Oriented Reactions to Power," in *Studies in Social Power*, Dorwin Cartwright, Ed. (Ann Arbor: University of Michigan, 1959), 35-52.
24. Cook, Walter W., "Some Effects of the Maintenance of High Standards of Promotion, *Elementary School Journal*, XLI (February, 1941), 430-437, as cited in *Educational Measurement*, E. F. Lindquist, Ed. (Washington, D. C.: American Council on Education, 1951), 20.
25. Cornell, Ethel L., "Effects of Ability Grouping Determinable from Published Studies," in *The Grouping of Pupils*, 35th Yearbook, Part I, NSSE, 1936, 289-304.
26. Cunningham, Ruth et al., *Understanding Group Behavior of Boys and Girls* (New York: Bureau of Publications, Teachers College, Columbia University, 1951).
27. Cunningham, Ruth, "Factors Affecting Group Behavior," *Baltimore Bulletin of Education*, XXIX (March-June, 1952), 9-15.
28. Davis, O. L., Jr., "Grouping for Instruction: Some Perspectives," *Educational Forum*, XXIV (January, 1960), 209-216.
29. Deutsch, Morton, "A Theory of Cooperation and Competition," *Human Relations*, II (April, 1949), 129-152.
30. Deutsch, Morton, "An Experimental Study of the Effects of Co-operation and Competition upon Group Process," *Human Relations*, II (July, 1949), 199-232.
31. Doll, Ronald C., "The High-School Pupils' Attitude Toward Teaching Procedures," *The School Review*, LV (April, 1947), 222-227.
32. Drawhorne, Curtis L., "Relation Between Pupil and Student-Teacher Interaction and Pupil Ratings of Teaching Effectiveness," *Educational Administration and Supervision*, XL (May, 1954), 283-296.
33. Ekman, Gösta, "The Four Effects of Cooperation," *Journal of Social Psychology*, XLI (February, 1955), 149-162.
34. Elias, George S., "An Experimental Study of Teaching Methods in Ninth Grade Social Studies Classes (Civics) (1957)" as reported in *NASSP Bulletin*, XLVI (February, 1962), 125-127.
35. Engle, Thelburn L., "A Study of the Effects of School Acceleration upon the Personality and Social Adjustments of High School and University Students," *Journal of Educational Psychology*, XXIX (October, 1938), 523-539.
36. Fair, Jean, "The Comparative Effectiveness of a Core and a Conventional Curriculum in Developing Social Concern," *The School Review*, LXII (September, 1954), 364-355.
37. Faunce, Roland and Bossing, Nelson, *Developing the Core Curriculum* (New York: Prentice Hall, 1951).
38. Feany, F. J., "A Survey of Instructional Practices and Equipment Used in Observed Lessons in the Social Studies in Grades VI to VIII in Selected Cities of the Midwest," *Journal of Educational Research* (January, 1937), 348-356.
39. Flanders, Ned A., *Teacher Influence: Pupil Attitudes and Achievement*, Final Report, Cooperative Research Project No. 397, University of Minnesota, Minneapolis, Minn., November 30, 1960.
40. Flesher, Marie A. and Pressey, Sidney L., "War Time Accelerates Ten Years After," *Journal of Educational Psychology*, XLVI (April, 1955), 228-238.

41. Foley, Grayce A., "Current Democratic Methods of Teaching at the Secondary Level in the United States," *Dissertation Abstracts*, XII (1952), 265-266.
42. Forlano, George and Wrightstone, J. Wayne, "Measuring the Quality of Social Acceptability Within a Class," *Educational and Psychological Measurement*, XV (Summer, 1955), 127-136.
43. Foshay, Arthur W. and Green, John Hawkes, "The Development of Social Processes," *Review of Educational Research*, XXIII (April, 1953), 146-150.
44. Fox, William M., "Group Reaction to Two Types of Conference Leadership," *Human Relations*, X (August, 1957), 279-289.
45. Frazier, Alexander, Ed., *Freeing Capacity to Learn* (Washington, D.C.: Association for Supervision and Curriculum Development, 1960).
46. Gale, Raymond, "The Progress of Students and Graduates of a Core Curriculum," *The School Review*, LXIII (October, 1955), 384-387.
47. Gebel, Arnold S., "Self Perception and Leaderless Group Discussion Status," *Journal of Social Psychology*, XL (November, 1954), 309-318.
48. Gerard, Harold B., "Some Effects of Status, Role Clarity, and Group Goal Clarity upon the Individual's Relations to Group Processes," *Journal of Personality*, XXV (June, 1957), 475-488.
49. Gilbert, Eugene, "What Young People Think: Teen-Agers Favor Code of Behavior," *The Philadelphia Inquirer*, April 4, 1958.
50. Gilchrist, Jack C. et al., "Some Effects of Unequal Distribution of Information in a Wheel Group Structure," *Journal of Abnormal and Social Psychology*, XLIX (October, 1954), 554-556.
51. Gill, Margaret, "A Look at Secondary Education Methods Courses," *Educational Leadership*, XVI (March, 1959), 355-367.
52. Goodlad, John I., "Classroom Organization," *The Encyclopedia of Educational Research*, Chester W. Harris, Ed. (New York: Macmillan Co., 1960), 224.
53. Goodlad, John I. and Anderson, Robert, *The Nongraded Elementary School* (New York: Harcourt Brace Co., 1959).
54. Gordon, Garford G., "A Study of Methods of Making Provision for Outstanding Science and Mathematics Students in High School," *Science Education*, XXXVIII (February, 1954), 24-33.
55. Gottheil, Edward, "Changes in Social Perception Contingent upon Competing or Cooperating," *Sociometry*, XVIII (May, 1955), 132-137.
56. Grann, Lloyd R. et al., "The Relationship Between Academic Achievement of Pupils and the Social Structure of the Classroom," *Rural Sociology*, XXI (June, 1956), 179-180.
57. Grossack, Martin M., "Some Effects of Cooperation and Competition upon Small Groups Behavior," *Journal of Abnormal and Social Psychology*, XLIX (July, 1954), 341-348.
58. Hanna, Paul R. and Lang, Arch D., "Integration," *Encyclopedia of Educational Research*, Walter S. Monroe, Ed. New York: Macmillan Co., 1952).
59. Hare, A. Paul, "A Study of Interaction and Consensus in Different Sized Groups," *American Sociological Review*, XVII (June, 1952), 261-267.
60. Hare, A. Paul, "Small Group Discussions with Participatory and Supervisory Leadership," *Journal of Abnormal and Social Psychology*, XLVIII (1953), 273-275.
61. Hare, A. Paul; Borgatta, Edgar F.; and Bales, Robert F., Eds., *Small Groups: Studies in Social Interaction* (New York: Alfred A. Knopf, 1955).
62. Harvey, Helen, "An Experimental Study of the Effect of Field Trips upon the Development of Scientific Attitudes in a Ninth Grade Science Class," *Science Education*, XXXV (December, 1951), 242-248.
63. Harvey, O. J. and Rutherford, Jeanne, "Gradual and Absolute Approaches to Attitude Change," *Sociometry*, XXI (March, 1958), 61-68.
64. Haythorn, William et al., "The Effects of Varying Combinations of Authori-

tarian and Equalitarian Leaders and Followers," *Journal of Abnormal and Social Psychology*, LIII (September, 1956), 210-219.

65. Hillson, Joseph S. et al., "The Field Trip as a Supplement to Teaching: An Experimental Study," *Journal of Educational Research*, LIII (September, 1959), 19-22.

66. Holmes, Darrell and Harvey, Lois, "An Evaluation of Two Methods of Grouping," *Educational Research Bulletin*, XXXV (November 14, 1956), 213-222.

67. Homans, George C., *The Human Group* (New York: Harcourt Brace and Co., 1950).

68. Horowitz, Milton W. and Perlmutter, Howard V., "The Concept of the Social Group," *Journal of Social Psychology*, XXXVII (February, 1953), 69-95.

69. Horowitz, Murray and Cartwright, Dorwin, "A Projective Method for the Diagnosis of Group Properties," *Human Relations*, VI (November, 1953), 397-410.

70. Horowitz, Milton W. and Perlmutter, Howard V., "The Discussion Group and Democratic Behavior," *Journal of Social Psychology*, XLI (May, 1955), 231-246.

71. Hoover, Kenneth H., "An Experiment on Grouping Within the Classroom," *California Journal of Secondary Education*, XXX (October, 1955), 326-331.

72. Hull, J. H., "Multigrade Teaching," *Education Digest*, XXIV (October, 1958), 5-7.

73. Jackson, Jay M., "The Effect of Changing the Leadership of Small Work Groups," *Human Relations*, VI (February, 1953), 25-45.

74. Jackson, Philip W. and Guba, Egon G., "The Need Structure of In-Service Teachers: An Occupational Analysis," *The School Review*, LXV (Summer, 1957), 176-192.

75. Jamrich, John X., "A Study of Current Practices in Conducting General Methods and Related Courses in the Preparation of Secondary School Teachers," *Journal of Educational Research*, XLVIII (September, 1954), 57-65.

76. Jenkins, William A., Ed., *The Nature of Knowledge* (Milwaukee: The University of Wisconsin at Milwaukee, 1961).

77. Jersild, A. T. et al., *Children's Interests and What They Suggest for Education* (New York: Bureau of Publications, Teachers College, Columbia University, 1949).

78. Jewett, Arno and Hull, Dan J., *"Teaching Rapid and Slow Learners in High Schools*, Bulletin No. 5, 1954. U. S. Dept. of Health, Education, and Welfare, Office of Education. Washington, D. C.

79. Kelley, Arthur C. and Beatty, Robert E., "Proof That Core Program Students Learn Basic Skills," *The School Review*, LXIV (January, 1956), 16-34.

80. Kelly, Harold and Pepitone, Albert, "An Evaluation of a College Course in Human Relations," *Journal of Educational Psychology*, XLIII (1942), 193-209.

81. Kerlinger, Fred N., "Progressivism and Traditionalism: Basic Factors of Educational Attitudes," *Journal of Social Psychology*, XLVIII (August, 1958), 111-135.

82. Kerr, Willard A., "Untangling the Liberalism-Conservatism Continuum," *Journal of Social Psychology*, XXXV (February, 1952), 111-125.

83. Kipnis, David, "The Effects of Leadership Style and Leadership Power upon the Inducement of an Attitude Change," *Journal of Abnormal and Social Psychology*, LVII (September, 1958), 173-180.

84. Kiszka, Joseph, "Describing the Effects of Experimentation in Teaching Science at the Eighth Grade Level," *Science Education*, XLII (October, 1958), 327-333.

85. Kight, S. S. and Mickelson, J. M., "Problems vs. Subject," *The Clearing House*, XXIV (September, 1949), 3-7.

86. Kruglak, Haym, "Achievements of Physics Students With and Without Laboratory Work," *Science Education*, XIV (February, 1954), 32-47.
87. Lagey, Joseph C., "Does Teaching Change Students' Attitudes?" *Journal of Educational Research* (December, 1956), 307-311.
88. Lewin, Kurt, "Group Decision and Social Change," *Readings in Social Psychology* (New York: Henry Holt Co., 1949).
89. Lewin, Kurt; Lippitt, Ronald; and White, R. K., "Patterns of Aggressive Behavior in Experimentally Created 'Social Climates,'" *Journal of Social Psychology*, X (May, 1939), 271-299.
90. Lewin, Kurt, "Experiments on Autocratic and Democratic Atmospheres," *Social Frontier*, IV (July, 1938), 316-319, as quoted in Fullagar, William A.; Lewis, Hal G.; and Cumbee, Carroll F., *Readings for Edueational Psychology* (New York: Thomas Y. Crowell Co., 410-417).
91. Lovell, John T., "The Bay High School Experiment," *Educational Leadership*, XVII (March, 1960), 383-387.
92. Lyle, Edwin, "An Exploration in the Teaching of Critical Thinking in General Psychology," *Journal of Educational Research,* LII (December, 1958), 129-133.
93. Maier, Norman R. F., "An Experimental Test of the Effect of Training on Discussion Leadership," *Human Relations*, VI (May, 1953), 161-173.
94. Maier, Norman R. F., "Screening Solutions to Upgrade Quality: A New Approach to Problem Solving Under Conditions of Uncertainty," *Journal of Psychology*, XLIX (April, 1960), 217-231.
95. Marquart, Dorothy Irene, "Group Problem Solving," *Journal of Social Psychology*, XLI (February, 1955), 103-113.
96. McGill, J. V., "How Valuable Is Homework?" *High Points*, XXXII (September, 1950), 48-53.
97. McKeachie, Wilbert J., "Individual Conformity to Attitudes of Classroom Groups," *Journal of Abnormal and Social Psychology*, XLIX (April, 1952), 282-289.
98. McKeachie, W. J., "Student-Centered Versus Instructor-Centered Instruction," *Journal of Educational Psychology*, XLV (March, 1954), 143-150.
99. Medley, D. M. and Mitzel, H. E., "A Technique for Measuring Classroom Behavior," *Journal of Educational Psychology*, XLIX (April, 1958), 86-92.
100. Meeks, Kenneth L., "Teacher and Pupil Judgments of Interpersonal Relations in the Classroom," *Dissertation Abstracts*, XVII (1957), Part I, 65.
101. Mellinger, Glen D., "Interpersonal Trust as a Factor in Communication," *Journal of Abnormal and Social Psychology*, LII (May, 1956), 304-309.
102. Mennes, A. H., "What Students Think of Integrated Curricular Practices in High School English and School Studies," *The School Review*, LXII (December, 1954), 535-541.
103. Merei, Ferenc, "Group Leadership and Institutionalization," *Human Relations*, II (January, 1949), 23-39.
104. Mills, Harriet C., "Thought Reform: Ideological Remolding in China," *The Atlantic Monthly*, CCIV (December, 1959), 70-77.
105. Moreno, J. L., "A Note on Sociometry and Group Dynamics," *Sociometry*, XV (August-November, 1952), 364-366.
106. National Education Association, "Teacher Opinion on Pupil Behavior, 1955-56," *NEA Research Bulletin*, XXXIV (April, 1956).
107. "Nation-Wide Sampling of Superintendents by Nation's Schools," *Nation's Schools*, LVIII (July, 1956), 57-58.
108. Passow, A. Harry, "The Maze of the Research on Ability Grouping," *Educational Forum*, XXVI (March, 1962), 281-288.
109. Pelz, Donald C., "Influence: A Key to Effective Leadership in the First-Line Supervisor," *Personnel*, XXIX (November, 1952), 209-217.

110. Perkins, Hugh V., "Climate Influences Group Learning," *Journal of Educational Research*, XLV (October, 1951), 115-119.
111. Phillips, Beeman N. and D'Amico, Louis A., "Effects of Cooperation and Competition on the Cohesiveness of Small, Face-to-Face Groups," *Journal of Educational Psychology*, XLVII (February, 1956), 65-70.
112. Polansky, Lucy, "Group Social Climate and the Teacher's Supportiveness of Group Status Systems," *Journal of Educational Sociology*, XXVIII (November, 1954), 115-123.
113. Preston, Malcom G. and Heintz, Roy K., "Effects of Participatory Versus Supervisory Leadership on Group Judgment," *Journal of Abnormal and Social Psychology*, XLIV (1949), 345-355.
114. Progressive Education Association, *Thirty Schools Tell Their Story* (New York: Harper and Bros., 1943).
115. Raths, Louis, "Power and Social Status," *Journal of Educational Sociology*, XXVIII (November, 1954), 97-103.
116. Raven, Bertram H., "Social Influence on Opinions and the Communication of Related Content," *Journal of Abnormal and Social Psychology*, LVIII (January, 1959), 119-128.
117. Rehage, Kenneth J., "A Comparison of Pupil-Teacher Planning and Teacher-Directed Procedures in Eighth Grade Social Studies Classes," *Journal of Educational Research*, XLV (October, 1951), 111-115.
118. Rogers, Maria, "Problems of Human Relations in Industry," *Sociometry*, IX (November, 1946), 350-371.
119. Roethlisberger, F. J., *Management and Morale* (Cambridge, Massachusetts: Harvard University Press, 1947).
120. Ruja, Harry, "Outcomes of Lecture and Discussion Procedures in Three College Courses," *Journal of Experimental Education*, XXII (June, 1954), 385-394.
121. Runkel, Philip J., "Cognitive Similarity in Facilitating Communication," *Sociometry*, XIX (September, 1956), 178-191.
122. Schneider, Samuel, "An Experiment on the Value of Homework," *High Points*, XXXV (April, 1953), 18-19.
123. Seashore, Stanley E., *Group Cohesiveness in the Industrial Work Group* (Ann Arbor: University of Michigan, Institute for Social Research, Survey Research Center, 1954).
124. Selznick, Philip, *Leadership in Administration: A Sociological Interpretation* (Evanston, Illinois: Row, Peterson and Co., 1957).
125. Shane, Harold G. and Polychrones, James Z., "Elementary Education—Organization and Administration," *Encyclopedia of Educational Research*, Chester W. Harris, Ed. (New York: Macmillan Co., 1960), 421-430.
126. Shane, Harold G., "Grouping in the Elementary School," *Phi Delta Kappan*, XLI (April, 1960), 313-319.
127. Shaw, Marvin E. and Gilchrist, Jack C., "Intra-Group Communication and Leader Choice," *Journal of Social Psychology*, XLIII (February, 1956), 133-138.
128. Smith, B. Othanel, *A Study of the Logic of Teaching*, USOE Project No. 258. College of Education, University of Illinois. Mimeographed. (no date)
129. Smith, Ewart E., "The Effects of Clear and Unclear Role Expectations on Group Productivity and Defensiveness," *Journal of Abnormal and Social Psychology*, LV (September, 1957), 213-217.
130. Somit, A. et al., "Effects of the Introductory Political Science Course on Student Attitudes Toward Personal Political Participation," *American Political Science Review*, LII (1953), 1129-1132.
131. Spence, Ralph B., "Lecture and Class Discussion in Teaching Educational Psychology," *Journal of Educational Psychology*, XIX (1928), 454-462.
132. Spivak, Monroe L., "Effectiveness of Departmental and Self-Contained

Seventh- and Eighth-Grade Classrooms," *The School Review*, LXIV (December, 1956), 391-396.

133. Stagner, Ross, "Attitude Toward Authority: An Exploratory Study," *Journal of Social Psychology*, XL (November, 1954), 197-210.

134. Stogdill, Ralph M., *Individual Behavior and Group Achievement: A Theory, the Experimental Evidence* (New York: Oxford University Press, 1959).

135. Taylor, Calvin W., "Possible Positive and Negative Effects of Instructional Media on Creativity," unpublished paper read at the ASCD seminar on Instructional Materials, St. Louis, April 19, 1960. Mimeographed.

136. Tear, Daniel Grant and Guthrie, George M., "The Relationship of Cooperation to the Sharpening-Leveling Continuum," *Journal of Social Psychology*, XLII (November, 1955), 203-208.

137. Thelen, Herbert A. et al., "Report on an Experiment Between a Group of Friends and a Group of Non-Friends," unpublished paper, 1953.

138. Thelen, Herbert A., "Educational Dynamics: Theory and Research," *The Journal of Social Issues*, VI (1950), 20.

139. Thelen, Herbert A. and Whithall, John, "Three Frames of Reference: A Description of Climate," *Human Relations*, II (April, 1949), 159-176.

140. Toops, Myrtle D., "The Core Program Does Improve Reading Proficiency," *Educational Administration and Supervision*, XL (1954), 494-503.

141. Torrance, E. Paul, "The Behavior of Small Groups Under the Stress Conditions of 'Survival,' " *American Sociological Review*, XIX (December, 1954), 751-755.

142. Torrance, E. Paul, "Perception of Group Functioning as a Predictor of Group Performance," *Journal of Social Psychology*, XLII (November, 1955), 271-282.

143. Volney, Faw, "A Psychotherapeutic Method of Teaching Psychology," *The American Psychologist*, (1949), 104-109.

144. Wall, Bartholomew D., "Some Attitudinal Differences Among Educational Specialists, Administrators and Teachers," *Journal of Educational Research*, LIII (November, 1959), 114-117.

145. Washburne, Carleton W. and Raths, Louis E., "The High-School Achievement of Children Trained Under the Individual Technique," *Elementary School Journal*, XXVIII (1927), 214-224.

146. Weiss, Robert S. and Jacobson, Eugene, "A Method for the Analysis of the Structure of Complex Organizations," *American Sociological Review*, XX (December, 1955), 661-668.

147. Weiss, Robert S., *Processes of Organization* (Ann Arbor: University of Michigan, Institute for Social Research, Survey Research Center, 1956).

148. Wickman, E. K., *Children's Behavior and Teacher Attitudes* (New York: The Commonwealth Fund, Division of Publications, 1928).

149. Wilkins, Walter L., "The Social Adjustment of Accelerated Pupils," *The School Review*, XLIV (June, 1936), 445-455.

150. Wingo, G. Max, "Methods of Teaching," *Encyclopedia of Educational Research*, Chester W. Harris, Ed. (New York: Macmillan Co., 1960), 848-861.

151. Wolman, Benjamin, "Leadership and Group Dynamics," *Journal of Social Psychology*, XLIII (February, 1956), 11-25.

152. Wright, Grace S., "Ten Years of Research on the Core Program," *The School Review*, LXIV (December, 1956), 397-401.

153. Wrightstone, J. Wayne, *What Research Says to the Teacher, No. 13, Class Organization for Instruction* (Washington, D. C.: National Education Association, 1957).

Chapter Seven

Using Structure Creatively

INTRODUCTION

In preceding chapters we have examined the concepts of learning, motivation, democracy, and structure. The purpose of this chapter is to blend these ideas into workable units so that teachers can use each effectively.

Learning

Learning has been described as the process of experiencing which results in changed behaviors. The organism engages in a series of activities designed to get the "outside" world inside his central nervous system. Once there, he attributes significance to his experiences by giving meaning to what he sees and hears. His perceptions are affected by how he sees himself, by his goals, and by the opportunities which he has to receive certain stimuli. Learning is only effective if the organism has a chance to explore ideas and information so that these stimuli have personal meaning for him. Mere contact is not enough. He must find ways and means of weaving the ideas into the fabric of his being before they can possibly affect his behavior.

Motivation

Motivation toward school is the result of an individual's personality and the kinds of values he holds. Those persons who are very perceptive and who believe in the worth of ideas are more apt to desire to do good work in school than those who feel otherwise. Persons whose perceptual

193

apparatus denies them experience of the world in which they live, who are cut off from their environment by psychological barriers and defense mechanisms, are seldom able to recognize the opportunities inherent in learning. They have built-in resistances which prevent them from acquiring the desire to know. They may possess high native ability, but they are prisoners of their own personalities, locked in isolation from their fellow man by prejudice and fear. These persons seldom display genuine desire to learn. Those who believe in the worth of ideas and in themselves, who are amenable to change, who do, in fact, seem to thrive on variations within their lives, are highly motivated. Their personal sense of adequacy and their particular value structure enables them to approach experiences so that they are continually finding chances to weave new ideas in with the old, and generate new concepts from experienced information. Their curiosity is almost childlike. They seek to learn.

Democracy

Democracy involves situations which are filled with opportunities to perceive. Two-way communication is apparent, and the purpose of communication is recognized as the need to examine ideas and information critically to subject them to the test of truth. Democracy is predicated upon the notion that each individual will learn to make wise choices, and in order for people to choose wisely, they must have access to vast amounts of information. This information must come to them in a way that is perceptible. Democracy also involves creating human relationships which enable people to think well of themselves and of their fellow man. It discourages degradation of either self or others. It seeks to foster relationships which culminate in independence of thought and action; independence which presupposes the worth and dignity of all men; independence which emanates from belief in the right of an individual to his own particular course of action. Democracy is learned by living it, and being democratic is more important than knowing what it is or being able to describe its parts.

Structure

Finally, structure has been described as that phase of the educational process which determines how a teacher develops various factors under his control: the communication patterns, the social relationships involved, the thought patterns encouraged, the sequence of ideas in the logic of subject matter, and the source and course of direction which the classroom group pursues. If the teacher dictates that the communication shall come primarily from a single source, and if distinct dominating-submissive relationships are fostered, more structure is practiced. Likewise, to evoke deductive thinking and determine what shall be taught and how, in isolation from student participation, would be evidence of considerable structure. On the other hand, if a teacher sought to establish equalitarian relationships within the room, if he worked with learners so that they had genuine opportunities to participate in determining the educational path to follow, and if many persons were contributing ideas and presenting information, this would be recognized as less structure. The effective teacher is the one who employs those particular structures which will be most in harmony with all of the forces within the classroom.

This chapter will be devoted to an exploration of ways in which teachers can use structure creatively. The creative teacher is the one who precisely understands many things about the situation in which he finds himself: his pupils and their peculiar needs; his own capabilities and his own preferences for teaching style; the nature of the subject matter; the types of instructional materials and facilities available, and the nature and importance of democracy. Finally, he needs to be able to weld all of these into a way of working which results in effective teaching. He needs to structure his teaching situation in such a way so that the students can learn effectively and democratically.

Teaching democratically but ineffectively is, by definition, impossible. Democracy thrives on intelligent behavior. Young people must experience ideas in order to be influenced by them. If the instruction is not effective, it denies the learner the opportunity to become a changed person by means of correct information.

On the other hand, increasing learning by violating the principles of democracy is self defeating. It is not possible to develop a free people by enslaving them while they are young. Our schools have kept us free. Our schools must keep us free. If freedom is worth fighting for and dying for, it is worth practicing in schools. Freedom is predicated upon the principles of democracy, and democracy must be practiced in classrooms as well as fought for on the battlefield. Schools must be democratic. Teachers must work in democratic ways toward democatic ends.

USING STRUCTURE DEMOCRATICALLY

Our task is clear. We must select or devise ways of structuring the learning situation so that students learn effectively and democratically. Structure is significant because it is the one thing over which the teacher has the most control: himself and his own behaviors.

It may be difficult to do more than acknowledge the fact that students have particular kinds of home backgrounds or come to school with different kinds of abilities. Some teachers use students' inadequacies as reasons why their youngsters do not learn, rather than trying to contrive ways of coping with the realities. Structure represents a manipulable variable in the educational process. Teachers can change what they do and how they do it. They can change themselves and their ways of working within the classroom. Teachers can use structure creatively by thoughtfully varying the kinds they employ, according to sound educational principles.

Allowing Choice

Using structure democratically demands that teachers assure learners of opportunities to exercise choice. Making decisions and exercising options is the democratic way; it is the stuff of freedom. If teachers want to help children learn to behave democratically and if they want their classrooms to reflect democracy in action, they must create opportunities for children to choose. Learning to make wise choices is like learning anything else; it follows instruction and practice. Intelligent decisions, calling for exact thinking, do not "just happen" unless people have had experience in the act.

Allowing students to make decisions, however, lies at the very core of some of the controversy about modern education. There are those who maintain that children should be deprived of any opportunity to make selection anywhere along the line. Their position runs something like this: "If you can hold the learner still long enough and get enough information into his head, he will be old enough and wise enough to make intelligent, responsible decisions." It hardly seems reasonable that you can teach young people to make wise decisions when they are older by denying them the right to try while they are young. Children have to learn to make choices, and they must learn by doing it.

Choice in education, however, can be real or apparent. Terminology may be misleading. An "elective" course in science for ninth-graders is really not a choice compared to a "required" course for college sophomores.

Teachers must recognize that choice in education may occur at either one of the two places, outside the classroom or within. Students may actually choose to take part in a particular course, and their decision has occurred outside the classroom itself. They can also make decisions and choices within the classroom, selecting topics for study and projects to develop. Unless students have genuine opportunities to choose and to make decisions, democracy is hardly possible inside the classroom or out. Whether these choices occur inside the classroom or before students enter is important, but in an entirely different way. The point is that they must occur.

Making decisions opens some doors and closes others. A satisfying existence presupposes the ability to open those doors which will be most meaningful to the person involved. At the same time he must learn to abide by the restrictions which he has imposed upon himself. For instance, if a person chooses to learn to fly an airplane, he may have to give up learning to be a good golfer. Both may appeal to him, but if time is limited, making one decision automatically negates another.

Securing Involvement

Choice is fundamental because it is one way to evoke involvement. When people have genuine opportunities to make decisions which affect their welfare, when they know that what they do and how they do it will influnce them personally, they become involved. Involvement is essential to effective learning. Unless students are psychologically committed to what they are doing, learning is a hollow affair. Teachers who are really interested in helping students change their ways work toward their involvement.

Involvement is attachment to the process, and follows choice. Significantly, learning follows involvement, but not until that involvement is proved. False choices or artificial efforts to guarantee participation may be successful for short periods, but they inevitably collapse when their true nature becomes known. Democracy demands a faith in people, and a way of working which is based on facts and on an honest way of working with them. Any effort at subversion, for whatever purposes, will backfire when the means become known. Teachers who disguise their own purposes by letting students think they make the decision are guaranteeing that learners will be deprived of a chance to grow. Students who discover that they "have been used" often lose all faith in the democratic way. Matching the opportunities to exercise choice with age and experience is one thing. Stating this and then pursuing your own ends through group participation and apparent voting is another. The classroom is no place for ulterior ways. Outright autocracy is better than a false democracy. People know how to react to those who openly deny them the right to choose. They can revolt.

Students' Sense of Adequacy

Choice and involvement are important parts of effective method, but another aspect is how students feel about themselves. Structuring a classroom must result in a sense of satisfaction or all else has failed. The learner must feel that what is going on is right and makes sense to him in light of his own purposes. He has to feel that what the teacher has done by directing the course of class action is compatible with his own needs and aspirations. He has to feel capable of responding to what has gone on and what will come. He must feel positively toward himself and his fellows. As he goes through the learning process and acquires information, new attitudes, and skills, he must interact with these so that he is able to make everything an integral part of himself. This is not possible if he feels threatened or anxious in any way.

Teacher's Sense of Adequacy

Likewise, whatever the teacher does to affect the structure must make sense to him as a person. He has to feel comfortable in his tasks. All of the research in the world could say that this way is better than that, but if a teacher does not feel adequate with the technique it will not be effective. Developing adequacy is a major teacher responsibilty. Though teachers may feel uncomfortable with new techniques, it does not mean they dare ignore them for long. What they must do is avail themselves of opportunities to keep up with current thinking about classroom methods. They have to practice these until they are a part of their professional repertoire. They have to feel at ease using many methods. This sensation comes with practice and skill.

When all of these conditions have been met, teachers are in a position to use structure creatively. If students have genuine opportunities to choose, if they can really become involved, and if students and teachers all feel comfortable in their work, teachers are in a position to employ structure creatively. Because the type of structure necessary may deviate from what students have known before, this idea might seem something of a paradox. If students must feel comfortable doing what the teacher requires, it may be disconcerting to be asked to do something new.

The wise teacher, however, recognizes that he must always start with students where they are. It is much easier to help students move from one experience to another if their present position is acceptable to them. The sensitive teacher incorporates enough of the known to assure familiarity, and adds enough of the unknown to make the process educational. In this way, idea by idea, teachers help students learn. There are no magic roads to intelligent behavior. There are only little steps, one at a time, which lead there.

This is the teacher's job. to organize the learning process so that persons who have less experience and less maturity than he can be helped to achieve understanding in an effective, democratic way. The skillful teacher does this by using himself as a teaching tool. He uses his personality and his ideas and his knowledge of how people learn to create a structure which will help his students grow.

RELATING STRUCTURE TO MOTIVATION

Motivation in School

Motivation manifests itself in many ways. One of the most common is apparent in young people's attitudes toward school. Many students have strong positive feelings about school. They like their teachers and they like to learn. They are attracted toward ideas, they seek new experiences, and they enjoy the chance to work hard to improve themselves.

Other students do not share these feelings. Some hate school with a passion. They dislike teachers. They do not like books. The very thought of going to school is distasteful. These persons are interested in learning, of course, but not in learning what the school teaches. They feel compelled to go to school.

The degree to which people feel compelled to go to school varies. Assume that compulsion refers to the personal sensation which any learner might possess about *having* to go to school; it is not his idea. Compulsion refers to a personal interpretation of the amount of external pressure exerted to get him there. It represents a state of mind ranging from extreme discomfort to pure joy at the prospect.

If we could determine the extent to which a hypothetical "average" student feels compelled to go to school, it would probably range from a fairly low point among six-year-olds up to a fairly high point among fifteen-year-olds, and then drop again for those boys and girls who continue their education. A motivation curve might look like the diagram in Figure 1.

It is probably safe to say that most children in early elementary school do not feel the external compulsion to attend school as strongly as do some older children. They are more highly motivated toward school. They want to learn.

When children want to learn, the problem of limits and requirements takes on an entirely different aspect than when their motivational level is low. When young people really want to learn they will meet almost any requirements and heed almost any limits. Structure here can be entirely different than when students hate school.

In the later elementary grades and junior high school, the extent to

Figure 1

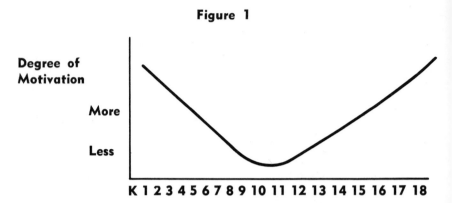

Degree of
Motivation

More

Less

K 1 2 3 4 5 6 7 8 9 10 11 12 13 14 15 16 17 18

**The Degree to Which Young People Probably Feel Motivated
to Do Good Work in School**

which many young people feel motivated to do good work decreases.
This probably reaches its lowest point somewhere between the ninth
and eleventh grades. Considering the compulsory attendance laws in
most states and the student mortality rate, one notes that the period of
greatest drop-out occurs at this time. Evidently those who leave school
at sixteen are not highly motivated toward school itself. Why else would
they leave?

Need for a Principle

It is the purpose of this book to attempt to outline a way of working
with students whatever their motivational patterns. What we need is a
principle to guide our actions. A principle is important because of the
varied degrees of motivation and the kinds of personalities which students bring to school. Everybody knows that children are different, but
a teacher must cope with these differences directly or fail himself.
Appreciating differences is not enough. The skillful teacher needs to
recognize the multitude of variations which exist among his students,
then treat them in a way which will be both democratic and effective
in helping them learn.

Students See the Classroom Situation Differently

How does the classroom look to different learners? If we can think of
structure as the positive and negative forces built into the situation by
the teacher, perhaps we can portray these feelings graphically. If we

summarize all that we know about structure to include the expectations and limitations imposed or developed either by the teacher himself (high structure) or in conjunction with his students (low structure), then it may be that we can present these ideas better spatially than verbally. Throughout the next few pages, expectations will be considered as the positive factors which are a part of structure within classrooms, and limitations will be considered as negative factors. This description is only partially correct, of course, since expectations may be negative to a learner if they are beyond his attainment. Likewise, limitations may be recognized in positive ways on some occasions; "getting bawled out" by the teacher may be rewarded under certain circumstances by peer approval. In the main, however, expectations are those aspects of structure which embody notions designed to attract learners. Limitations involve curtailments of students' freedoms for particular ends. In the following illustrations, the hurdles represent the students conceptions, of classroom expectations and limitations.

The parallel expectation-limitation situation shown in Figure 2 symbolically outlines some teachers' images of the classroom structure. They see in their classrooms many attractive features (positive values), as well as certain definite limitations (negative values). These teachers might well believe that their classroom structure encourages psychological exploration of increased learning. To the students, however, this naïve perspective is unrealistic. They see the classroom structure more accurately, as suggested in Figures 3 and 4.

Figure 3 illustrates the image of the classroom as it appears to a student whose motivational level is low. He feels compelled to be in school; he sees himself surrounded by uninteresting but definite expectations and limitations. Achievement of the expected goals seems impossible for him, and he feels trapped. He gives in quickly to defeat, and his only positive outlook is to quit.

Conversely, the highly motivated student sees the classroom as optimistic and challenging. Figure 4 illustrates his image of the expectations and limitations confronting him. This view of the classroom is more apparent with a graduate student, who is highly involved in his major study area. His motivation for learning is increased because he has a greater area for intellectual movement and a definite goal at the end of the hurdles. He sees the many requirements before him as positive values and does not exercise his option to leave until he has attained his goal even though he may freely leave at any time. Leaving prematurely is undesirable to him.

To point to these few illustrations is simply to underscore the fact that students view differently the way a teacher structures a class. The

Figure 2

**Naïve Teachers' Estimate
of Classroom Structure**

graduate student in Figure 4, for instance, does not see the situation in negative terms because he selected it in the first place. He chose to be there. The demands are exactly what he wants. He expects the instructor to lay out a narrow and rigorous course for him to follow, and he will pursue it.

Look again at our learner in Figure 3, however. Here we see a kind of structure which, from the student's point of view, it very narrow. Faced on all sides with barriers, confronted with requirements which he does not desire, the entire situation is overwhelming in many ways. The learning experiences built into the course are not recognized as challenges but as threats. The student is not attracted toward the new experiences because they are exciting or worthwhile; he is repelled by them because they are too difficult or unrelated to his own needs. Even though the result of the entire course may be attractive, if he must survive these negative experiences to get there, the entire process will be avoided, if at all possible.

Figure 3

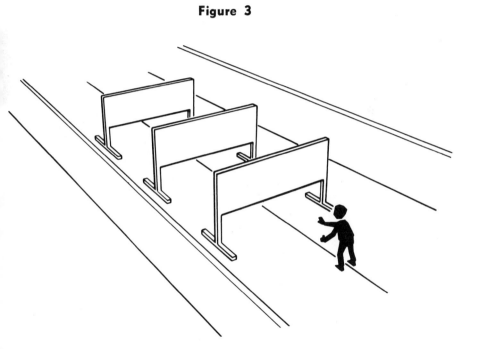

Low Motivated Students' Perception of Classroom

If all school is seen in these terms, this student will undoubtedly quit when the time allows. Until that time, he may "drop out while he is still in school," psychologically, at least. He may skip school or feign sickness whenever possible, or retreat into his own little world while he is there within the building. Fortunately or unfortunately, the human mind has a way of compensating by withdrawing into a world of fantasy when the pressures mount too high. Teachers who assume that all students who are present really want to learn are fooling themselves. Students are not all highly motivated. Deploring this fact is one possible course of action for a teacher. Devising a way of working with such young people is a different approach. Effective teachers are those who structure the situation in such a way that students who dislike school are attracted toward it, so they will feel pulled not pushed, encouraged not discouraged, accepted not rejected.

Figure 4

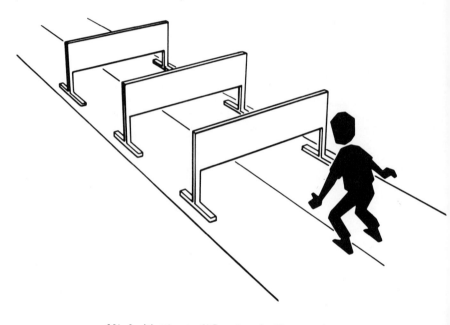

**High Motivated Student's Perception
of Classroom Structure**

A Step Toward Effective Structure

Knowing that students see the classroom in different ways should give us clues as to how to structure for maximum learning. If a sensitive teacher recognizes that his students feel the way our learner does in Figure 3, he can arrange things so that the situation is seen differently. He tries to help the student feel the way the learner does in Figure 2: surrounded, but with a bit more room. Since there is no physical way out of the classroom because of the compulsory attendance laws, then perhaps the teacher can try to make "intellectual leg room" *inside.*

Perhaps he can interest the student in ways which will allow him to move about within certain limits and create objectives for himself which are both realistic and inviting. Since no choices were involved in determining whether or not he would be included in the first place, maybe the teacher can contrive opportunities for the student to become involved by working with him, slowly and carefully.

If the student feels compelled to be in school, the teacher actually has one of two directions in which to move. Either he can work for more restriction or less. Either he can "clamp down" or he can "let up." He can attempt to "demand" attention or he can try to "evoke" participation. He can employ more structure or less. What would you do?

Many teachers working in junior high school tend to feel that if students "get out of line" as youngsters often do when they are trying to evade unpleasantness, they must be held in check. The teacher who feels this way tends to "tighten the screws" on the educational lid. He deprives students of opportunities to leave the room, to speak, or to work on activities of their own choosing. He may prevent them from participating in extracurricular activities or keep them after school. In any one of a thousand different ways the teacher may impose greater structure upon the student.

On the other hand, given these circumstances, another teacher might choose to move in the other direction. He could make fewer requests and fewer demands. He could be more tolerant of late papers or minor oversights. He might also work to find out what his students' interests are, and he might try to encourage systematic investigation of some of these interests as legitimate classroom activities.

Faced with one student or an entire class who see themselves as our student does in Figure 3, hemmed in and disliking school, a teacher can attempt to move with these students' purposes or against them. He can seek to "fence them in" and push them toward his goal, or he can try to pull them by involving them deeply in concerns of their own making, recognizing that once he has their attention and cooperation, he can help. Less structure, not more, is clearly called for here. This does not mean that the student will do whatever he desires. It does mean that the teacher and the student together can pool their ambitions, knowledge, and skill, and out of this joint effort and less structure can come effective learning.

Parts of our principle begin to stand clear now. There are times when a teacher should deliberately use less structure. Should he ever use more? Let us go back to our graduate student of Figure 4. Here we see a learner deeply engrossed in a field of study, the field of English, perhaps, highly motivated to learn, and desirous of instructor help. The student is already involved. He has chosen to take the course and he embraces the idea of being "allowed" to proceed through a series of demanding experiences.

Structure here takes on an entirely different aspect. The more that is demanded of this student, the better he likes it. More structure appeals to him because he is highly motivated. Less structure would probably be interpreted as a sign of weakness on the part of the instructor or "softness" on the part of the course. This student wants great demands to be made on him.

A Principle of Educational Method

Already we can see that there is no single way of structuring a class without being aware of students' motivations and varying the structure according to these needs. Our principle seems fairly clear.

> *The amount of structure in a classroom should vary directly with the degree of student motivation. The greater the motivation, the more the structure. The less the motivation, the less the structure.*

This principle of educational method is democratic and firmly rooted in learning theory. By capitalizing upon student motivation, the principle incorporates the idea that involvement facilitates learning. By creating situations in which student choice is emphasized, the principle embodies the very spirit of democracy itself.

If we can accept the notion that motivation toward school starts at a relatively high level, decreases to a low point somewhere during the junior or senior high school years, and then increases again at the upper college level, how should the structure pattern look? Figure 5 shows the amount of structure which, according to the principle just described, should be employed.

Translating the Principle into Practice

Recognizing that a teacher should vary the way in which he structures his students' motivation is one thing. Finding ways to accomplish this in actual practice may be another. The discussion thus far has revolved around motivation as tied directly to age and the compulsory attendance laws. There is some relation between these factors, obviously, but the relationship is neither as simple nor as direct as has been implied. Most students, who start school at about six years of age actually want to go, but there are some who abhor the whole idea. Many students feel the compulsory aspects of education very strongly when they are about fifteen years old; their motivational level is quite low. However, great

Figure 5

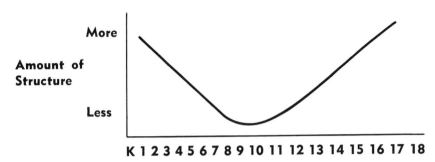

K 1 2 3 4 5 6 7 8 9 10 11 12 13 14 15 16 17 18

Variations in Structure Which Should Be Employed in "Average" Situations

numbers of other children at this age want to do good work and really want to learn. During the pages which follow we will examine some specific examples to make the discussion more realistic.

The important point under consideration is this: *It is not unreasonable to structure to a high degree.* However, the amount and kind of structure should vary according to some defensible criterion, and motivation is such a factor. Likewise, *it is not unreasonable to use less structure.* If students' motivations toward school are relatively low, less structure will be both more feasible and more effective.

Some Examples of Different Types of Motivation

It is not uncommon for junior high schools to require a course in English grammar. Frequently students are expected to learn the parts of speech, to be able to diagram sentences, punctuate correctly, spell properly, and, hopefully, by the end of the year to express themselves legibly and effectively in written form.

Faced with this, many adolescents, particularly boys, respond quite negatively. They see little relationship between labeling words within a sentence and learning to write precisely and communicate well. They fail to see the significance of diagramming sentences and studying parts of speech. Going through an explosive period of their own physical growth, acquiring new interests and knowledge outside of school, and facing difficult decisions regarding moral standards and ethical problems, adolescent boys frequently find other things much more interesting than school. Their motivation drops. For some, the prospect of "dropping out" within a short period of time is appealing. With this kind of student, how should a teacher structure his class for best results?

Let us consider for a moment our graduate student working toward his doctorate in English Literature. Thinking of his future life as a professor of English, intrigued by the intricacies of language, attracted toward the academic life and learning in general, this student relishes the opportunity to work hard in English grammar. Whatever the instructor suggests, he will pursue, not because he is dependent or afraid, but because he is sincerely interested in learning all he can about the subject. If the professor suggests he read this book or write that paper, such request is readily accepted as a resonable and desirable part of the course. When his papers are returned with criticisms and comments, they only spur him on to greater effort. The more the instructor demands the more he likes it. Increasing the structure is a positive means to a desirable end; his own competence in the field of English.

Another illustration might be helpful. Games and physical education activities are often appealing to boys in senior high school. Let us look at two examples. Varsity football coaches often approach their charges at the beginning of the year with something like this: "If you want to play football here you will have to do these things: Get to bed every night before nine o'clock. Keep your grades up. Be out here for practice every day at three o'clock sharp and work till five. You cannot smoke, drink, swear, or carouse at all. You will have to work very hard keeping yourself in shape physically and psychologically for the game. There are many plays to learn, and you may get hurt. For all of this I may give you a chance to play, but the odds are that many of you will be on the bench a lot of the time. Are there any questions?" To this kind of structure, many boys say: "Good! I am ready to start. When can I begin?"

The situation just described, of course, is highly structured. The coach imposes many limitations and expectations upon his team. *He* plans the practice sessions, *he* selects the plays, *he* decides who will and who will not be allowed to play. Yet through all of this, many boys are eager to join the squad, willing to try, if he will have them. They want to learn. Why do they accept such a rigid structure?

The answer is obvious. It is because they want to play. They are very highly motivated. *They* decide whether they want to play varsity football or not. *They* choose whether or not they want to enter this learning area, and abide by the coach's rules. Having made this choice, they are willing to submit to the teacher-imposed restrictions and demands because they want to learn. Structure is not really a problem unless the coach uses too little.

On the other hand, suppose that same coach also teaches a required course in physical education for boys of the same age. Suppose that he decides to use the same techniques and the same structure with his required course, since it worked so well with the varsity team. What do you think will happen?

Without question, rigid structure imposed by a teacher on a large group of students less interested in physical education than the football team is in playing football is apt to bring dire consequences. Making students do difficult exercises, run exacting plays time after time for perfect performance, play till exhaustion, then play some more—these exactions meet with a different response. Much structure is perfectly acceptable to members of a voluntary team; they have chosen to participate. Rigid structure for those required to take physical education whether they want to or not gets a different reaction.

The question is basically whether the teacher will decide to work with the learners' natural grain or against it. The physical education teacher who makes a recalcitrant student "take five laps around the field for being slow" may be teaching the boy the value of physical exercise. The odds are he is also teaching him to dislike physical education. Isn't it interesting how many teachers use their basic subject matter for punishment when students get out of hand? Maintaining that "learning to write is an important skill," and punishing an unruly youngster by making him write a theme of 500 words on "Why I Will Do as I Am Told" seems somewhat contradictory. If an experience is good, why is it selected as a punishing device?

Consider another illustration. Mathematics is required of all sixth grade students. Physics is generally available for those who want to take it about grade twelve. Students' attitudes toward sixth grade arithmetic vary from positive to negative; some are highly motivated and some are not. Most of the students enrolled in physics, however, are there because they want to be. They have decided that physics is something which will be of value to them. They are highly motivated to learn.

For the sixth grade teacher, structuring the classroom is quite complex. For those students who are attracted toward mathematics and want to learn, he can employ more structure. For those who resist the idea of learning quantitative relationships, less structure is more appropriate. By the very nature of the situation, however, most of the physics students can be assumed to be highly motivated, thus more structure is in line.

As one last example, many schools today are teaching elementary school children a foreign language. Children's reactions to learning a second language vary, but in the main they are excited about it and want to learn. Especially if the program proceeds at a conversational level, most youngsters will be enthusiastic about the opportunity to study a foreign language and culture. It is novel, it is something they may have heard about, and it is frequently taught by an especially competent teacher, who may be out of the ordinary and even somewhat exotic. All things considered, many boys and girls in the early elementary grades who have an opportunity to learn a foreign language are quite highly motivated.

Suppose, on the other hand, that a man majoring in electrical engineering is required to master a foreign language in order to get his college degree. Here we have a student working in a field of his choice who has to take a course not even closely related to it. Assume, further, that this particular man dislikes foreign languages. Now we have a situation with complex motivational factors. The boy wants an engineering degree but he does not like languages. He has chosen to go to college and study engineering, but a part of that choice involves studying some things completely unrelated to his interests, as he sees them. He wants to be successful, he wants to learn, and he wants the degree, but he dislikes studying foreign languages.

In the first instance it is probably quite appropriate for an elementary foreign language teacher to use considerable structure. In the second case, less structure would undoubtedly be most effective.

Thus far only pure motivational factors have been discussed, but many other things are important. The motivations of a six-year-old who wants to learn to read are not identical to those of a graduate student working on his dissertation. Both are highly motivated, but in different ways. High structure is called for in working with both students, but because experience and maturity differ, these structures also ought to differ. The accomplished teacher will be able to build the kinds of experience each learner needs by relating the fine points of their interests and achievements to his understanding of the dynamics of structure in action.

Other complications also arise. Certain kinds of "false" motivation may distract the teacher from using the best type of structure. Many students will want to work hard only because good grades will guarantee them certain advantages or rewards outside of school. If a student has been promised a dollar for every "A" or a new car if he graduates from college, such factors introduce a new set of variables which affect the structure. No longer is the student really interested in trying to do good work for its own sake. His motivations have been contaminated.

In a similar manner, many parents push their children so hard that they develop fears of various kinds if they do not succeed in school. Their fundamental academic motivations are really rooted in apprehensions about loss of parental affection or fear of reprimand. These factors cloud real motivations to a point that it will be difficult for teachers to know which forces are really operating. The problem becomes especially involved when students who fear the consequences of bad grades appear to be moving toward higher levels of motivation but are actually becoming dependent in their efforts to achieve. These factors are things of which the effective teacher must be aware and must seek to interpret and understand. His real skill rests on his ability to make structural sense out of the maze of dynamic factors evident in that most complex of social institutions, the school.

Faced with such students, teachers who want to work democratically but effectively must employ structure precisely, so that it will fit their students' needs. They must match their own techniques to their students' motivations.

There are two courses of action. Either teachers can work with their administrators to group students into classes in which these students' motivational patterns are fairly similar, or they can vary their instructional ways according to their learners' needs within their own classrooms.

Grouping Students Within a School

Schools have to organize their students into units. Grouping students has long been accomplished according to age, sex, intellectual ability, reading achievement or interest. What is suggested here is that it might be more productive and more satisfying if students were grouped according to their desire to do good work.

Students who are highly motivated tend to respond positively to high structure. Students who dislike school respond most effectively to lesser structure. If students were grouped according to their motivations toward school, teachers might be able to tailor their teaching to meet the needs of the group. This is the same kind of argument often proposed for grouping students according to ability. The difficulty in that case, however, is that even though students may have similar abilities, if their motivational levels vary they tend to respond differently to different types of instruction. On the other hand, students of differing abilities but similar motivations are much more apt to learn effectively if the structure employed is matched with their ambitions rather than with their abilities.

Since both ability and maturation influence learning, what would be most effective would be to employ both factors: able students who are highly motivated, able students who are not highly motivated, less able students who are highly motivated, and less able students who are not highly motivated. Grouping students according to their abilities without taking into account their motivations is probably much less effective than grouping them primarily according to their desire to do good work in school. Motivations are more basic to learning, even, than ability, as far as teaching methods are concerned.

One other point deserves attention if schools consider grouping students in any way. Teachers must be matched with groups to be effective. Teachers must be "fitted" to students whose motivational levels demand the kind of teaching style which is most appropriate for them. Many teachers "feel more at ease" using one kind of structure than another. The wise administrator will see to it that these teachers are placed with students whose motivational needs allow a minimum of conflict and a maximum of personal satisfaction for all involved. Placing students in particular groups makes no sense at all unless they are confronted with teachers whose basic style will harmonize with their own particular ambitions.

Working with Students Within a Classroom

Many teachers, however, will find themselves unable to work with groups of students who have been placed together according to their motivation toward school. Recognizing this, teachers can ascertain certain facts about each of their students, and then select the type of structure which will be most productive for the majority.

Still other teachers, however, can even relate to different students differently according to their desire to do good work. A fundamental notion of learning is that we must start with people where they are. Where there are many different kinds of student motivation present in one classroom, it is most advisable to use types of structure which will be most effective at the moment, according to each student's motivational needs. Wherever possible, each teacher should provide each student with the experiences and opportunities to develop that will enable him to move from where he is to where he ought to be. The "best" teachers are those who are most flexible, most able to build a structure which corresponds to their students' needs.

Imagine a classroom in which a teacher is simultaneously working with three groups of students using three types of structure. With one small group he is behaving very directly, telling them precisely what to do and how to do it. With a second group he is participating in discussion, pooling ideas and generating direction from everyone's participation. With two individuals he is being supportive, allowing them to strike out in directions which mean most to them, but backing them up with suggestions and criticisms. The point here is that teachers must capitalize upon paramount factors of student development and need and turn them to advantage. The wise and sensitive teacher is one who studies his students ceaselessly for any indication of variation in these factors. Being sensitive, he is able to modify the classroom structure of the moment for a more timely approach. He varies his teaching procedures with his students' own aspirations.

This is not to say that his teaching techniques are "will-o'-the-wisp." Every function of his behavior is designed to stimulate a positive reaction among his students, and the only reason he ever modifies his procedures is so that he can increase his students' learning. Students' action patterns are seldom so erratic as to call for drastic overhaul of teaching method every day. The sophisticated and competent instructor, however, is constantly alert to cues and clues.

Reviewing our eight examples, how would you structure your classroom to cope with these different students? For the eighth-grade grammar student a discussive type of structure might be most effective. For the graduate student in English, supportive might be most appropriate. For the varsity football players a very directive type of structure would seem to be most useful; for the physical education class the persuasive might be of greatest value. The twelfth grade physics teacher might do best using directive and persuasive means, whereas the sixth grade arithmetic teacher most certainly would find discussive more effective. For the teacher working with elementary students learning a foreign language either the direct or persuasive would seem to fit most precisely. For the college language teacher with the reluctant engineering student the persuasive would seem to lend itself most readily to the learner's needs.

It is not possible to prescribe the types of structure any teacher should employ without knowing more about the circumstances than it has been possible to outline here. The best teachers are those who seek all possible information about their students, and then devise teaching procedures to match these learners' ambitions so that the classroom operation proceeds smoothly and surely. You can use structure creatively.

GENERAL OBSERVATIONS AND SUMMARY

Many critics of American education speak only from their own experience in the academic world. Suppose that you were a college professor of history working primarily with advanced undergraduate and graduate students. You probably would have observed that your students come to you highly motivated, and you have also found out over the years that the more you demand of them the more you get. By bearing down, you note that your students respond favorably. They like to be told what to do and how to do it. They like the idea of having the course laid out completely by the instructor before they arrive. In this way they can immediately master the required experiences and go on.

From where you stand in your university post, when you "get tough" with students and "bear down" they seem to like it. It is very natural to generalize from your experiences to the whole field of education, but if you do you are in serious error. Just because college students who are highly-motivated react favorably to presure does not mean that it will be effective all up and down the line.

Consider the education professor who *lectures* to his students that they ought to use discussion. Is he being undemocratic? Is he violating what he believes? Is he failing to practice what he preaches? The answer to these questions is "not necessarily." Since college students' motivations are apt to be entirely different from the motivations of the youngsters with whom these prospective teachers will be working, there is nothing inherently incorrect in being directive while urging future teachers to be more discussive. The principle is constant, but the novice may fail to see it. However, the education professor who *insists* that his students participate in group activities and make decisions about what they will do in his course is really being quite directive.

Other teachers must be careful not to generalize about educational method strictly from their own frame of reference. Most teachers are academically oriented. They like school and books and learning; that is why they are where they are. All boys and girls, however, do not have these same feelings toward school. Any teacher who unconsciously projects his own motivations and values into his teaching methods to the point that he ignores his students' desires to learn will find himself in serious difficulty, and perhaps not know why.

This is not to say that teachers should not be enthusiastic about what they teach. Being enthusiastic, however, is not to assume that, because teachers generally like books and ideas and school, all other persons do. There may be many youngsters in their classes even more highly motivated to learn than they are. Others will be much less interested in every respect. To cope with these differing students, teachers must strive to understand each one as an individual human being; how he sees school; how he feels about himself; what his values and his interests are; how he strives to learn. Knowing these things, then, the creative teacher presents an educational experience tailored to the need pattern of each student. Teaching is an art based on a science. The best teachers are those who fully comprehend the great mass of personal and social factors operating within the classroom, then, by sensitive observations and exacting methods, construct learning experiences which will be congruent with and moving in the same direction as their pupils' expectations.

Keeping students within limits and maintaining discipline is a result, not an action itself. Students who are actively pursuing their own purposes have little time to get into trouble. Teachers who structure their classrooms according to their students' motivations generate entirely different attitudes among their learners than those who proceed as if they ought merely to do as they are told.

Learning is a very personal affair. Clarifying expectations and limitations will be helpful in gaining and maintaining classroom control. Unless students know exactly where they stand and what they can and cannot do, they move to find out. They try to "see how far they can go." Establishing rigid limits is no real solution. To make sure that some reasonable expectations are clearly understood, as well as compatible with students' purposes, will simplify the problem. No one wants to live in a world without limits, but young people have a way of testing limits. These testing actions are seldom designed to be destructive, though they are surely meant to gauge better the nature of the structure which is employed. Wise teachers expect students to test the limits, but they also know that if learners have helped establish these limitations and expectations, or have chosen them in some general way, discipline becomes a way of achieving mutually acceptable goals by involvement and choice.

In summary, the purpose of this chapter has been to outline a way of working with students so that the principles of democracy and learning theory are apparent. It suggests that teachers should vary the structure which they employ according to their students' motivational levels. Further, each teacher should also attempt to fashion his structuring procedures so that he can match his ways with his students' learning needs, individually or collectively. This is the art of teaching. Some teachers do these things intuitively. Most have to learn through effort and continuous study.

REFERENCES

1. Aaron, I. E. et al., "Fourth Grade Teachers Experiment with Cross-Class Grouping for Reading Instruction," *Elementary English*, XXXVI (May, 1959), 305-307.
2. Aaron, Ida S., "Teachers' Attitudes Toward Children's Behavior: A Study of Teachers' Attitudes Toward Children's Behavior Problems and Their Relation to Pupil-Teacher Morale," *Dissertation Abstracts*, XIX (1958), 1024.
3. Abramson, David A., "The Effectiveness of Grouping for Students of High Ability," *Educational Research Bulletin*, XXXVIII (October 14, 1959), 169-182.

4. Aeleny, Leslie Day, "Leadership," *Encyclopedia of Educational Research,* Walter S. Monroe, Ed. (New York: Macmillan Co., 1952), 662-668.

5. Albers, Mary E. and Seagoe, May V., "Enrichment for Superior Students in Algebra Classes," *Journal of Educational Research,* XL (March, 1947), 481-495.

6. Albrecht, Milton and Gross, Llewellyn, "Nondirective Teaching," *Sociology and Social Research,* XXXII (May-June, 1948), 874-881.

7. Alexander, Theron, "The Prediction of Teacher-Pupil Interaction with a Projective Test," *Journal of Clinical Psychology,* VI (July, 1950), 273-276.

8. Alder, Henry L. and Norton, Donald A., "Intermediate Algebra in High School or College?" *Journal of Educational Research,* LII (October, 1958), 61-63.

9. Amatora, Sister Mary, "Highs and Lows in the Teacher Personality," *Journal of Educational Research,* XLVIII (May, 1955), 693-698.

10. Amidon, Edmund and Flanders, Ned A., "The Effects of Direct and Indirect Teacher Influence on Dependent-Prone Students Learning Geometry," *Journal of Educational Psychology,* LII (December, 1961), 286-291.

11. Anderson, H. H. and Brewer, H. M., "Dominative and Socially Integrative Behavior of Kindergarten Teachers," in *Studies of Teacher's Classroom Personalities,* I (Stanford University Press, 1955).

12. Anderson, H. H. et al., "Image of the Teacher by Adolescent Children in Four Countries: Germany, England, Mexico, United States," *Journal of Social Psychology,* L (August, 1959), 47-55.

13. Anderson, Kenneth E. et al., "An Evaluation of the Introductory Chemistry Course on Film," *Science Education,* XLV (April, 1961), 254-269.

14. Anderson, Kenneth E. and Montgomery, Fred S., "An Evaluation of the Introductory Chemistry Course on Film by the Factorial Design and Covariance with Method and Sex as the Main Variables," *Science Education,* XLV (April, 1961), 269-274.

15. Anderson, Lester W., "Teacher Morale and Student Achievement," *Journal of Educational Research,* XLVII (May, 1953), 693-698.

16. Anfinson, Rudolph D., "School Progress and Pupil Adjustment," *The Elementary School Journal,* XLI (March, 1941), 507-514.

17. Asch, M. J., "Nondirective Teaching in Psychology: An Experimental Study," *Psychological Monographs,* LXV (1951), Whole No. 321.

18. Astin, Alexander W., " 'Productivity' of Undergraduate Institutions," *Science,* CXXXVI (April 13, 1962), 129-135.

19. Baldauf, Robert J., "A Comparison of the Extent of Educational Growth of Mentally Advanced Pupils in the Cedar Rapids Experiment," *Journal of Educational Research,* LII (January, 1959), 181-183.

20. Baker, Marvin E., "A Comparison of Grades Between Grouped Classes," Unpublished Master's Thesis (The Ohio State University, 1961).

21. Banghart, Frank W., "Group Structure, Anxiety, and Problem-Solving Efficiency," *Journal of Experimental Education,* XXVIII (December, 1959), 171-174.

22. Barbe, Walter B., "Evaluation of Special Classes for Gifted Children," *Exceptional Children,* XXII (November, 1955), 60-62.

23. Barbe, Walter B. and Waterhouse, Tina S., "An Experimental Program in Reading," *Elementary English,* XXXIII (February, 1956), 102-104.

24. Barbe, Walter B., "What Happens to Graduates of Special Classes for the Gifted," *Educational Research Bulletin,* XXXVI (January, 1957), 13-16.

25. Barr, A. S., "Teaching Competencies," *Encyclopedia of Educational Research,* Walter S. Monroe, Ed. (New York: Macmillan Co., 1952), 1446-1454.

26. Barr, A. S. et al., "The Measurement and Prediction of Teacher Effectiveness," *Journal of Experimental Education,* XXX (December, 1961).

27. Barrett-Lennard, G. T., "Dimensions of Perceived Therapist Response Related

to Therapeutic Change," Unpublished Doctoral Dissertation (University of Chicago, 1959).

28. Barry, R. F. and Smith, P. E., "An Experiment in Ninth-Grade Reading Improvement," *Journal of Educational Psychology*, XLV (November, 1954), 407-414.

29. Barthelmess, H. M. and Boyer, P. A., "An Evaluation of Ability Grouping," *Journal of Educational Research*, XXVI (December, 1932), 284-294.

30. Bavelas, Alex and Lewin, Kurt, "Short Articles and Notes on the Training in Democratic Leadership," *Journal of Abnormal and Social Psychology*, XXXVII (1942), 115-119.

31. Baymur, Feriha B. and Patterson, C. H., "A Comparison of Three Methods of Assisting Underachieving High School Students," *Journal of Counseling Psychology*, VII (Summer, 1960), 83-90.

32. Bearmer, George C. and Ledbetter, Elaine W., "The Relation Between Teacher Attitudes and Social Service Interests," *Journal of Educational Research*, L (May, 1957), 655-666.

33. Bendig, A. W., "Ability and Personality Characteristics of Introductory Psychology Instructors Rated by Their Students," *Journal of Educational Research*, XLVIII (May, 1955), 705-710.

34. Billet, R. O., "A Controlled Experiment to Determine the Advantages of Homogeneous Grouping," *Educational Research Bulletin*, VII (April and May, 1928), 133-140, 165-172, 190-196.

35. Bills, Robert E., "An Investigation of Student Centered Teaching," *Journal of Educational Research*, XLVI (December, 1952), 313-319.

36. Bills, Robert E., "Personality Changes During Student Centered Teaching," *Journal of Educational Research*, L (October, 1956), 121-126.

37. Bills, Robert E., "About People and Teaching," *Bulletin of the Bureau of School Service*, XXVIII (December, 1955).

38. Blumberg, Arthur and Amidon, Edmund, "Students' Reactions to Group Teaching Methods," *Journal of Teacher Education*, XII (December, 1961), 458-462.

39. Bostwick, Prudence, Ed., "The Importance of People, Authoritative or Authoritarian," *Educational Leadership*, XIX (October, 1961), 45-50.

40. Branson, Ernest P., "An Experiment in Arranging High School Sections on the Basis of General Ability," *Journal of Educational Research*, III (January, 1921), 53-55.

41. Braun, R. H. and Steffensen, James, "Grouping, Acceleration, and Teacher Aides Experiments in Urbana Secondary Schools," *The Bulletin of the National Association of Secondary School Principals*, XLIV (January, 1960), 305-315.

42. Breidenstine, A. G., "The Educational Achievement of Pupils in Differentiated and Undifferentiated Groups," *Journal of Experimental Education*, V (September, 1936), 91-135.

43. Breslow, Alice et al., "Forces Influencing Curriculum," *Review of Educational Research*, XXX (June, 1960), 199-225.

44. Borg, Walter R., "Personality and Interests Measures as Related to Criteria of Instructor Effectiveness," *Journal of Educational Research*, L (May, 1957), 701-709.

45. Bush, Robert N., *The Teacher-Pupil Relationship* (New York: Prentice-Hall, Inc., 1954).

46. Callihan, T. W., "An Experiment in the Use of Intelligence Tests as a Basis for Proper Grouping and Promotions in the Eighth Grade," *The Elementary School Journal*, XXI (February, 1921), 465-469.

47. Cappa, Dan and Schubert, Delwyn G., "Are Teachers Meeting the Reading Needs of the Gifted?" *California Journal of Educational Research*, XII (January, 1961), 42-44.

48. Cathell, Dorothy, "Honors English: A Break for Bright Students," *Clearing House*, XXIX (February, 1955), 331-337.

49. Coch, Lester and French, John, "Overcoming Resistance to Change," *Human Relations*, I (August, 1948), 512-532.

50. Cochran, John R., "Grouping Students in Junior High School," *Educational Leadership*, XVIII (April, 1961), 414-419.

51. Coffield, William H., "Effects of Non-Promotion on Educational Achievement in the Elementary School," *The Journal of Educational Psychology*, XLVII (April, 1956), 235-250.

52. Coffman, William E., "Determining Students' Concepts of Effective Teaching from Their Ratings of Instructors," *Journal of Educational Psychology*, XLV (May, 1954), 277-286.

53. Cogan, Morris L., "The Behavior of Teachers and the Productive Behavior of Their Pupils," *Journal of Experimental Education*, XXVII (December, 1958), 89-124.

54. Coleman, James S., *Social Climates in High School* (Washington, D. C.: U. S. Department of Health, Education, and Welfare), Cooperative Research Monograph No. 4, 1961.

55. Combs, Arthur W. and Taylor, Charles, "The Effect of the Perception of Mild Degrees of Threat on Performance," *Journal of Abnormal and Social Psychology*, XLVII (1952), 420-424.

56. Combs, Arthur W., Ed., *Personality Theory and Counseling Practice* (Gainesville, Florida: University of Florida).

57. Cook, Inez M. and Goodrich, T. V., "How High-School Pupils Spend Their Time," *School Review*, XXXVI (December, 1928), 771-778.

58. Cook, R. R., "A Study of the Results of Homogeneous Grouping of Abilities in High School Classes," *The Education of Gifted Children*, 23rd Yearbook, N.S.S.E., Part I. 1924, 302-312.

59. Cooper, James G. and Lewis, Roland B., "Quantitative Rorschach Factors in the Evaluation of Teacher Effectiveness," *Journal of Educational Research*, XLIV (May, 1951), 703-707.

60. Corey, Fay L., *Values of Future Teachers* (New York: Bureau of Publications, Teachers College, Columbia University, 1955).

61. Cressman, Harry, "Opportunity in Junior High Science," *The Science Teacher*, XXVII (November, 1960), 55-57.

62. Daniels, J. C., "Effects of Streaming in the Primary School," *British Journal of Educational Psychology*, XXXI (June, 1961), 69-78.

63. Doll, Ronald C., "High-School Pupils' Attitudes Toward Teaching Procedures," *School Review*, LV (April, 1947), 222-227.

64. Dressel, Paul L. and Grabow, John M., "The Gifted Evaluate Their High School Experience," *Exceptional Children*, XXIV (May, 1958), 394-396.

65. Dreyer, Albert S. and Haupt, Dorothy, "The Assertion of Authority: Differences Between Teachers, Student-Teachers, and Mothers of Young Children," *Journal of Educational Research*, LIV (October, 1960), 63-66.

66. Durr, William K., "Provisions for the Gifted in Relation to School Size and System Size at the Elementary Level," *Journal of Educational Research*, LV (December-January, 1962), 149-158.

67. Eales, John et al., "Grouping Practices in the Secondary Schools of Los Angeles County," *California Journal of Secondary Education*, XXX (January, 1955), 54-57.

68. Eberman, Paul W., "Personal Relationships: One Key to Instructional Improvement," *Educational Leadership*, IX (March, 1952), 389-392.

69. Eckert, Ruth E., "Colleges and Universities—Programs," *Encyclopedia of Educational Research*, Chester W. Harris, Ed. (New York: Macmillan Co., 1960), 268-285.

70. Edminston, R. W. and Benfer, J. G., "The Relationship Between Group

Achievement and Range of Abilities Within the Groups," *Journal of Educational Research*, XLII (March, 1949), 547-548.

71. Edmiston, R. W. and Braddock, R. W., "A Study of the Effect of Various Teaching Procedures upon Observed Group Attention in the Secondary School," *Journal of Educational Psychology*, XXXII (December, 1941), 665-672.

72. Engle, Thelburn L., "Achievements of Pupils Who Have Had Double Promotions in Elementary School," *The Elementary School Journal*, XXXVI (November, 1935), 185-189.

73. Fair, Jean, "The Comparative Effectiveness of a Core and a Conventional Curriculum in Developing Social Concern," *The School Review*, LXII (May, 1954), 274-282 and (September, 1954), 346-353.

74. Farnsworth, B. K. and Casper, J. B., "A Study of Pupil Failure in High School," *The School Review*, XLIX (May, 1941), 380-383.

75. Faw, Volney, "A Psychotherapeutic Method of Teaching Psychology," *The American Psychologist*, IV (April, 1949), 104-109.

76. Flanagan, John et al., "A Survey and Follow-Up Study of Educational Plans and Decisions in Relation to Aptitude Patterns," United States Office of Education, Cooperative Research Project No. 226 (1962).

77. Flanders, Ned A., "Personal-Social Anxiety as a Factor in Experimental Learning Situations," *Journal of Educational Research*, XLV (October, 1951), 100-110.

78. Flanders, Ned A. et al., "Measuring Dependence Proneness in the Classroom," *Educational and Psychological Measurement*, XXI (Autumn, 1961), 575-587.

79. Flanders, Ned A., *Teacher Influence: Pupil Attitudes and Achievement.* Final Report, Cooperative Research Project No. 397, University of Minnesota, Minneapolis, Minnesota, November 30, 1960.

80. Flesher, Marie A., "Did They Graduate Too Young?" *Educational Research Bulletin*, XXIV (November, 1945), 218-221.

81. Fliedner, L. J., "A Comparison of the Achievement of an Honor School Class and a Regular Class in Chemistry," *High Points*, XXVIII (November, 1946), 67-70.

82. Foley, Grayce A., "Current Democratic Methods of Teaching in the Secondary Schools in the United States," *Dissertation Abstracts*, XII (1952), 265-266.

83. Fosmire, Frederick R., "The Role of Ego Defense in Academic Reputations," *Journal of Social Psychology*, XLIX (February, 1959), 41-45.

84. Frazier, Alexander, Ed., *Learning More About Learning* (Washington, D. C.: Association for Supervision and Curriculum Development, NEA, 1959).

85. French, John W., "Evidence from School Records on the Effectiveness of Ability Grouping," *Journal of Educational Research*, LIV (November, 1960), 83-91.

86. Frymier, Jack R., "Prospective Teachers' Estimates of Adolescents' Responses to F-Scale Items," *Journal of Experimental Education*, XXIX (December, 1960), 183-188.

87. Frymier, Jack R., "Teachers' Estimates of Adolescents' Responses to F-Scale Items," *Journal of Educational Research*, LV (May, 1962), 353-357.

88. Gage, Nathaniel L. and Succi, George, "Social Perception and Teacher-Pupil Relationships," *Journal of Educational Psychology*, XLII (March, 1951), 144-152.

89. Gale, Raymond F., "The Progress of Students and Graduates of a Core Curriculum," *The School Review*, LXIII (October, 1955), 384-387.

90. Garside, Leonard J., "A Comparison of the Effectiveness of Two Methods of Instruction in High School Physics as Measured by Levels of Achievement of Students of High and Low Intelligence," *Dissertation Abstracts*, XX (1959), 2172.

91. Gerberich, Joseph R. and Warner, K. O., "Relative Instructional Efficiencies

of the Lecture and Discussion Methods in a University Course in American National Government," *Journal of Educational Research*, XXIX (April, 1936), 574-579.

92. Gibb, Lorraine M. and Gibb, Jack R., "The Effects of the Use of 'Participative Action' Groups in a Course of General Psychology," *The American Psychologist*, VII (June, 1952), 247-248.

93. Goldberg, Miriam L., "Studies in Underachievement Among the Academically Talented," in *Freeing Capacity to Learn*, Alexander Frazier, Ed. (Washington, D. C.: The Association for Supervision and Curriculum Development, 1960), 56-73.

94. Goldberg, Miriam L. and associates, "A Three Year Experimental Program at DeWitt Clinton High School to Help Bright Underachievers," *High Points*, XLI (January, 1959), 5-35.

95. Goldberg, Miriam L. and Passow, A. Harry, "The Effects of Ability Grouping," *Education*, LXXXII (April, 1962), 482-487.

96. Goldstein, Phillip, "Concerning Ninth-Year Biology," *The Science Teacher*, XXV (December, 1958), 454-457.

97. Goldworth, Mary, "Measuring Social Relationships in a Special-Grouping Program for Fast Learners," *California Journal of Educational Research*, IX (September, 1958), 167-173.

98. Goodenough, Eva, "The Forced Choice Technique as a Method for Discovering Effective Teacher Personality," *Journal of Educational Research*, LI (September, 1957), 25-31.

99. Gowan, John C., "Self-Report Tests in the Prediction of Teaching Effectiveness," *The School Review*, LXVIII (Winter, 1960), 409-419.

100. Grace, Arthur, "A Study of the Achievement of Sixth Grade I Repeaters as Compared with That of Non-Repeaters of the Same Mental Age," *Journal of Experimental Education*, V (December, 1936), 203-205.

101. Grace, Harry A. and Booth, Nancy Lou, "Is the Gifted Child a Social Isolate?" *Peabody Journal of Education*, XXXV (January, 1958), 195-196.

102. Grassell, Edward M., "An Evaluation of Educational Films in the Teaching of High School Physics in Oregon," *Dissertation Abstracts*, XXI (1960).

103. Graves, Walter A., "Today's College Students," *National Educational Association Journal*, XLVII (October, 1958), 498-500.

104. Gray, Howard A. and Hollingworth, Leta S., "The Achievement of Gifted Children Enrolled and Not Enrolled in Special Opportunity Classes," *Journal of Educational Research*, XXIV (November, 1931), 255-261.

105. Grime, Herschel E., "Aptitude and Ability in Elementary Algebra," *School Science and Mathematics*, XLVII (December, 1947), 781-784.

106. Guba, E. G. and Getzels, J. W., "Personality and Teacher Effectiveness: A Problem in Theoretical Research," *Journal of Educational Psychology*, XLVI (October, 1955), 330-344.

107. Haigh, Gerard V. and Schmidt, Warren, "The Learning of Subject Matter in Teacher-Centered and Group-Centered Classes," *Journal of Educational Psychology*, XLVII (May, 1956), 295-301.

108. Hardwick, F. T., "Classification by Chronological Age," 6th Yearbook, Elementary School Principals (1927), 211-216.

109. Heil, Louis M. and Washburne, Carleton, "Brooklyn College Research in Teacher Effectiveness," *Journal of Educational Research*, LV (May, 1962), 347-351.

110. Herrold, Earle E., Michael, W. B. and Cryan, Eugene E., "A Survey of Student-Teacher Relationships," *Journal of Educational Research*, XLIV (1950-1951), 657-673.

111. Herschi, L. Edwin, "An Experiment in the Teaching of Elementary Algebra," *The School Review*, LXVI (Summer, 1958), 185-194.

112. Hipsher, Warren L., "A Study of High School Physics Achievement," *The Science Teacher*, XXVIII (October, 1961), 36-37.
113. Holmes, Darrell and Harvey, Lois, "An Evaluation of Two Methods of Grouping," *Educational Research Bulletin*, XXXV (November, 1956), 213-222.
114. Holy, T. C. and Sutton, D. H., "Ability Grouping in the Ninth Grade," *Educational Research Bulletin*, IX (October 22, 1930), 419-422.
115. Homman, Guy Burger, "A Study of Several Factors and Their Relationship to Achievement in High School Chemistry by Use of Factorial Design and Covariance," *Dissertation Abstracts*, XXII (1962), 3949.
116. Hoover, Kenneth, "An Experiment on Grouping Within the Classroom," *California Journal of Secondary Education*, XXX (October, 1955), 326-331.
117. Hoyt, Kenneth B., "A Study of the Effects of Teacher Knowledge of Pupil Characteristics on Pupil Achievement and Attitudes Toward Classwork," *Journal of Educational Psychology*, XLVI (May, 1955), 302-310.
118. Husen, Thorsten and Svensson, Nils-Eric, "Pedagogic Milieu and Development of Intellectual Skills," *The School Review*, LXVIII (Spring, 1960), 36-51.
119. Jackson, Joseph, "The Effect of Classroom Organization and Guidance Practice upon the Personality Adjustment and Academic Growth of Students," *Journal of Genetic Psychology*, LXXXIII (September, 1953), 159-170.
120. Jackson, Philip W. and Guba, Egon G., "The Need Structure of In-Service Teachers: An Occupational Analysis," *The School Review*, LXV (June, 1957), 176-192.
121. Jacob, Philip E., *Changing Values in College: A Study of the Impact of College Teaching* (New York: Harper and Bros., 1957).
122. Jenkins, David H. and Lippitt, Ronald, *Interpersonal Perceptions of Teachers, Students, and Parents* (Washington, D. C.: Adult Education Service, NEA, 1951).
123. Jensen, Vern H., "Influence of Personality Traits on Academic Success," *Personnel and Guidance Journal*, XXXVI (March, 1958), 497-500.
124. Jersild, Arthur T., *When Teachers Face Themselves* (New York: Teachers College, Columbia University, 1955).
125. Johnson, Granville B. Jr., "An Evaluation Instrument for the Analysis of Teacher Effectiveness," *Journal of Experimental Education*, XXIII (June, 1955), 331-344.
126. Johnson, Granville B. Jr., "An Experimental Technique for Prediction of Teacher Effectiveness," *Journal of Educational Research*, L (May, 1957), 679-689.
127. Jones, Edward S. and Ortner, Gloria K., "Advanced Standing for Superior Students," *National Educational Association Journal*, XLIII (February, 1954), 107-108.
128. Justman, Joseph, "Academic Achievement of Intellectually Gifted Accelerants and Non-Accelerants in Senior High School," *The School Review*, LXII (November, 1954), 469-473.
129. Karp, Mark, "An Evaluation of an Individual Method and a Group Method of Teaching College Freshmen the Mechanics of English Composition," *Journal of Experimental Education*, XI (September, 1942), 9-15.
130. Keener, E. E., "Results of Homogeneous Classification of Junior High School Pupils," XIV (June, 1926), 14-20.
131. Kelley, Arthur C. and Beatty, Robert E., "Core Program Students Learn Basic Skills," *The School Executive*, LXXII (February, 1953), 54-55.
132. Kelley, Earl C. and Rasey, Marie I., *Education and the Nature of Man* (New York: Harper and Bros., 1952).
133. Kelley, Earl C., *The Workshop Way of Learning* (New York: Harper and Bros., 1951).
134. Kingston, Albert J. and Newsome, George L., "The Relationship of Two

Measures of Authoritarianism to the Minnesota Teacher Attitude Inventory," *Journal of Psychology*, XLIX (April, 1960), 333-338.

135. Koontz, William F., "A Study of Achievements as a Function of Homogeneous Grouping," *Journal of Experimental Education*, XXX (December, 1961), 249-253.

136. Knapp, Leda A. and Seidman, J. M., "Teacher Likes and Dislikes of Student Behavior and Student Perceptions of These Attitudes," *Journal of Educational Research*, XLVII (October, 1953), 143-150.

137. Knoell, Dorthy, "A Second Attempt to Predict Teaching Success from Word Fluency Data," *Journal of Educational Research*, XLIX (September, 1955), 13-25.

138. Kuenzli, Alfred E., "Preference for High and Low Structure Among Prospective Teachers," *Journal of Social Psychology*, XL (May, 1959), 243-248.

139. Lambert, Philip, "Interaction Between Authoritarian and Nonauthoritarian Principals and Teachers," *Genetic Psychology Monographs*, LVIII (November, 1958), 163-205.

140. Lamke, Tom A., "Personality and Teaching Success," *Journal of Experimental Education*, XX (December, 1951), 217-259.

141. Leeds, Carroll H., "A Scale for Measuring Teacher-Pupil Attitudes and Teacher-Pupil Rapport," *Psychological Monographs*, LXIV (1950), 1-24.

142. Levine, Jacob and Butler, John, "Lecture vs. Group Decision in Changing Behavior," *Journal of Applied Psychology*, XXXVI (February, 1952), 29-33.

143. Lewin, Kurt, "Frontiers in Group Dynamics," *Human Relations*, I (1947), 5-41.

144. Lindquist, E. F., "The Gap Between Promise and Fulfilment in Ninth Grade Algebra," *The School Review*, XLII (December, 1934), 726-771.

145. Lindvall, C. M. and Hooker, Clifford P., "Teachers Colleges vs. Liberal Arts Colleges in Teacher Preparation," *Phi Delta Kappan*, XLI (March, 1960), 260-263.

146. Lippitt, R., "An Experimental Study of Democratic and Authoritarian Group Atmospheres," *Child Welfare*, XVI (1940), 43-195.

147. Longenecker, E. D., "Perceptual Recognition as a Function of Anxiety, Motivation, and the Testing Situation," *Journal of Abnormal and Social Psychology*, LXIV, 215-221.

148. Lovell, John T., "A Study of the Relationship Between the Style of Teacher Participation in the Total Classroom Group and the Internal Structure of Sub-Groups in the Classroom," Unpublished Doctoral Dissertation (University of Florida, 1954).

149. Lundin, Robert W. and Kuhn, Jerald P., "The Relationship Between Scholarship Achievement and Changes in Personality Adjustment in Men After Four Years of College Attendance," *Journal of General Psychology*, LXIII (July, 1960), 35-42.

150. Mahan, Thomas, "Human Judgment: Can the Classroom Improve It?" *Journal of Educational Research*, XLIX (November, 1955), 161-169.

151. Maltzman, Irving et al., "Some Relationships Between Methods of Instruction, Personality Variables, and Problem-Solving Behavior," *Journal of Educational Psychology*, XLVII (February, 1956), 71-78.

152. Mandler, George and Sarason, Seymour B., "A Study of Anxiety and Learning," *Journal of Abnormal and Social Psychology*, XLVII (1952), 166-173.

153. Mann, Horace, "How *Real* Are Friendships of Gifted and Typical Children in a Program of Partial Segregation?" *Exceptional Children*, XXIII (February, 1957), 199-201.

154. Marie, Sister Ernestine, "A Comparison of Inductive and Deductive Methods of Teaching High School Chemistry," *Science Education*, XLV (December, 1961), 436-443.

155. Mark, Steven J., "Experimental Study Involving the Comparison of Two

Methods of Performing Experiments in High School Chemistry," *Science Education*, XLV (December, 1961), 410-412.

156. Maslow, A. H. and Zimmerman, W., "College Teaching Ability, Scholarly Activity, and Personality," *Journal of Educational Psychology*, XLVII (March, 1956), 185-189.

157. Mason, John M., "An Experimental Study in the Teaching of Scientific Thinking in Biological Science at the College Level," *Science Education*, XXXVI (December, 1952), 270-284.

158. Mathes, George E. and Blanc, Sam, "Biology Achievement in Grades Nine and Ten," *The Science Teacher*, XXVII (March, 1960), 23-26.

159. Mathewson, Angell and Michelson, H. R., "The Nature and Worth of a Program of Remedial Reading," *The Bulletin of the National Association of Secondary School Principals*, XLI (September, 1957), 83-89.

160. McCall, William A. and Krause, Gertrude R., "Measurement of Teacher Merit for Salary Purposes," *Journal of Educational Research*, LIII (October, 1959), 73-75.

161. McConnell, T. R., "Education Articulation," *Journal of Higher Education*, V (1934), 253-258.

162. McElwee, Edna W., "A Comparison of the Personality Traits of 300 Accelerated, Normal, and Retarded Children," *Journal of Educational Research*, XXVI (September, 1932), 31-34.

163. McGuire, Carson, "Factors Influencing Individual Mental Health," *Review of Educational Research*, XXVI (December, 1956), 451-478.

164. Mennes, Arthur H., "What Parents Think of the Multiple Period," *The Clearing House*, XXIX (January, 1955), 280-283.

165. Mennes, Arthur H., "The Effectiveness of Multiple Period Curricular Practices in High School English and Social Studies," *Journal of Educational Research*, L (September, 1956), 59-69.

166. Meredith, Charles E., "Development of Problem Solving Skills in High School Physical Science," *Dissertation Abstracts*, XXII (1962), 3550.

167. Michael, William B. et al., "Survey of Student-Teacher Relationships," *Journal of Educational Research*, XLIV (May, 1951), 657-673.

168. Mickelson, John M., "What Does Research Say About the Effectiveness of the Core Curriculum?" *The School Review*, LXV (June, 1957), 144-160.

169. Miller, K. M. and Biggs, J. B., "Attitude Change Through Undirected Group Discussion," *Journal of Educational Psychology*, XLIX (August, 1958), 224-228.

170. Miller, Leonard M., Ed., *Guidance for the Underachiever with Superior Ability* (Washington, D. C.: U. S. Department of Health, Education, and Welfare, 1961), Bulletin No. 25.

171. Miller, Vera M., "Education of the Gifted: A Progress Report on an Experiment Begun in 1956," *The American School Board Journal*, CXXXIX (September, 1959), 23-26.

172. Moore, Clark H. and Cole, David, "The Relation of MMPI Scores to Practice Teaching Ratings," *Journal of Educational Research*, L (May, 1957), 711-716.

173. Montross, Harold W., "Temperament and Teaching Success," *Journal of Experimental Education*, XXIII (September, 1954), 73-97.

174. Morse, Grant D., "A Differentiated Program for Duller Higher School Pupils," *Journal of Experimental Education*, X (September, 1941), 38-40.

175. Morse, Nancy C., *Satisfactions in the White Collar Job* (Ann Arbor: Survey Research Center, Institute for Social Research, University of Michigan, 1953).

176. Morsh, Joseph E. et al., "Student Achievement as a Measure of Instructor Effectiveness," *Journal of Educational Psychology*, XLVII (February, 1956), 79-88.

177. Moyer, Edward L., "A Study of the Effects of Classification by Intelligence

Tests," 23rd Yearbook, National Society for the Study of Education, Part I, 313-322.

178. Mussen, Paul H. and Wyszynski, Anne B., "Personality and Political Participation," *Human Relations*, V (February, 1952), 65-82.

179. Newman, Earl N., "A Comparison of the Effectiveness of Three Teaching Methods in High School Biology," *Dissertation Abstracts*, XVII (1959), 2940.

180. Otto, Henry J. and Melby, Ernest O., "An Attempt to Evaluate the Threat of Failure as a Factor in Achievement," *The Elementary School Journal*, XXXV (April, 1935), 588-596.

181. Ozinonu, Ahmet Kemal, "Integrating Recent Scientific Concepts into the Ninth-Grade Science Curriculum," *Dissertation Abstracts*, XX (1959), 2716.

182. Parker, Clyde, "Mentally Advanced Children," *American School Board Journal*, CXXXIII (December, 1956), 23-24.

183. Passow, A. Harry and Goldberg, Miriam L., "Study of Underachieving Gifted," *Educational Leadership*, XVI (November, 1958), 121-125.

184. Pella, Milton et al., "The Use of the White Films in the Teaching of Physics," *Science Education*, XLVI (February, 1962), 6-21.

185. Perkins, Hugh V., "The Effects of Climate and Curriculum on Group Learning of In-Service Teachers," Unpublished Doctoral Dissertation (University of Chicago, 1948).

186. Perlmutter, Howard and de Montmollin, Germaine, "Group Learning of Nonsense Syllables," *Journal of Abnormal and Social Psychology*, XLVII (1952), 762-769.

187. Pistor, F. A., *Evaluating Newer School Practices by the Observation Method*, Sixteenth Yearbook, Department of Elementary School Principals, 1937.

188. Portenier, Lillian, "A Twelve Year Study of Differentiated Groups of High School Pupils," *Journal of Educational Psychology*, XXIX (January, 1938), 1-13.

189. Potter, Donald G., "Extra Class Science Activities in Accredited Colorado High Schools and Their Relationship to Certain Measures of Student Interest in Science," *Dissertation Abstracts*, XXII (1962), 3553.

190. Provus, Malcolm M., "Ability Grouping in Arithmetic," *The Elementary School Journal*, LX (April, 1960), 391-398.

191. Pruitt, Coy C., "An Experimental Program in Mathematics," *Mathematics Teacher*, LIII (February, 1960), 102-105.

192. Rainey, Homer P. and Anderson, Hilma, "An Experiment in Classifying High School Pupils on the Basis of Achievement," *Educational Administration and Supervision*, XIII (November, 1927), 528-544.

193. Rankin, Paul T. et al., "Ability Grouping in the Detroit Individualization Experiment," 35th Yearbook, National Society for the Study of Education, Part I, 277-288.

194. Rasmussen, Glen R., "An Evaluation of a Student-Centered and Instructor-Centered Method of Conducting a Graduate Course in Education," *Journal of Educational Psychology*, XLVII (December, 1956), 449-461.

195. Raven, Bertram H. and French, John R., "Legitimate Power, Coercive Power, and Observability in Social Influence," *Sociometry*, XXI (June, 1958), 83-97.

196. Reed, Harold J., "An Investigation of the Relationship Between Teaching Effectiveness and the Teacher's Attitude of Acceptance," *Journal of Experimental Education*, XXI (June, 1953), 277-325.

197. Reiss, Albert J. Jr. and Rhodes, Albert Lewis, "A Socio Psychological Study of Adolescent Conformity and Deviation," Cooperative Research Program Project No. 507, OE-33020, October 31, 1959.

198. Remmers, H. W. et al., "Interrelationships of Various Teaching Criteria," *American Psychologist*, IV (July, 1949), 288.

199. Rickard, Paul B., "An Experimental Study of the Effectiveness of Group Dis-

cussion in the Teaching of Factual Content," Unpublished Doctoral Dissertation (Northwestern University, 1946).

200. Roberts, Helen Erskine, "The Reactions of a Group of High School Sophomores to Their Experiences in Special Classes," *California Journal of Educational Research*, X (November, 1959), 220-225.

201. Rothrock, Dayton, G., "Heterogeneous, Homogeneous, or Individualized Approach to Reading?" *Elementary English*, XXXVIII (April, 1961), 233-235.

202. Russell, Ivan L. and Thalman, W. A., "Personality: Does It Influence Teachers' Marks?" *Journal of Educational Research*, XLVIII (April, 1955), 561-564.

203. Ryan, W. Carson, "The Emerging Concept of Mental Health in Education," *Review of Educational Research*, XXVI (December, 1956), 417-428.

204. Ryans, David G., "An Analysis of Teacher Examination Scores of College Seniors Who Expect to Become Teachers," *American Psychologist*, IV (July, 1949), 288.

205. Ryans, David G., "A Study of the Extent of Association of Certain Professional and Personal Data with Judged Effectiveness of Teacher Behavior," *Journal of Experimental Education*, XX (September, 1951), 67-77.

206. Ryans, David G., "Some Correlates of Teacher Behavior," *Educational and Psychological Measurement*, XIX (Spring, 1959), 3-12.

207. Sadnavitch, J. M. et al., "Retention Value of Filmed Science Courses," *Science Education*, XLVI (February, 1962), 22-27.

208. Sarason, Irwin G., "The Effects of Anxiety and Threat on the Solution of a Difficult Task," *Journal of Abnormal and Social Psychology*, LXII (1961), 165-168.

209. Scarborough, G. C. et al., "Improvement of Reading Through Ability-Level Assignments," *The School Review*, LXV (December, 1957), 474-480.

210. Scates, Douglas E., Ed., "With The Researchers," *Journal of Teacher Education*, VII (September, 1956), 276-277.

211. Schaaf, Oscar, "Student Discovery of Algebraic Principles as a Means of Developing Ability to Generalize," *Mathematics Teacher*, XLVIII (May, 1955), 324-327.

212. Schwartz, Anthony N., "A Study of the Discriminating Efficiency of Certain Tests of the Primary Source Personality Traits of Teachers," *Journal of Experimental Education*, XIX (September, 1950), 63-93.

213. Schwartz, Bernard, "An Investigation of the Effects of a Seventh and Eighth Grade Core Program," *Journal of Educational Research*, LIII (December, 1959), 149-152.

214. Seagoe, M. V., "Prediction of In-Service Success in Teaching," *Journal of Educational Research*, XXXIX (May, 1946), 658-663.

215. Seidman, Jerome M. and Knapp, Leda B., "Teacher Likes and Dislikes of Student Behavior and Student Perception of These Attitudes," *Journal of Educational Research*, XLVII (September, 1953), 143-148.

216. Singer, Arthur, "Social Competence and Success in Teaching," *Journal of Experimental Education*, XXIII (December, 1954), 99-131.

217. Singer, Jerome L. and Goldman, George D., "Experimentally Contrasted Social Atmospheres in Group Psychotherapy with Chronic Schizophrenics," *Journal of Social Psychology*, XL (August, 1954), 23-37.

218. Smith, Louis M., "What Research Says to the Teacher No. 19: Group Processes in Elementary and Secondary Schools" (Washington, D. C.: National Education Association, 1959).

219. Smith, William F. and Rockett, Frederick C., "Test Performance as a Function of Anxiety, Instructor, and Instructions," *Journal of Educational Research*, LII (December, 1958), 138-141.

220. Sobel, Max A., "Concept Learning in Algebra," *Mathematics Teacher*, XLIX (October, 1956), 425-430.

221. Stiles, Lindley, J. et al., "Methods of Teaching," *Encyclopedia of Educational Research*, Walter S. Monroe, Ed. (New York: Macmillan Co., 1952), 745-752.
222. Stouffer, George A. W. Jr. and Owens, Jennie, "Behavior Problems of Children as Identified by Today's Teachers and Compared with Those Reported by E. K. Wickman," *Journal of Educational Research*, XLVIII (January, 1955), 321-331.
223. Symonds, Percival M., "Education for the Development of Personality," in *Readings for Educational Psychology*, William Fullager et al., Eds.
224. Symonds, Percival M., "Characteristics of the Effective Teacher Based on Pupil Evaluations," *Journal of Experimental Education*, XXIII (June, 1955), 289-310.
225. Templin, R. J. W., "A Check-Up of Non-Promotions," *The Journal of Education*, CXXIII (November, 1940), 259-260.
226. Thistlethwaite, Donald L., "College Environments and the Development of Talent," *Science*, CXXX (July, 1959), 72-74.
227. Thompson, Orville E. and Tom, Frederick K. T., "Comparison of the Effectiveness of a Pupil-Centered versus a Teacher-Centered Pattern for Teaching Vocational Agriculture," *Journal of Educational Research*, L (May, 1957), 667-678.
228. Torbet, David P., "The Attitude of a Select Group of Colorado Secondary School Teachers Toward Informal Teacher-Made Tests as Measured by a Projective Interview," *Journal of Educational Research*, L (May, 1957), 691-700.
229. Turner, Carla S., "Improving Selection of Pupils for Remedial Reading: A Report of Research," *The English Journal*, L (January, 1961), 23-33.
230. Ulrich, Arthur H., "The Accelerated and Enriched Biology Course," *The Science Teacher*, XXVIII (February, 1961), 35-39.
231. Waetjen, Walter B., Ed., *Human Variability and Learning* (Washington, D. C.: The Association for Supervision and Curriculum Development, NEA, 1961).
232. Ward, John, "Group Study versus Lecture-Demonstration Method in Physical Science Instruction for General Education College Students," *Journal of Experimental Education*, XXIV (March, 1956), 197-210.
233. West, Jeff and Sievers, Callie, "Experiment in Cross Grouping," *Journal of Educational Research*, LIV (October, 1960), 70-72.
234. West, Jessee W., "A Study of Grouping, the Grouping Procedure at the Galion Junior High School, and the Procedures of Thirty Junior High Schools Throughout Ohio," Unpublished Master's Thesis (The Ohio State University, 1961).
235. Wheeler, Edwin E. and Bass, Thomas A., "A Study of Control Grouping in High School Biology," *American Biology Teacher*, XIX (December, 1957), 243-245.
236. Wiles, Kimball and Patterson, Franklin, "The High School We Need" (Washington, D. C.: Association for Supervision and Curriculum Development, NEA, 1959).
237. Willard, Ruth A., "A Study of the Relationship Between the Valued-Behaviors of Selected Teachers and the Learning Experiences Provided in their Classrooms," *Journal of Educational Research*, XLIX (September, 1955), 45-51.
238. Wispé, Lauren G., "Evaluation Section Teaching Methods in an Introductory Course in Social Relations," *Journal of Educational Research*, XLV (November, 1951), 161-186.
239. Witty, Paul, "An Analysis of the Personality Traits of the Effective Teacher," *Journal of Educational Research*, L (1957), 662-679.
240. Wren, F. L., "A Survey of Research in the Teaching of Secondary Algebra," *Journal of Educational Research*, XXVIII (April, 1935), 597-610.

241. Wrightstone, J. W., *Appraisal of Experimental High School Practices* (New York: Teachers College, Columbia University, 1936).

242. Wrightstone, J. W., *Appraisal of Newer Elementary School Practices* (New York: Teachers College, Columbia University, 1938).

243. Wrightstone, J. Wayne, "Evaluation of the Experiment with the Activity Program in the New York City Elementary Schools," *Journal of Educational Research,* XXXVIII (December, 1944), 252-257.

244. Wrightstone, J. Wayne and Forlano, George, "Evaluation of the Experience Curriculum at Midwood High School," *High Points,* XXX (December, 1948), 35-42.

245. Wrightstone, J. Wayne, "Evaluating the Effectiveness of an Integrated Ninth Grade Curriculum," *The Teachers College Journal,* XIX (November, 1947), 2-3.

246. Yeager, Robert E., "Grade Placement of High School Chemistry," *The Science Teacher,* XXIX (April, 1962), 27-29.

247. Yourglich, Anita, "Study on Correlations Between Teachers' and Students' Concepts of Ideal-Student and Ideal-Teacher," *Journal of Educational Research,* XLIX (September, 1955), 59-64.

Chapter Eight

Encouraging and Evaluating
Achievement

INTRODUCTION

How would you like to fly in an airplane with a pilot who made a score of 70 per cent on his flight examination? All pilots *learn* to fly. Somebody teaches them and somebody evaluates their learning. There are definite facts, skills, and attitudes which must be acquired. And there are also standards. Some student pilots "pass" and some "fail."

What is passing? What is failing? What are standards? How *do* teachers evaluate students' attainments? How *should* teachers evaluate educational growth?

As used in schools, evaluation and grading are almost synonymous terms. With regard to the differences, the purpose of this chapter will be to examine the concept of grading, and all its implications. Inherent are many ideas which properly belong in the area of evaluation, but because most teachers use the two terms interchangeably, the effort here will be to outline a way of working with students so that the ideas of evaluation are incorporated into educational grading practice.

Grading students is an involved process, and although it causes more headaches and heartaches than any other single task which teachers face, they still have to give grades. They dare not "throw out the baby with the bath." Generations of students are accustomed to getting grades as periodic reports of their achievement. The problems in grading are difficult but not insurmountable. Perhaps teachers can change both the concept and the process of grading for more effective results.

228

Let us examine some of the factors in evaluating student accomplishment and growth. We will start with several illustrations of present practice. Then we will explore the grading process in some detail. Following this, we will analyze the total concept of grading. Finally, a way of encouraging and evaluating achievement will be described which attempts to satisfy the tenets of democracy and learning upon which this book is based.

A LOOK AT CURRENT PRACTICE

Described below are several illustrations of procedures which teachers have used to grade their students. Some are excerpts from the total experience of a learner. Some are more complex. Each example illustrates a point about the process and problem of grading.

Grading in Arithmetic

These ten problems appeared recently on a third grade arithmetic test:

$$\begin{array}{cccccccccc} 7 & 2 & 3 & 6 & 4 & 2 & 5 & 6 & 8 & 4 \\ + & + & + & + & + & + & + & + & + & + \\ \hline 8 & 4 & 5 & 9 & 9 & 5 & 9 & 7 & 9 & 6 \end{array}$$

The ten items, each counting ten points, made a total possible score on the examination of 100 per cent. There are at least three possible ways to arrive at the correct answer: counting, subtracting, or adding to the addend. Note, however, that the plus sign implies addition *only*. If you were a teacher, how would you have graded the following paper?

$$\begin{array}{cccccccccc} 7 & 2 & 3 & 6 & 4 & 2 & 5 & 6 & 8 & 4 \\ 15 + & 6 + & 8 + & 15 + & 13 + & 7 + & 14 + & 13 + & 17 + & 10 \\ \hline 8 & 4 & 5 & 9 & 9 & 5 & 9 & 7 & 9 & 6 \end{array}$$

Are these problems worked correctly or incorrectly? Are they to be graded "right" or "wrong"? According to conventional arithmetical procedures they are incorrect. According to the mathematical problem implied they are correct. That is, 2 and 4 coupled with the action symbol

+ imply addition, and when these numbers are added together one gets 6. That was not what the teacher meant but obviously he did not communicate adequately to the student the process expected. Depending upon his mood for the day, a teacher might count these items as "right," "wrong," "partially correct," or refuse to score them for purposes of grading.

The teacher could have also used this testing experience as a teaching opportunity; a point from which to depart for instructional purposes. He did not, however, and the student, who thought she had actually performed the mathematical operations correctly, was disheartened because all of the answers were considered wrong, and she got a zero on the test. The implicit lesson of this "failure" far outweighed the explicit learning intended.

Should examinations be used primarily to determine students' accomplishments or should they fulfill an instructional purpose? Should tests be used to diagnose learning problems, determine teacher effectiveness, or help students learn? It is simple to say that they should be used to achieve all of these ends. It is much more difficult to try to accomplish such purposes in the classroom.

Grading College Students in Golf

Imagine that you are a physical education instructor working with college sophomores who are learning to play golf. Assume further that after two months of instruction, the final month is devoted to actual play on the course every day for a full 18 holes. At the completion of this month of play, two students in your class made the following scores:

	John Smith's Scores					William Jones' Scores				
First Week	115	107	109	104	102	85	84	86	84	81
Second Week	105	96	102	99	98	82	83	80	79	81
Third Week	97	94	96	95	93	80	75	75	79	83
Fourth Week	94	89	90	90	89	78	80	79	79	81

In studying these two sets of data we can observe that John Smith's first score was 115 and his last score 89 while Jones' first score was 85 and his final score 81. If we total each student's daily scores and compute the average, we note that for the one-month period Smith had an average of more than 95 while Jones' average was 80. Compared to par, a hypothetical perfect score, Smith made the greatest progress but Jones most nearly attained perfection.

How should this segment of these students' experiences be graded?

On their growth? Their average? Their final accomplishment? Their relationship to par? What should be the basis for imposing standards?

Grading in Ninth Grade Mathematics

Many school systems evaluate academic achievement by means of yearly standardized tests administered to all pupils. In one school system the following achievement profiles for three different junior high schools were compiled following the annual testing program in mathematics.

The distribution of scores varies significantly for these three schools. Note, however, that ten students in Glencoe Junior High School achieved at the 35th percentile, as did twenty students at Wilson and forty students at Hardy Junior High School. Although the standardized tests results were not used as a basis for grading, it was interesting that the ninth graders enrolled at Glencoe who achieved at the 35th percentile failed

Figure 1

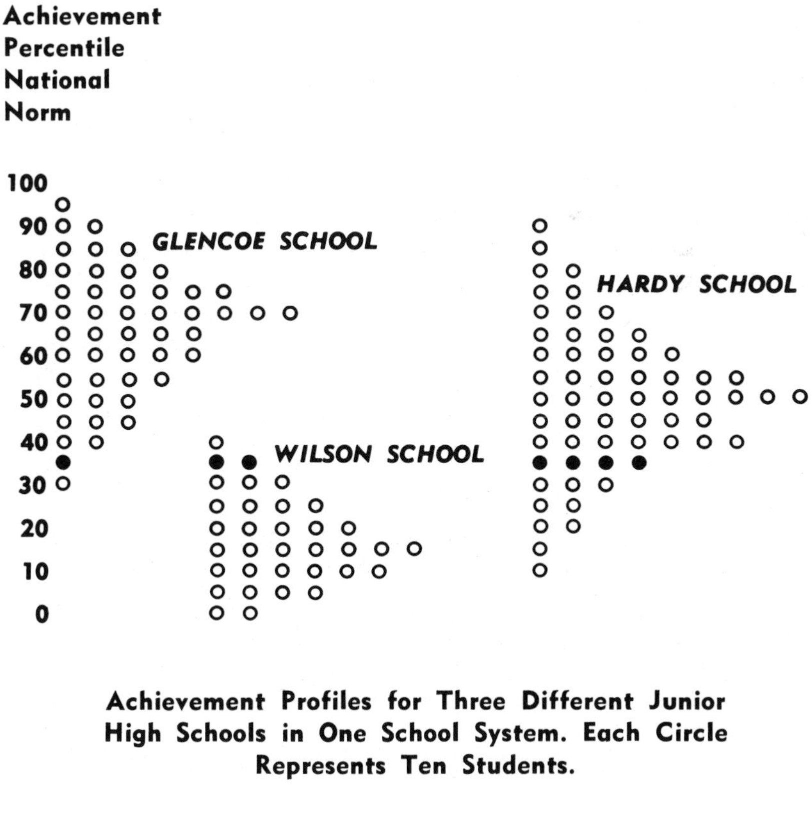

Achievement
Percentile
National
Norm

Achievement Profiles for Three Different Junior
High Schools in One School System. Each Circle
Represents Ten Students.

mathematics in their school, while those at Wilson who made similar scores on the standardized test got "A's." Most of those who were at this level at Hardy received average grades, "C's." In other words, grading was more a function of the way this school system drew its attendance lines than how particular students achieved. This illustration, by the way, is not a hypothetical case. It is from a real school system which prides itself on its academic standards.

What does a grade mean, then? What does an "A" represent? A "C"? An "F"? What do such symbols mean from schools that are not more than four miles apart in the same school district? What do grades mean from schools widely separated?

Grading in Latin II

A sixteen-year-old boy named John was enrolled in Latin II. On his first six weeks' grade report he got a "C," on the second a "D," on the third an "F," and on the fourth an "F." After the fourth report he went home, wrote a note to his mother apologizing for not getting better grades, took a shotgun and killed himself.

Two weeks later his father, who was living in another community (the parents were separated), asked the Latin teacher if she could provide him with any more details. She replied: "Mr. Ross, I was so very sorry about John, but you know, he never should have been allowed to enroll in Latin II. He did not know how to conjugate verbs."

This incident happened exactly as described. Although not common, a school year never passes without some students committing suicide because they get poor grades in school. These are extreme cases, but how do grades affect students? How are they interpreted by parents at home? By other students? By college admission officers? By prospective employers? What do grades say to people and how do they say it? These are important questions which must be explored in great detail.

Grading in American History

The following questions appeared recently on an eleventh grade test in American History:

> (1) The issuance of the Declaration of Independence was followed by
> (a) The first fighting of the revolution
> (b) The appointment of Washington as Commander-in-Chief
> (c) The calling of the Second Continental Congress
> (d) Conclusion of an alliance with France

(2) The American Revolution would probably not have occurred if
   (a) The French Revolution had not taken place
   (b) America had been allowed as much freedom of worship as was permitted in England
   (c) Agriculture rather than industry had been the major interests of the American colonies
   (d) England had followed the same policy toward her American colonies that she now follows toward Canada and Australia

(3) Which of the following originated the Committees of Correspondence?
   (a) Patrick Henry
   (b) James Madison
   (c) John Adams
   (d) Samuel Adams

Other questions which appeared on a different teacher's six-week examination at a later date are listed below:

(4) _____ built hospitals, took care of sick in the war.
(5) _____ Senator from Ohio during the war, and
_____.
(6) _____ (woman) Nurse in the war.
(7) _____ The leading North General in the West (Mississippi).
(8) _____ A negro minister that tried to free them too.
(9) _____ "Lost Cause" refers to.
(10) _____ Spy in Civil War.
(11) _____ How was the war financed?

Do *you* know which answers are correct? Do you suppose that all history teachers would agree? Are the questions all of equal value? Is the recall demanded in Question 3 as significant as the reasoning called for in Question 2? Are Questions 4 through 11 clear? Are the two examinations comparable in terms of standards? Are the questions objective? What learnings are being measured?

Ninth Grade English Test

The following ten items were selected from a 190-item final examination prepared for a ninth grade English class:

(1) A conjunction which introduces an adverb clause is called a
_____.

(2) An adjective which tells how many is called

_____.

(3) LOOSE—LOSE: Which one means "to suffer loss"?

_____.

(4) CAPITAL—CAPITOL: Which one is a building?

_____.

(5) Past participle of WRITE: _____.
(6) Present perfect tense of TEAR: _____.
(7) Nominative case, first person, singular:

_____.

(8) Objective case, third person, singular, feminine gender:

_____.

(9) Speculative degree of INDUSTRIOUS

_____.

(10) Comparative degree of MUCH _____.

Will an ability to answer these questions correctly improve a student's skill in communication? How many college professors of physics could answer all of these questions accurately? Is it unreasonable to suppose that a professor should be able to demonstrate high levels of proficiency in a junior high school English examination?

Fourth Grade Spelling

This letter was actually received by a parents who had a child in fourth grade:

Dear Mrs. Smith:

Martha's speling is very poor. I hope you can help her practise at home each day so she will be able to improve.

Sincerely,

Beatrice Jones
Fourth Grade Teacher

The examples described have illustrated some of the questions with which we must concern ourselves. There are also other important facets of evaluation. The following questions pose some of the issues: Should students who try get passing grades, even if their achievement scores are unsatisfactory? Should a juvenile delinquent be allowed to graduate from high school if he has a criminal record? Should students be retained or failed if they miss school because of an extended illness, even when no homebound teachers are provided?

Suppose we teach a boy to high jump and keep a record of his progress during a three-month period. He may start out by being able to get over a bar set at three feet six inches, but after three months of instruction be able consistently to clear a bar five feet two inches. Would an averaging of his achievements during the previous 90 days be an accurate indicator of his achievement?

Given all of these illustrations as background, we will now look at the grading process more closely.

THE PROCESS AND PROBLEMS IN GRADING

Grading involves three different processes: the teacher arrives at a grade somehow, this information is communicated to various persons, and the communication has an impact upon the recipients.

Arriving at Grades

Grading follows testing or observation by teachers. They can have confidence in their tests to the degree that they sample appropriate behaviors adequately. But sampling behaviors by testing in education is like standing by a river with a cup, dipping into the stream as it moves by. In assessing learning, like dipping the cup into the river, one seldom gets an adequate sample. Besides, unless he is especially careful, the sampler often muddies the very waters he is trying to dip out. The process of collecting information through testing often affects the learner so that the sampled behaviors are "contaminated" in various ways. Just as a visit to a physician's office may accelerate the heart beat and increase the blood pressure, something which the doctor may be actually attempting to lower, so do certain teacher behaviors affect their procedures for arriving at grades.

Some students "clam up" on examinations, and what may be assessed is actually their degree of "test anxiety." It may be that test anxiety is what the teacher hopes to measure, but probably not. In the process of giving an examination, however, if certain students' responses are inhibited by their prevailing state of "test anxiety," then the score will be misleading to the teacher seeking a valid grade.

In similar fashion, many teachers value some behaviors more than others on examinations, and impose these values unconsciously to the point that grades are affected. For instance, neatness often adds as much to a student's score as accuracy. Typed papers almost invariably receive higher marks than those in longhand. To write on both sides of the paper irritates some teachers to the extent that it influences the grades they give.

These illustrations are examples of the way teachers themselves sometimes contaminate the very thing they are striving to look at precisely —student behavior. To overcome these problems, many teachers resort to objective tests, which supposedly enable a teacher to sample a wide variety of behaviors, and permit a fair interpretation of the results. Ross quotes Brownell on these tests (99):

> Well, first of all, in the practical circumstances of teaching, one decides to give a test. The decision is surely not based upon purely objective considerations. Second, one determines whether to make a test or to buy one. . . . Third, one makes up one's mind regarding the kind of test—whether it is to be of the traditional type, of the newer types, or a combination—judgment again. Fourth, one settles upon the scope of the test—judgment once more. Fifth, one selects the items to be included—little objectivity here. Sixth, one chooses the form to be employed—true-false, multiple choice, or what not—again little objectivity. Seventh, one frames the items as carefully as one can—and once more has only his judgment for guidance. Eighth, one prepares a key by listing the correct answers—a judgment which may not be acceptable to other teachers even of the same subject. Ninth, through opinion one defines the conditions of administering the test. Tenth, one scores the papers—at last objectivity. But eleventh, one assigns marks—another increment of judgment, and a big one.

This incisive analysis demonstrates the subjectiveness of so-called objective tests. Throughout each of the phases involved in measuring student accomplishments, there are many pitfalls. Some are semantic, such as the "objective" test situation, which Brownell explodes above. Other problems are logical. For example, teachers, students, and parents are often misled into believing that "figures do not lie," primarily because they have not carefully examined the assumptions underlying the grading system. They have convinced themselves that the system is really satisfactory.

In the process of devising ways to cope with the problem of evaluating students' achievements, many teachers have in fact deluded themselves into thinking they were doing a good job. They have become victims of their own arithmetical manipulations, imprisoned in a verbal cocoon of their own fabrication. For instance, it is not uncommon for some teachers to determine all grades from percentages. To make the process mathematical, they give so many points for each question involved; two points, say, for a fifty question examination. If a student gets 33 questions correct, he gets a score of 66 per cent, which will probably be considered failing, although not necessarily so. And if there are several examinations during any grading period, such a procedure enables the teacher to add up all the scores, divide them by the number of tests involved, and reach an arithmetical average which both he and the student understand. It is not at all unusual for a teacher in such circumstances to say: "You got these scores on this many examinations, which average out to this, so your grade is this. Isn't that clear?" Almost without exception both the student and the teacher accept the grade without real question because the logic of the system seems irrefutable.

But is it? What if the teacher had made the questions more difficult? That would not be hard to do. What if he had made them easier? What if he had doubled the number of items? In any of these instances, each student would probably have scored differently, even though the tests were "objective." The odds are very great that the degree of difficulty of any item will always be a matter of chance, since only through extended studies can the actual difficulty level of any question become apparent. Most teachers, though, do not engage in extensive item analysis studies of the questions on their particular examinations.

Furthermore, such a system as described above presupposes that each test question is equal in value to every other. This is seldom true. Some questions are much more important than others. Unless every test also has an identical number of items, the influence of any one item on the total score will vary from examination to examination. Worse yet, in an effort to follow a system which converts readily to percentages, many items are intentionally or inadvertently included which are not as important as other items. They are just there to make the final scores come out in even numbers. Any resulting grade inevitably reflects the teacher's subjective judgment to a great degree.

However, it is not the purpose of this chapter to condemn so-called objective examinations. Rather, it is to encourage each teacher to examine exhaustively and critically the assumptions underlying any rationale which he may hold regarding the use of such test data for grading purposes. "Figures do not lie, but liars can figure." In teaching, some persons lie even to themselves because they have not had the courage or the interest to study carefully their own practices in grading. The consequences of such inaction are too serious to be continued.

Consider, if you will, whether or not the tests with which you are familiar require the student to master the questions which he misses before he goes on to new material. Does he have to "get them right" before he proceeds? If so, are the original errors "held against him?" If he misses an item, does his first score go down in the grade book to be averaged in with all subsequent scores, or is he encouraged to master that bit of learning without penalty before he goes on? Recording the first score that a student makes on an examination in the grade book, or worse yet, expecting him to transfer what he did not learn from one test to a new and entirely different one at a later date ("try harder next time, John") hardly makes sense from a *teaching* point of view. Testing is one thing, teaching another. It may be, and it should be, that testing contributes to learning, but this is not always true in schools today.

Testing in most schools requires a student to perform competently the first time he is tested in any subject. If he is unsuccessful in any phase of the experience, he is then expected to apply the knowledge of this inadequacy to the next testing situation, but this, of course, includes new behaviors rather than the ones originally failed. In other words, the typical learning situation requires students to go from one testing and grading experience to another, never fully mastering or comprehending that which is deemed essential in the first place. Most teachers never give a student a chance to improve his grade on any particular test. All he can do is try to bring up his average by doing well on the next test. This is really beside the point. The next test will be based on new experiences and new learning, and he will be allowed—in fact, required—to proceed to those new experiences not having fully learned those he did not know in the first place. In this way the conventional procedures restrict a teacher's opportunity to teach. Following the conventional pattern, students who do not achieve high levels of proficiency pass, but at much lower levels. The irony of the conventional grading system is that it encourages low standards. The compulsion to "cover the ground" results in just that; those learnings which are not mastered initially are buried deep and covered completely. The learning ground is covered, very, very well.

Let us return to our original question. How would you like to fly in an airplane with a pilot who got a score of 70 per cent on his flight examination? Commercial pilots must demonstrate that they know and have achieved *all* that is essential about flying any particular aircraft safely. The minimal or acceptable standards are really very high. The pilot who fails his examination, however, gets another chance to study and to try again. The authorities are much more interested in helping him learn to achieve mastery than they are in the low score he made initially. Pilots, when they are students, *must* perform at very high levels. A score of 70 is far too low.

Arriving at grades and determining standards is one phase of the grading process. We will have much more to say about this later, but let us now look at the communication facet of grading.

Grades Communicate

Once grades have been determined, they then become agents of communication. Grades must give at least five kinds of information to three different groups of people. Consider those with whom grades must communicate, first of all.

Students are very concerned about their grades. The grade should tell the student something about himself and his educational achievement. Further, it should encourage him, if possible, toward more and better learning.

Parents also gain information from grades. Probably the major purpose of grades is to report students' educational accomplishments to parents so they will be accurately and frequently informed.

Finally grades communicate to various segments of the general public: employers, college admission officers, or the armed services. These groups need reliable information about students' achievements, and grades must at least partially provide it.

To acknowledge the fact that grades must "say something" to three entirely different groups of persons presents one problem. To realize that these same grades must simultaneously convey several different types of information to diverse groups magnifies the chore. For instance, one or more of the above named groups expect information from the schools regarding at least five kinds of educational achievement.

First, how much change has taken place? How much development has come about? These questions reflect a concern for information about achievement over a period of time. This information tells both the student and his parents about the kind of progress he is making. "Am I moving ahead? Do I really know more than I did six months ago?" Information about learning growth is extremely important.

Second, grades also communicate information about achievement in relation to ability. Parents expect more achievement from an able child, less from a youngster who has less growth potential. No one expects a blind child to learn to read print or a crippled child to learn to walk. All parents, however, want to know how well their child is doing compared to how well he could be doing. This is information which grades must endeavor to communicate.

Third, parents and employers both want to know how students succeed in terms of their effort. How hard do they try? Our Puritan background seems to value hard work and effort, and this important information is sought by various persons. No employer wants a lazy worker, and if a student is not really attempting to get ahead, parents need to know if they should seek special assistance in counseling, or perhaps to continue supporting their child in college. Grades must communicate information relating achievement to effort.

Fourth, both students and parents want to know how students' achievement compares to their peers'. "How are the other students in the class progressing? Is my boy doing as well as most of the others in that room?" College admission officers want to know a senior's rank in class. To be valedictorian is significant only in relation to the other students in a group. Being the brightest of the bright is one kind of achievement. Being the brightest of the slow provides information of a different order.

Finally, colleges and employers especially want to know how well any student compares with a larger norm, or a national average. Teachers and parents need some outside criterion on which they can base their judgments. Superintendents sometimes feel compelled to find out if students in their school system "are doing as well as or better than the national norm." Comparisons with larger groups are also important functions of grades in school.

Trying to communicate five kinds of information at once is a considerable chore. Trying to say these things to three distinctly different groups of people is yet more difficult. One is almost forced to conclude that, in such a task, any person or group who deliberately selected the barest unit of language available to do the job—the single letter—would seem to be plainly idiotic.

That seems to be exactly where much of the teaching profession stands today. Confronted with such a responsibility, teachers cling tenaciously to the most minute segment of the system at their disposal, the letter grade. One would think it almost sinful to attempt to describe all of the richness of development and achievement represented in educational growth by a single letter. The tradition persists, however, in spite of many efforts to change.

Teachers are not people who shy from hard work, however. For years they have attempted many different ways of communicating with students, parents, and society. Most of these efforts have been less than satisfactory; witness the perpetual discussion and attempted innovations regarding grading. What is needed is some kind of symbol system which will adequately communicate different kinds of information to many people.

I must assume, at least for the present, that letter grades are here to stay, and only slight modifications are possible. This I do with resignation. In later portions of this chapter improvements are suggested. No modification of the system itself is actually contemplated. Such modification is needed, however, but the general unwillingness of the profession to detach itself from anything so archaic as the traditional grading system seems beyond present attainment. This book does not try to describe high sounding theories which are impossible to translate into practice. The grading procedure described in later sections is practical, although it falls short of what is truly needed—a major change. Devising a different way of arriving at grades, however, may affect the communication and the impact which they produce.

The Effect of Grades

After grades have been determined, they communicate something to somebody. As a result of this communication, there is impact.

Some students who get poor grades become depressed to the point of suicide. Others drop out and look for jobs. Others retreat to a less troublesome world of movies, TV, 'True Romances' and dates. Others just run away from home—and school. A good many are impenetrably indifferent.

Many students, however, respond positively to their grades. They feel happy and satisfied, and are encouraged to continue their studies, and to go to college. Some researchers suggest that only about half of any group of typical students is really affected by their grades. And of this number, half are encouraged if they get good grades, while the remainder put forth their greatest effort if they receive poor marks. In other words, about 25 per cent of them supposedly work harder in school when they get good grades, another 25 per cent work harder when they get poor grades, and the remaining 50 per cent are not affected one way or the other.

This means that a teacher who uses grades to try to get students to work harder is only being successful with a minor fraction of them. Individual admonitions would be a different thing. Teachers who try to use grades as motivating levers, however, are generally assured of failure, except with certain students. Because most teachers are academically oriented, and because they themselves have responded favorably to grades, they are apt to generalize from their own experience. This is an extremely dangerous practice at any time, but especially with regard to grades.

Parents are also affected by students' grades. In some cases it is seen as a direct attack upon their personal integrity if their youngsters receive poor marks. Generally, however, when poor grades have an effect upon parents, the youngsters are put in double jeopardy. Some parents whip children who bring home poor grades, and physical punishment is seldom interpreted as a sign of affection. Other parents reward their youngsters with money for every "A," and any poor grade may be interpreted as a potential loss of parental love. It is easy for a child to assume that if he is beaten for an "F" or if his parents deprive him of a dollar if he does not get an "A," what he is really losing is their love and faith in him. It hardly makes any difference that this is seldom true. If a youngster thinks that it is true, for him it is.

The net result of these feelings is a tendency to cheat in examinations or try to get good grades in any way he can. From a student's point of view, cheating is perfectly justifiable if it means not losing his parents' affection. Studies have repeatedly shown that most students cheat much of the time, and few of them are really concerned about this behavior at all. Most persons who have studied cheating feel that our present grading system encourages it. Earl Kelley once lamented the fact that "about the worst sin a child can commit in school is to help another learner." One can only conclude that our value system is awry somewhere.

Other persons are also concerned about students' grades. Employers seek people who have been successful in their school efforts. Since the best single predictor of college success is high school grades, college admission officers are affected by students' grades. Admissions practices have expanded in recent years to consider other data (College Entrance Examination Boards, principal's recommendations, counselor's evaluation, or the reputation which a given school has for turning out good students), but with the increasing pressure on college gates, grades are again becoming a major factor. Rightly or wrongly, because of the very simplicity of their single letter form, grades have a way of persisting after other factors have been forgotten.

In essence, teachers arrive at grades, these grades communicate a variety of information to different groups, and some kind of impact follows. This is the grading process. In the section which follows we will explore the idea of "standards" and grading.

THE CLASSIFICATION OF EDUCATIONAL OBJECTIVES

The concept of standards in education is very fuzzy. Some schools supposedly have higher standards than others. Some teachers are also said to have higher standards than other teachers. What these standards are or how they come to be is seldom known. In most cases a general "toughening up" is apparent, but aside from more failures and fewer "A's," other manifestations of standards in action are not often found.

Some teachers cite with approval the number of students they fail as evidence of high standards. Carrying this logic further, dare we assume that if they failed everybody they would then be doing a perfect job? The author knows of one situation in which only 26 students out of more than four thousand enrolled in a beginning college course got "A's." Is this a high standard or poor teaching?

Certainly in some institutions noted for academic prowess, the scramble for high grades results in students learning how to cheat effectively. In one academic high school, for example, where admissions are carefully controlled and scholarships abound for graduates with good records, the one thing that everybody learns, according to the students themselves, is how to cheat. The stakes are too high not to try to get good grades, one way or another—or so these students feel. Telling them they ought not to feel this way is of little use. Imposing harsher punishment for offenders simply drives them to new approaches. The basic system must be changed.

It will be our purpose later in this chapter to outline an educational system in which students can learn, rather than simply be tested and graded according to unstated assumptions which actually militate against continued achievement.

There is now some evidence that many teachers inadvertently apply an economic theory out of context when they are evaluating students' achievements. The principle of scarcity presupposes that of certain commodities there is "not enough to go around." Grading on the curve presupposes similar notions. It implies that all children should not be able to learn all things, even if teachers could teach them. To urge some kind of normal distribution of grades is to predetermine the learning limits. Teachers who do this are restricting their opportunities in the very thing they are trying to accomplish: helping students learn. Such an idea as grading on a curve is contrary to the very premises of education, which imply that *everybody should learn everything there is to know*, if that is possible.

From experience we realize that all children will not be able to learn all things. This does not excuse teachers from trying. Specifically, it does not warrant teachers in justifying their grading procedures as fitting a normal probability curve because "all things fit such a distribution." All aspects of existence do not fit any such a normal curve.

Some learnings do distribute themselves in fairly symmetrical fashion around a central point. To assume that, because such learnings apparently follow a pattern, grades in school should also follow such a pattern is a most serious error. In the first place, seldom is there a sample of adequate size to check such a distribution. Only if there were several hundred students, at least, whose learnings had been carefully and uniformly observed in realistic manner would it be possible at all.

It is not uncommon for some teachers to devise tests in such a way that they "rig" the difficulty level according to the group. For example, if a group of slow learners all got the answers all right on an easy test, some instructors would then say: "I'll have to make the test more difficult next time so none of them will think they ought to get an 'A.' After all, standards are standards, you know."

Some school systems even legislate through school board policy that no student in an honors class shall make less than a "C," nor any student who is not in an honors class make more than a "B." Imagine the problem facing a teacher who has to give a "B" to a student who scores perfectly on a given test. What that teacher does, of course, is simply make the tests more difficult, add essay questions which he can score in another way without having to defend his actions, or move the student up to the honors group. These actions, however, are all avoiding the problem rather than confronting it.

Ideas are not property. Copyrights and patent laws are efforts to deny this fact, and ideas can be "owned" for short periods of time this way. But for all practical purposes ideas are non-economic entities, and they do not answer to the laws of economic distribution. The teacher's job is not to arrange the circumstances so that he gets a distribution of grades, but to endeavor to help all students learn all things. Theoretically the perfect teacher would give all "A's," simply because every student learned everything there was to know.

The plea here is not to grade according to unexamined assumptions. Undoubtedly there are both real and imagined factors which limit students' learnings. Probably no person has ever actually realized his full potential, however, therefore teachers must have hope. They must be optimistic about how much children can learn. Unless teachers believe that the human organism can be modified, their effectiveness is reduced from the very start. They must believe that what they do can help students learn. If they believe otherwise they are in the wrong profession.

What do we need? Specifically, we need a clarification of the levels or standards of achievement and a statement of the student's relation to these standards. Grading must always be seen in terms of specific objectives. Clarifying and determining standards is philosophy. Reaching the standards is teaching. Deciding when the standards have been met is evaluation. Reporting the achievements is grading. The place to start is with the standards themselves.

Kinds of Learning

Many different kinds of learning are taught in school. At least five types seem important here, and will be discussed in detail. Not all of these are taught directly, of course, but, because they are learned behaviors and because they often are predicated upon previous teachings, they will be outlined here.

Social learnings are important in any school. Students of all ages are taught to work effectively and easily with other learners. Cooperation is the keystone of our democratic way. Tolerance, acceptance, understanding, sympathy, kindness, generosity, compassion—all these are social learnings and social skills. Schools teach these ways of behaving, directly or indirectly, as part of the complex.

Physical learnings are a second category. Students learn to write, to run, to jump. Some are taught to draw and some to carve. Some learn to fill teeth or dissect cadavers, to drive tractors or to type letters. Others learn shorthand while still others are taught to saw a straight line or run a machine. Physical skills are important learnings, and they are taught in school.

Intellectual learnings are a third type of activity taught in school. Recognition, recall, and reasoning might be labeled as the important three R's in this sphere of teaching. Knowing certain ideas, the meaning of words, the relationship of particular events, or when to apply certain formulae or generalizations are illustrations of intellectual learnings. Understanding why particular conditions develop, how various phenomena occur, or in what manner energy is transformed are intellectual learnings. Facts, knowledge, concepts, data, relationships, causes, effects, are all taught in school.

Affective learnings, or attitudes, are also taught. The ability to enjoy poetry or music, for instance, is an attitude. Liking mathematics or geography is also attitudinal. Valuing truth or believing in the worth and dignity of all men are affective learnings. These ways of behaving, which we sometimes call emotions or attitudes, are learned and they are taught. Some teachers do not especially relish the idea of working with attitudes, but affective learnings are a part of the educator's domain.

Finally, there are behaviors which can be characterized as judgmental or decision-making kinds of learnings. These actions, more than any others, involve relating intellectual, social, physical, and attitudinal behaviors simultaneously into functional behavioral units. Deciding how to vote, which route to follow, when to trade automobiles, whether to rent or buy a home, what church to attend, which persons to select as intimate friends, are all examples of judgmental activities. Learning to make decisions is taught, as well as learned, in schools.

Degree of Mastery Required

These five kinds of learning represent one aspect of our classification of educational objectives. For each of these learning areas, however, there are at least three different degrees of mastery required. Some skills *must* be learned perfectly. There is no room for error. Teaching a pilot to land an aircraft safely is one example. Eighty per cent, 90 per cent, even 99 per cent accuracy is far too low a standard. If commercial pilots could be depended upon only 999 times out of a thousand to make safe, sure landings, this standard would not be high enough. This skill must be mastered to perfection.

Our first degree of mastery, then, is the imperative level. Some things must be learned so well there is *never* any error, if at all humanly possible. Mistakes and errors do occur, but the degree of competence sought is 100 per cent—perfect learning. Anything less may be disastrous. Surgeons *must* tie sutures perfectly every time. Truck drivers *must* apply their brakes properly at icy intersections perfectly every time. Electricians *must* ground their installations correctly every time. Housewives *must* keep poisons out of the reach of little children every time.

In the main, learnings on the imperative level assume greater significance because life itself is often at stake. This is not a necessary characteristic of the imperative learnings, however, since even typists must make errors less than one per cent of the time. But many kinds of imperative learnings do fall into this life and death classification.

There are others which are important but which need not be learned that well. The degree of mastery required is fairly high, somewhere in the neighborhood of 85 per cent proficiency, but perfection is neither necessary nor possible in many instances. This level of mastery might be called the desirable level.

No medical student should be allowed to graduate unless he can satisfactorily perform a spinal tap. But no physician need be able to do it perfectly every time. He must learn this skill—it must be taught—but if he is unsuccessful on occasions, this can be remedied by a second attempt or assistance from another doctor. Performing properly almost every time is good enough.

Every truck driver must learn to back his rig to the loading dock. This he must learn to do with considerable skill, but perfection is not necessary. Any truck driver who can only back his truck successfully 30 per cent of the time will probably find himself seeking other employment, but 100 per cent achievement is hardly essential. A desirable degree of mastery will suffice.

On the other hand, there are certain kinds of learnings in which even lower levels of mastery are satisfactory, depending upon circumstances. Learning to putt perfectly in golf is imperative for the professional golfer. If the physician, playing a relaxing round, can stroke the ball properly half the time, however, this is perfectly acceptable. It would be helpful if every truck driver could accurately diagnose every motor difficulty in his vehicle, but this is hardly essential. If his truck's temperature gauge shows "hot," it may be of some value for every trucker to know that a hot engine may mean a broken fan belt, which in turn could mean generator trouble. However, all he really has to know is that something is wrong, and that he ought to get it checked quickly. The degree of mastery required is this instance is much less imperative than that of being able to brake safely at an icy intersection or the desirability of being able to back his truck correctly.

The point is this: some things must be taught in such a way that they are learned perfectly, others must be learned quite well, but others may be learned only half as well to be satisfactory. Acceptable levels of performance vary according to the particular learning involved, and defining that level of acceptability is one responsibility of a teacher.

The Importance of Time

There is, however, another dimension to the classification of educational objectives. In the course of performing learned behaviors, time plays a major role in some instances and not in others. Consider a physician confronted with two patients: one has just suffered a coronary attack and the other has pneumonia. Diagnosing these difficulties is obviously judgmental learning at the imperative level; he must make an accurate assessment of the available data in each instance and prescribe appropriate therapy. In the case of the patient with a severe heart attack, the physician only has one chance. For all practical purposes, either he will decide and prescribe correctly, or there will be no second opportunity.

On the other hand, if his first estimate of the patient with pneumonia proves incorrect, he will probably have time for alternative courses of action. He must ultimately make the correct decisions, of course, but he has extended time opportunities in the pneumonia case which are not available in the coronary case.

In other words, there are some circumstances in which immediate learned behavior is important. In others there are extended time opportunities. These variations exist at every level and with every type of learning.

To return to our golf illustration, we can note that putting in golf is an example of immediate performance. A golfer has one chance each time he putts. He may not be successful but every effort will count against his score. For the engineer or writer, there are always opportunities to perform and then correct. If the mathematical problem is not worked properly, there is time for another trial. If the sentence is not acceptably written, the writer can do it over and over again until it does suit him. Not so with the actor on the stage. Once his lines are said, his chance is gone. Either the truck driver applies his brakes properly or he does not. Either the pilot lands his plane safely or he does not. There are no second chances in some activities.

This is only partially correct, of course. There will always be another play for the actor who misses his lines. There are always other tournaments to win for the professional golfer. There may or not be other chances for the victims of airplane mishaps or faulty diagnoses. The main point is that learning may be so thought of that the kinds and levels required can also be considered in terms of time.

These ideas are described graphically in Figure 2. Here we can note the three dimensions of our classification: the kinds of learning demanded along the base, the degree of mastery required represented by the vertical, and the time dimension along the other side.

This classification outlines thirty categories of educational objectives according to the kinds, the degree of mastery required, and the significance time plays in the performance of each. In one sense this model may appear restrictive to the educational practitioner, but it should add power to the teacher's thinking. Just as a telescope restricts the visual field of the astronomer, simultaneously it deepens tremendously that segment of the heavens he does survey. Similarly, the mathematician's formulae give rigor and power to his applications which are not possible in a

Figure 2

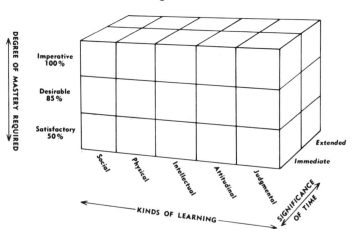

Classification of Educational Objectives

random approach to quantitative phenomena. Hopefully, this syntactical model will enable teachers to gain clearer ideas of educational standards.

Given this theoretical framework, teachers should be able to categorize their objectives and thereby improve their efforts. No single dimension is adequate. Recognizing that some learnings must be mastered perfectly while others are less important should assist teachers in clarifying their notions about standards of excellence.

The typing teacher understands that final proficiency in typing is more important than progress, and that acceptable typing standards demand almost perfect performance at reasonable speed. No typist who errs once every hundred strokes can expect to keep a position unless greater achievement is made. No typist who types perfectly at five words per minute can expect to find employment. Acceptability in typing standards demands accuracy in excess of 99 per cent with sufficient speed.

In basketball, however, no coach can expect over 50 per cent accuracy from his players shooting from the floor, yet no coach dare accept less than 80 per cent accuracy from those players at the foul line. Expectations must vary, and the skillful teacher is one who clarifies to himself and his students which learnings are imperative, which desirable, and which are satisfactory. The accomplished teacher then devises a way of translating these ideas into educational practice: he grades according to this principle.

It is not the purpose of this book to outline in detail those learnings which are appropriate for all teachers and students in all situations. What desirable skills does the historian or journalist or truck driver need? Which intellectual or social or judgmental learnings are imperative for the prospective accountant, carpenter, teacher, housewife, machinist, architect, X-ray technician, data processing specialist, chemical engineer, dairy farmer, citrus grower, nurse?

Only those persons who are specialists in their particular fields could complete the pattern by defining all appropriate learnings. Only fourth grade teachers or vocational agriculture teachers or English teachers or professors of political science or sociology or biology could make the necessary decisions for their fields at their particular levels. But this must be done. Bloom (13) and his associates have shown part of the way. Unless teachers identify outcomes precisely and in relationship to other factors, evaluation will remain a morass.

Related Problems

Let us examine one final point before we move on. Defining the imperative and desirable levels in any educational context is extremely important, but it is especially difficult for teachers working in the public schools. To teach the children of all sorts of people and to determine imperatives, particularly, is a serious responsibility. Two factors must be considered: the importance of the particular learning to society, and the abilities of the students to acquire those behavior changes through teaching. Only the second problem will be considered here.

Think about the decisions facing a public elementary school faculty, for example. How many children *should* learn how to add, subtract, multiply, and divide accurately before they are passed to junior high school? Is it reasonable to insist that *every* youngster demonstrate proficiency in these areas before he is promoted?

The use of the word "should" implies a philosophical meaning, an "ought-to" kind of thinking. To expect *every* child to accomplish all of these learnings may be expecting the impossible. Some children simply do not have the intellectual ability. Should they be retained? Should they be promoted? How many children reasonably should be expected to reach the imperative level?

Retaining only 10 per cent of any given group each year diminishes a beginning first grade class of 30 to less than 10 students 12 years later. The chart below describes the loss:

Grade	Number Enrolled	Number Retained
1	30	3
2	27	3
3	24	2
4	22	2
5	20	2
6	18	2
7	16	2
8	14	1
9	13	1
10	12	1
11	11	1
12	10	1
Number graduating	9	

The reader may want to quarrel with this arithmetic. Obviously those students who have been retained would have to be included in the new totals each year at the lower level, and the problem gets much more involved than this simple illustration shows. The point is that a retention rate of only 10 per cent imposes a very severe standard of excellence— one which is neither practical nor defensible. Nothing succeeds like success, and retention is hardly success.

People will only attempt those things in which they feel they have some opportunity for success. Few elementary teachers would compete in a push-up contest with their high school coach, even though all would agree as to the importance of physical fitness for everybody. Very few high school English teachers would compete with bright eighth graders in extracting the square root from eight-digit numbers. The same thing is true of students. They will only make attempts where they have some chance of success and whether they are successful or not depends upon the kind of feedback information they receive from their teacher, usually in the form of grades.

Yet teachers must decide what is passing and what is failing. They must also decide *who* shall pass and *who* shall fail. Unless their objectives are clear both to themselves and their students, any efforts at evaluation may be disastrous. Teachers must spell out to themselves and to their students just which learnings are imperatives, which desirable and which satisfactory. If these decisions can be achieved in concert with students and parents, so much the better. Helping teachers determine which achievements should be classified as imperatives or otherwise is a legitimate role for non-professionals. Determining whether these degrees of mastery have been achieved is a professional responsibility.

One of the characteristics of a profession is that the practitioner makes judgments which the recipient is in no position to know about himself. That is, if a doctor or lawyer advises an individual to act in a certain way, he is dependent upon the professional for his advice and is seldom capable of "second guessing" his recommendations. It is essential, therefore, for professional persons to perform their services in the best of faith, because the recipient cannot make valid decisions himself. Ethics hinge upon this point. For a physician to continue scheduling appointments for a patient who has progressed beyond the need of his services is a violation of medical ethics.

Neither students nor parents are in a position to judge achievements as well as a teacher, who must generally stand alone on his professional decisions about achievement and grades. But these decisions must be reasonable. They must be based on valid evidence and unquestionable assumptions.

Many teachers believe that almost every fifth grade child *should* achieve at or above fifth grade level on a standardized achievement test in reading. If a youngster scores below fifth grade level, this is considered bad, and that student must be helped to get up to grade level.

Grade level, however, is a statistical concept in educational measurement. It is a figure which describes the mean achievement of a typical group of students from all over the nation who were at that grade level when they were tested. By definition, half the students must achieve at fifth grade level or above, and half must achieve at fifth grade level or below. Nothing else is possible. For any teacher to expect all or most of his students to achieve at fifth grade level or above is unreasonable. Such a teacher might as well deplore the fact that half the people in the United States have an I.Q. of 100 or below. It is not possible for all children to achieve at or above grade level because grade level is that point at which the average student achieves. To hope that more than 50 or 60 per cent exceed that point in any classroom is to attempt to translate a statistical description of what is true for an average child (grade level is the arithmetical mode or mean) into a philosophical statement of what ought to be true for all youngsters. This is dangerous if not downright fallacious thinking.

In the example just cited, any teacher who expects most children in his class to achieve at or above grade level is really saying that grade level ought to be higher than it actually is. He is implying that a new mean achievement for fifth graders should be far enough above the present grade level so that almost all students in his class would fall within the "acceptable" limits.

Raising standards is certainly commendable on the part of teachers, and over a period of several years, by improving teaching methods and instructional materials, especially, achievement norms can be increased appreciably. Any teacher who approaches the area of evaluation without at least a basic understanding of elementary statistical concepts, however, may very well violate principles of ethical conduct because he does not know when he is basing decisions on erroneous assumptions. This is an extremely important point. The truly professional teacher must consciously and consistently explore the assumptions underlying his evaluations, discarding those which are unreasonable and modifying those which hold some kernel of validity.

THE CONTRACT IDEA

Thus far in this chapter we have looked at several illustrations of educational evaluation, explored some of the problems and processes involved in grading, and examined in some detail a structural model designed to assist teachers. This is a book on methodology, however, and the time has come to suggest specific ways and means for coping with some of the problems.

The remaining portion of this chapter is devoted to this end. One way of grading which is both democratic and effective in terms of learning theory is outlined in detail. Examples of this method in operation among college students and junior high school students are included. Finally, the principles upon which this method are based have been isolated and explained.

The purpose of this elaboration is, first of all, to demonstrate the relationship of these ideas to the thesis of this book. More importantly it is hoped that an analysis of the reasoning may help the reader find new approaches and modifications to the problem of encouraging and evaluating student achievement. Without question, there are more real problems in educational methodology than almost any other aspect of the educational enterprise. Hopefully, *you* may be encouraged to think seriously about some of these problems and propose new hypotheses to test. Modification of the grading system might well be among these contributions.

What Is a Grade Contract?

The contract idea, hardly new in education, is based upon the fact that one student and one teacher together spell out in writing exactly what will be accomplished during a period of time for a particular grade. The contract is prepared in two copies, the instructor and student each sign both copies, and each keeps one for his own use. The contract is a mutually agreed program of learning covering certain common and certain different experiences for each student, specifying particular times and dates and forms, and predicated upon the assumption that the teacher should teach and the student should learn. Finally, the contract idea in operation is a fulfillment of democratic principles and learning theory in that it is based upon cooperative decisions, involvement, maximum communication, high standards of academic excellence, and genuine mutual trust.

If we examine a grade contract in detail these points may become more apparent. Please note as we go along that the contract idea is both simple and complex. The basic notion is deceptively easy to understand; for the contract to be effective in actual use, however, many special conditions must be met. These conditions are as important as the contract idea itself. Without them, the entire procedure becomes another 'gimmick" for teachers' use.

Described in Figure 3 is an actual copy of a grade contract which has been used with college students in an introductory psychology course. Note first that the contract, which is prepared in two copies by each student, actually represents a signed agreement between the student and the instructor for a particular grade. The student himself decides to which grade he aspires. After this, he and the instructor together work out a series of agreements about how this grade shall be achieved. These agreements should free the learner to participate and explore ideas more in class. No student should have to parrot an instructor in order to get a particular grade. If he meets the agreed-upon requirements, that grade would be forthcoming because he fulfilled the conditions of the contract. Likewise, if only part of the agreement was met, only that part of the contract would be binding. And the contract is binding both ways; upon

Figure 3

GRADE CONTRACT

NAME_____ COURSE_____ SEMESTER_____

I will do the following things for a grade of:	I will demonstrate that I have done these things by:
A 1. Do an original study on:**	1. Submitting a written report* to instructor January 15 and give oral report in class after January 15
B 2. Do a study of studies on:**	2. Submitting a written report* to instructor December 16
C 3. Visit one of the following: (a) School for retarded (b) State school for insane (c) Children Psychiatric Hospital	3.
D 4. Attend class 5. Read *Introduction to Psychology* by Morgan	4. Instructor's record 5. Pass Examination* October 17 December 3 January 31
6. Fill out contract	6. Submitting contract to instructor September 24

* Will be graded pass or fail. If failed, may be repeated.

** See attached sheets

INSTRUCTOR _____

STUDENT _____

A Grade Contract

the student and upon the teacher. Neither can withdraw from the agreement without the full knowledge and consent of the other.

Observe that the grade contract is cumulative. To get a grade of "D" any student must meet all of the requirements specified under "D" on the contract. To get a "C," he must meet all of the "D" requirements plus all of the "C" requirements. Should he want to strive for a "B," he would have to meet all of the "D" and "C" requirements satisfactorily, as well as those for a "B." Finally, if he decided to work for an "A," he would agree to do everything specified on the contract sheet. The grade contract is predicated upon the idea that the amount of work a student does will be one factor involved in determining his grade. In this sense a grade contract is quantitative in nature.

Quality is also extremely important, however, in the way assignments are handled. Note that under "D" requirement 5, for instance, there will be three examinations given during the course of the semester, which the student must pass to get a "D." Passing, however, will be defined perhaps as a grade of 85 per cent on an objective test or a conventional "B" on an essay examination. If the student does not make a passing grade the first time, however, the test may be repeated.

Here is an important point: if the student does not at first succeed, let him try and try again. In each instance his effort is simply graded pass or fail, but by keeping the passing level high, rigid standards can be imposed —imposed, however, by insisting upon accomplishment rather than by penalizing through failure.

Suppose a student fails a test the first time around. He should study his material and prepare again. The second time it may be well to have another sequence of items available in order to discourage rote memory of symbols in a multiple-choice test. The second time it is also reasonable to raise the performance level required for passing from 85 to 90 per cent, if the teacher can assume that knowing the correct answers to his test questions is a satisfactory proof of understanding.

Should the student fail a second time, the teacher can even permit a third effort, perhaps this time demanding a score of 95 per cent. Each instructor can plan such repetitions only for himself by trial and error and careful thought. Note, however, several fundamental points in this approach to grading by contract.

First, the emphasis is upon learning and success rather than testing and failure. What if a student does not meet a high level of proficiency his first effort? As long as this unsatisfactory score, which may be as high as an 82, is not held against him and averaged in with his other grades, the testing can be a learning experience. If he can study for the same examination again, his performance level may be satisfactory. If permitting a student to take the same examination a second time seems illogical, one can only assume that the examination was not appropriate to use even once. Either it measures the important factors or it does not.

Second, note that the "D" requirement constitutes the instructor's major responsibility for the course. This is the part of the curriculum which the teacher can certify as meeting institutional expectations—class attendance and the basic course content—and this insures that any student passing the course has demonstrated proficient behavior if the class sessions were conducted meaningfully and the examinations utilized were realistic representations of the basic material. If these conditions were not met, whatever grade a student might receive would be meaningless.

For this "D" requirement to be successful, and for the contract to work satisfactorily, the specific expectations regarding number of absences allowed, kind and length of examinations, number of re-testing sessions permitted, and other such problems would have to be spelled out *before* the contract went into effect. Unless such provisions were clarified first, misunderstandings and distrust would be apt to arise.

This brings up another advantage of the contract. Used properly, relations between students and instructor improve markedly. No longer are students out to "beat the teacher at his own game" by cheating or shirking responsibility. Each student strives for whatever grade he desires. The conditions for achieving that grade are understood clearly in advance. Either the learning occurs or it does not. If it does, the grade is granted. If it does not, all parties involved understand exactly how and why the conditions were not fulfilled.

One of the characteristics of the contract is to insure a maximum of communication between teacher and student about course objectives, evaluation procedures, and analysis of results. To be effective, each instructor should arrange at least two short conferences with each student during the course of any grading period. The first enables both teacher and student to raise any question either might have about the requirements for a particular grade or how these learnings will be demonstrated. In the case of an "A" requirement, exactly what original study would be undertaken, how this study would be accomplished, what methods of observation would be employed, when the data would be gathered, and similar questions, can all be resolved in clear fashion at an early planning session.

The second conference at the end of the grading period allows teacher and student to go over together each detail of the contractual arrangement and agree on the grade to be received. They are thus brought face to face with the agreed-upon contract and evidence of learning presented. Such opportunities for personal communication are essential for the contract idea to work satisfactorily. Finding time to meet with each student may be a problem, but if helping individual students is an important part of teaching, ingenious teachers can find ways of overcoming the difficulty.

One final word about the "D" requirement: observe in this contract that class attendance is required. In actual practice, of course, there are times when it is more important for students to be somewhere else than in class. Illness, trouble at home, or other problems may be more demanding. Reasonable limits for absence must be allowed.

Even more important than that, note that class participation is not evaluated in this particular contract at all. As defined here, students must attend class, but beyond that point their activities are not scored in any way. The instructor assumes that if students are present he will find ways of influencing their behavior. Some instructors might prefer some other arrangement. The important point is that *everything which is included in the evaluation must be spelled out and graded "pass" or "fail."* It might be that the questions students asked, their responses under pressure, or other such behaviors should be assessed. These objectives would be identified and classified so that both teachers and students would know the bases for grading. One thing which a contract can do is specify educational objectives in writing. When students know exactly what is expected of them, and when and how, much of the difficulty of teaching has already been overcome.

Now let us look at the "C" requirements in this particular contract. Remember, first of all, that if a student wants a grade of "C," he must first do all of the work required for a "D" satisfactorily and then complete the "C" requirements. Note also that this requirement is an entirely different type of learning experience from the basic "D" requirement.

For the contract idea to be successful, students should not be required to do more and more of the same thing to get a higher grade. Varying the educational experiences they will have is essential to planning the contract.

Note here, also, that the student has at least two choice in fulfilling this requirement, if the instructor agrees. In this case, the student may elect to visit any one of three specified institutions, and he may also determine how he will show he has made the visit, since that space in the contract has been purposely left blank. He may choose to present an oral report to the teacher, have a tape recording of his interview with the director to present before the class, bring the institutional psychologist to class to discuss the institution, or report in any way which seems appropriate and educational to him—any way, that is, to which the instructor will agree. During the planning conference the teacher must exercise judgment about what he will accept as proof of the learning.

In certain cases he might be permissive, in others more demanding. The wise teacher is one who can encourage each student in an activity which will be rewarding personally and beneficial educationally. By allowing students to propose how they will solve this problem, the contract is encouraging individual involvement.

Look now at the "B" requirement. Again you will recall that a student will have to complete all of the "D" and "C" requirements in addition to the "B" stipulations. Here you can see another feature of the contract: choice within limits. By specifying a particular type of activity, a "study of studies," the instructor has limited the kind of experience considerably. Any student who wants a "B" in that course will have to undertake to read ten or fifteen original research reports on a psychological problem of his choice, summarize each carefully, see what conclusions are apparent, then write a detailed report of his investigation. Additional instructions and suggestions would be provided by attaching supplementary materials, as indicated on the contract itself. By insisting that the students dig deeply into original research reports, the instructor is assuring himself that these students will have at least some experience with good psychological sources. If the student chooses, with the instructor's approval, an area of special interest, several possibilities unfold.

First, the student is attracted to the more advanced work because he has a chance to probe deeply in areas with which he is not familiar, but in which he may have some general interest. Second, by working through a series of topics with each student, the instructor is in an excellent position to offer suggestions about references, authors and title indices. He is in a position to assist each individual learner. Finally the "choice within limits" provides a structure which is generally comforting to most undergraduate college students: a framework which outlines the course, but a flexibility within that framework which allows for creativity and growth. Given different circumstances and different students, the instructor might vary these conditions one way or another for maximum gain. Teachers can structure the experience more highly or less highly by increasing or decreasing the number and kinds of options in the contract. In some cases, all requirements might be predetermined completely; in others there might be no limits whatsoever. The student might be allowed to propose his own approach for a particular grade.

For a student to get an "A" in this particular psychology course he must, in addition to all of the other requirements, do a study of his own. As spelled out in the supplementary sheets, an original study would involve asking some kind of sensible question, then seeking an answer through empirical means. The student must define a problem in the general area of psychology, then solve it through his own efforts.

A quick look again at all of the requirements makes evident the fact that each experience required for each grade is unique. For a "D" the student goes to class and reads a book. For a "C" he visits an institution. For a "B" he reads and abstracts original research reports, and for an "A" he conducts some simple research project on his own.

In terms of the time involved, the "D" requirement probably takes more than any other, though not necessarily so. The "A" requirement, on the other hand, may only take a few hours of the student's working time for satisfactory completion. The important thing is that the experiences all be different in kind and quality, and that they fulfill the educational objective desired.

Reading is one kind of learning activity. It is slow, at times tedious, and invariably passive. Conceptualizing a study, however, is a different kind of mental process. It requires the active participation of the learner at every step. Guided by a creative teacher, the student who seeks to strive for an "A" might, in a psychology class, want to compare responses of white and Negro college students to a measure of ethnocentrism, study the learning rates of rats in a maze under varying conditions over a period of time, investigate the reasons expressed by men over 21 regarding their preferences for vocations, or compare adolescents' retention of nonsense syllables with and without monetary rewards. In any instance, the student should have an opportunity to move out in an unknown field and pursue a problem of special concern to him. Any student who would want to do this would also have to do extensive reading even before he could discuss the problem intelligently. But learning is what the instructor hopes for, so that would be a part of the experience.

If the student's first efforts are not satisfactory, since he will probably not have had much experience with research methods, his grades will not suffer because he selects a difficult problem. The teacher will simply work with him until the appropriate learning does occur. The quality of performance must be defined in terms that are observable and measurable, and some kind of acceptable behavior described. This means that the lowest possible level of satisfactory achievement must be spelled out in detail. The lowest possible level, however, can actually be quite high, if students have more than one opportunity. The important thing is that the level should be reasonable in terms of what the experience purports to accomplish.

The contract idea presents teachers with an unusual opportunity to individualize instruction, achieve course objectives, raise educational standards, and satisfy everybody's demands for a fair means of evaluation. Throughout the entire process the emphasis is always upon learning, and both students and teachers inevitably feel better about grades arrived at this way. The reasons for satisfaction rest in part with the contract idea itself, but more in the manner in which it is used.

When teachers and students trust each other and work together, honestly and openly, learning and personal satisfaction can both follow. There must be good communication and there must be clarification of expectations. Limitations must be obvious and reasonable. If these conditions are met, encouraging and evaluating educational achievement are both possible and enjoyable for all concerned.

Other Suggestions for Using the Contract Idea

In preceding pages specific ways of incorporating the use of a grade contract into teaching procedures have been described. Other suggestions might also be noted. Any teacher who decides to use the contract probably would do well to try it with one class experimentally until he gets the "feel" of grading this way. He should also expect to spend some additional time initially, since the mechanisms of using a grade contract will be different than conventionnal procedures. It is most important, also, for a teacher to honor any student's aspiration level; the grade for which he strives. If students who usually make poor grades want to try for an "A," this must be permitted. Likewise, any good student who wants to set his sights lower must have this privilege. Subtle attempts to manipulate this phase of the contract will surely raise doubts in the minds of students. Only by assuring every student of the chance to establish his own grade is the real force of the contract idea demonstrated.

Finally, it must be recognized that students should receive grades according to what they finish. If a student contracts for an "A" but only completes the "D" and "C" requirements, he should not fail the course. His grade becomes a "C." This is not an "all or none" contract even though each segment functions thus. Certain requirements, however, may be made mandatory for any kind of passing grade. It is reasonable to say that no person shall pass unless he satisfactorily completes the "D" requirement. If a student finishes only his "D," "C," and "A" requirements, however, his final grade should probably become a "B." This provision is important because after students get underway, conditions may allow them to finish some requirements but not others. This should be allowed.

The example of the grade contract described has been selected to represent college level work because most of the readers of this book will be college students and it is hoped that such an illustration will be more meaningful to them.

Let us now consider a contract at another level. All this chapter can do is to outline the principles and illustrate the major ideas of a grade contract. Each practicing teacher, in the final analysis, must employ the concept in his own way. Variations in length of grading period, number of students, facilities for experiences, library resources, size of community and many other factors require each teacher to analyze his own situation and adapt the contract idea to his peculiar circumstances. He must devise a way of grading which satisfies his own professional aspirations while meeting the emotional and learning needs of his students. The contract idea holds real promise for fulfilling these obligations.

A Junior High School Contract

We have examined the idea of a grading contract by using a college level example. Look now at junior high school instance. Described in Figure 4 is a contract for use with a seventh grade science group.

Because of the previous lengthy analysis, only a brief summary will be presented here. Note again how all requirements are graded "pass" or "fail," how each level of requirement incorporates a different kind of activity, and how there is always opportunity for repeating to insure satisfactory performance. Note also that this particular contract is prepared for a semester. Most junior high schools make out grade cards more frequently than twice a year. In this case the instructor would need a clear-cut understanding of how he would determine six-weeks' grades.

Observe also that this contract provides choice within limits, since the student can select the grade he wants to strive for and can also determine, with the teacher's approval, what kind of science project to initiate. Still other choices are available within the "B" requirements. Because of the individual aspirations and interests of students, those who elect to do advanced study will probably be working in entirely different areas than others. This permits the teacher to work with each learner so that he can design an experience precisely to that student's motivational and intellectual needs.

PRINCIPLES UNDERLYING THE CONTRACT IDEA

Further illustrations might be presented. Since each teacher must interpret the contract in his own way at this point we will move on to an examination of some of its fundamental principles. Each of these principles has been implied already, but an explicit statement may make them more clearly usable.

Clarification of Expectations and Limitations

Using the grade contract enables a teacher to come to grips with educational objectives. Developing and utilizing the contract idea forces a

Figure 4

```
GRADE CONTRACT
```

NAME_____ SEMESTER_____

I will do the following things for a grade of:	I will demonstrate that I have done these things by:

A 1. Develop the following exhibit for the science fair:

    1. Display my project at local science fair February 17 according to rules** established for entering projects. Submit weekly progress reports to instructor in writing.

B 2a. Maintain a science notebook on:

    2a. Submit to instructor last school day of each month.***

OR

  2b. Visit one of the following science exhibits each month:
(1) Planetarium
(2) Technical Institute
(3) Industrial Research Center
(4)
(5)

    2b.   ***

OR

  2c. Read one of the following biographies of scientists each month:
(1)
(2)
(3)
(4)
(5)

    2c.   ***

C 3. Participate in class activities

    3. Pass oral exam on laboratory practice*

D 4. Read the textbook

    4. Pass weekly exams*
Pass six-week exams*

   5. Learn the technical vocabulary

    5. Pass weekly spelling and definition exams*

   * Will be graded pass or fail. If failed, may be repeated following day after school.
** See attached sheets.
*** Will be graded pass or fail. If failed, may be revised and resubmitted following week.

STUDENT _____

INSTRUCTOR _____

Junior High School Contract

teacher to spell out in writing exactly what is expected of students and what will not be allowed. By providing a written agreement with appropriate supplementary material, both the teacher and the students have access to a reference stipulating expectations and limitations. Students need security, but they also need opportunities to make choices and decisions. The contract idea provides flexibility within limits, freeing students to explore ideas, to disagree with the teacher, and to examine information critically before they incorporate it into their own behavior.

Emphasizes Success and Teaching

Teachers who use the grade contract as described here emphasize success for their students. They teach more than they test, and tests are used primarily for teaching. Errors are not held against students by being incorporated into the teacher's record. Rather, they serve as springboards to higher learning. The final level of performance is considered more important than the rate or route of learning. Students are not always expected to demonstrate all they know "between two bells"—testing sessions confined to one class period. Contract grading lends itself especially well, also, to take-home and open-book examinations, as well as other out-of-class activities. It enables instructors to make greater demands on their students and at the same time insist on higher levels of performance.

Insisting on high levels of achievement is possible because students have more than one opportunity to reach such levels. The expectations are that almost any one who tries hard enough and works long enough can satisfy his own aspirations. Because it involves individualized activities, contract grading result in much less cheating than conventional grading. If everybody is learning a different thing in a different way, nobody can cheat.

Using Students' Aspiration Levels

Allowing students to decide which grade they wish to strive for, which activities they will engage in, and how they will demonstrate that they have satisfactorily completed their studies permits a teacher to seize upon powerful motivating forces within individual students. No one *has* to try for an "A." Likewise, anyone *can* try. This notion shifts responsibility for learning from the teacher to the student, but at the same time offers an incentive by insuring success under known conditions. There are no secret, unstated assumptions operating within a teacher's mind when he grades students with the contract plan. Involvement is a natural product of the process, making for more satisfying learning. Students are challenged without being threatened. By being allowed to establish their own aspiration levels, students learn to undertake what they can accomplish and be satisfied with what they gain. Students are almost never dissatisfied with grades, whatever they may be. If they receive good marks, they recognize that they have done definite, legitimate things. If their grades are low, they accept them without hesitation or shame. Using the contract allows students to devote more attention to some segments of their education than others, purposely accepting a lower grade in one course to make a particular gain in another. Conventional grading tends to make students who do this feel guilty; as if they had "let somebody down." This is not the case when the contract grading plan is used.

Democracy in Action

Democracy involves communication, self direction, cooperative planning and action, high performance levels, choice, involvement, and good human relationships. All of these things are possible with the contract idea. Teachers and students work jointly to define objectives, map out procedures to gain those ends, and devise ways of assessing whether those objectives have been achieved. The teacher plays an important role by establishing the framework, providing counsel and encouragement, and assisting the student to define and channel his efforts. The student participates by indicating a level to strive for, choosing projects he would like to work on, and assuming responsibility for his own learning. By designing the experience so that the student is free to become creative, the teacher can establish good personal relationships. By demanding top proficiency but allowing students to profit by their errors, the teacher creates an atmosphere in which accomplishment is prized. He proves in action that ideas are important, but that people are important, too. The teacher's job is to teach and the students' job is to learn. Together they make a powerful team. Working at cross purposes brings sure defeat. The contract idea encourages joint teacher-pupil effort for educational gain.

SUMMARY

The purpose of this chapter has been to look critically at the conventional grading practices now used in American schools. The study disclosed that there are many purposes which grades must serve. They communicate different kinds of information to several different recipients.

The nature of life in general and education in particular demands that teachers clarify standards of performance logically. A framework for doing this was outlined.

Finally, one way of grading was examined which offers opportunity for coping with various aspects of the dilemma. The contract idea was advanced as a way of encouraging and evaluating educational achievement. It is no panacea. If used wisely the grade contract does overcome certain objections to present practice.

Other possibilities could also be successful. The intent here has been to stimulate teachers to examine their own assumptions regarding grading so that they may devise new procedures for evaluating achievements. The conventional method is obsolete. Fundamental changes are required. Only teachers who know themselves and their methods well can produce needed techniques which will be both democratic and effective.

REFERENCES

1. Adams, W. L., "Why Teachers Say They Fail Pupils," *Educational Administration and Supervision*, XVIII (November, 1932), 594-600.
2. Alpert, Harvey and Stripling, Robert O., "A Comparison of Marking Practices," *Educational Research Bulletin*, XXXIV (January, 1955), 10-14.
3. Anderson, Robert H. and Steadman, Edward R., "Pupils' Reactions to a Reporting System," *The Elementary School Journal*, LI (October, 1950), 136-142.
4. Anderson, William E., "An Attempt Through the Use of Experimental Techniques to Determine the Effect of Home Assignments upon Scholastic Success," *Journal of Educational Research*, XL (October, 1946), 141-143.
5. Arthur, Mary Grace, "A Study of the Achievement of Sixty Grade 1 Repeaters as Compared with That of Non-repeaters of the Same Mental Age," *Journal of Experimental Education*, V (December, 1936), 203-205.
6. Ashbaugh, E. J., "Reducing the Variability in Teachers' Marks," *Journal of Educational Research*, XI (March, 1924), 185-198.
7. Ashburn, Robert, "An Experiment in the Essay-type Question," *Journal of Experimental Education*, VII (September, 1938), 1-3.
8. Baker, Robert L and Doyle, Roy P., "Teacher Knowledge of Pupil Data and Marking Practices at the Elementary School," *Personnel and Guidance Journal*, XXXVII (May, 1956), 644-648.
9. Baldwin, Alfred L. and Levin, Harry, "Effects of Public and Private Success or Failure on Children's Repetitive Motor Behavior," *Child Development*, XXIX (September, 1958), 363-372.
10. Battle, Haron J., "Relation Between Personal Values and Scholastic Achievement," *Journal of Experimental Education*, XXVI (September, 1957), 27-41.
11. Bendig, A. W., "The Reliability of Letter Grades," *Educational and Psychological Measurement*, XIII (Summer, 1953), 311-321.
12. Bixler, Roy W., "Variable Standards of Marking in High Schools," *School and Society*, XXXVIII (July 29, 1933), 159-160.
13. Bloom, Benjamin et al., *Taxonomy of Educational Objectives*, Handbook I. *Cognitive Domain* (New York: David McKay Co., Inc., 1956).

14. Bolmeier, E. C., "What's in a Mark?" *The School Executive*, LXII (May, 1943), 25.
15. Bolmeier, E. C., "Principles Pertaining to Marking and Reporting Pupil Progress," *The School Review*, LIX (1951), 15-24.
16. Bond, Jessie A., "Analysis of Factors Adversely Affecting Scholarship of High School Pupils," *Journal of Educational Research*, XLVI (September, 1952), 1-15.
17. Brooks, Fowler and Heston, Joseph C., "The Validity of Items in a Study Habits Inventory," *Journal of Educational Psychology*, XXXVI (1945), 257-270.
18. Brooks, Samuel S., *Improving Schools by Standardized Tests* (Boston: Houghton Mifflin Co., 1922).
19. Brown, C. W., "The Study Habits of Failing and Successful Students in the First Two Years of College," *Journal of Experimental Education*, IX (1941), 205-208.
20. Brink, William G., "Assignment Procedures of 1000 High School Teachers," *Educational Trends*, L (April, 1932), 6-14.
21. Brundage, Ervin, "A Staff Study of Student Failures," *Educational Administration and Supervision*, XLII (November, 1956), 428-435.
22. Buckingham, B. R., "An Experiment in Promotion," *Journal of Educational Research*, III (May, 1921), 326-335.
23. Carrothers, George E., "Why Do High School Pupils Fail?" *Bulletin of the National Association of Secondary School Principals*, No. 137 (March, 1946), 29-36.
24. Carter, Harold D., "Correlations Between Intelligence Tests, Study Methods Tests, and Marks in a College Course," *Journal of Psychology*, XXX (1950), 333-340.
25. Carter, Robert S., "Non-Intellectual Variables Involved in Teachers' Marks," *Journal of Educational Research*, XLVII (October, 1953), 81-95.
26. Cavanaugh, Joseph A., "A Survey of Opinion on Examinations," *The Educational Research Bulletin*, XXIX (May, 1950), 120-125.
27. Class, E. C., "The Effect of the Kind of Test Announcement on Students' Preparation," *Journal of Educational Research*, XXVIII (January, 1935), 358-361.
28. Coffield, William H. and Blommers, Paul, "Effects of Non-Promotion on Educational Achievement in the Elementary School," *Journal of Educational Psychology*, XLVII (1956), 235-250.
29. Combs, Arthur W., "Statement of Teaching Methods" (Gainesville: College of Education, University of Florida). Mimeographed.
30. Cook, Walter W. and Kearney, N. C., "Effects of Nonpromotion on Achievement and Personality Traits," reported in *Grouping and Promotion in the Elementary Schools* (Minneapolis: University of Minnesota Press, 1941), 34-39.
31. Conant, James B., *The American High School Today* (New York: McGraw-Hill, 1959).
32. Cornell, Charlotte, "Why Pupils Fail: From the Pupil's Viewpoint," *Texas Outlook*, XXVI (September, 1942), 16.
33. Curtis, Francis D. and Woods, G. G., "A Study of the Relative Teaching Value of Four Common Practices in Correcting Examination Papers," *School Review*, XXXVII (1929), 615-623.
34. Crawford, D. H., "An Introductory Study of the Consistency of Marking Mathematics Papers in Schools," *The Alberta Journal of Educational Research*, V (March, 1959), 31-40.
35. Cuff, Noel B., "Study Habits in Grades Four to Twelve," *Journal of Educational Psychology*, XXVIII (1937), 295-301.

36. Day, C. L., "Boys and Girls Honor Ranks," *School Review*, XLVI (1938), 288-300.
37. Delaney, John F., "That Vacant High School Seat," *American School Board Journal*, CXXI (November, 1950), 22-23.
38. Dexter, Emily S., "The Effect of Fatigue or Boredom on Teachers' Marks," *Journal of Educational Research*, XXVIII (May, 1935), 664-667.
39. Douglas, H. R. and Tallmadge, Margaret, "How University Students Prepare for New Types of Examinations," *School and Society*, XXXIX (March, 1934), 318-320.
40. Douglass, Harl R. and Olson, Newman, "The Relation of High School Marks to Sex in Four Minnesota Senior High Schools," *School Review*, XLV (April, 1937), 385-388.
41. Douglass, Harl R. and Bauer, Harold C., "The Study Practices of Three Hundred Ninety-Five High-School Pupils," *Journal of Educational Psychology*, XXIX (1938), 36-43.
42. Durrell, Donald D., "Learning Difficulties Among Children of Normal Intelligence," *Elementary School Journal*, LV (1954), 201-208.
43. Edmiston, R. W., "Do Teachers Show Partiality?" *Peabody Journal of Education*, XX (1943), 234-238.
44. Falls, J. D., "Research in Secondary Education," *Kentucky School Journal*, VI (March, 1928), 42-45.
45. Farnsworth, Burton K. and Casper, Jesse B., "A Study of Pupil Failure in High School, *The School Review*, XLIX (May, 1941), 380-383.
46. Farrell, M. S. and Gilbert, N., "A Type of Bias in Marking Examination Scripts," *British Journal of Educational Psychology*, XXX (February, 1960), 47-52.
47. Fensch, Edwin A., "Failed Without Good Cause," *Clearing House*, XVIII (February, 1944), 326-328.
48. Gaier, Eugene L., "Student Self Estimates of Final Course Grades," *Journal of Genetic Psychology*, XCVIII (March, 1961), 63-67.
49. Gardner, C. A., "A Study of School Failures," *School Review*, XXXIII (February, 1927), 108-112.
50. Goodlad, John, "Some Effects of Promotion and Nonpromotion upon the Social and Personal Adjustment of Children," *Journal of Experimental Education*, XXII (June, 1954), 301-328.
51. Goodman, Delmar and Knipe, William, "An Experimental Unit in American History," *Bulletin of the National Association of Secondary School Principals*, XLV (September, 1961), 91-96.
52. Guilford, C. C., "Why Pupils Fail," *Educational Method*, XII (January, 1933), 219-222.
53. Hack, Barbara H., "The Effect of Nonpromotion on Personal and Social Adjustment," Unpublished Master's Thesis (The Ohio State University, 1959).
54. Hadley, S. Trevor, "A School Mark—Fact or Fancy?" *Educational Administration and Supervision*, XL (May, 1954), 305-312.
55. Halliwell, Joseph W., "The Relationship of Certain Factors to Marking Practices in Individualized Reporting Programs," *Journal of Educational Research*, LIV (October, 1960), 76-80.
56. Handlin, Oscar, "Are the Colleges Killing Education?" *The Atlantic Monthly*, CCIX (May, 1962), 41-45.
57. Hastings, J. Thomas, "Tensions and School Achievement Examinations," *Journal of Experimental Education*, XII (March, 1944), 143-164.
58. Hawley, W. E. and Pechstein, L. A., "Diminishing Returns in Reducing Nonpromotion," *Elementary School Journal*, XXII (April, 1922), 584-596.
59. Hines, Vynce A., "Homework and Achievement in Plane Geometry," *Mathematics Teacher*, L (January, 1957), 27-29.

60. Holland, John L., "Some Limitations of Teacher Ratings as Predictors of Creativity," *Journal of Educational Psychology*, L (October, 1959), 219-223.
61. Hollingshead, August B., *Elmtown's Youth* (New York: John Wiley and Sons, Inc., 1949).
62. Hulten, C. E., "The Personal Element in Teachers' Marks," *Journal of Educational Research*, XII (June, 1925), 49-55.
63. Hurd, A. W., "A Suggested Technique for Selecting High School Pupils Who May Be Allowed to Plan Their Own Lesson Assignments," *School Review*, XXXIV (October, 1926), 618-626.
64. Inglis, Alexander, "Variability of Judgments in Equating Values in Grading," *Educational Administration and Supervision*, II (January, 1916), 25-30.
65. James, H. W., "The Effect of Handwriting upon Grading," *English Journal*, XVI (March, 1927), 180-185.
66. Johnson, Frank W., "A Study of High-School Grades," *School Review*, XIX (January, 1911), 13-24.
67. Keisler, Evan R., "Peer Group Ratings of High School Pupils with High and Low School Marks," *Journal of Experimental Education*, XXIII (June, 1955), 375-378.
68. Kellog, W. N. and Payne, Bryan, "The True-False Question as an Aid in Studying," *Journal of Educational Psychology*, XXIX (January, 1938), 581-589.
69. Kelly, Eldon G., "A Study of Consistent Discrepancies Between Instructor Grades and Term-End Examination Grades," *Journal of Educational Psychology*, XLIX (December, 1958), 328-334.
70. Keller, Irvin A., "An Evaluation of the Dual Grading System," *Bulletin of the National Association of Secondary School Principals*, XXXIX (November, 1955), 38-45.
71. Keyes, Charles H., *Progress Through the Grades of City Schools* (New York: Teachers College, Columbia University, 1911).
72. Lafferty, Harry M., "Reasons for Pupil Failure: A Progress Report," *American School Board Journal*, CXVII (July, 1948), 18-20.
73. Lentz, Theodore F., "Sex Differences in School Marks with Achievement Test Scores Constant," *School and Society*, XXIX (January 12, 1929), 65-68.
74. Lobaugh, Dean, "Girls and Grades," *School Science and Mathematics*, XLVII (1947), 763-773.
75. Lobdell, Laurence O., "Results of a Nonpromotion Policy in One School District," *Elementary School Journal*, LIV (February, 1954), 333-337.
76. Maney, Charles A., "Sex Bias in College Marking," *Journal of Higher Education*, IV (January, 1933), 29-31.
77. Meyer, George, "An Experimental Study of the Old and New Types of Examination: I. The Effect of the Examination Set on Memory," *Journal of Educational Psychology*, XXV (December, 1934), 641-661.
78. Meyer, George, "An Experimental Study of the Old and New Types of Examination: II. Methods of Study," *Journal of Educational Psychology*, XXVI (January, 1935), 30-40.
79. Meyer, George, "The Effect on Recall and Recognition of the Examination Set in Classroom Situations," *Journal of Educational Psychology*, XVII (February, 1936), 81-99.
80. Meyer, Max, "The Grading of Students," *Science*, XXVIII (August, 1908), 243-250.
81. Michael, William B. and Reeder, Douglas E., "The Development and Validation of a Preliminary Form of a Study Habits Inventory," *Educational and Psychological Measurement*, XII (1952), 236-247.
82. Moore, C. C., "The Relation of Teachers' Marks to Standardized Tests," *Journal of Experimental Education*, VIII (September, 1939), 49-50.

83. Morton, R. L., "The Influence of Pupil Conduct on Teachers' Marks," *Educational Research Bulletin*, XI (February 3, 1932), 57-60.
84. Muessig, Raymond H., "How Do I Grade Thee? Let Me Count The Ways," *Clearing House*, XXXVI (March, 1962), 414-416.
85. McGill, J. V., "How Valuable Is Homework?" *High Points*, XXXII (September, 1950), 49-53.
86. McWhinney, Lucille G., "Parents Approve Homework," *Clearing House*, XXIX (April, 1955), 456-458.
87. National Education Association, "Reports on Pupil Progress and Elementary School Promotion Policies," Research Memo 1960-36, (Washington, D. C.: National Education Association, December, 1960).
88. Newton, Robert F., "Do Men Teachers Record Higher Grades Than Women Teachers?" *School and Society*, VI (July, 1925), 72.
89. Otto, Henry J. and Melby, Ernest O., "An Attempt to Evaluate the Threat of Failure as a Factor in Achievement," *Elementary School Journal*, XXXV (April, 1935), 588-596.
90. Page, Ellis Batten, "Teacher Comments and Student Performance: A Seventy-Four Classroom Experiment in School Motivation," *Journal of Educational Psychology*, XLIX (August, 1958), 173-181.
91. Pease, Glen R., "Should Teachers Give Warning of Tests and Examinations?" *Journal of Educational Psychology*, XXI (1930), 273-277.
92. Priday, P. R., "A Study of Dishonesty Among Tenth Grade Economics Students," Unpublished Paper (The Ohio State University, 1963).
93. Riffenburgh, Robert H., "Fitting Asymmetric Student Grade Distributions," *Journal of Educational Research*, LXII (December, 1959), 123-129.
94. Robertson, Malcolm H., "Counselor and Student Estimates of Grades as Predictors of Academic Achievement," *Journal of Educational Research*, LIV (October, 1960), 73-75.
95. Rocchio, Patrick D. and Kearney, Noland C., "Teacher-Pupil Attitudes as Related to Nonpromotion of Secondary School Pupils," *Educational and Psychological Measurement*, XVII (1956), 244-252.
96. Rogers, D. C., "A Study of Pupils' Failures and Subject Failures in Chicago," *Journal of Educational Research*, XIV (November, 1926), 247-255.
97. Rogers, Herbert W., "The Reliability of College Grades," *School and Society*, XLV (May 29, 1937), 758-760.
98. Rosenstengel, W. E. and Turner, Charles, "Supervised School Study vs. Home Study," *American School Board Journal*, XCII (April, 1936), 42.
99. Ross, C. C., *Measurement in Today's Schools*, 3rd ed., revised by G. C. Stanley (Englewood Cliffs, N. J.: Prentice-Hall, Inc., 1954).
100. Russell, Ivan L. and Thalman, W. A., "Personality: Does It Influence Teachers' Marks?" *Journal of Educational Research*, XLVIII (April, 1955), 561-564.
101. Sandin, Adolph A., *Social and Emotional Adjustments of Regularly Promoted and Nonpromoted Pupils* (New York: Teachers College, Columbia University, 1944).
102. Sarason, Seymour B., "What Research Says About Test Anxiety in Elementary School Children," *National Education Association Journal*, XLVIII (November, 1959), 26-27.
103. Saunders, Carleton M., *Promotion or Failure* (New York: Teachers College, Columbia University, 1941).
104. Schain, Robert L., "Another Homework Experiment in the Social Studies," *High Points*, XXXVI (February, 1954), 5-12.
105. Schiller, Belle, "A Questionnaire Study of Junior High School Students' Reactions to Homework," *High Points*, XXXVI (June, 1954), 23-36.
106. Schinnerer, Mark C., "Failure Ratio: 2 Boys to 1 Girl," *Clearing House*, XVIII (January, 1944), 264-270.

107. Schneider, Samuel, "An Experiment on the Value of Homework," *High Points*, XXXV (April, 1953), 18-19.
108. Schutte, Tenjes H., "Is There Value in the Final Examination?" *Journal of Educational Research*, XII (1935), 204-213.
109. Smith, Eugene R. and Tyler, Ralph W., *Appraising and Recording Student Progress* (New York: Harper and Bros., 1942).
110. Starch, Daniel and Elliott, Edward C., "Reliability of the Grading of High-School Work in English," *School Review*, XX (September, 1912), 442-457.
111. Starch, Daniel and Elliott, Edward C. "Reliability of Grading Work in Mathematics," *School Review*, XXI (April, 1913), 254-259.
112. Starch, Daniel, "Reliability and Distribution on Grades," *Science*, XXXVIII (October, 1913), 630-636.
113. Starch, Daniel, "Can the Variability of Marks Be Reduced?" *School and Society*, II August 14, 1915), 242-243.
114. Steele, A. G., "Training Teachers to Grade," *Pedagogical Seminary*, XVIII (December, 1911), 523-532.
115. Steiner, M. A., "Value of Home-Study Assignments," *School and Society*, XL (July 7, 1934), 20-24.
116. Stevens, S. S., "Measurement and Man," *Science*, CXXVII (February 21, 1958), 383-389.
117. Swenson, Clifford C., "Packing the Honor Society," *Clearing House*, XVI (September, 1941), 521-524.
118. Swenson, Clifford C., "The Girls Are Teachers' Pets," *Clearing House*, XVII (May, 1943), 537-540.
119. Terry, Paul W., "How Students Review for Objective and Essay Tests," *Elementary School Journal*, XXXIII (April, 1933), 592-603.
120. Terry, Paul W., "How Students Study for Three Types of Objective Tests," *Journal of Educational Research*, XXVII (January, 1934), 333-343.
121. Travers, R. M. W. and Gronlund, Norman, E., "The Meaning of Marks," *Journal of Higher Education*, XXI (October, 1950), 369-375.
122. Troutner, Howard L., "An Investigation into the Apparent Effects of Retainment on the Growth and Behavior Trait Characteristic Patterns of Elementary School Children in Three Socioeconomic Areas," Unpublished Master's Thesis (The Ohio State University, 1961).
123. Tyson, Robert, "Grades Through Students' Eyes," *Journal of Education*, CXXIV (1941), 124-136.
124. U. S. Department of Health, Education, and Welfare, Office of Education, Reporting Pupil Progress to Parents," Mimeographed paper No. 34 (December, 1956).
125. Vallance, Theodore R., "A Comparison of Essay and Objective Examinations as Learning Experiences," *Journal of Educational Research*, XLI (December, 1947), 279-288.
126. Vincent, H. D., "An Experimental Test of the Value of Homework in Grades Five and Six," *National Elementary Principal*, XVI (June, 1937), 199-203.
127. Vredevoe, Lawrence E., "How May We Make the Recording and Reporting of Pupil Achievement More Meaningful?" *Bulletin of National Association of Secondary School Principals*, XXXVII (April, 1953), 179-182.
128. Wheeler, Norman E., "A Comparison of the Objectives Considered Important by High School Teachers of Plane Geometry and by College Teachers and Administrators in Scientific and Mathematical Fields," Unpublished Master's Thesis (The Ohio State University, 1958).
129. White, Hubert, "Testing as an Aid to Learning," *Educational Administration and Supervision*, XVIII (January, 1932), 41-46.
130. Williamson, Edmund G., "The Relationship of Number of Hours of Study to Scholarship," *Journal of Educational Psychology*, XXVI (December, 1935), 682-688.

131. Worth, Walter H., "The Effects of Promotion and Nonpromotion on Pupil Achievement and Social-Personal Development in the Elementary School," *Educational Administration and Supervision*, XLVI (January, 1960), 16-26.
132. Wrenn, Gilbert C. and Humber, Wilbur J., "Study Habits Associated with High and Low Scholarship," *Journal of Educational Psychology*, XXXII (1941), 611-616.
133. Wrinkle, William L., *Improving Marking and Reporting Practices in Elementary and Secondary Schools* (New York: Rinehart and Co., Inc., 1947).
134. Yauch, Wilbur A., "What Research Says About School Marks and Their Reporting," *National Education Association Journal*, L (May, 1961), 50-52.
135. Zeisler, Donald E., "A Study of Marking and Reporting System Used in the Marion, Ohio Junior High School," Unpublished Master's Thesis (The Ohio State University, 1956).

Chapter Nine

The Dynamics of Improvement

INTRODUCTION

During recent years some critics of education have claimed that children today are not learning as much or as well as children did in years gone by. Some of those who criticize are seriously concerned with purposes and accomplishments; others (43, 53) apparently have other motives.

How effective is the educational effort today? How well do children learn, and how well are young people prepared for satisfying and productive lives?

Before we attempt to answer these difficult questions let's look first at some aspects of the situation as it affects teachers and teaching. Since some data are currently available that will affect life fifty or more years from now, and since most of the young people in school today will be living throughout this period, this is not an abstract problem.

First, and perhaps most important, the human race is undergoing what some have called a "population explosion." The increasing birth rate has reached a point where men in all walks of life are addressing their attention to the problem (59). Paul Sears, then president of the American Association for the Advancement of Science, wrote in 1958:

> Man's physical body occupies space, somewhere between two and four cubic feet of it. At his present rate of increase in the United States, he is set to double the aggregate volume occupied by human bodies in about 41 years. Continuing at this rate, it would be less than 700 years—say 22 generations—until there is standing room only, with each space of 3 by 2 feet, or 6 square feet, occupied . . .
> A little after this the hypothetical human population would weigh more than the planet.

In 1850, for example, the population of the United States was 23 million. In 1900 this number had increased to 75 million, and by 1950 over 150 million (22). Even though about 40 million of these were immigrants, to continue at this rate will mean more than 300 million persons living in the United States by the year 2000, and by 2050 over half a billion. And the children of the youngsters now in school will be living then. Preparing youth to cope with the problems inherent in an increasingly crowded world is one need the school must meet.

Though it is more difficult to state objectively, most experts agree that we are also witnessing an "explosion of knowledge." Ideas and facts are being produced at an accelerating pace. Expenditures for library materials, monies allocated for research, and the number of technical journals devoting space to original research are all evidence of increasing amounts of knowledge. It has even been estimated that it would take 12,000 men working eight hours a day, seven days a week, just to read the new research which is published every day. Gerald Holton (30) states:

> When future generations look back to our day, they will envy us for having lived at a time of brilliant achievement in many fields, and not least in science and technology. We are at the threshold of basic knowledge concerning the origins of life, the chemical elements, and the galaxies. We are near an understanding of the fundamental constituents of matter, of the process by which the brain works, and of the factors governing behavior. . . . Hand in hand with the quality of excitement in scientific work today goes an astonishing quantity. The world-wide output is vast. There are now over 50,000 scientific and technical journals, publishing annually about 1,200,000 articles of significance for some branch of research and engineering in the physical and life sciences. Every year there are about 60,000 new science books and 100,000 research reports. And the amount of scientific work being done is increasing at a rapid rate, doubling approximately every 20 years.

Gray cites Price (23) who pointed out that most non-scientific aspects of our culture double every 30 to 50 years, but that science is doubling every 10 years in this country. Whether such estimates are correct or not is beside the point: there is more knowledge, and schoolmen must be concerned about it since it is their chief commodity.

In other areas, even a casual observer of events realizes that mankind is experiencing some kind of social revolution. Racial strife in America, emerging nations in Africa, explorations in outer space, and innovations in government, social relations and economics all over the world are proof that we live in a state of constant change. Heraclitus maintained that no man could step into the same river twice. However one expresses it, change is part of our way of life. And change today is threatening.

But apart from these dramatic changes, many remarkable alterations are occurring inside education itself. Some of these are obvious, such as new kinds of school buildings and equipment, programmed learning, use of TV in teaching, generative grammer, foreign languages in early grades.

Other changes are much more subtle, difficult to see and more difficult to understand. The number of students taking college boards increased more than a thousand per cent in the last ten years. Certain national science curriculum groups copyrighted textual materials which had been developed with millions of taxpayer's dollars. Why have some foundations put so much money into demonstrations of educational change only when such changes were predicated upon the guarantee that they would *not* be studied? Why have those who work regularly with curriculum problems been ignored in the development of new programs? Why have educators generally become defensive when faced with opportunities for curriculum change? Why are teachers and administrators afraid?

THE NATURE OF TEACHERS' FEARS AND FEELINGS

To ask " why are teachers afraid?" implies that many are afraid, and as a teacher I hesitate to make such an accusation about myself and those with whom I labor, but I must. I think we are afraid. We do resist change. We are not forward-looking. Why else would the progressive movement die if we were not fearful? Does anyone really believe in *re-gressive* education? Is there anyone who sincerely believes that the road ahead lies back?

We live in a time and place in which education is worshipped like a god but supported like a church. Talked about, condemned, cajoled, threatened and abused, the teaching profession has been subjected to a psychological mauling the like of which no other group has ever experienced. No group in America has been so heavily criticized and maligned as teachers have been in recent years. In dozens of magazines we find articles complaining about the poor preparation of teachers or the poor quality of teaching, or some other fault of the schools. To live on a steady diet of being told how poor he is hardly helps anyone's ego or his capacity to cope with change.

Added to these pressures are such national issues as integration—in the main, a school problem. And neither the pharamacists nor the farmers were blamed for America's missile lag after Sputnik; again it was the schools. Finally, there is the cold war and its related problems. The loss of academic freedom reported by Commager (11) and others (43) and antidiscussion trends stemming from the McCarthy era, are cases in point.

The Russian menace has affected education in more obvious ways. With such groups as the National Science Foundation and Congress itself taking steps to encourage the development of new areas in the curriculum, important changes were bound to occur. Sudden availability of federal funds has assured educators of plenty of push to get things changed.

Teaching is no longer carried on in a friendly atmosphere of helping and developing. Schoolmen suddenly find themselves working in a competitive world of big business and organization politics, forced to pull wires for tax dollars, foundation funds and professional prestige. They recognize that education is political business, and politics means power. Teachers and administrators are forced to accept procedures once disdained. Altruism is still present, but it is rapidly giving way to pressure politics, mass communications and public relations.

All of these forces and factors exist in a period of the greatest threat to man since the beginning of time—extermination of the species itself. "Overkill," more than a catch phrase, is an ominous threat which each man understands in some vague way to affect his very being.

Little wonder teachers are afraid. But knowing we are afraid is the key to the problem. Describing our fears in words is now the most important thing that we can do.

How Effective Are Schools Today?

People working in education have long been concerned about keeping pace with the times and improving their effectiveness. Teachers and administrators have continuously studied the educational situation for clues to different methods to maximize the learning experience for children. They have experimented with large classes and small classes, lecture and discussion, core programs and conventional programs, homogeneous grouping and heterogeneous grouping, new textual materials, traditional materials, television, teaching machines, science fairs, team teaching, and a whole host of other procedures, all designed to improve the quality of learning in youth.

How effective have these changes been? Lynd states that (38):

> . . . while neo-pedagogues palaver more and more about the "real" needs of youngsters, the pupils are learning less and less about the arts of word and number, the history and the literature, the science

and the esthetics, and the rest of the painfully accumulated culture of this harassed civilization.

But are the youngsters in schools now more poorly prepared than children were 30 years ago? The answer is "no." Studies made in recent years have compared the achievements of today's children with those of other generations, using the same instruments, and almost without exception young people today do better than their earlier counterparts. Lanton describes his research result, involving more than 1200 elementary students, like this (35):

> The composite achievement of the children in 1953 in the third and fifth grades was significantly higher than that of children in 1934 . . .

Young people today read better, spell better, add, subtract, multiply, and divide better than did the children 20 or 30 years ago. They know more science and history. In almost every measure they do better than students of another era. *But just a little bit better.* Considering the fact that we have better buildings and equipment, better prepared teachers and textbooks, more and better libraries, along with teaching films and other innovations, why is it that students today do only a little better than their predecessors?

The reluctance of educators to look at themselves as the most crucial variable in the classroom may have resulted in a kind of professional "perseveration," a term by which psychologists imply a persistence in error, a repetition of mistakes. Consider the areas in which experimentation and innovation have usually occurred in American schools.

First, teachers and administrators have generally behaved as if they thought that grouping children according to ability for instructional purposes would bring about significant changes in learning. From the scores of studies on grouping that have been made in this country since the 1920's, we know fairly conclusively that such grouping will probably not affect learning. Teachers, if they can have the top or an average group, will probably like it better, but learning will seldom be much affected.

How about the effect of lecture or discussion on learning? No difference has been noted. Large classes versus small classes? No difference, except perhaps in the very early years. Television versus conventional classes? Again, no differences appear. After reviewing 393 studies in this area, Schramm reported (58) that 65 per cent of the reports indicated no significant differences in learning between television and conventionally taught classes, whereas in 21 per cent of the studies TV-taught students learned more, and in 14 per cent they learned less.

In recent years educators have moved more into experimental programs involving direct changes in subject matter. Do the children who study SMSG mathematics or PSSC physics or BSCS biology or CHEM Study materials or structural linguistics or generative grammar learn more, faster, better, than students participating in traditional programs? To date there is very little evidence relating to these programs. Apart from the results reported by the groups actually developing the new materials, the literature about the effectiveness of these innovations is very limited. Judging from that which is available, however, including that from the organizations which have prepared the new textbooks and procedures, the results are about the same: students in the "new" programs do as well as those in conventional classes; seldom worse, but seldom much better. There do seem to be some important changes in attitudes, and teachers generally like the new programs better, but nobody knows whether these changes are lasting.

The story is the same for almost any segment of the educational system one cares to examine. Whether teachers use certain materials, certain procedures, certain grouping practices, certain equipment, or not, they get about the same results.

How Effective Are Other Professional Groups?

It is not quite the same in other fields. In 1920, for instance, a physician spent approximately twelve hours with each patient who had pneumonia, and he was successful in his efforts about 80 per cent of the time. In 1960 a physician spent two hours and 15 minutes, on the average, with a pneumonia patient and over 95 per cent got well. This kind of change, plus the fact that the ratio of physicians to the total population (22) is almost exactly what it was 40 years ago (1920: 1/746; 1959 1/751) implies that medicine is making progress.

Some data in education also reflect steady improvement such as the holding power of the school, the proportion of high school graduates going on to college, and literacy rate, but improvements in communications and transportation as well as significant improvements in agricultural production, manufacture and sources of power, indicate that professionals in some areas are bringing about very significant change. Educators lament the fact that they seem only to be holding their own, because learning is difficult to define and more difficult to promote. However, it seems unreasonable to suppose that learning is any more complex than life itself, and some professional groups have made remarkable progress in their efforts to improve man's lot.

From a description (8) of the rehabilitation of chronic schizophrenic patients we learn that the percentage discharged increased from approximately 55 per cent after one year's therapy to over 80 per cent after a change in effort. And working with schizophrenics is at least as difficult as working with youngsters in school.

The point is, educators seem to have developed ways of working which in some instances correspond to the psychologists' "perseveration." While *perseverance* is a positive trait, to do the same *wrong* thing again and again is self-defeating. Some insecure persons, unable to view their problems from another angle, work diligently, if not creatively, to solve them by repeated efforts of the same old routine. Even though research shows no significant results from a particular procedure, there are teachers and administrators who can only respond with "more of the same."

"What we need is more and better grouping, more homework, more tests, and more demands on students' time." Or, "If we only had more teachers, more money, more classrooms, and more books we could do a better job." More and more of what has already been tried and found wanting hardly seems to be the answer. The needs are for new concepts and new relationships and new skills. Keeping the best of the old and selecting the best from the new, the educator's task now is to re-define his role and re-allocate his efforts in order to make an educational difference. Teachers must effect a significant change in the lives and minds of boys and girls or they have reached a point of technological and professional obsolescence.

What Does Make a Difference?

If this is the problem, then, what can be done? Any careful assessment of the research in education indicates time and again that there is one thing which makes a difference: the teacher himself. Changing the size of a class has far less impact than changing the teacher of a class. How children are grouped, or whether they use modern or traditional texts, is far less important than the personality of those who teach them. The way to change education is to change the quality of people who do the teaching.

Teachers, being the most important variable in the classroom, must improve themselves. They must devise ways of working which enable them to become better, richer personalities, people who can use themselves as the means of helping children learn. Somehow, someway, they must find a way to shape their efforts and their energies so that their effectiveness can be increased through what they do and what they are. Teachers must find a way to lift themselves by their own bootstraps— to wind their own springs, so to speak. Administrators and supervisors, college professors and publishers, may help, but the task, essentially, is one for each professional teacher to accomplish alone.

THE POWER OF EXPERIMENTATION

The problem is clear. Teachers must select or devise ways of working which will assure them of maximum effectiveness for energy expended. Any organism has only so much energy. Persons who are most successful find ways of concentrating their efforts. In part, this is a problem for all the profession, and Chapter Ten will explore this idea at greater length. For the individual teacher, however, the problem is always present. Each one, if he is sincerely concerned about making an educational difference, must be able to utilize all of his own creative abilities for teaching.

There are many ways to do it. Thoughtful supervisors will help, and being introspective also is important. Continuous study and scholarship is an essential. Attending conferences, talking with fellow teachers, reading professional journals, and observing new practices in other schools are all important keys to improved teaching

One other avenue, experimentation, seems unusually promising, especially if it is combined with the approaches described above. Teachers who seek to improve their effectiveness by continuous experimentation in their classrooms develop an attitude toward teaching and an openness to experience which inevitably results in important changes in their students. The power of experimentation arises from three main factors: (a) The so-called "Hawthorne effect," (b) the fact that the teacher is "freed" to change, and (c) that he adds to his knowledge about himself, his students, and his subject field.

The "Hawthorne Effect"

Research involving people often results in unpredicted changes because the persons doing the research and those being experimented upon become psychologically involved and often committed to some aspect of the study itself. This involvement usually results in improvement, whatever is done.

In the Western Electric projects initiated in 1924 as studies of the relationship between illumination and productivity in a factory, the researchers discovered that when they isolated groups of workers for experimental purposes production always increased, regardless of how they manipulated the variables. When they increased the illumination, production went up; when they decreased it production went up. If they shortened the work week it rose; if they lengthened the work week it rose. Providing rest periods and eliminating rest periods—all changes resulted in increased productivity.

Cook quotes Pennock about this point as follows: (14):

> From the tests have come some startling results, startling because
> they were unexpected as well as because they were sometimes con-
> trary to accepted opinion. In the first place, there was a gradual yet
> steady increase in production, regardless, to a certain extent, of test
> conditions imposed. . . . Now this unexpected and continual up-
> ward trend in the productivity throughout the periods, even . . .
> when the girls were put on a full 48-hour week with no rest period
> or lunch period, led us to seek some explanation or analysis. . . .
> [We are] convinced that *the rather remarkable results we have been
> able to obtain with this group are due mainly to changes in their
> mental attitude. This we consider a major accomplishment of our
> entire study.* [Italics added]

This notion, later dubbed the "Hawthorne effect" because the studies
had been conducted in Western Electric's Hawthorne plant outside Chicago, has since become a formidable problem for educational researchers.
In some instances it means that, however the problem is posed, the
hypothesized results are almost bound to appear. Rosenbloom says (14)
"that in educational experimentation, no matter what the hypothesis is,
the experimental classes do better than the control classes." In other
situations it may very well account for the "no significant difference"
which so often occurs. On this point Cook elaborates (14):

> The Hawthorne effect can also be used to account for situations
> where no differences are observed between the experimental and
> control groups at the end of an experimental period. How can such
> a situation occur? It might occur when an experimenter approaches
> a classroom to measure student performance before conducting the
> experiment. The pretesting of not only the experimental but the
> control group can become a signal to the latter group that they are
> the subjects of an experiment. They might also be able to identify
> the experimenter's purpose. Consequently, the control group en-
> gages in activities leading to such improvement that the final result
> is that both groups perform equally well at the end of the experi-
> mental period.

Recalling the general pattern of research results in education cited
earlier—no significant differences observed—it now seems reasonable
to suppose that part of that pattern, at least, might be explained by the
"Hawthorne effect." This point is even clearer if one examines the specific research results in education which are apparent from many studies
in the same area.

Some of the "no significant differences" observed are just that; study after study reports experimental and control groups doing equally well. In other areas one can note that some of the studies show significant differences in favor of one group or the other. The general conclusion must always be vague, but it would appear that instances in which some of the studies indicate one thing and some another might well be illustrations of the first "Hawthorne effect"—"no matter what the hypothesis, the experimental classes do better than the control classes." The areas in which there generally are no significant differences between experimental and control groups could be those described by Cook in which both groups made extra effort and both progressed.

It is precisely this dilemma for researchers, however, that also holds real promise for classroom teachers. When teachers experiment in their classrooms, if the students know they are involved in a genuine experimental venture they apparently put forth extra effort toward learning. This extra effort generally results in greater learning, so *whatever the teacher does, if he experiments the students gain.*

The principles behind the "Hawthorne effect" which influences students' efforts are based on what is known about how people learn. When students are involved in the teaching-learning process, when they feel that they are truly a part of an on-going experience, they are affected. Their perceptual processes are influenced so that they give more meaning to the stimuli which come their way. The organism apparently reaches out and draws stimuli toward itself; it "needs" to know.

Teachers Freed to Change

When a teacher experiments in his own classroom he is immediately faced with the question: "How do I know that this new way will be better than what I did before?" To answer this question some kind of evidence is necessary; he will have to gather information pertinent to the innovation. If he is systematic and if the data prove to have real validity, he allows himself to change. The data, in effect, free him from the traditional role of proponent or opponent of educational change and permit him to focus his attention on the problem.

When new ideas have been proposed in education they have often been examined verbally but not experimentally. Discussion about whether a proposition will work or not often kills the notion completely without its ever being tried. Purely on the basis of logic and common sense, many suggestions for change have been rejected because they did not seem worthwhile or effective. Considering the stalemate in the profession in producing better results, such an approach hardly seems defensible.

Even among researchers, however, resistance to new ideas is widespread, so it is certainly understandable among teachers. For example, Stevenson says (65):

> We owe to Francis Bacon much of the foundation of scientific method. He said: "We have sit it down as a law to ourselves that we have to examine things to the bottom; and not to receive upon credit or reject upon improbabilities, until these have passed a due examination." Yet Bacon could not believe that the Earth goes around the Sun. Galileo, who could not persuade fellow astronomers to look into his telescope, could not himself accept Kepler's evidence that the planets move in ellipses.

Deciding to accept or reject an innovation in education only on the basis of talk places everyone in difficult positions. If some one has an idea that he believes would prove worthwhile in practice, persuading others of its merit *before* it is tried makes people tend to "choose up sides." Some, seeing the possible advantages of the proposal, move to adopt the new idea, at least temporarily. Others, sincerely believing the idea is not sound, or perhaps dreading the thought of an unfamiliar technique which might be required of them, resist the change. In any event, such a proposal often results in sharp division within a professional staff. Over a period of time this split may widen and create other problems.

However, if a teacher himself decides to try something new, or if a group of teachers working together makes such a decision, the opportunity for change presents itself. Change may not come, but when schoolmen are neither advocates nor opponents of innovation, and decide, instead, to try it out and see what happens, they are exposing themselves to the possibility of change.

This possibility for change, though, can be realized only if there is a genuine effort to *study* the change. Innovation in the name of experimentation has no place in education today, nor has change for the sake of change. Unless the change grows out of a real concern for improvement, and unless it is studied exhaustively, there is little reasons to believe that any significant developments can ever occur, *for it is in the process of studying the change that those involved allow themselves to be affected by the facts.*

Committing oneself to an experiment in which careful observations will result in accummulated evidence regarding the feasibility and effectiveness of the change, enables a teacher to get to the point where he can say: "Now that's interesting, but I wonder if it would have come out the same if I had done it this way." Or, "I thought the kids really were excited about this new technique, but according to these test results it didn't make much difference. Do you suppose these tests are really measuring what I'm trying to teach?"

As soon as a teacher places himself in the position of studying evidence regarding the effectiveness of his own procedures, he is also freeing himself to change. Change within the practicing teacher can occur only when he is open to experience, when he is ready to learn. Studying *data* about his own classroom practice allows the professional to take a detached view of his efforts and study his operation objectively. No doubt his observations will be quite subjective, at least at the start, but if he works at clarifying precisely what he is trying to do and makes careful observations to determine whether he is attaining his goal, he becomes a different person. As he struggles to "keep himself out of it," he develops more objective assessment procedures but ends up being more involved. Thus introspection becomes useful if the teacher studies what he is doing as conscientiously as possible. The act of looking carefully at himself and what he does gives him deeper insight into his classroom practice and makes him a better human being.

The Teacher Learns

When a teacher studies his own classroom experiments, he also learns. As he experiments, he collects information about himself, his students, and the idea he is teaching. The teacher who experiments becomes, by so doing, a scientist, and Thistle has this to say about scientists (70):

> Certain other attitudes of our scientists seem to me to be worth pondering: the desire to find out what is really going on, instead of being content with what other people say is going on; the determination to take no man's word, not even your own, for a material fact unless you can put it to the test and observe for yourself; the confident expectation that whatever you do will soon become outmoded and surpassed, and that this does not matter in the least; the expectation that other people will be markedly different from you, and this is an excellent arrangement; the convictions that doing your best to think straight is a worthy occupation for a full-grown man, that this is a strange and wonderful universe whose ultimate secrets we will never quite plumb, that it is nevertheless the best sport in the world to try to plumb them, that you *never* get something for nothing, that you *always* get less than you expect—and that *never* and *always* are very dangerous words.

One thesis of this book is that the teacher must be a scientist of sorts; a student of himself and his pupils and his discipline. Experimentation in teaching encourages a teacher to adapt the spirit of science to his daily practice. An alternate approach would be to assume that teaching is primarily a technical accomplishment, and if a teacher could master a sufficient number of techniques he could employ the appropriate skill at the most appropriate time.

Physicians face a similar choice. Baldwin describes the ways in which physicians may approach the problems in medicine (3):

> There are two ways of viewing the practicing physician. On the one hand he may be thought of as primarily a diagnostician, who, having identified a disease process, treats it in accordance with general recommendations originating in medical research centers. In doing so he takes into account certain parameters in the individual patient and modifies the suggested treatment accordingly. This view of the physician pertains to the concept of medical care as a public utility and to situations involving large numbers of patients and standardization of services, where variation in treatment due to variation in the intellectual and educational qualifications of the individual physician is minimized. The physician, viewed in this way, is essentially an engineer, exploiting general knowledge acquired through biological research.
>
> Alternatively, the physician may be regarded as primarily an investigator attempting to understand the complex process of disease as it exists in each patient. As such, he is expected to theorize about, and to investigate, his problem (in this case, the human patient) and to introduce variation and innovation in arriving at a diagnosis and a plan of treatment. This view implies quite emphatically that disease and the means of modifying it are largely not understood and that regimentation of diseased individuals into broad treatment categories is a waste of scientific effort.
>
> The first view implies a degree of uniformity in the patient population as well as a degree of diagnostic reliability as yet unattained in medicine. . . . The second view implies that the practicing physician is a competent scientist—that he has a knowledge of medicine sufficient for making sound and responsible judgments. Both views, as stated, are idealizations, and a more realistic appraisal would recognize the need for a blend of the two. However, as between the two, I believe that the better situation results when the practicing physician recognizes that the diagnosis and treatment of disease has all the elements of an experimental situation—that is, observation, data collection, judgment or conclusion (diagnosis), and treatment on the basis of the conclusion (indirect verification).

This idea, applied to teaching, would make each classroom teacher a researcher of sorts. Spieker states a viable position for teachers working at the college level (64):

Unless a college teacher is actively engaged in grappling with the unknown somewhere on the forefront of knowledge, he will not bring into the classroom the point of view, the frame of mind, the mode of attack, the general air of the investigator, and these qualities are just what is essential to show, in the presence of the student, by various forms of example, how to go about dealing with the problems in his subject.

What better place is there for a teacher to study than his own classroom? What better subjects are there for him to study than himself and his students? What better discipline is there for him to explore than those ideas which attracted him to teaching in the first place? The professional teacher turns his observations inwardly upon himself, outwardly upon his students, and downwardly into the depths of the subject matter with which he works for improvement in teaching. He uses the ways of science to help him see more clearly and profoundly. There is real power in experimentation for the teacher who seeks to change and grow.

STUDYING EXPERIMENTATION IN THE CLASSROOM

So far in this chapter the effort has been to describe reasons why educators are cautious and conservative in their practice, and how they might overcome these hesitant ways by experimentation. There has been some effort to outline the advantages of experimental work in the classroom as a means of improving teaching and helping children learn. Perhaps it is unreasonable to hope for dramatic changes in educational effectiveness, but we need a breakthrough in education. Repeating old mistakes is not enough. What is called for is a completely new concept of educational effort, a bold new approach casting all component parts into a new mold. Tinkering with what we already do is not enough, but it is a place to start. "Big oaks from little acorns grow."

Should Teachers Experiment?

The classroom is the only laboratory a teacher has, and insights can only follow extensive experience and detailed experimentation. Accepting the fact that methods must change considerably if the educational effort is to be upgraded significantly, every professional teacher must be a practicing student of himself and his ways. He must experiment within the classroom and he must study everything he does most carefully.

There are some who say that teachers have no right to experiment with their teaching. It is unethical and unprofessional to use youngsters like guinea pigs, they say.

Such a criticism has some validity, depending upon the motives of the experimenter involved. If a teacher seeks innovation to increase his own prestige, then experimentation is unwarranted. On the other hand, accepting the traditional way as right and best just because it has evolved historically hardly makes sense either. It is unfortunate that each new venture should have to be compared to conventional teaching, since such a comparison presupposes that the way things are done now is satisfactory. This is not at all possible to demonstrate.

The proposition advanced here is that studying innovations in the classroom is one of the most effective ways for a teacher to do better what he is expected to do—teach. Experimentation simply sensitizes him to the whole process in a way that promotes his effective use of himself to help children learn. Such a notion is predicated upon the assumption that a truly professional teacher is much more than a high-level technician; he is a student of himself and his pupils and his discipline. He is a scientist, if you please, in the business of teaching.

How Can a Teacher Start to Study What He Is Doing?

How can a practicing teacher experiment with himself and his classes while he is teaching? Where does he begin? What is research in education?

Far from being a lofty, abstract process, research in any area starts with a question. After the question is asked, one must work to answer it in any objective way that he possibly can. The secret is to ask the right question, since the question profoundly influences the course of action which follows.

The power of question-asking is described by Norbert Wiener in a discussion of secrecy in government regarding armament developments (76):

> . . . when we consider a problem of nature such as that of atomic reactions and atomic explosives, the largest single item of information which we can make public is that they exist. Once a scientist attacks a problem which he knows to have an answer, his entire attitude is changed. He is already fifty percent of his way toward that answer.

Knowing that something actually is possible, that is, that someone has asked a question which can be answered, spurs scientists on to answer the question for themselves. In the problem of armaments, when scientists in one country learn that scientists in another country have developed a new weapon, this means to them that an answerable question has been asked. And, as Wiener points out, if they *know* the question can be answered, they can begin at once to bring to bear their professional energies to get that information themselves. When one nation develops new weaponry and makes these developments known, what it really does is provide impetus to its enemies by proving that a question has been asked which can be answered. Wiener continues (76):

> I have already said that the dissemination of any scientific secret whatever is merely a matter of time, that in this game a decade is a long time, and that in the long run, there is no distinction between arming ourselves and arming our enemies.

That such a state of affairs can be is mute testimony to the power of asking the appropriate question.

Wendell Johnson makes similar observations (33):

> We may say, in briefest summary, that the method of science consists in (a) asking clear answerable questions in order to direct one's (b) observations, which are made in a calm and unprejudiced manner, and which are then (c) reported as accurately as possible and in such a way as to answer the questions that we asked to begin with, after which (d) any pertinent beliefs or assumptions that we held before the observations were made are raised in light of the observations made and the answers obtained. Then more questions are asked in accordance with the newly revised notions, further observations are made, new answers are arrived at, beliefs and assumptions again revised, after which the whole process starts over again. In fact, it never stops. Science as method is continuous. All its conclusions are held subject to the further revision that new observations may require. It is a method of keeping one's information, beliefs, and theories up to date. It is above all, a method of "changing one's mind"—sufficiently often.

Teachers who hope to use the power of experimentation to improve their teaching must learn to ask answerable questions about themselves and their classroom operation. Good questions come in many ways— from uncomfortable feelings that certain procedures are not really effective; from an awareness of a student's difficulty in comprehending a particular concept; from discussions with other teachers about classroom practice; from listening to tape recordings of themselves in action in class; from reading, from ideas proposed by consultants, from thoughtful reminiscence coupled with the desire to improve.

"Will children studying SMSG mathematics materials develop more favorable attitudes towards mathematics than those who use the conventional books?" "What motivates Billy to try so hard to do good work in school?" "Does Mary dislike school? If she does, why? And if she does not, is something else wrong?" "Can eighth grade students learn algebra as effectively as ninth grade youngsters?" "Is Jean rejected by the other members of the class? If she is rejected, as she seems to be, will changing the seating arrangement or talking with other girls help overcome this problem?" "How can I deepen this student's insight into Milton's *Areopagitica*? If he reads Commager's *Freedom, Loyalty, Dissent* and John Stuart Mill's *Essay on Liberty*, will he have a better understanding of Milton's "cloistered virtue"? "Why do I seem to resent having George in class? Is it because he is Jewish? I did not think that I was prejudiced. Is it possible that he aware of my negative feelings and that this influences his learning?"

Asking important questions is the first step in experimentation. The questions above are just beginnings. They all describe areas of concern, but none is precise enough yet to guide one's observations. From questions such as these the teacher can develop more specific queries which grow out of his actual situation. One specific example is described in Appendix B, and though it is not a highly sophisticated theoretical study, it is an example of classroom experimentation which caused the teacher to change.

Answering the Question

Once a question is posed it must be answered, or at least an effort can be made. In the process scientists find it necessary to bring all of their intellectual abilities and observational powers to bear. There is no such thing as "the scientific method," but there is what has been referred to as "interior" science—that which comes after the fact. Schilling maintains that the process of "science as the scientist himself knows it remains essentially unknown." He then goes on to say (57):

> Consider, for instance, the great difference between the science of the intellectual frontier and that of the interior. These are as different as the laws, politics, or social and economic structures on a national frontier are typically different from those behind the frontier. Frontier science is exploratory and adventurous. Here ideas are tentative and impermanent, coming and going rapidly. More often than not they are audacious guesses or vague hunches that rarely conform to established patterns of thought. Often they are thoroughly unorthodox and what many people would even

regard as "unscientific." This is science in the raw—controversial, competitive, inefficient, governed to a considerable extent by the demands and urgencies of the moment, and employing predominantly *ad hoc* methods. It is the science of the restless explorer, always on the trek, never stopping anywhere very long—always looking for new horizons and taking the frontier with him.

The science of the interior, by contrast, is that of the intellectual colonizers who follow the pioneers, consolidate gains, and establish order and respectability. It is characterized by much less fluctuation and change, and therefore by relative permanence; by system, precedence, and closer adherence to established canons of methodology and thought; by logic more than hunch. Here is where the straightforward "proofs" or "logical developments" put in their appearance, and where everything seems to be orderly and logically interdependent.

Now it is the teacher's and interpreter's preoccupation with this systematic, rational science of the hinterland that is largely responsible for the overabstracted, formalized stereotype to which I have been referring. Certainly such an oversimplification as that of the "scientific method" could not possibly have arisen out of careful contemplation of frontier physics.

Science in the raw, then, is what we need in classrooms. Once a teacher has posed a question about his techniques or materials or students, then he must work to get answers to that question. Answering questions involves making observations and garnering relevant facts.

Suppose that a teacher has a vague suspicion that one student in his class is being left out of things and that this rejection affects his learning. Watching the class in action may be enough to confirm or deny the first hypothesis, that the student is rejected. If other students never sit with him, talk to him, play with him, or walk to school or home with him, a teacher might be safe in concluding that he was not accepted by the rest of the group. Now, whether such lack of acceptance was actually rejection, and how such a relationship affected that particular youngster's learning would be another problem. Research tends to substantiate the idea that rejected students learn less well than those who are accepted, but whether such a conclusion would be warranted in a particular instance would be a different matter. The teacher might attempt an experimental situation in which acceptance would be encouraged, and observations of the student's behavior undertaken to see if changes did in fact occur. He might assign particular tasks to small groups and note the behavior of the student involved. He might rearrange the seating and watch for indications of greater or lesser acceptance. If he is a social studies teacher, he might consider the possibility of studying a unit on social relationships which would include a consideration of the problems of discrimination, rejection, or ghettos, and then teach for generalizations so that similar problems in his own classrooms might be brought to light.

Collecting socio-metric data, on the other hand, might indicate that the student was actually not so much rejected as let alone; that other students held no ill feelings toward him and that his behaviors were really deliberate efforts to use his time in non-social activities to achieve other ends. In such a case the teacher might do best to let well enough alone. Unless he gets precise data about the particular youngster he could do more harm than good by working to foster social relationships unrelated to school. In either event, only careful observation and pertinent data would enable a teacher to fulfill his professional obligations effectively.

This reveals one of the pitfalls awaiting teachers who hope to improve their efforts through careful study of what they do and how they do it. It shows how their activities rest upon an interpretation of what is a means and what is an end. For instance, many teachers value homework, and their judgments of students' achievements and growth are based upon the assumption that homework is important. Homework, however, is actually a means to an end. Unless it affects their learning, whether students complete their homework assignment or how much time they spend on it are completely irrelevant. Either homework helps a student to master certain skills or other objectives or it does not, and whether assignments are turned in on time, or how parents feel about the values of homework are interesting but unrelated information.

In other words, when a teacher seeks to answer a question about his teaching it is extremely important for him to keep his eye fixed upon his basic objectives and the question asked. The data must answer the question. All sorts of incidental, unimportant information can clutter up his efforts. Unless he is careful, he will find himself confronted with observations of his own making which pertain only indirectly to the question at hand.

Parental *estimates* of how much homework helps students is not nearly as important as data which relate *directly* to desired changes in students' behavior: their responses on examinations or their measured attitudes toward learning, for example. If the examination questions are not measuring the hoped-for learnings, why are they given in the first place? Whether youngsters like a particular approach to studying history is less important than whether such an approach evokes the changes in their attitudes and understandings and ways of behaving which were considered desirable at the time it was decided to include history in the curriculum.

By way of illustration, consider two approaches to the teaching of American history to high school students. There are many other ways of organizing the subject matter of history for instructional purposes, but these two will serve to illustrate the problem. One approach might be based upon reading and discussing and thinking about historical facts in chronological sequence. A second approach might consider these same ideas in reverse order; from the present back to the past. Either way has merit.

In the first place, there is an observable sequence to events which have occurred, and to follow this sequence faithfully may enable a student to gain the behavioral changes desired. That is, tracing President Wilson's actions and speeches from his election until his death might provide a framework for understanding the downfall of the League of Nations and the problems which led to the Second World War.

An alternative hypothesis, however, might very well suggest the opposite approach. Since much of history is a study of cause and effect, and since exploring effects *first* might lead one *back* to their causes, perhaps organizing instructional materials so that results are related to the causes in reverse order might be more effective. To start with present activities in the United Nations might uncover some of the problems which face that organization today. By exploring these problems backwards, the structure and function of the League of Nations might be unearthed, then its failure could very well lead back again to its founding, the opposition in the United States to participation in the League, the majority vote in the Senate in favor of the League (which was not enough), arguments advanced by Wilson and others, the Fourteen Points, and so on. In this way the multiplicity of causes might be better understood, since an exploration of the many relationships among historical events could be more apparent. Such an approach would surely be more problem-centered, since the purpose of studying each effect would be to uncover the causes which produced it, and these causes would then be viewed in turn as effects themselves, and the entire process continued for greater understanding.

Endeavoring to resolve such a problem by talk leads one either way he chooses to go. There are good arguments on both sides. Coming at the alternative approaches experimentally, though, is something else again. Working strictly within the confines of his own classroom, any teacher could could attempt to find out which of the two was more effective for him. He might work with one class one way, with another class the other way. He might try one approach one year and the other the following year. In either case, if he controls all of the variables he can, clarifies his objectives carefully, and then works to collect information which relates directly in these objectives, the chances are great that his students will profit much more than they would if he simply teaches the class routinely.

First, they will probably catch some sense of his involvement and his experimental approach—the "Hawthorne effect." Second, as he struggles to control the variables and define the differences precisely, he will inevitably give increased attention to his teaching and to his students. All of this means more effective instruction. As he tries first one approach and then another he develops insights into himself and his ways of working which allow him to capitalize upon his strengths and overcome his weaknesses. No man can do all things equally well. Uncovering his assets and limitations for himself is a concomitant result of educational experimentation which gives power to any teacher's way of working. Finally, grappling with such a problem forces a teacher to think about his subject matter. Continued scholarship becomes natural, helpful and important for him. He may utimately hit upon such techniques or materials or ways of organizing experiences that students may make much more significant growth than they would otherwise.

SUMMARY

Specific suggestions for answering educational questions have not been set forth here. None can be. Thoughtful reading of research reports may lead to some helpful conclusions. For the teacher who earnestly wants to improve his effectiveness, adopting an experimental attitude and devising experimental procedures will help him learn and grow. But he will have to study himself and his way as he goes along.

Such an attitude on the part of any teacher lightens his psychological burden. There are no routines to slip into if one tries to use experimentation to improve his teaching. Every day is different and exciting. Teaching is a challenge and not a chore. Converting logical arguments into researchable problems brings teaching alive. Students recognize their teacher as one who is interested and interesting. Inquiry is the heart of every significant learning experience, and devising ways of inquiring into his methods and himself and his area of interest gives a teacher insights and generalizations unknown to him before.

REFERENCES

1. Abramson, David A., "The Effectiveness of Grouping for Students of High Ability," *Educational Research Bulletin*, XXXVIII (October, 1959), 169-182.

2. Allardice, D. et al., "Curricular Innovations," *National Association of Secondary School Principals Bulletin* (May, 1963), 127-128.
3. Baldwin, Richard D., "Impediments to the Acquisition and Use of Medical Knowledge," *Science*, CXLI (September 27, 1963), 1237-1238.
4. Banning, Evelyn I., "Teacher Attitudes Toward Curriculum Change: The Effect of Personal Relationships on the Degree of Favorableness," *Journal of Experimental Education* (December, 1954), 133-147.
5. Brickell, Henry M., *Organizing New York State for Educational Change* (Albany: State Department of Education, 1961).
6. Bronowski, J., *Science and Human Values* (New York: Julian Messner, Inc., 1956).
7. Bullington, R. E., "Experimental Curriculum for the 'More Able' Students," *Journal of Experimental Education* (March, 1963), 291-296.
8. Chittick, Rupert A. et al., *The Vermont Story: Rehabilitation of Chronic Schizophrenic Patients*, Report of a research and demonstration grant (No. 180) from the Office of Vocational Rehabilitation, Department of Health, Education, and Welfare (Washington, D. C.: January, 1961).
9. Clary, William Max, "A Study of the Role of the Principal in Coordinating Curriculum Improvement in the Elementary Schools of Indiana," *Dissertation Abstracts*, XX (1959), 1240.
10. Cogan, Morris L., "The Behavior of Teachers and the Productive Behavior of Their Pupils: I. Perception Analysis," *Journal of Experimental Education*, XXVII (December, 1958), 89-124.
11. Commager, Henry S., *Freedom, Loyalty, Dissent* (New Haven: Yale University Press, 1954).
12. Commoner, Barry et al., "Science and the Race Problem," *Science*, CXLII (November 1, 1963), 558-561.
13. Compton, Arthur H., "Science and Man's Freedom," *The Atlantic Monthly*, CC (October, 1957), 71-74.
14. Cook, Desmond L., "The Hawthorne Effect in Educational Research," *Phi Delta Kappan*, XLIV (December, 1962), 116-122.
15. Coxe, Ross M., "A Suburban School System Faculty Looks at and Improves Its Program in Social Studies for Children and Youth," Doctoral Dissertation (Wayne State University. 1957).
16. Crawford, Dean A., "The Administrative Organization of the Curriculum in Midwestern High Schools," *Dissertation Abstracts*, XV (1955), 2058-2059.
17. Davidson, Helen H. and Lang, Gerhard, "Children's Perceptions of Their Teachers' Feelings Toward Them Related to Self-Perception, School Achievement, and Behavior," *Journal of Experimental Education*, XXIX (December, 1960), 107-118.
18. Drucker, Peter F., "The New Philosophy Comes to Life," *Harper's Magazine*, CCXV (August, 1957), 36-40.
19. Gardner, Richard N., "The Politics of Population," *Saturday Review* (September 7, 1963), 10-38.
20. Glaser, Barney G., "Comparative Failure in Science," *Science*, CXLIII (March 6, 1964), 1012-1014.
21. Goldberg, Miriam L. and Passow, A. H., "The Effects of Ability Grouping," *Education*, LXXXII (April, 1962), 482-487.
22. Goldfield, Edwin D., Ed., *Statistical Abstract of the United States, 1961* (Washington, D. C.: U. S. Department of Commerce).
23. Gray, Dwight E., "Information and Research—Blood Relatives or In-Laws?" *Science*, CXXXVII (July 27, 1962), 263-266.
24. Graybeal, William S., "Contributions of Teacher Judgments of Test Item Relevance to Planning for Instructional Improvement," *Dissertation Abstracts*, XXIII (April, 1963), 3686-3687.

25. Harrington, Gordon M., "Smiling as a Measure of Teacher Effectiveness," *Journal of Educational Research*, XLVIII (May, 1955), 715-717.
26. Heath, R. W. and Stickell, D. W., "CHEM and CBA Effects on Achievement in Chemistry," *The Science Teacher* (September, 1963), 45-56.
27. Heidel, R. H., "A Comparison of the Outcomes of Instruction of the Conventional High School Physics Course and the Generalized High School Senior Science Course," *Science Education* (March, 1944), 88-89.
28. Helfant, Kenneth, "Group Psychotherapy with Teachers and Administrators in a Public School," *Educational Leadership*, XIX (December, 1961), 187-193.
29. Hillkirk, John M., "Action Research as Applied in Curriculum Development, Grades K-12, A Case Study," *Dissertation Abstracts*, XXIII (April, 1963) 3722-3723.
30. Holton, Gerald, "Modern Science and the Intellectual Tradition," *Science*, CXXXI (April 22, 1960), 1187-1190.
31. Hyram, G. H., "An Experiment in Developing Critical Thinking in Children," *Journal of Experimental Education*, (December, 1957), 125-132.
32. Jensen, A. M., "An Experimental Evaluation of Two Different Programs of Teaching Health in the Sixth Grade and the Administrative Implications Involved," *Journal of Experimental Education*, (March, 1959), 203-210.
33. Johnson, Wendell, *People in Quandries*, (New York: Harper and Row, Publishers, 1946).
34. Kaplan, S. J., "An Appraisal of an Interdisciplinary Social Science Course," *The Journal of Educational Sociology* (October, 1960), 70-77.
35. Lanton, Wendell C., "Comparison of the Reading, Arithmetic, and Spelling Achievement of Third and Fifth Grade Pupils in 1953 and in 1934," *Dissertation Abstracts*, XIV (1954), 1619-1620.
36. Livermore, A. H. and Ferris, F. L., "The Chemical Bond Approach Course in the Classroom," *Science*, CXXXVIII (December 7, 1962), 1077-1080.
37. Lynch, J. J., "An Experiment with the Theme Conference in the High School," *Journal of Secondary Education* (October, 1963), 22-26.
38. Lynd, Albert, *Quackery in the Public Schools* (New York: Grosset and Dunlap, 1953).
39. McNally, Harold J. and Passow, A. Harry, *Improving the Quality of Public School Programs* (New York: Teachers College, Columbia University, 1960).
40. McQuigg, Robert B., "Participation in Curriculum Committees by Classroom Teachers in Selected Colorado School Systems," *Dissertation Abstracts*, XXIII (1963), 3733.
41. Medley, Donald M. and Mitzel, Harold E., "Some Behavioral Correlates of Teacher Effectiveness," *Journal of Educational Psychology*, L (December, 1959), 239-246.
42. Nelson, C. B., "An Experimental Evaluation of Two Methods of Teaching Music in the Fourth and Fifth Grades," *Journal of Experimental Education* (March, 1955), 231-238.
43. Nelson, Jack and Roberts, Gene Jr., *The Censors and the School* (Boston: Little, Brown and Co., 1963).
44. Novak, J. D., "An Experimental Comparison of a Conventional and a Project Centered Method of Teaching a College Botany Course," *Journal of Experimental Education* (March, 1958), 217-230.
45. Oppenheimer, J. Robert, "The Tree of Knowledge," *Harper's Magazine*, CCXVII (October, 1958), 55-60.
46. Overton, Harvey W., "The Image of Conflict and Change in Secondary Education Held by Two Groups of Teachers in the Secondary Schools of a Community in Cultural Transition," *Dissertation Abstracts*, XXII (January, 1962), 2309.
47. Pauley, B. G., "An Evaluation of a Secondary-School Mathematics Program for Able Students," *The Mathematics Teacher*, LIV (May, 1961), 324-332.

48. Perlman, J. S., "An Historical vs. Contemporary Problem Solving Use of the College Physical Science Laboratory Period for General Education," *Journal of Experimental Education* (March, 1953), 251-257.
49. Peterson, Clarence E., "The Role of the Principal in Curriculum Development," *Dissertation Abstracts*, XIII (1953), 709.
50. Peterson, Shailer, "The Evaluation of a One-Year Course, the Fusion of Physics and Chemistry, with Other Physical Science Courses," *Science Education*, XXIX (December, 1945), 255-264.
51. Piel, Gerard, *Science in the Cause of Man* (New York: Alfred A. Knopf, 1961).
52. Rasschaert, William M., "A Descriptive Analysis of a Departmental Curriculum Improvement Project in an Urban Junior High School," *Journal of Experimental Education* (September, 1958), 37-48.
53. Raywid, Mary, *The Ax-Grinders* (New York: Macmillan, 1963).
54. Ross, Walter E., "A Study of Personnel Factors Affecting the Morale Status of Teachers of Two Rural School Systems in New York State and Including Comparisons of Findings with Those of a Similar Study Completed for a New Jersey Suburban School System," *Dissertation Abstracts*, XXI (1960), 110-111.
55. Russell, Bertrand, "The Social Responsibilities of Scientists," *Science*, CXXXI (February 12, 1960), 391-392.
56. Sand, O. and Miller, Richard I., "Curricular Innovations," *National Association of Secondary School Principals Bulletin* (May, 1963), 121-122.
57. Schilling, Harold K., "A Human Enterprise," *Science*, CXXVII (June 6, 1958), 1324-1327.
58. Schramm, Wilbur, "Learning from Instructional Television," *Review of Educational Research*, XXXII (April, 1962), 156-167.
59. Sears, Paul B., "The Inexorable Problem of Space," *Science*, CXXVII (January 3, 1958), 9-16.
60. Shumsky, Abraham, "Teachers' Insecurity and Action Research," *Educational Research Bulletin*, XXXV (October, 1956), 183-186.
61. Simons, Joseph H., "Scientific Research in the University," *American Scientist*, XLVIII (March, 1960).
62. Slesnick, I. L., "The Effectiveness of a Unified Science in the High School Curriculum," Unpublished Doctoral Dissertation (The Ohio State University, 1962).
63. Snow, Charles P., "The Moral Un-Neutrality of Science," *Science*, CXXXIII (January 27, 1961), 256-259.
64. Spieker, Edmund M., "Teaching and Research," *Science*, CXXIX (May 15, 1959), 1324.
65. Stevenson, Ian, "Scientists with Half Closed Minds," *Harper's Magazine*, CCXVII (November, 1958), 64-71.
66. Street, Scott, W., "A Description and Evaluation of Cooperative Curriculum Planning by Staff and Parents at the Andrew Jackson School and the Paul L. Best School, Ferndale School District, Michigan," *Dissertation Abstracts*, XIX (1959), 3197-3198.
67. Symonds, Percival, "Characteristics of the Effective Teacher Based on Pupil Evaluation," *Journal of Experimental Education*, XXIII (1955), 289-310.
68. Taylor, Bob L., "Factors Influencing In-Service Teacher Education Programs," *Journal of Educational Research*, LII (May, 1959), 336-338.
69. Taylor, Calvin W., "Bridging the Gap," *National Education Journal* (January, 1962).
70. Thistle, M. W., "Popularizing Science," *Science*, CXXVII (April 25, 1958), 951-955.
71. Verduin, John R., "An Evaluation of a Cooperative Approach to Curriculum Change," *Dissertation Abstracts*, XXIII (June, 1963), 4581.

72. Wallace, W. L., "The BSCS 1961-62 Evaluation Program—A Statistical Report," *BSCS Newsletter*, XIX (September, 1963).
73. Wallen, N. E. et al., "The Outcomes of Curriculum Modifications Designed to Foster Critical Thinking," *The Journal of Educational Research* (July, 1963), 529-534.
74. Walters, James, "The Effects of an Introductory Course in Child Development on the Attitudes of College Women Toward Child Guidance," *Journal of Experimental Education*, XXVII (June, 1959), 311-321.
75. Weiss, Paul, "Knowledge: A Growth Process," *Science*, CXXXI (June 10, 1960), 1716-1719.
76. Wiener, Norbert, *The Human Use of Human Beings: Cybernetics and Society* (Boston: Houghton Mifflin Company, 1954).
77. Wilk, Roger E. et al., *Student Teacher Activities and Pupil Responses: A Report to Participants*, Research Memorandum BER-60-7 (University of Minnesota, July, 1960).
78. Willink, Ross J., "Inservice Training of Junior High School Teachers," *National Association of Secondary School Principals Bulletin*, XLIII (December, 1959), 13-17.
79. Zagona, Salvatore V. and MacKinnon, William J., "Open-Mindedness and Hypotheses Interdependence Between Libertarian and Equalitarian Processes," *Journal of Psychology*, LII (October, 1961), 347-361.

Chapter Ten

Drawing a Circle

INTRODUCTION

What is teaching? Some say that "if nothing has been learned, then nothing has been taught." Negative statements help, but they hardly answer the question. Any analysis of teaching indicates at least two answers to the question: teaching is a process and teaching is a profession. Helping children learn is the heart of the process. Seeing yourself and being seen by others as performing this role is teaching as a profession.

Teachers must draw a circle around themselves so that what they do and how they do it differentiates them from other members of society to the extent that they are recognized as professionals.

Being a professional teacher involves more than teaching. Any one can teach, and many do. Professional teachers, however, differ from others who teach in that they have drawn a second circle in such a way that some persons are included and some exclued from their group.

Professional teaching involves these two things. The purpose of this chapter is to trace the boundaries of these two circles. One defines a role and the other defines a group. Teaching is a process and it is a profession. Those things which make the process professional are explored in the pages which follow.

DEFINING THE TEACHING PROCESS

An exasperated third grade teacher, unable to keep her classroom under satisfactory control, punishes the class by refusing to allow any youngster to go to the bathroom for half a day. Is this teaching? An upset junior high school teacher requires a student who has broken a rule, to kneel, place his nose upon a thumbtack which has been pushed into the floor, and to hold this position for fifteen minutes. Is this teaching? A senior high school teacher requires a student to write a 1000-word theme for smirking in class. A college professor assigns a book to read but gives tests on his lectures. Are these things teaching?

Defining the teaching process involves drawing a line between activities which contribute directly to educational goals and those which do not. Understanding what teaching is not helps one to understand what teaching is. Looking carefully at the part which punishment plays is an important step.

Think for a moment about the contradictions involved in punishing children by making them write long themes. Learning to communicate effectively in written form is considered important. Writing is a worthwhile skill, and learning how to write well is a noble educational goal. Imagine how that goal is seen by the child who *has* to write because he has done something wrong. If writing is worthwhile, why is it selected as a means of punishment? Is it possible for learners to appreciate writing and want to write well if those who are supposed to know misuse it so?

Drawing a circle around what is teaching involves more than a mere description of what occurs in classrooms. A verbal picture of what now exists would help to define teaching, but would pose many problems. This chapter draws a circle around teaching in an effort to describe it as it ought to be rather than as it actually is. Some aspects of teaching as defined here will differ sharply from present practice; others will be the same.

Teaching Process and Educational Goals

One cannot describe the teaching process until it is clear what it is intended to achieve. Society commits schools to particular ends. Schools exist to help children learn.

During the last half century repeated statements about the purposes of schools have been made. These statements, which are society's effort to make articulate what it expects of schools, illustrate forcefully the concepts of positive control described in Chapter One. Teachers are expected to help youth become worthy home members rather than unworthy, critical rather than uncritical thinkers, vocationally efficient rather than inefficient, good citizens rather than poor, democratic rather than undemocratic. When teachers help children learn to behave in these ways they are participating directly in the teaching process.

Professional teaching includes those activities which facilitate the achievement of educational purposes: it excludes those which impede their attainment. In principle, our first circle is drawn. Doing things which lie within that circle is appropriate teacher behavior. Initiating, informing, explaining, demonstrating, clarifying, diagnosing, evaluating, and reporting are some of them. Teaching is to engage in these activities in such a way that youngsters develop democratic behavior and learn to become what they can, and what society expects them to become.

What is teaching *not*, then? What actions on the part of a teacher should be excluded from the teaching act? Those things which inhibit the achievement of desirable goals are excluded from the process.[1]

Let us return to the problem of punishments. What do children learn who are punished by being forced to write a theme? What do boys in a physical education class learn about the importance of physical activity when they are punished by being made to "take ten laps around the field"? What do children learn about school being a good place to be when they are made to "stay after school" for one reason or another?

These punishments, all fairly common in schools today, do not help young people learn to develop expected behaviors. Punishment probably has a place in the educative process, if for no other reason than that teachers sometimes "run out of brains." There probably *are* better ways of helping children learn to behave appropriately than by punishing them, but sometimes these ways are not apparent when a crucial moment arrives, so teachers punish. A nation-wide study (44) of over 4000 teachers disclosed that 77 per cent of the elementary teachers, 62 per cent of the junior high school teachers, and 37 per cent of the senior high school teachers favored having the authority to administer corporal punishment. That makes one wonder precisely how some of them see their role.

Teachers must be especially careful to avoid actions which are designed to accomplish educational goals but which actually are mis-educative in their results. Any act or deed which causes or encourages students to move away from democratic behaviors is not teaching.

Between the extremes are many activities whose direct contribution to educational goals are of questionable value. Somebody has to check

---

[1] Implicit in this argument is the notion that teaching is good. Children can be taught to behave in ways which are undesirable but this is not teaching. Technically, this is not a valid statement. In an effort to circumscribe the process, however, these ways of teaching are excluded because of the conflict which they produce in their relationship to acceptable goals.

and record attendance, but is this teaching? Somebody has to open the windows and score test papers, but is this teaching? Somebody occasionally has to help little children put on their galoshes or go to the bathroom or blow their noses, but is this teaching? Is collecting lunch money, keeping records on the magazine sale drive, collecting tickets at the football game or chaperoning dances, teaching? Is keeping order in a study hall or lunchroom or at the bus stop teaching, or is it policing? Is typing stencils and running the ditto machine teaching or secretarial work? If one is qualified to teach mathematics but required also to take on an English class "out of field" each day, can this be teaching?

We gather from these illustrations that many tasks connected with a teacher's work are not, in fact, teaching.

In a hospital somebody must change the sheets and empty the bed pans, somebody performs the blood studies and administers the pills, but this is not the physician's role. Somebody types the contract or files the deed, but this is not to practice law. Separating the essential from the unessential is not defining professional duties.

Many activities are important in the educative process, but not all are teaching. Teachers must draw a circle around those functions so that every act contributes *directly* to the educational goal. Those activities which are peripheral must be excluded from the teaching act. Tangential roles may be very important—nobody denies the fact that a hospital patient needs clean linen or that attendance must be kept in school—but unless they contribute directly to the task at hand, such processes should be considered outside the sphere of the professional teacher.

The purpose of drawing a circle is not to be "better than" or "different from" some other persons. Basically, each person has only so much energy to expend. Defining the teacher's role precisely and in detail allows the professional teacher to achieve his goals. By concentrating his abilities, he is best able to accomplish that which he was prepared to do —teach. Scoring objective tests is an important job, but interpreting test results is more nearly teaching. If scoring test papers will actually enable a teacher to know each student better and to understand his learning problem, then it is part of teaching. But if scoring stacks of papers or supervising study halls or collecting tickets at ball games do not make a direct contribution to educational objectives, then they are not teaching.

The professional is one who knows exactly what his objectives are, which activities on his part will attain those goals, and behaves accordingly. He recognizes that many things are important, but his job is to teach. Drawing a circle around his role is one place to start. A carefully defined role does not make a teacher less human, only more able to accomplish his task.

DEFINING THE TEACHING PROFESSION

Understanding the teaching process is one thing. Working with others to insure its practice is another. Though no clearcut set of criteria has been accepted as applicable to all professions, several general characteristics prevail: service to mankind, extensive training, intellectual and judgmental activities, self-discipline through organization, and an enforced code of ethics.[2]

Service to Mankind

First and foremost, all professional groups have as their major purpose to serve mankind. Personal satisfaction, financial remuneration and social prestige are often associated with the professions. The fact that they generally do accrue is largely a reflection of the extent to which society appreciates the service. This does not mean that some do not enter the professions for those secondary reasons, because they do. Through organization, however, the profession tries to insure that its members' activities conform to professional expectations—serving mankind.

The professional practitioner's activities are unique and essential to those he serves. The principle of uniqueness has been discussed above as drawing a circle. What has not been pointed out is that mankind *must* have the service performed if it is to live satisfactorily. Somebody has to prescribe medicine and perform surgery, minister to man's spiritual needs, and represent the one against the many and the many against the one in court. These are services which men need, and they fall within the professional's sphere.

Extensive Training

Becoming a professional person is a long, involved process. Because of the nature of the service to be performed, those who seek to become practitioners must engage in extensive training. This presupposes that there is a body of knowledge and set of techniques which are appropriate and that these can be taught. No man is born knowing how to be a doctor or lawyer or teacher. Professional behavior is not acquired either through the genes or by casual contact. Those who pursue this path

---

[2] For a more extensive description of this problem see Myron Lieberman, *Education as a Profession* (Prentice-Hall, Inc.; Englewood Cliffs, N.J.), 1956, 540 pp.

undertake systematic study of a body of information unique to the profession, as well as broad programs of general education. Sometimes described as "broad men sharpened to a point," professionals must acquire liberal amounts of general education plus the precise knowledge and skill peculiar to their group.

Intellectual and Judgmental

Although many of the day to day activities of the professional involve dexterity or technical skill, it is characteristic that his basic training and practice are primarily intellectual. Even the physical skills of preparing a dental plate or extracting a tooth, for example, are based first on broad understanding. Knowing when to fill or when to extract a tooth, or whether to prescribe drug therapy or surgery, are intellectual and judgmental concerns. Accomplishing the tasks may or may not themselves be an intellectual exercise. The broad base upon which professional activity rests, however, is intellectual.

Being professional includes being responsible, and the heavy responsibility comes from the fact that the recipient of the service seldom knows whether the decisions made are the right ones. If I decide to buy a piece of property and want to know if the title is clear, I ask my lawyer. After his study of the abstracts, he tells me that in his judgment the title either is or is not clear. Whatever he says, I must trust his judgment. I am in no position to know if what he says is true. I may go from lawyer to lawyer, if I like, double checking on the first one's information, but this is usually unnecessary. Even if I asked other attorneys, I would still have only their word.

A second example may better clarify the point. In the process of treating an individual, a physician may prescribe medicine and subsequent office visits. Suppose that after the first few visits the patient recovers, but, for purposes of illustration, suppose also that he did not know that he was well. Assume that the illness was some sort of blood infection which was not apparent to the patient, and was only detected in the first place through a routine physical examination. It would be highly unethical for a physician to continue treatment and require additional observations if the patient actually had recovered. It is precisely this fact, that those who receive a professional serivce are seldom able to evaluate its worth, which makes it imperative for those in the professions to base their judgments upon a code of ethics.

An analaogy in the field of business illustrates the point again. After World War II when automobiles were scarce, buyers were often forced to purchase unwanted accessories in order to get a new car. Because the automobile dealers were either unwilling or unable to refrain from such practices, the federal government had to legislate such activities out of existence. Compelling people to pay for a service they neither want nor need is hardly professional.

Professional Groups Are Self Disciplining

This last illustration points up a difference between professional and non-professional groups. In the case of the retailers described, outside pressures finally forced a curtailment of questionable practice. Those who sell automobiles are obviously not members of a professional group, and one of the basic distinctions revolves around the concept of jurisdiction and control. Who shall say whether what a group does is professional?

The answer clearly lies with the organization itself. Those groups which are truly professional are so organized that they impose discipline upon their members according to a single code of ethics. If members of the profession stray from the code, they are admonished or expelled. Persons seeking membership within the profession assume obligations and agree to abide by the code of ethics. Beyond this, the various segments of the profession have organized themselves so that they are able to *demand* compliance from their peers. Control comes from within the profession. This control is rooted in the professional's trust in his fellow practitioners. The organizational basis through which this control operates is predicated upon a common code of ethics.

Professional Groups Have a Common Code of Ethics

Undergirding the professions, providing visible points of reference and guides for action, codes of ethics set forth those principles which give rise to professional effort. Not laws, codes of ethics can have more force than any law. Principles and standards, they provide continuity and cohesiveness, direction and inspiration, strength and fiber, to professional groups. A brief quotation from "Principles of Medical Ethics" of the American Medical Association may illustrate these points (1):

> These principles are intended to serve the physician as a guide to ethical conduct as he strives to accomplish his prime purpose of serving the common good and improving the health of mankind. They provide a sound basis for solution of many of the problems which arise in his relationship with patients, with other physicians, and with the public. They are not immutable laws to govern the physician, for the ethical practitioner needs no such laws; rather

they are standards by which he may determine the propriety of his own conduct. Undoubtedly, interpretation of these principles by an appropriate authority will be required at times. As a rule, however, the physician who is capable, honest, decent, courteous, vigilant, and an observer of the Golden Rule, and who conducts his affairs in the light of his own conscientious interpretation of these principles will find no difficulty in the discharge of his professional obligations. [p. 1.]

Reference is made to the medical profession, not because teachers should emulate another group, but rather because most observers would agree that medicine *is* a profession, and provides a kind of case study for insights into the nature of teaching as a profession. Other citations from the medical source already mentioned may prove helpful. For example:

> There is but one code of ethics for all, be they group, clinic, or individual and be they great and prominent, or small and unknown. [p. 2.]

Again:

> The prime object of the medical profession is to render service to humanity; reward or financial gain is a subordinate consideration. Whoever chooses this profession assumes the obligation to conduct himself in accord with its ideals. [p. 7.]

Or;

> Physicians should strive continually to improve medical knowledge and skill, and should make available to their patients and colleagues the benefits of professional attainments.
>
> A physician may patent surgical instruments, appliances, and medicines or copyright publications, methods, and procedures. The use of such patents or copyrights or the receipt of remuneration from them which retards or inhibits research or restricts the benefits derivable is therefore unethical. [p. 13.]

At another point a basic tenet is declared:

> A physician should practice a method of healing founded on a scientific basis; and he should not voluntarily associate professionally with anyone who violates this principle.

In order that a physician may best serve his patients he is expected to exalt the standards of his profession and to extend its sphere of usefulness. To the same end, he should not base his practice on an exclusive dogma, or a sectarian system, for "sects are implacable despots; to accept their thralldom is to take away all liberty from one's action and thought." A sectarian or cultist as applied to medicine is one who alleges to follow or in his practice follows a dogma, tenet or principle based on the authority of its promulgator to the exclusion of demonstration and scientific experience. All voluntary associated activities with cultists are unethical. [p. 17.]

Trust in their fellow physicians is projected in the fourth principle:

The medical profession should safeguard the public and itself against physicians deficient in moral character or professional competence. Physicians should observe all laws, uphold the dignity and honor of the profession and accept its self-imposed disciplines. They should expose, without hesitation, illegal or unethical conduct of fellow members of the profession.

The reader will note in the references cited that in medicine the burden of responsibility for ethical conduct is placed squarely on the individual physician and the larger group of physicians of which he is a member. This is not a hollow responsibility. During 1962 the American Medical Association reported that 783 physicians were cited for disciplinary action. Of these, 111 were penalized by license revocations, expulsions or suspensions (67). Since 1919 the National Education Association has expelled one member for violation of its ethical code (18). Unquestionably many teachers have been relieved of their teaching positions for unethical practice, but these teachers often move from one community to another to teach in different schools.

Several years ago the need for a single code of ethics for the teaching profession was recognized, and one has recently been proposed. In any group as large and diverse as that of teachers, enthusiasm for compliance with a single code varies. Because it is the best step forward in recent years, the code of ethics is reproduced here. In the pages which follow the code, efforts will be made to draw this professional circle to a close. Defining teaching as a profession involves drawing into the group those persons whose training and behavior merit the label, "professional teacher." Those whose preparation or conduct is unbefitting the profession must be denied admittance or expelled. In either instance, the profession itself must draw the line. The formula for the circle lies within the code.

THE CODE OF ETHICS OF THE EDUCATION PROFESSION

Preamble

We, professional educators of the United States of America, affirm our belief in the worth and dignity of man. We recognize the supreme importance of the pursuit of truth, the encouragement of scholarship, and the promotion of democratic citizenship. We regard as essential to these goals the protection of freedom to learn and to teach and the guarantee of equal educational opportunity for all. We affirm and accept our responsibility to practice our profession according to the highest ethical standards.

We acknowledge the magnitude of the profession we have chosen, and engage ourselves, individually and collectively, to judge our colleagues and to be judged by them in accordance with the applicable provisions of this code.

Principle I
Commitment to the Student

We measure success by the progress of each student toward achievement of his maximum potential. We therefore work to stimulate the spirit of inquiry, the acquisition of knowledge and understanding, and the thoughtful formulation of worthy goals. We recognize the importance of cooperative relationships with other community institutions, especially the home.

In fulfilling our obligations to the student, we—

1. Deal justly and considerately with each student.
2. Encourage the student to study varying points of view and respect his right to form his own judgment.
3. Withhold confidential information about a student or his home unless we deem that its release serves professional purposes, benefits the student, or is required by law.
4. Make discreet use of available information about the student.
5. Conduct conferences with or concerning students in an appropriate place and manner.
6. Refrain from commenting unprofessionally about a student or his home.
7. Avoid exploiting our professional relationship with any student.
8. Tutor only in accordance with officially approved policies.
9. Inform appropriate individuals and agencies of the student's educational needs and assist in providing an understanding of his educational experiences.

10. Seek constantly to improve learning facilities and opportunities.

Principle II
Commitment to the Community

We believe that patriotism in its highest form requires dedication to the principles of our democratic heritage. We share with all other citizens the responsibility for the development of sound public policy. As educators, we are particularly accountable for participating in the development of educational programs and policies and for interpreting them to the public.

In fulfilling our obligations to the community, we—

1. Share the responsibility for improving the educational opportunities for all.
2. Recognize that each educational institution may have a person authorized to interpret its official policies.
3. Acknowledge the right and responsibility of the public to participate in the formulation of educational policy.
4. Evaluate through appropriate professional procedures conditions within a district or institution of learning, make known serious deficiencies, and take any action deemed necessary and proper.
5. Use educational facilities for intended purposes consistent with applicable policy, law, and regulation.
6. Assume full political and citizenship responsibilities, but refrain from exploiting the institutional privileges of our professional positions to promote political candidates or partisan activities.
7. Protect the educational program against undesirable infringement.

Principle III
Commitment to the Profession

We believe that the quality of the services of the education profession directly influences the future of the nation and its citizens. We therefore exert every effort to raise educational standards, to improve our service, to promote a climate in which the exercise of professional judgment is encouraged, and to achieve conditions which attract persons worthy of the trust to careers in education. Aware of the value of united effort, we contribute actively to the support, planning, and programs of our professional organizations.

In fulfilling our obligations to the profession, we—

1. Recognize that a profession must accept responsibility for the conduct of its members and understand that our own conduct may be regarded as representative.
2. Participate and conduct ourselves in a responsible manner in the development and implementation of policies affecting education.
3. Cooperate in the selective recruitment of prospective teachers and in the orientation of student teachers, interns, and those colleagues new to their positions.
4. Accord just and equitable treatment to all members of the profession in the exercise of their professional rights and responsibilities, and support them when unjustly accused or mistreated.
5. Refrain from assigning professional duties to non-professional personnel when such assignment is not in the best interest of the student.
6. Provide, upon request, a statement of specific reason for administrative recommendations that lead to the denial of increments, significant changes in employment, or termination of employment.
7. Refrain from exerting undue influence based on the authority of our positions in the determination of professional decisions by colleagues.
8. Keep the trust under which confidential information is exchanged.
9. Make appropriate use of time granted for professional purposes.
10. Interpret and use the writings of others and the findings of educational research with intellectual honesty.
11. Maintain our integrity when dissenting by basing our public criticism of education on valid assumptions as established by careful evaluation of facts or hypotheses.
12. Represent honestly our professional qualifications and identify ourselves only with reputable educational institutions.
13. Respond accurately to requests for evaluations of colleagues seeking professional positions.
14. Provide applicants seeking information about a position with an honest description of the assignment, the conditions of work, and related matters.

Principle IV
Commitment to Professional Employment Practices

We regard the employment agreement as a solemn pledge to be executed both in spirit and in fact in a manner consistent with the highest ideals of professional service. Sound professional personnel relationships with governing boards are built upon personal integrity, dignity, and mutual respect.

In fulfilling our obligations to professional employment practices, we—

1. Apply for or offer a position on the basis of professional and legal qualifications.

2. Apply for a specific position only when it is known to be vacant and refrain from such practices as underbidding or commenting adversely about other candidates.

3. Fill no vacancy except where the terms, conditions, policies, and practices permit the exercise of our professional judgment and skill, and where a climate conducive to professional service exists.

4. Adhere to the conditions of a contract or to the terms of an appointment until either has been terminated legally or by mutual consent.

5. Give prompt notice of any change in availability of service, in status of applications, or in change in position.

6. Conduct professional business through the recognized educational and professional channels.

7. Accept no gratuities or gifts of significance that might influence our judgment in the exercise of our professional duties.

8. Engage in no outside employment that will impair the effectiveness of our professional service and permit no commercial exploitation of our professional position.

IMPLEMENTING A CODE OF ETHICS

This code of ethics provides a framework for a professional circle. It draws no lines and neither includes nor excludes any person as it stands. It now remains for educators in local districts to devise by-laws whereby these principles can be implemented.

Just as the operational group in medicine is the country medical society, so it seems appropriate that teachers might best exercise control over their membership at the local level. Not all professional groups are organized so that their main strength lies in local groups. Law, for example, typically exerts influence through state bar associations. Other professional groups' controlling efforts vary, according to their numbers and purposes. It would seem most practical for teachers to band together at the district level with a view toward adopting a common code of ethics for their own locale.

As a professional group, teachers do not now function according to a code of ethics. This does not mean that most teachers are unethical. It does mean that teachers have not devised ways of disciplining themselves and their fellow teachers according to a common code. An illustration or two may clarify this point.

Examples of Unethical Actions

Some teachers sell encyclopedias to supplement their income. According to Principle IV, obligation number eight, a teacher "engages in no outside employment that will impair the effectiveness of our professional service and permit no commercial exploitation of our professional position."

Is selling encyclopedias a violation of this principle? It depends upon the particulars involved. If a teacher "suggests" to the parents of a child in his class that having encyclopedias available will probably improve a student's grades, the practice borders on being unethical. Many parents, desirous of their child's welfare, and interpreting the teacher's statements as either a promise or a threat, feel compelled to buy the books. Whether teachers intend such interpretations is not the point. Under such circumstances, if parents *feel* compelled to buy the books to help their child in his work, the practice approaches a violation of Principle IV. And though it would be difficult to assess, there is also logical reason to believe that, if teachers spend out-of-school time selling encyclopedias, they will not be devoting that time to their professional activities of preparing lessons, counseling with individual students, reading student themes, or interpreting test data.

Consider another example. A professor, chairman of a department in his college, becomes a chronic alcoholic. During the course of any given semester this professor misses more than half of his assigned class meetings. His absences are never announced and during those times when he is present it is often evident to students and staff alike that his physical condition and his conduct are not acceptable. Here we have a clear violation of Principle III in that a member of the profession can "recognize that a profession must accept responsibility for the conduct of its members and understand that our own conduct may be regarded as representative." Obligation No. 6 under the same principle suggests a course of action, since it directs that a member of the profession "provide, upon request, a statement of specific reason for administrative recommendations that lead to the denial of increments, significant changes in employment, or termination of employment."

Without question the responsibility rests on the shoulders of those members of the staff whose conduct is above reproach. What often happens in a case like this is that other professors "look the other way," hoping that eventually the college administration will note the problem and handle it somehow. If students complain or ask what they can do, other professors usually shrug their shoulders and say, "It's out of my hands."

More often than not, however, administrators also sidestep the problem. They know that if they take steps to terminate the professor's employment, they may find themselves confronted with a law suit over tenure, or a general fracas involving accusations about academic freedom. Administrative action may explode into editorial attack by student or local newspapers.

If the situation is as clear-cut as this, it seems reasonable to suppose that the dean or other college administrator would still proceed to terminate the professor's employment, or insist that he seek special help. If the professor is within three or four years of retirement, or is a close friend of one of the college trustees, the chances are that there will be no administrative action.

Here is one final illustration. Some persons, by virtue of their personality and experience, develop into social deviates of one kind or another. Homosexuality, for instance, exists. Some men molest young boys. On occasions these persons are found in the teaching profession. Some even become school principals.

Confronted with a problem such as this, the profession is often at a loss. Sooner or later different persons become aware of the problem. Teachers know, some parents know, the superintendent knows, the school board knows. Everybody knows, but nobody wants to act.

Teachers are afraid that the principal, who can recommend their reappointment may jeopardize their positions. The parents generally want no publicity which could hurt their child. The superintendent may be afraid that any undesirable publicity might cause an upcoming bond issue to be defeated. The board agrees.

All persons concerned are aware of the problem, but nobody wants to take steps to eliminate such a person from the profession.

Likely as not, this deviate will be encouraged to resign, and helped to get another job somewhere else through the innocuous practice of a vague letter of recommendation. The new position may even be in another state and all parties breathe a sigh of relief that they have solved the problem.

But did they? Unless the profession acts to guarantee that such a person's certificate is revoked, and information made available about his deviant ways, he is free to move from one community to another, exploiting young people wherever he goes.

These three cases are not imagined. Each one is well known to the writer. We need not deplore the fact that all teachers are not perfect. Teachers are human, and, like members of the other professions, some stray from the ethical way.

It seems significant that there is no term comparable to "quack" or "shyster" to describe unethical teachers. There is every reason to believe that the demeanor of teachers in general is better than that of almost any other professional group.

But some still violate the ethical code. How, then, can the profession exercise the power of the code to draw a circle around those who abide, and exclude those whose behavior is unprofessional?

Achieving Professional Status

There are four steps to achieving professional status: satisfactory completion of a college degree; satisfactory completion of a teacher-education program; certification by the state; and acceptance into the professional group. The first three will be discussed here briefly, then acceptance into the group will be explored at greater length.

Extended college preparation is the first step toward becoming professional. Programs in higher education for teachers are designed to assure a broad experience in the areas of general education—the arts and sciences, primarily. Special emphasis in those areas in which the prospective professional expects to teach is also mandatory. Persons hoping to become teachers of English take basic courses in English, then go on to study both more intensively and extensively in that field. The same is true for teachers of vocational agriculture or French or physical education or any other specialty.

In addition to, or as a part of, their requirements for a college degree, prospective teachers also take special work designed to help them become competent teachers. One of the criteria of a profession, you will recall, is that there exists a specialized body of techniques and knowledge, and that these can be taught. Understanding the role of the school in the social order, how children learn, ways of assessing academic achievement, methods of presenting information and leading discussions, and supervised teaching are some of the experiences. Whether these come before or after completion of the bachelor's degree varies, but all states require professional work before they certify teachers.

Should any person who can pass all his college courses be allowed to teach?—definitely not. A major difference between professional preparation and college work in general rests on the fact that teacher education institutions must screen out those whose personality or value structure would present risks. Many phychotics could successfully complete college course requirements, but no one would want to have them work with a group of children.

Students who are unsuitable teacher-material should be eliminated from professional training. Prospective teachers should demonstrate respect for their profession, and belief in the worth of every human being. Knowledge and skill are not enough, but must go hand in hand with a proper attitude. Those entrusted with the training of teachers recognize that their first responsibility is to the children these young men and women may teach. They must consider the next generation—their students' students—as well as those immediately before them.

Granting a certificate or a license to teach is a function of state governments. Just as doctors and dentists and barbers are licensed by a state agency, teachers are also certified by state departments of education. The usual pattern is for states to issue certificates to those who have satisfactorily completed a college degree, taken certain professional courses, passed a physical examination, and been recommended by the graduating institution. Most states also have provisions for issuing special certificates for those who do not meet all of the requirements imposed.

Problem in Achieving Professional Status

Teacher certification ha been widely discussed (62, 64) in recent years, and several observations seem pertinent at this point. The licensing boards for attorneys, physicians, and dentists in all of the states are composed of professional practitioners. Even 42 states have barbers on that group's licensing board, and in 38 states beauticians serve on the boards which license them. However, only five states require teachers on their certification boards, and some states even prohibit them from serving. (34, pp. 95ff). Here is one area, clearly, in which the teaching profession does not exert control over its own destiny and its own membership.

Why is this so? Why is there so much discussion and concern about teacher certification and professionalization today? Without making any effort to explore the problem in depth, certain basic notions seem worth mention.

First, throughout our history this nation has steadily moved in the direction of expanding educational opportunities for more of its youth. Because of the population growth, the need for teachers has been phenomenal. More hopes for more people mean that more teachers are necessary.

Second, most of the educational effort in this country has been public, and the problems of persons seeking to attain professional status as public employees has been complicated by the fact that they are public employees. Salaries and working conditions are usually not matters over which teachers have any direct control. This is not to say that they do not exert any influence over these matters, but being on the public payroll creates circumstances which persons who are self-employed do not face.

Third, and perhaps most important, there is a legal hierarchy within teaching which works against professional strength. Because they are public, all schools exist within a tight structure of statutes. These laws prescribe the power and responsibilities inherent in various roles. School board members and superintendents are told exactly what they can and cannot do by legislative decree. The authority of principals and teachers is defined in detail. The precise relationship each of these groups has with the others and with the state are also delineated. A chain of authority, extending downward from the state through local boards to superintendents and principals and teachers, imposes a legal hierarchy which binds the profession.

Such a structure creates a series of *authority* levels within the profession which tend to be seen as *competence* levels. A principal is recognized as having the authority to tell teachers what and how to teach, even though very few principals in any large high school could possibly do so. The distinction between *authority* and *authoritative* is extremely important to professional groups, but in most school systems this distinction is seldom made.

Few hospital administrators would think of telling a doctor how he should treat his patients, but most persons think that a school administrator ought to function that way with the teachers in his building. Very few superintendents are ever in a position to know what instructional materials or teaching techniques are most appropriate in a classroom, yet if one or two parents complain about teaching procedures, some act as though their legal authority and educational competence are on the same plane. Some school administrators do not confuse these issues, but any observer of the educational scene is generally forced to conclude that they are relatively few. "When push comes to shove," as the saying goes, most educational executives equate legal authority and professional competence, though this assumption is seldom valid.

Only if the profession polices its own ranks can it be assured of reducing attacks from outside. Demands that teachers be fingerprinted, sign loyalty oaths, make certain scores on standardized tests, or be denied opportunity to travel outside their state to professional meetings, are all examples of unjust and damaging regulations. Only if the profession assumes full responsibility for exercising control over its own membership can it strengthen itself so that its importance and force will be recog-- nized.

Gaining Membership in the Profession

Once a college degree and professional training have been attained, and after a state has certified a person to teach, there remains the final step of being received into the professional group. At the present time the first three steps are all that are generally required. If teachers are to achieve true professional status, however, the fourth step in the process must be acceptance into the group and adherence to its ethical way. Without this, teaching will never be truly professional. But, more important, without this, professional aspirations can never be realized fully. *If schools exist to help children learn, professional behavior is important because this is the only way the profession can assure itself that learning occurs.*

To determine the importance of learning is not a professional matter. Physicians do not decide that health is an important social objective. Society makes that determination. Physicians accept the objective as worthy and organize themselves to achieve it. Deciding that children should learn to become literate, sensitive citizens is not the prerogative of educators alone; society makes the stipulation. Recognizing a service to be performed, teachers strive to meet the requirement. Defining the *goal* is for society; defining the *way* is for the professional. Educators must draw a circle around their group and around their procedures.

Acceptance by one's fellow professionals is not an empty social gesture, but an essential element of teaching success. Professional behavior is insurance that those who are competent and prepared control the educational procedures, which otherwise rests by default with non- professionals.

A Plan for Action

Faced with the alternatives of striving for full professional stature or accepting less is a simple choice. Teachers must become truly profes- sional or they will be ineffective in helping children learn.

Though the American educational system has produced definite ac- complishments, the list of inadequacies is almost as long. Widespread dis- taste for learning and distruct of intellectuals is evident everywhere. Drop-outs, failing school bond issues, low level participation in political affairs, inadequate salaries for teachers and increasing delinquency are a few instances that come to mind. Though there has been some recent progress in these areas, the gains seem small compared to the attainments of modern medicine or engineering.

It is proposed here that teachers accept the challenge of professional discipline as a means of realizing their educational objectives. Instituting such a program involves four things: a commitment to the idea; general acceptance of the code; permission of constituted authorities; and a written legal instrument.

Initially, those who desire full professional status must be committed to the notion of self-discipline. They must understand that confining their efforts to professional activities and membership in their group to professional persons is simply a means to an end—helping children learn. They must be firmly convinced that only through professional organization can they hope to narrow their efforts and focus their energies in such a way that ethical practice is assured. Minor gains dare not be confused with major advances.

Following commitment to full professional stature must come widespread agreement upon a binding code of ethics. Principle by principle, point by point, and word by word, the code must be considered by every member of the organization. Full understanding and approval of the spirit of the code is mandatory. Serious reservations by any major segment of the group in the district involved would undermine the cause. Each person must participate to the point that he has a real "feel" for the basic code as a guide to ethical behavior, and agrees with its thesis.

Since school systems exist within a legal framework, it is necessary next to gain permission from the local school board to admit and to expel persons from the local professional group. Such a step might mean changes in contractual arrangements. Teachers might be required to agree to accept the basic code of ethics as a condition of employment. If such a requirement were imposed by the school board it would represent external control; demanded by the profession itself, it has a different significance.

School boards would also have to agree to let the professional organization recommend persons for appointment. Such a step would be a drastic change from present practice, but would only mean that candidates would be screened by the professional group in addition to those who now consider applicants. Such a screening might not involve more than perfunctory examination of the applicant's credentials and certification, but the fact that the profession itself could recommend *not* hiring unqualified persons would be an important move toward full professional standing.

Finally, the professional organization would have to be free to recommend dismissal of persons whose conduct violated the ethical code. The image of any group of teachers which recommended dismissal of one of its own members for unethical conduct would be improved in the eyes of the public. Still free to champion the cause of those who might be dismissed for unjust or political reasons, teachers would win new public support for their own disciplinary procedures. This improved status would be a natural by-product. The important factor would be that the members of the professional group would be better able to accomplish their objectives by insisting that their members' teaching practice and behavior conform to ethical principles.

Some persons may feel that abiding by an ethical code should be a matter of conscience and not decree. It should, and for almost all practical purposes this would be true. For those few who violate the code of ethics, it would still be necessary for the group to bring the full weight of its membership to bear upon the offender to cease and desist. Hopes that unprofessional teachers will "go away" are never fulfilled. Stronger measures, instituted by the profession itself, are needed to guarantee children the best education.

Permission by a school board to inaugurate such a plan as this would hinge upon the existence of appropriate judicial procedures for the profession to employ. It might be necessary to gain the approval of both the membership and the governing board, so it seems appropriate here to suggest certain particulars.

Judicial procedures would have to exist in writing as by-laws of the professional organization. They would need to be predicated upon the principles of democratic action so important to our way of life: involvement, representation, and appeal. This would probably mean that each school district might have as a sub-group of its local professional group an ethics committee charged with the responsibility of investigating the activities of those accused of unethical teaching practices. Such a committee would necessarily be elected by members of the profession at large.

All persons in the community—parents, students, teachers, administrators, and the general public—would have to have access to this committee. A known procedure for making complaints would have to be available.

Such a committee might at first deal with many minor and unjust complaints, but as the profession and the public had wider experience in the way the group handled complaints, confidence would grow.

Such an ethics committee would need (as part of the by-laws) specific policies to guide its investigations. The accused should always know who is the accuser, he should be entitled to counsel, and a complete record of all hearings and testimony should be maintained in permanent form. There should be definite provisions for appeal. If the original investigating group finds sufficient cause for continuing, subsequent investigating bodies should take a new look at the problem. No one man or single group should be allowed to reach decisions which affect the lives of professional practitioners without recourse to appeal. As a general rule, it would seem that any case should pass through at least three levels of investigation, all involving different judges and all keeping permanent transcripts for record and study, before any disciplinary action is imposed.

Finally, several different types of disciplinary action would be specified, ranging from complete refutation of the charges as unwarranted, through private admonition, public admonition, temporary dismissal, or permanent dismissal, including revocation of teaching certificates and notification of all certification boards of the action taken.

If such investigations were handled entirely by the membership, conducted with the full knowledge of the profession but apart from the public view, and if they could result in recommendations to the governing board, it seems likely that teachers could in time acquire full professional status, based on a clear commitment to educational purposes and framed within the context of an inspiring and powerful code of ethics.

Teachers are the heart of educational method. Their every act must further educational goals. Drawing a tight circle around their kind and around their way should free teachers to accomplish their purposes. To accept less may be too little.

REFERENCES

1. American Medical Association, *Opinions and Reports of the Judicial Council* (Chicago: American Medical Association, 1960).
2. Anderson, William F., "The Sociology of Teaching I: A Study of Parental Attitudes Toward the Teaching Profession," *Dissertation Abstracts*, XII (1952), 692.
3. Andrews, John H. M., "A Deterrent to Harmony Among Teachers," *Administrator's Notebook*, VI (March, 1958).
4. Beamer, George and Ledbetter, Elaine, "The Relation Between Teacher Attitudes and the Social Service Interest," *Journal of Educational Research* (May, 1957), 655-666.
5. Beery, John R., "Does Professional Preparation Make a Difference?" *Journal of Teacher Education*, XIII (December, 1962), 386-395.
6. Belok, M. V., "Social Attitudes Toward the Professor in Novels," *Journal of Educational Sociology*, XXXIV (May, 1961), 404-408.

7. Blumberg, Arthur and Amidon, Edmund, "Teacher Attitudes and School Faculty Meetings," Paper delivered at American Educational Research Association meeting in Atlantic City (February, 1962).

8. Byrnes, Arthur F., "A Study of Job Satisfactions and Dissatisfactions of Teachers in Selected Schools of Indiana," *Microfilm Abstracts*, XI (1951), 885-887.

9. Callaway, Albert B., "Some Environmental Factors and Community Influences That Are Brought to Bear upon the Lives of Missouri Teachers and Administrators," *Microfilm Abstracts*, XI (1951), 554-555.

10. Carter, Richard F., "Voters and Their Schools," *Phi Delta Kappan*, XLII (March, 1961), 244-249.

11. Cobb, Paul R., "High School Seniors' Attitudes Toward Teachers and the Teaching Profession," *Bulletin of the National Association of Secondary School Principals*, XXXVI (January, 1952), 140-144.

12. Cook, Lloyd A. et al., "Teacher and Community Relations," *American Sociological Review*, III (1938), 167-174.

13. Cottrell, Donald P., Ed., *Teacher Education for a Free People* (Oneonta: American Association of Colleges for Teacher Education, 1956).

14. Dutton, Wilbur H. and Keislar, Evan R., "Attitudes Toward Teaching," *Journal of Teacher Education*, XII (June, 1961), 165-171.

15. Edson, William H. and Wilk, Roger E., "An Experimental Study of the Admissions Interview in Teacher Education for Predicting Success in Teaching," Cooperative Research Program, USOE, Final Report (July, 1958).

16. Edwards, Nathan A., "Sociology of Teaching II: A Study of the Male Classroom Teacher," *Dissertation Abstracts*, XII (1952), 700-701.

17. Fielstar, Clarence, "An Analysis of Factors Influencing the Decision to Become a Teacher," *Journal of Educational Research* (May, 1955), 659-688.

18. Firth, Gerald R., "Teachers Must Discipline Their Professional Colleagues," *Phi Delta Kappan*, XLII (October, 1960), 24-27.

19. Fishburn, C. E., "Teacher Role Perception in the Secondary School," *Journal of Teacher Education*, XIII (March, 1962), 55-59.

20. Fischer, John H., "Pressures on Education and Their Effect on School People," *Public Opinion Quarterly*, XXIV (Fall, 1960), 471-472.

21. Fischer, Louis, "A Profession Without Members," *Journal of Teacher Education*, XII (June, 1961), 139-142.

22. Fox, Raymond B., "Factors Influencing the Career Choice of Prospective Teachers," *Journal of Teacher Education*, XII (December, 1961), 427-432.

23. Getzels, J. W. and Guba, E. G., "The Structure of Roles and Role Conflict in the Teaching Situation," *Journal of Educational Sociology*, XXXIX (September, 1955), 30-40.

24. Hill, Henry H., "Wanted: Professional Teachers," *The Atlantic Monthly*, CCV (May, 1960), 37-40.

25. Hill, Walter W., "Factors Contributing to the Problems of Teachers in the Secondary Schools of Maryland Leaving the Profession from 1950 to 1955," *Dissertation Abstracts* (1957), 453.

26. Hlavoc, Rene Edson, "Characteristics of Teachers' College Graduates and of Teachers Employed in Secondary Schools in 1959-1960 in Relation to Career Status in 1960-1961," *Dissertation Abstracts* (1962), 1969-1970.

27. Jackson, Phillip W. and Guba, Egon G., "The Need Structure of In-Service Teachers: An Occupational Analysis," *School Review*, LXV (June, 1957), 176-192.

28. Jewett, Robert E., "Why the Able Public School Teacher Is Dissatisfied," *Educational Research Bulletin*, XXXVI (October, 1957), 223-234.

29. Jones, Harry E., "Some Aspects of an Occupational Stereotype: The American Public School Teacher," *Dissertation Abstracts*, XVII (1957), 2880.

30. Kaplan, Louis, "More Men for Elementary Schools!" *Phi Delta Kappan*, XXIX (March, 1948), 299-302.
31. Kearney, Nolan and Rocchio, Patrick D., "The Effect of Teacher Education on the Teacher's Attitudes," *Journal of Educational Research*, XLIX (May, 1956), 703-708.
32. Knapp, Robert, "Changing Functions of the College Professor," in *The American College*, Nevitt Sanford, Ed. (New York: John Wiley and Sons, Inc., 1962), 290-311.
33. La Bue, Anthony C., "A Study of Motivation of Persistent vs. Non-Persistent Students in Teacher Education," *Journal of Teacher Education*, V (September, 1954), 242-243.
34. Lieberman, Myron, *Education as a Profession* (Englewood Cliffs, N. J.: Prentice-Hall, Inc., 1956).
35. Lynd, Albert, *Quackery in the Public Schools* (New York: Grosset and Dunlap, 1952).
36. Mason, W. S. and Bain, R. K., "Outgoing Teachers," in *Teacher Turnover in the Public Schools 1957-58* (Washington: U. S. Office of Education), 1-9.
37. Mason, W. S.; Dressel, R. J.; and Bain, R. K., "Sex Role and the Career Orientation of Beginning Teachers," *Harvard Educational Review*, XXIX (Fall, 1959), 370-383.
38. Manwiller, Lloyd V., "Expectations Regarding Teachers," *Dissertation Abstracts*, XVII (1957), 2215-2216.
39. Mooney, Ross L., "The Problem of Leadership in the University," *Harvard Educational Review*, XXXIII (Winter, 1963), 42-57.
40. Moore, Clark H. and Cole, David, "The Relation of MMPI Scores to Practice Teaching Ratings," *Journal of Educational Research* (May, 1957), 711-716.
41. Mueller, Kate H. and Mueller, John H., "Class Structure and Academic and Social Success," *Educational and Psychological Measurement*, XIII, No. 3 (1953), 486-496.
42. Murray, Thomas H., "An Investigation into the Annoyances and Frustrations Which Cause Alberta Teachers to Quit Teaching," *The Alberta Journal of Educational Research*, I (September, 1955), 17-33.
43. Nation's Schools, "Opinion Poll," *The Nation's Schools* (May, 1956), 92-94.
44. National Education Association, "Teacher Opinion on Pupil Behavior," *Research Bulletin*, XXXIV, No. 2 (April, 1956), 51-107.
45. National Education Association, "Ten Criticisms of Public Education," *Research Bulletin*, XXXV, No. 4 (December, 1957), 129-175.
46. National Education Association, "Loyalty Requirements," *Research Bulletin*, XXXVII (December, 1959), 116-117.
47. National Education Association, "Code of Ethics" (1963).
48. National Education Association, "Guidelines for Professional Negotiation" (Washington, D. C.: National Education Association, 1963).
49. Peck, Robert F., "Predicting Principals' Ratings of Teacher Performance from Personality Data," *Journal of Educational Psychology*, L (April, 1959), 70-74.
50. Peckham, Dorthy Reed et al., "High School Seniors' Opinion of Teaching," *California Journal of Educational Research*, XIII (January, 1962), 17-30.
51. Phillips, W. S. and Greene, J. E., "A Preliminary Study of the Relationship of Age, Hobbies, and Civil Status to Neuroticism Among Women Teachers," *Journal of Educational Psychology*, XXXIX (September, 1939), 440-444.
52. Powell, M. and Ferrano, C. D., "Sources of Tension in Married and Single Women Teachers of Different Ages," *Journal of Educational Psychology*, LI (April, 1960), 92-101.
53. Prince, Richard, "Individual Values and Administrative Effectiveness," *Administrator's Notebook*, VI (December, 1957).
54. Reed, Robert, "Blueprint for Merit Rating," *School Executive*, LXXVII (June, 1958), 52-55.

55. Reiner, Hyman L., "A Study of the Factors Which Have Caused Elementary School Teachers to Leave the Profession," *Dissertation Abstracts* (1957), 5230.
56. Rettig, Salomon and Passmanick, Benjamin, "Status and Job Satisfaction of Public School Teachers," *School and Society*, LXXXVII (March, 1959), 113-116.
57. Richey, Robert W. et al., "Prestige Ranks of Teaching," Occupations, XXX (October, 1951), 33-36.
58. Saltz, Joanne W., "Teacher Stereotype—Liability in Recruiting?" *School Review*, LXVIII (Spring, 1960), 105-111.
59. Seagoe, May V., "A Follow Up of 314 Students Whose Fitness for Teaching Was Questioned," *Journal of Educational Research*, L (May, 1957), 641-653.
60. Stewart, Lawrence H., "A Study of the Critical Training Requirements for Teaching Success," *Journal of Educational Research*, XLIX (May, 1956), 651-661.
61. Stinnett, T. M. and Huggett, Albert J., *Professional Problems of Teachers* (Second Edition), (New York: Macmillan Co., 1963).
62. Stout, Lydia, "What Strangles American Teaching: The Certification Racket," *The Atlantic Monthly*, CCI (April, 1958), 59-63.
63. Sweeney, Thomas J., "Do Graduate Students at The Ohio State University Believe Teaching Is a Profession?" Unpublished paper, 1962.
64. Tanner, Daniel et al., "The Certification Racket: Florida and Elsewhere," *The Atlantic Monthly*, CCII (July, 1958), 34-39.
65. Tate, Merle W. and Haughey, Charles F., "Teachers Rate Merit Rating," *The Nation's Schools*, LXII (September, 1958), 48-50.
66. Thomas, Donald R., "Our Professional Expectations for Teachers," *Educational Forum*, XXIV (May, 1960), 421-427.
67. Troan, John, "102 Errant Medics Lose Licenses," *Columbus Citizen-Journal*, August 14, 1962 (Editorial Page).
68. White, J. B. et al., *Florida Study of Teacher Education* (Tallahassee: Florida Teacher Education Advisory Council, 1958).
69. Wolf, Willavene and Wolf, William, "Teacher Drop-Outs—A Professional Lament," in *Teaching in America* by Anthony Riccio and Frederick Cyphert, Eds. (Columbus: Charles E. Merrill Books, Inc., 1962), 323-329.
70. Wolfe, Dael, *America's Resources of Specialized Talent* (New York: Harper and Bros., 1954), 226-239.
71. Woodring, Paul, *New Directions in Teacher Education* (New York: Fund for the Advancement of Education, 1957).
72. Woodring, Paul, *A Fourth of a Nation* (New York: McGraw-Hill Book Co., 1957).

Appendix B*

Acceptance and Rejection
of New Students

Several months ago the author, who teaches tenth-grade core in a laboratory school, felt that something was amiss in his particular class. The group actually appeared to be split into two distinct sections. Study of the situation over an extended period of time indicated an apparent relationship between these groupings and the length of time the students had attended school together. One part of the class seemed to be composed of those students who had attended school together since kindergarten or the early elementary grades. Another group, about equal in size but less well defined, seemed to be made up primarily of those who had entered this particular school from various other schools at the ninth-grade level.[1] Further, it appeared that the group which had attended there the longest time served as a power faction. On the other hand, the members who had most recently joined the class often appeared to be rejected, apparently for no real reason at all.

To provide something other than a teacher's subjective estimate of the situation, each of the students in the class was asked six simple questions. Essentially these questions comprised a sociometric-type questionnaire. Two of the questions related to preference regarding seating arrangements. Two other questions involved preference for associates in committee work. One question asked each class member to point out any persons he felt were members of a power faction. Finally, each was asked to list any persons he felt were isolates.

In an effort to bring the picture of this tenth grade core class into sharp focus in the over-all school picture, four other teachers were asked to

---

[1] This laboratory school maintains one section at each grade level kindergarten-8. At grade 9, grade level enrollment is doubled, and two sections are carried in grades 9-12.

* This originally appeared in *Progressive Education* (January, 1957). Reprinted by permission.

collect similar information from their core students. In all, 141 students from five core classes, grades nine through twelve, participated. In general terms their responses indicated several trends:[2]

(1) Oldtimers accept oldtimers
(2) Oldtimers reject newcomers
(3) Newcomers accept oldtimers
(4) Newcomers accept newcomers
(5) More oldtimers are members of power factions
(6) More newcomers are isolates

CONSISTENCY OF REJECTION

Throughout the five groups there was considerable consistency in the way oldtimers accepted other oldtimers but rejected the newer students. And though this rejection diminished during the four-year period of ninth through twelfth grade, the differences did continue throughout all levels. Considered together, these differences were statistically significant at the .001 confidence level. The extent to which oldtimers were pointed out as being members of power factions and newcomers were labeled as isolates was also highly significant statistically.

The only factor accounted for was the length of time the students had attended this particular school together. Therefore it seems noteworthy that these differences were consistent and extreme.

Since, to some extent, all schools face the problem of orienting new students, and the pattern of rejection found in this one school may be repeated elsewhere, some observations on this acceptance-rejection pattern seem indicated.

Individuals who come into a ready-made situation in which there is an existing extablished group, seem to experience considerable difficulty becoming accepted. It appears, actually, that incoming members are rejected simply because they have not been a part of the established group over an extended period of time.

Further, those individuals who come into an established group seem forced by the situation to do one of two things: (a) try to gain acceptance by forcing themselves into the established group, or (b) wait until the established group extends acceptance to them. Either solution seems undesirable. If a person attempts to force acceptance he will probably

---

[2] Jack R. Frymier, "Acceptance and Rejection as Related to Length of School Residence," Unpublished study. University of Florida, 1955.

only insure his own rejection. On the other hand, if he waits for acceptance it may never come unless or until he "proves" himself.

NEWCOMERS MUST PROVE THEMSELVES

There also seems to be a rather widespread, undesirable attitude on the part of the established group members involving individual value and worth. It seems reasonable to assume that acceptance should be extended by members of an established group to incoming members simply on the basis of common courtesy and because the newer members are human beings of integrity and worth. Inherent in the situation is the fact that the established group members are in a position to extend or withhold this acceptance. It appears, however, that established groups tend to reserve their acceptance until incoming members "prove" themselves. This they may do socially, athletically, or otherwise.

For example, an examination of the data and the situation itself indicates that the incoming members who have been accepted to any great degree generally are those who are extremely proficient in athletics, possess exceptional beauty or charm, dance exceedingly well, or have some other highly desirable teen-age quality. However, for those persons who can not or do not "prove" themselves in one way or another, there seems to be an extended waiting period before acceptance occurs. Indeed, there are indications that it may never be achieved in many cases.

Such an attitude and atmosphere is not conducive to optimum human growth and personality development.

If a considerable number of individuals come into an established group at one time the rejection pattern seems to be particularly noticeable, it may unite the original members into a strong, cohesive, defensive unit. In turn they tend to increase acceptance of their own members but to reject incoming members. In other words, it is within the oldtimer groups that this extreme acceptance and rejection actually begins, where the power factions originate, where the cliques develop, and where isolation almost never occurs. However, these are probably very natural reactions. These oldtimers undoubtedly see their self-concepts being endangered; hence they unite with those they know and feel secure with and reject the new and unknown persons in their midst.

OLDTIMERS AS POWER FACTIONS

When the original members of a group are confronted with a situation in which their group status is disturbed by the influx of several additional members, those persons who comprise the established group also tend to do things which cause them to be recognized as power factions. In turn, this appears to create a dual atmosphere of extreme acceptance and extreme rejection. At best, this dichotomy must seem confusing to incoming students and difficult to comprehend. At worst, it means that a large proportion of the group members find themselves part of a physical group but not part of the functioning group. Perhaps members of an established group could effectively cope with a situation in which their self-concept was not in danger if, for example, only one or just a few new members were introduced. But confronting them with a large number of new persons apparently causes them to become defensive in their attitudes and actions.

The curriculum and structural organization of a school may be responsible in part or in whole for such a situation as described here. For example, if an established group does tend to reject incoming members, any situation in which they are required to come together and spend a considerable portion of their day together, as they are in core, may actually maximize rather than minimize the degree of acceptance and rejection.

For instance, if a core class spends two or more hours per day together, working cooperatively on problems of the group's own choice, it may be fallacious to assume that a positive learning situation exists if there is an atmosphere of rejection enshrouding a large segment of the class. The very idea of core, or for that matter almost any good school situation, is predicated upon the effective functioning of the group. However, if there is not one real group, but rather two, the situation may be doomed to mediocrity from the very start. Further, if groups are obliged to spend as much time together as they do in this particular situation, it may be difficult for them not to exert the extensive interactions upon one another, and thus accept or reject one another, as severely as they apparently do.

"BUILT IN REJECTION PATTERNS"

In this particular school, core groups function by making decisions. They select units, determine procedures, reports, deadlines, field trips and other things, all with the teacher's assistance and counsel, of course. Perhaps such a process inherently creates tensions between group members, thus creating and perpetuating a situation in which there are inclinations toward power factions on one hand and isolation on the other. This may actually "build in" acceptance and rejection patterns right from the very start, patterns which are difficult, if not impossible, to erase.

Possibly if an approach not involving group decision-making were employed, the established group members might not be forced together for security, as they now seem to be. In other words, if their status and self-concept were no longer endangered, as they now are when group selection and decision-making occur, there might not be the tendency for severe acceptance in the form of power factions, and severe rejection in the form of isolation, to develop. This problem itself deserves serious study and further consideration.

Certainly a careful program of evaluation is urgent in such an organizational structure as this, where an established group is forced by the situation to take in a sizable number of incoming members from other schools or where they are required by the situation to employ group procedures in reaching decisions.

If such a situation requiring introduction of large numbers of new persons does exist, it might be possible to deal with it most effectively if every effort were made to "bring it out into the open." If teachers and students could work on such a problem honestly and openly, could recognize it as the result of a situational rather than an individual's error, it is conceivable that the extreme differences between established and incoming members reflected in this particular study might be resolved in less time than was required here. Perhaps these differences could be effectively reduced before the end of the first school year.

Finally, how justified can a school faculty be in effecting or continuing a situation which inherently creates a tendency for the rejection of a major portion of its student body? How justified are they in permitting a situation to continue in which great numbers of their students are isolates, apparently just sitting through four years of school? How much and what kind of personality damage does this kind of experience have on people over an extended period of time? And, of course, what types of attitudes are being fostered and developed within those persons who comprise the established groups?

INDEX

Index